Biomedical Hegemony and Democracy in South Africa

International Comparative Social Studies

Editor-in-Chief

Mehdi P. Amineh (*Amsterdam Institute for Social Science Research, University of Amsterdam*, and *International Institute for Asian Studies, Leiden University*)

Editorial Board

Shahrough Akhavi (*Columbia University*)
W.A. Arts (*University College Utrecht*)
Sjoerd Beugelsdijk (*Radboud University*)
Mark-Anthony Falzon (*University of Malta*)
Harald Fuhr (*University of Potsdam*)
Joyeeta Gupta (*University of Amsterdam*)
Xiaoming Huang (*Victoria University Wellington*)
Nilgün Önder (*University of Regina*)
Gerhard Preyer (*Goethe University Frankfurt am Main*)
Islam Qasem (*Webster University, Leiden*)
Kurt W. Radtke (*International Institute for Asian Studies, Leiden University*)
Mahmoud Sadri (*Texas Woman's University*)
Jeremy Smith (*University of Eastern Finland*)
Ngo Tak-Wing (*Leiden University*)
L.A. Visano (*York University*)

VOLUME 51

The titles published in this series are listed at *brill.com/icss*

Biomedical Hegemony and Democracy in South Africa

By

Ngambouk Vitalis Pemunta
Tabi Chama-James Tabenyang

BRILL

LEIDEN | BOSTON

Cover illustrations: *Ancistrocladus Korupensis* (commonly called Cameroonian vine), photo by Emmanuel O. Buea, Cameroon; a bone thrower (*izangoma esichita amathambo*) at work, photo by Zona Dotwana; stripped bark of *Prunus Africana* (Pygeum, Wotango, African prune, Red stinkwood), photo by Emmanuel O. Buea, Cameroon.

Library of Congress Cataloging-in-Publication Data

Names: Pemunta, Ngambouk Vitalis, author. | Tabenyang, Tabi Chama-James, author.
Title: Biomedical hegemony and democracy in South Africa / by Ngambouk Vitalis Pemunta, Tabi Chama-James Tabenyang.
Description: Leiden ; Boston : Brill, 2021. | Series: International comparative social studies, 1568-4474 ; volume 51 | Includes bibliographical references and index. |
Identifiers: LCCN 2020038830 (print) | LCCN 2020038831 (ebook) | ISBN 9789004436411 (hardback) | ISBN 9789004436428 (ebook)
Subjects: LCSH: Medical care--South Africa. | Traditional medicine--South Africa. | Alternative medicine--South Africa. | Medical anthropology--South Africa. | South Africa--Politics and government.
Classification: LCC RA418.3.S6 P46 2021 (print) | LCC RA418.3.S6 (ebook) | DDC 362.10968--dc23
LC record available at https://lccn.loc.gov/2020038830
LC ebook record available at https://lccn.loc.gov/2020038831

Typeface for the Latin, Greek, and Cyrillic scripts: "Brill". See and download: brill.com/brill-typeface.

ISSN 1568-4474
ISBN 978-90-04-43641-1 (hardback)
ISBN 978-90-04-43642-8 (e-book)

Copyright 2021 by Koninklijke Brill NV, Leiden, The Netherlands.
Koninklijke Brill NV incorporates the imprints Brill, Brill Hes & De Graaf, Brill Nijhoff, Brill Rodopi, Brill Sense, Hotei Publishing, mentis Verlag, Verlag Ferdinand Schöningh and Wilhelm Fink Verlag.
All rights reserved. No part of this publication may be reproduced, translated, stored in a retrieval system, or transmitted in any form or by any means, electronic, mechanical, photocopying, recording or otherwise, without prior written permission from the publisher. Requests for re-use and/or translations must be addressed to Koninklijke Brill NV via brill.com or copyright.com.

This book is printed on acid-free paper and produced in a sustainable manner.

*To Professors Don Kalb and Ronnie G. Moore
for mentorship over the years*

and

*In memory of late Professor Canasseus Masilo Lamla
for prefacing this book prior to his death;
May his gentle soul rest in perfect peace*

Contents

Foreword XI
Acknowledgements XIII
List of Illustrations XIV
Abbreviations XVI
Local Words and Expressions XIX

1 Prelude: the Globalization of Traditional Knowledge Systems 1
 1.1 Introduction 1
 1.2 Definition of Concepts 2
 1.3 The International Context of TCAM Practices 5
 1.4 Different but Complimentary? 15
 1.5 Layout of This Work 24

2 Subject Matter, Method and Theoretical Framework 27
 2.1 Introduction 27
 2.2 Choice of Study Area 31
 2.3 Methodological and Theoretical Framework 32
 2.4 Data Analysis 37
 2.5 Ethical Considerations and Reflexivity 39
 2.6 Theoretical Framework 40
 2.7 Conclusion 46

3 Traditional Medicine, Colonialism and Apartheid in South Africa 47
 3.1 Introduction 47
 3.2 Biomedical Capitalism 48
 3.3 Colonialism, Biomedical Hegemony and Alternative Healthcare 52
 3.4 The Pre-Colonial Era 55
 3.5 The Colonial Era 58
 3.6 The Post-Colonial Era 68
 3.7 Conclusion 75

4 Democracy, Witchcraft and Traditional Medicine 77
 4.1 Introduction 77
 4.2 The HIV/AIDS Policy Context, Traditional Medicine and Democracy 78

		4.3 The Lingering Socioeconomic Inequalities of the Apartheid Era 80
		4.4 The "Return to Tradition" Policy 80
		4.5 Shortages of Human Resources for Health 82
		4.6 The Adoption of Democracy and the Promotion of Cultural Rights 84
		4.7 Traditional Medicine as Cure and a Curse for HIV/AIDS 86
		4.8 The Preference for Traditional Healers 87
		4.9 Biomedical Hegemony? 96
		4.10 Conclusion 100

5   The Sociocultural Context of HIV/AIDS in the Eastern Cape Region 102
    5.1 Introduction 102
    5.2 The Eastern Cape Region and the Legacy of Apartheid Era Policies 103
    5.3 The Sociocultural Context of HIV/AIDS 110
        5.3.1 *Labour-related Migration* 112
        5.3.2 *Gender Identity and Unprotected Sex* 113
        5.3.3 *Multiple Partnering and Intergenerational Relationships* 113
        5.3.4 *Gender Inequality and Gender-based Violence* 114
        5.3.5 *Teenage Pregnancies* 114
        5.3.6 *Substance Abuse* 116
        5.3.7 *Cultural Factors: Initiation Rituals* 117
            5.3.7.1 Ukuthwala 118
            5.3.7.2 Virginity Testing 118
    5.4 Conclusion 120

6   The Debate on the Integration of Traditional Medicine into the Mainstream Healthcare Delivery System in South Africa 121
    6.1 Introduction 121
    6.2 The Debate for and against Traditional Medicine 124
    6.3 Primary Healthcare and the Changing Pattern of Disease 139
    6.4 Traditional Medicine and the HIV/AIDS Pandemic 140
    6.5 Conclusion 157

7   "African Diseases" and the Epistemology of South African Healers' Knowledge 159
    7.1 Introduction 159
    7.2 The African Concept of Health 160

7.3 The Process of Becoming a Healer 164
7.4 Typology of African Traditional Healers 165
    7.4.1 *Disease as Prelude to Divinership* 168
7.5 Prospects for the Integration of Traditional Medicine into Official Healthcare 184
7.6 Enhancing Cooperation between Traditional Healers and Biomedicine 187
7.7 Conclusion 188

8 The Integration of Modern and Traditional Medicine in Qokolweni Location 190
8.1 Introduction 190
8.2 Respondents' Opinions on Traditional Medicine 192
8.3 Opinions on Traditional Medicine 194
    8.3.1 *Case Study 1: Vuyo (Fictitious Name)* 211
    8.3.2 *Case Study 2: Bate (Fictious Name)* 211
    8.3.3 *Case Study 3: Monde (Fictious Name)* 212
8.4 Perception of Nurses and Traditional Healers 215
8.5 Conclusion 218

9 The Daily Use of Traditional Medicine in Qokolweni Location 221
9.1 Introduction 221
9.2 The African Concept of Health 221
9.3 The Concept of Traditional Medicine in Qokolweni 222
9.4 The Use of Traditional Medicine in Qokolweni 230
9.5 Attitudes and Perceptions towards African Traditional Medicine in Qokolweni 232
9.6 Users of African Traditional Medicine 234
9.7 Recommendations 236
9.8 Conclusion 239

Bibliography 241
Index 276

Foreword

Scientifically based medicine has accumulated a great amount of knowledge about the causes of ailments and their cures. Against this background, traditional healers and their practices appear as a mainstay of the grossest darkness, which holds the human mind. This study by Ngambouk Vitalis Pemunta and Tabi Chama-James Tabenyang shows that in spite of this assumption, there is good reason to investigate the often surprising effectiveness of traditional healing.

The study reveals that the traditional healer undergoes an initiation into the healing practices through experiencing the destructive force of sickness and the redeeming effect of healing in a religious frame of thought. In this context, healing appears as the application of natural means against supernatural forces. In such a context, sickness is more than merely an ailment: it is the incapacitated personality. Thus healing is redeeming rather than curing. The healer, his medicine and the patient belong to a closed system of thought. Traditional healing is the operation of that system. This particular orientation makes traditional healing effective, sometimes even more effective than scientific medicine as in the case of "African" sicknesses.

In a certain sense, sicknesses and their cures are culturally conditioned. This situation is part of a person's self- understanding. Thus it is certainly an anthropological issue to investigate the condition of traditional healers and their medicines. It is an investigation of practical concern for the scientifically based physician.

The manuscript itself focusses on the role of traditional medicine in an era of predominantly bio-medical research. It is a commendable attempt to fill in the knowledge gaps created by colonial parlances and inconsistencies.

The fact that this work has been done by persons who understand the cultural nuances and intricacies of local communities gives it some freshness and a depth that might not otherwise have been possible. The work is characterized by the use of such primary sources as traditional healers, bio-medical practitioners, observers and patients. Their words and their strong emotions in relation to the process of healing, impart to the reader, a sense that he /she is actually there. In this sense, an analytic reader may be inclined to view traditional healing as a community resource.

This work is highly commendable. It is hoped that it will inspire many more researchers and social scientists to explore this and similar topics in order to bring the role of traditional healing, in an era of largely bio-medical research, into the main stream of our literature for the common good.

>*Prof. C.M. Lamla*
>School of Social Sciences and Humanities, Walter Sisulu University,
>Mthatha, Eastern Cape

Acknowledgements

The lengthy period of research on this book led to the accumulation of many debts to both individuals and institutions, a few of these individuals and institutions deserve mention. Our sincere gratitude goes to the Centre for Concurrences in Colonial and Postcolonial Studies at Linnaeus University for financial support towards the realization of this work. We fervently thank Prof. C.M. Lamla, Mr. P.N. Nyoni, Ms K.H. Ngqila, and Dr. C.L. Petkou of Walter Sisulu University (WSU) for their generosity with their time, for continued interest and intellectual stimulations that have greatly enhanced this work.

We sincerely thank Chief N.D. Zwelihle Sangoni of Qokolweni for granting us access into the research sites. Our appreciation also goes to Mr. W.N. Mshumpela and other officials of the Department of Traditional Affairs (Mthatha) for authorizing the study.

Tabi Chama-James wishes to acknowledge the friendship and conviviality of Dr. Gladys Ashu, D.M.E. Matike, W.D. Dzemo, Dr. Derick Forbanka and W. Masomera, Mvunyiswa N., Zona Dotwana, Buqindlela K. (RIP), Dlaba N. and Mpaka N. as well as family support and encouragement from Mrs. Frida Okpu and her husband, Cyprian Tabi, Charity Tabi, Ben Tabi, Victor Tabi, Susan Tabi, Sophy Tabi, Alex Tabi, Otang Bernadette and his dearest Godson Tabi. Special thanks to our colleagues Rosemary Niba and Vera Shey of WSU for moral support and the common vision we share.

We would also like to sincerely thank the anonymous reviewers for their helpful comments that have greatly shaped this work. Ngo Valery Ngo provided great research assistance at various points, including the indexing of this book for which we are immensely grateful.

Last but not the least; we are grateful to Julienne Ebangha and Emilia Nkoyo for not complaining more than they did when we were completely absorbed in the completion of this work. We sincerely thank the staff at Brill, especially Pieter van Roon and Pieter te Velde, production editors, for their patience and professionalism all through the production process. The responsibility for any deficiencies and omissions are solely ours.

Ngambouk Vitalis Pemunta and Tabi Chama-James Tabeyang
Gothenburg, Sweden, and Roubaix, France, 18 March 2020

Illustrations

Maps

1. Location of Mthatha in the Eastern Cape Region of South Africa. Source: https://www.britannica.com/place/Eastern-Cape-province-South-Africa/media/1/176933/129602   32
2. Position on the map of Qokolweni suburb of Mthatha, Eastern Cape, South Africa. © Open Street Map, https://www.roadonmap.com/za/where-is/Qokolweni-Umtata,eastern_cape   33
3. Map of the Eastern Cape Region. Source: https://municipalities.co.za/provinces/view/1/eastern-cape   105

Photos

1. A herbalist (*amaXhwele*) at work. Photo by Tanyi Besong   170
2. *Ancistrocladus Korupensis* (commonly called Cameroonian vine). Photo by Emmanuel O. Buea, Cameroon   172
3. A priestess diviner (*amagqirha*). Photo by Zona Dotwana   173
4. A bone thrower (*izangoma esichitha amathambo*) at work. Photo by Zona Dotwana   176
5. Faith healer T.B. Joshua exorcising a patient. Photo by Tabi Chama   178
6. A diviner's shrine Upper Ngqwarha. Photo by Tabi Chama   181
7. The dispensary of a traditional healer. Photo by Zona Dotwana   182
8. Leaves and stripped bark of *Prunus Africana* (Pygeum, Wotango, African prune, Red stinkwood). Photos by Emmanuel O. Buea, Cameroon   186

Figures

1. Defining African traditional medicine   195
2. Usage of traditional medicine   198
3. Respondents who use and encourage others to use traditional medicine   201
4. Traditional vs Biomedicine   203
5. Collaboration between traditional healers and biomedical doctors   204
6. Challenges experienced in the use of traditional medicine   205
7. Difference between traditional medicine and modern medicine   207
8. Opinions on improving traditional medicine   210

Tables

1 Traditional healing agencies in South Africa. Source: *Traditional Healing Agencies in South Africa* (McFarlane, 2015: 66)   166
2 Demographic characteristics of respondents   192
3 Marital status and religious affiliation of respondents   194
4 Effectiveness of traditional medicine   210
5 Number of patients visiting Obale's shrine   214
6 Number of patients visiting Enow's shrine   214
7 Number of patients visiting Sangoni Community Health Centre   214

Abbreviations

AACHRD	African Advisory Committee for Health Research and Development
ADR	Adverse Drug Reactions
AIDS	Acquired Immune Deficiency Syndrome
AMA-PM	American Medical Association Physician Masterfile
ANC	African National Congress
ART	Antiretroviral therapy
AU	African Union
ATM	African Traditional Medicine
AVR	Antiretroviral
BMA	British Medical Association
CAM	Conventional, Complementary and Alternative Medicine
CNCR	Chief Native Commissioner's Report
CITES	Convention on International Trade in Endangered Species of Flora and Fauna
CGE	Commission on Gender Equality
CWA	Catholic Women's Association
DOH	South African Department of Health
EBM	Evidence Based Medicine
ECA	Economic Commission for Africa
ENE	Estimate of National Expenditure
FAO	Food and Agriculture Organization
GHS	General Household Survey
HAART	Highly active antiretroviral therapy
HIV	Human Immuno-deficiency Virus
HSRC	Human Sciences Research Council
IDP	Integrated Development Plan
IK	Indigenous Knowledge
IMF	International Monetary Fund
IMPD	Institute for Multi-party Democracy
IPR	Intellectual Property Rights
IIDMM	Institute for Infectious Diseases and Molecular Medicine
IMPD	Institute for Multi-Party Democracy
KSD	King Sabatha Dalindyebo
KZNTHC	KwaZulu-Natal Traditional Healer's Council
MDGS	Millennium Development Goals
MRC	Medical Research Council
MINSANTE	Ministère de la Santé Publique (Ministry of Public Health)

ABBREVIATIONS

NAPRALERT	Natural Product Alert database
NACOTHA	National Council of Traditional Healers and Herbalists Association
NCCAM	National Centre for Complementary and Alternative Medicine
NEPAD	New Partnership for Africa's Development
MDI	Multidimensional Poverty Index
NIH	National Institute of Health
NTM	Natural and Traditional Medicine
NRCATM	National Reference Centre for African Traditional Medicines
NTFPS	Non-Timber Forestry Products
OAU	Organization of African Unity
PEPFAR	United States Presidents Emergency Plan for AIDS Relief
PrEP	pre-exposure prophylaxis
PHC	Primary Health Care
PLHIV	People Living with HIV
PRC	People's Republic of China
RCTS	Randomized Controlled Trials
RDP	Reconstruction and Development Plan
RSA	Republic of South Africa
SAHPRA	South African Health Product Regulatory Authority
SAP	Structural Adjustment Programme
SSA	Sub-Saharan Africa
SAHSMI	South African Herbal Science and Medicine Institute
SDA	Sustainable Development Agenda
Stats SA	Statistics South Africa
STD	Sexually Transmitted Disease
STIS	Sexually Transmissible Infections
TAC	Treatment Action Campaign
TasP	Universal Treatment as Prevention Strategy for HIV
TBAS	Traditional Birth Attendants
THCPS	Traditional Health Care Practitioners
TCAM	Traditional, Alternative and Complementary Medicine
TCHM	Traditional Chinese Herbal Medicine
TCM	Traditional Chinese Medicine
TK	Traditional Knowledge
UN	United Nations
UNCTAD	United Nations Industrial Organization
UNEP	United Nations Environment Programme
UNIDO	United Nations Industrial Organization
US	United States of America

UNAIDS	United Nations Programme on HIV/AIDS
UNAID	United Nations Agency for International Development
UNESCO	United Nations Economic Social and Cultural Organization
VCT	Voluntary Counselling and Testing
WHO	World Health Organization
WIPO	World Intellectual Property Rights Organization
WSU	Walter Sisulu University

Local Words and Expressions

abathandazeli	faith healer
amaXhwele	herbalists
Amagqirha or izangoma	priest diviners
amagqirha	priest diviner
Abathandazeli	faith healers
Amafufunyane	disease targeting girls and believed to be caused by a sorcerer("isizwe")
Amagqirha	priest diviners
Amagumbiokuxilongela	traditional healer's consultation lodge
Amakhubalo	protective charms/amulets
EtaMandem	high god (Kenyang of Cameroon)
Idliso	poisoning by spirits (literally, "that which has been eaten")
Impilo	medicine used for restoring health/a state of total well-being
Impundulu	lightening bird
Intawaso	animistic force responsible for psychiatric disorder
Intwaso or ukuthwasa	entry into, meaning initiation into priest divinership
Inanuse	diviners
Ilishwa	misfortune
Isimnyama	repulsiveness
Ingqongqo	cowhide
Imixube	herbal mixture
Izinyamazane	protective remedies
Izinyanga Ezixube Nolwazi ewabelungu	homeopathic herbalists
Isimnyama	disease caused by mystical force, which leads to intense suffering
Imihlanti	a goatskin bag
Inyanga (Zulu)	herbalist
Ixhwele (Xhosa)	herbalist
Iqgirha lentloko	"head diviner/chief"
Izangoma esichitha amathambo	diviner who uses bone throwing/ bone thrower
Igqirha lemilozi	"whistling diviners"
Marabou (French)	medicine man

Mwari	high god (Zezuru of Zimbabwe)
Ngaka	apprentice
Ochitha	herbal vendor
Omazala	mother-in-laws
Omakhulu	grandmothers
Siyavuma	to agree/especially with a diviner's divination
Thwasa	a calling for priest divinership
Uganga	(Zaramo, Tanzania) expertise in traditional medicine
Ukubhodla	acidity
Ukukhutywa	uncontrollable hiccup
Umrhawule/umsamo	traditional healer's shrine
Umvelingqangi	high god (Zulu)
Umlozi	whistling
Umthandazeli	faith healer

CHAPTER 1

Prelude: the Globalization of Traditional Knowledge Systems

1.1 Introduction

This book examines the prospects of integrating traditional medicine into the dominant biomedical healthcare system within the context of the social crises orchestrated by the HIV/AIDS pandemic and the simultaneous "return to tradition" policy—adopted by the African National Congress (ANC)-government in the Republic of South Africa (RSA) after 1994. Although the "return to tradition" policy implied the revalorization of African cultural traditions and practices as well as of the African personality, it was however, diametrically opposed and antithetical to the fight against the ravaging HIV/AIDS pandemic. While the effervescence of some of these practices including masculine and feminine coming of age rites of passage and initiations are capable of fueling the spread of the epidemic, it simultaneously dissuaded HIV/AIDS patients from taking life-saving antiretroviral therapy (ART) (see Chapter 5). The reasons forwarded were the alleged unproven efficacy and toxicity of antiretroviral drugs by the Thabo Mbeki adminsitsration and the South African political class (Shutter et al., 2009: 9121; Ashford, 2005) who felt the roots of the epidemic was poverty and sought an "African solution" to an alleged "African problem" (Ashford, 2005). The Mbeki administration's AIDS denialist policy was concuurent with a hostile and dangerous campaign against evidence-based medicine (EBM) in general and ART medicine as part of a global conspiracy by multinational pharmaceutical companies to reap profits from ill health. Led by Dr Rath Health Foundation, the campaign summarily rejected biomedicine and claimed that a mixture of micronutrients and unspecified traditional medicines (Hassim et al., 2014: 218, http://www.tac.org.za) can cure ailments including HIV. Under the presidency of Jacob Zuma, there was, however, a radical break away from this ultra-conservative and AIDS denialist policy whose overall implication was a death sentence for HIV/AIDS patients. Zuma's policies eventuated in the scaling up of ART and increased health promotion at the population level (Zuma et al., 2016) (see Chapter 6).

This opening chapter examines how the consumption of herbal remedies became a global industry—"contributing at least R2.9 billion (US$2.2 million)" to the South African economy (Mander, 2007: 189)—and the pharmaceutical industry's appropriation of local knowledge systems. It further examines the factors underpinning individual choices for the recourse to traditional/complementary and alternative medicine (TCAM) in both the developed and less developed world. Some key concepts deserve clarification at the very onset of this work.

1.2 Definition of Concepts

In this study, the expressions "modern medicine," "scientific medicine," "allopathic medicine," "Western medicine," "orthodox medicine" and "biomedicine," are used interchangeably to refer to conventional medicine. They are juxtaposed against traditional medicine that is a constitutive element of TCAM. Regardless of the difficulties in nailing a precise meaning or of assigning one definition to the broad range of characteristics and elements of traditional medicine and healers, Marlise provided the following working definition:

> African traditional medicine includes diverse health practices, approaches, knowledge and beliefs incorporating plant, animal and or mineral based medicines, spiritual therapies, manual techniques and exercises applied singularly or in combination to maintain well-being, as well as to treat, diagnose, or prevent illnesses. This leads to the restoration of life. (2003: 17)

On its part, the World Health Organization (WHO) has provided the following working definition of African traditional medicine:

> the sum total of all knowledge and practices, whether explicable or not, used in diagnosis, prevention and elimination of physical, mental, or societal imbalance, and relying exclusively on practical experience and observation handed down from generation to generation, be it verbally or in writing. (WHO, 1990: 65)

Traditional medicine refers to all substances including—herbal plants, animal parts, material and other substances such as soils—be they in powder or liquid form, used by members of any particular cultural milieu for the treatment and prevention of diseases (used to restore health- *impilo*). Traditionally, the art of healing diseases involves the use of roots, stems, leaves, barks and flowers used for preparing medicines. Traditional medicine usually consists of a concoction of animal fats, skins, and snakes, just to name a few (Donda, 1997: 1). There is growing interest in traditional medical knowledge and thus, its widespread recognition in development policies, the media and the scientific literature because African traditional healers and their remedies play an important role in the health of many people (Flint, 2016; Sterk & Del Rio, 2008). A traditional healer is a person who is recognized by the community in which he or she lives as competent to provide healthcare by using plants, animal, mineral substances and other methods based on the patient's socio-cultural and religious background. Healing is also based on knowledge, attitudes and beliefs that are prevalent in the community regarding the physical, mental and social wellbeing of the patient (Zubane, 2001). Healing is based on the causative agents of disease and disability (Helman, 2001: 50–72). African traditional healers have been categorized into three distinct groups: herbalists (*amaXhwele*), faith healers (*abathandazeli*) and priest diviners (*amagqirha*) (Fyhrquist, 2007: 23–25). The different types of traditional healers in South Africa and their method of their treatment is discussed in Chapter 4. They play different but complementary roles and are considered by John Mbiti (1966) as 'the friends of the community.' This is a reflection of the wide range of health and social issues traditional healers deal with to maintain harmony and wellbeing within their communities.

The African concept of health is all-encompassing. It includes physical, mental and social wellbeing. Although it reflects the idealistic WHO's definition of health as "a state of complete physical, mental and social well-being and not merely the absence of disease or infirmity" (Constitution of the WHO, 1946), it however goes beyond that. It is a reflection of the African worldview as relational in which man depends on other human beings and his ancestors— in which the world of the living and the dead is believed to be intertwined (de Roubaix, 2016: 160; Menketi, 2004; Mbiti, 1990). "Every human being without distinction of race, religion, political belief, economic or social condition is entitled to the highest culturally and socially attainable standard of health" (Constitution of the WHO, 1946). This implies that one system of medicine (biomedicine) should not be perceived as superior to all others (alternative therapies). The concept of biomedical hegemony implies the domination of a culturally diverse society by the ruling class who manipulate the culture of that society—the beliefs, explanations, perceptions, values, and mores—so that their imposed, ruling-class worldview about illness, disease and therapy becomes the accepted cultural norm as universally valid (Benedetto, 2008) (see Chapter 4). The pervasive poverty of South Africa's Eastern Cape Region makes the concept of biomedical 'hegemony' a theoretical framework rather than a reality for the healthcare of the majority (see Chapter 5).

Although this case study focuses on health decision making between modern and traditional medicine in the Qokolweni Location of the southern Nguni community, examples are also drawn from other communities within the African continent and beyond. This does not however, presuppose the idea of a unilineal or monologic Africa (African traditional medicine) since even in South Africa, traditional medical practices and practitioners differ (see Chapter 7). This is simply an articulation of the fact that there are similar beliefs and practices that are widespread all over the continent (but differ) and that TCAM in various guises has become a global business enterprise generating billions of dollars annually.

The so-called "TCAM" encapsulates heterogeneous healthcare practices, including Ayurvedic medicine, Yoga, various varieties of Chinese medicine, homeopathy, Swedish massage, Qi Gong, as well as various variants and nuances of these that fall outside the 'conventional' category called biomedicine (WHO, 2013; Coulter & Willis, 2004). In Africa, it includes "local herbal medicines or products, indigenous healthcare practices (traditional bone setting), as well as imported complementary and alternative medicine products (e.g., acupuncture or chiropractic)" (James et al., 2018:1). Furthermore, these different health-restoring practices are underpinned by a wide variety of cosmologies and approaches, which tend to fall outside of the province of biomedicine (or the so-called biomedical paradigm) (Tovey et al., 2004). Medical pluralism can be defined as the employment of more than one medical system or the use of both TCAM for health and illness.

An estimated 80% of Africans rely on traditional medicine for their primary health needs (Olayede, 2010; WHO, 2008; Flint, 2008). Although traditional medicine has been used for millennia and is today a multi-billion industry, it does not hold up to the rigour of scientific evidence (de Roubaix, 2016; Sobiecki, 2014). It is therefore still in need of 'perfection.' Its 'perfection' through the standardization of its dosage, some advocates of the integration of indigenous medical systems into the dominant allopatic medical system maintain, should precede its formal integration into biomedicine (de Roubaix, 2016; Bruce, 2002). The presumed imperfection of traditional healing practices suggests that these amalgams of practices are unevolving, whereas traditional health practices are opened to modernization through cultural contact and the appropriation of elements from other medical traditions. It is therefore, "not-so-traditional," but rather, inherently dynamic and responsive to sociopolitical changes (Flint, 2008; Flint, 2016: 4326; Leslie, 1992).

In what follows, we set the macro-international context of the globalization of traditional and alternative medicine and their imbrication in global frameworks of action to deliver healthcare worldwide, as well as the 'green economy' choices of patients and their desire to take control of their healthcare needs that has given rise to the massive consumption of alternative therapies. We show how the pharmaceutical industry is increasingly involved in the transformation and commercialization of medicinal plants ("pharmaceutization"). We further examine how, although both traditional and modern medicine are based on different and competing epistemologies, they are however considered as complementary by patients and members of their "therapy seeking group" (Hsu, 2008; Hsu, 2002). This suggests that the integration of both systems of healthcare will lead to improvements in the overall health of the South African population.

1.3 The International Context of TCAM Practices

The increasing global recourse to TCAM practices by patients (see below) and practitioners emphasizes the need to integrate traditional and modern medicine to deliver better and culturally appropriate healthcare to the masses. Patients use TCAM alone or in combination with biomedicine and for specific health conditions in Sub-Saharan Africa (SSA) (James et al., 2018) and globally. At the landmark ALMA ATA Conference of 1978 governments worldwide were exhorted to harness the skills of indigenous medicine practitioners in their primary healthcare initiatives. However, benevolent calls for the integration of traditional medicine and its practitioners into the dominant biomedical health care system have always implied the need for evidence of quality, efficacy and safety, or of well-defined close/effect relationships (Roubaix, 2016; Sobiecki, 2014; Olayede, 2010). Such good intentioned calls are partly informed by the social acceptability of indigenous therapies, and therefore the social legitimacy of TCAM (Moore and McClean, 2012). Furthermore, the numerical superiority of traditional healers when compared to biomedical doctors, and the upsurge in communicable and non-communicable diseases including the HIV/AIDS pandemic that has inordinately taxed healthcare systems and health budgets are other push factors militating in favour of TCAM (de Roubaix, George et al., 2013; Mander et al., 2007). However, the basis and the standard norm for the integration of traditional health care systems into biomedicine emains the hegemonic biomedical mindset of "well-controlled clinical trials including placebo controlled trials" (Olayede, 2010: 74–75) that is dependent on appropriate evidence adduced from the bioavailability of pharmacokinetic studies (Olayede, 2010: 74–75; Roubaix, 2016; Sobiecki, 2014). This is happening against the backdrop of the integration of local knowledge systems into the circuit of a global capitalist enterprise controlled by governments, pharmaceutical companies, herbal entrepreneurs and entrepreneurs of healing, transnational research partnerships between Northern and Southern-based institutions, and overtures from international organizations such as the World Bank and the WHO. These powerful actors pushed for the integration of traditional medicine systems into the mainstream biomedical healthcare system for the achievement of the health-related Millennium Development Goals (MDGs). Similar ambitions have been expressed as part of the health-related Sustainable Development Agenda (SDA) adopted by world leaders. The SDA are a set of goals to end poverty, protect the planet and ensure prosperity for all. Simultaneously, traditional healers remain at the margins of the integration debate. They are rarely included in key decision-making, action agendas and community programme discussions.

Despite its avowed 'imperfections,' local knowledge as instantiated by the millions of dollars traditional medicine generates has become global business through a simultaneous process of rejection and appropriation partly through biopiracy. As one indigenous healer poignantly pointed out:

> Biomedical doctors adopt some of our procedures, but refuse us in public. Like pharmaceutical companies, they steal our products. They treat us like prostitutes who are solicited for sex only at night, but denigrated in broad day light like lepers. (Nwene, interview of December 10, 2010)

Early anthropologists who studied so-called "primitive" medical systems and the colonial masters were complicit in the balkanization (framed as ethnomedicine) as well as the subsequent appropriation, through biomedicalization and pharmaceutization of traditional knowledge systems. In fact, alternative systems of healthcare and knowledge systems have since the epistemological conquest unleashed by colonialism been vigorously promoted by postcolonial regimes. In South Africa, traditional medicine was imbricated in the maintenance of cultural boundaries during the apartheid era. This is despite the fact that cultural boundaries are not impermeable (Chapter 3). Today both tangible and intangible forms of local knowledge systems are increasingly under pressure from powerful international actors including the World Bank and the WHO "to commercialise and technologise [their] goods and services" (McClean and Moore, 2012: 1). The dual processes of "economic liberalisation and the democratisation of health care have encouraged the increased commodification of complementary health services" (Ibid.). In fact, the process involving the commodification and subsequent marketization of health care, McClean and Moore further argue should be seen against the backdrop of the personalization of various forms of complementary health care, including folk healing.

This development, they maintain, calls for a whole health-care systems analysis framework (McClean and Moore, 2012; Moore, 2010). In addition, there is the need to take into consideration local health narratives/ "subaltern health narratives" (King, 2010; King, 2012). Such a whole health-care systems analysis paradigm is important and should form the basis of efforts geared towards the integration of TCAM into biomedicine.

Apart from myriad global health initiatives including the achievement of the MDGs, the SDA, the WHO has churned out several key policy documents for the promotion and development, regulation, guidelines and standards for safety, efficacy, good manufacturing, research, assessment, clinical trials, rational use of TCAM, the training of traditional health practitioners, standardization of vocabularies in specific disciplinary fields such as acupuncture, relevance of indigenous medicine to HIV/AIDS, consumer information, good agricultural practices, the conservation of natural resources and intellectual property rights among others (WHO, 2007). Furthermore, the ability to use traditional medicine is embedded in the United Nations Environment Programme's (UNEP) conceptual framework on poverty and ecosystems as one of the 10 resources for well-being (UNEP, 2013). The UNEP's Convention on International Trade in Endangered Species of Flora and Fauna (CITES) promotes the sustainable use of natural resources by monitoring the trade in endangered species of flora and fauna. Among the policy resources developed by the Food and Agriculture Organization (FAO) is a policy resource on non-timber forest products (NTFPs) that includes policy, conservation and research on medicinal plants (Ibid.). The UN Conference on Trade and Development (UNCTAD) protects traditional knowledge systems and promotes trade and development opportunities for developing countries through traditional medicine (Payyappallimana, 2009). While the industrial production and use of traditional medicine is the focus of the UN Industrial Development Organization (UNIDO), it also encourages improved technologies for the standardization of traditional medicine as well as support for the capacity building of member countries (De Silva, 1993; Tcheknavorian-Asenbauer, 1993). The World Intellectual Property Organization (WIPO) has vigorously championed initiatives for Intellectual Property Rights (IPR) including for custodians of traditional medicinal knowledge (Payyappallimana, 2009: 65–69). Are these policy initiatives geared towards the promotion of indigenous medical and traditional knowledge (TK) systems acts of philanthropy?

Local knowledge systems as commodities in the global business chain are now subjected to the process of biomedicalization and pharmaceutization. Worldwide, governments, international organizations and corporate bodies are appropriating traditional medicinal and knowledge systems in the name of meeting the primary healthcare needs of their population. An estimated 80% of people in Africa, Asia and Latin America continue to use traditional medicine while in industrialized economies, almost half the population regularly use some form of TCAM (United States 42%, Australia, 48%, France 49%, Canada, 70%) (Bodeker and kronenberg, 2002). The prevalence of TM use by the general population was higher in East Asian countries (South Korea: 45.8–69%, China: 90% or Lao PDR: 77%) (Tran et al., 2016; Shin et al., 2013; Sydara et al., 2005; WHO, 2002) in comparison with developed countries with around 50% in Australia, 42% in both USA and France: 49% respectively (Tran et al., 2016; Bodeker and kronenberg, 2002). These figures are a testament to the social acceptability of TCAM.

Contrary to Western Europe where the revival of TCAM is attributed to the "'green' life style economic interests and new images of doctor-patient relationships" in Eastern Europe, the easing of social restrictions led to renewed interests in TCAM. The European parliament has vigorously pushed for the official recognition of all TCAM practices through the putting in place of appropriate commissions charged with safety, efficacy and areas of applicability (Payyappallimana, 2010: 64). In fact, the European Union (EU)'s complementary health care sector is under immense economic and regulatory pressure to commercialise, technologise and commoditise its goods and services, and for entrepreneurism among its practitioners (Andrews and Phillips, 2005). This tendency towards the commercialization, technologization and commodification of alternative health services and products is reflexive of a "general trend towards consumerism in healthcare; involving the commodification of health and the emergence of diverse health markets" (Bury and Taylor, 2008; cf. McClean and Moore, 2012: 2).

The annual global consumption of traditional medicine is estimated at US$60 billion (WHO, 2002), while the global spa industry which is a derivative of traditional medicine is valued at US$255 billion annually (Cohen and Bodeker, 2008). Traditional knowledge and medicinal products are of great economic value, providing employment opportunities to a significant number of individuals (Farnsworth, 1998: 95; cf. Payyappallimana, 2010: 63). Out of pocket expenses on TCAM continue to grow exponentially: Malaysia-US$500 million, USA,-$2,700 million (1997), Australia-$80 million, Canada, $2,400 million and United Kingdom-$2,300 million (WHO, 2002). Concurrently, medicinal plants are increasingly under the threat of extinction while the cost of herbal products in domestic markets is increasing rapidly (Williams et al., 2013; UNEP, 2013; Mander, 1998). For instance, a study of South Africa's Red List assessments of 20,456 indigenous vascular plant taxa shows that an estimated 2062 indigenous plant species (10% of the total flora) were determined as being employed for traditional medicine recipes. Of this total national flora, 82 species (0.4%) face the threat of extinction in the short and medium-term. A further 100 species are reportedly of conservation concern. This includes two species that are already extinct in the wild. Thirty-two percent of the taxa have been recorded in traditional medicine markets in KwaZulu-Natal, Gauteng, Eastern Cape, Mpumalanga and Limpopo Provinces (Williams et al., 2013).

The pharmaceutical industry is appropriating local knowledge systems for the production of drugs, what Cathy Fournier (2013) refers to as "the pharmaceutization of traditional medicine." The Natural Product Alert database (NAPRALERT) of the University of Illinois, Chicago concedes "that 74% of the 119 pure compound based modern drugs derived from plants are based on leads from custodians of traditional medical knowledge [systems] and that modern applications are similar to the traditional ones." Similarly, Jean-Francois Sobiecki's ethnographic and phytopharmacological research among Southern Bantu healers in South Africa demonstrates that some of the plants have an empirical basis for their use in divination "by producing things such as clarity of thought and dreams" (Sobiecki, 2014: 7). He simultaneously reveals "the phytochemical and biomedical foundations of the African traditional healer's explanations of why and how various spiritually used plants have medicinal value" (Ibid.). He concludes that phytopharmacological and phytochemical (scientific) studies provide the basis for the culturally defined descriptions and explanations of spiritual plant use. One example is the verified psychoactive relaxing properties of *imphepho*. These properties have been shown to be conducive to the promotion of an altered state of consciousness and as facilitating its traditional spiritual use (Stafford et al., 2005 cf. Sobiecki, 2014: 7). Concurrently, the pharmaceutical industry and non-specialists who now pass around as self-styled healers are diluting traditional knowledge systems and practices (Fournier, 2013). This scenario calls for the need for regulatory governance and surveillance to ensure environmental sustainability and sustainability for future generations.

In most of the Global South, most people depend on traditional medicine for their primary healthcare needs. There is, however, also evidence suggesting that most people do seek out and have some access to biomedical treatment as their first therapeutic recourse. For instance, data from the 2016 South African General Household Survey (GHS) suggests that an estimated seven in every ten (71,4%) households reported that they first sought biomedical treatment regimens (from public clinics and hospitals) whenever household members took ill or were injured. In comparison, only 27,0% of households indicated they would consult private doctors, private clinics or hospitals (Statistics South Africa [Stats SA], 2017a).

Contrary to the developed world, in resource constrained countries access to healthcare is for the privileged few. Furthermore, there is an acute crisis of health-related human resources, inadequacies in healthcare financing by most Third World states[1] and a double burden of both communicable and non-communicable diseases, the privatization of health care services, migration of health care personnel, environmental changes and the constant outbreak of epidemics (Tran et al., 2016; Hughes et al., 2013). In these contexts, traditional medicine is seen as an affordable health care option that is 'culturally appropriate' (Tran et al., 2016; Flint, 2016). In developed countries, higher income and higher education underpin the preference of patients for traditional medicine (Kew et al., 2015; Hughes et al., 2013). Simultaneously, migrant groups face difficulties in accessing healthcare due to economic and social disadvantage and often resort to TCAM as their first therapeutic option, thereby making it non-complementary (Bodeker et al., 2007). This is happening against the backdrop of what could be called the globalization of TCAM. In some instances, TCAM appears as an add-on, rather than an alternative to conventional medical care (for the United States and Canada, see among others Mcfarland, 2002: 1617; Tataryn and Verhof, 2001; Fournier, 2013; for the UK and Europe, see McClean and Moore, 2012; Moore, 2010). Chinese doctors are increasingly combining TCAM with biomedicine to produce 'rapid effects' in Tanzania (Hsu, 2002). The structural integration of TCAM is happening both at the level of patients and within national healthcare institutions including in South Africa, especially within the context of the HIV/AIDS pandemic. The push and pull factors for the use of TCAM include: ethnic diversity and the influx of immigrants, and its integration by both patients and practitioners in the management of the former's health (Andrews and Boon, 2005; Kelner and Wellman, 1997a; Kelner and Welman, 1997b; Andrews, 2003). A significant number of physicians and physiotherapists are including acupuncture into their practices (Andrews, 2003). Like traditional medicine (a sub component of TCAM) which is sometimes erroneously perceived as medicine for the poor (the majority), the use of TCAM is no longer restricted to the more highly educated and affluent in society, neither is it age-specific (Tran et al., 2016; Sobiecki, 2014; Bodeker and kronenberg, 2002). Furthermore, the inadequacies of biomedicine and the attractions of TCAM as integrative medicine are some of the other pull factors that have increased the global recourse to it (de Roubaix, 2016; Bodeker and

---

1   South Africa is classified as a mixture of both a developing and a developed country (Mothibe & Sibanda, 2019). In terms of infrastructure, the country's metropolitan and surrounding areas tend to be that of a developed nation whereas the rural countryside has all the hallmarks of an underdeveloped nation with poor infrastructure.

kronenberg, 2002). Additionally, geographically diverse political, economic and cultural contexts, factors significantly influence health and healthcare (see King, 2012; King, 2010; Farmer, 2006; Andrews and Boon, 2005). Medical pluralism has become global business, and corporate actors including pharmaceutical companies are appropriating traditional knowledge systems.

This book argues that the 'benevolent' global optimism articulated by powerful international actors such as the WHO and the World Bank who are uncritically pushing for the mainstreaming of diverse healthcare systems and practices into the public healthcare system are insensitive to the local context of traditional health practices and knowledge systems for a good number of reasons. First, there is a disjuncture between the personal choices the public makes in terms of integrating different medical systems on the one hand and on the other, between the TCAM policy formulation and their implementation. Challenges such as safety, efficacy, quality and the rational use of traditional medicine stand on the way of this policy (Sobiecki, 2014; Oloyede, 2010; WHO, 2002). Secondly, the debate on efficacy (scientific evidence) about the effectiveness of traditional medicinal therapies is happening in a context where even evidence for the effectiveness of the renowned and highly researched and popular Chinese and Indian medical systems is meagre (Bode & Payyapplallimana, 2013). The EBM approach whose epistemological foundation is biomedically-oriented Randomized Controlled Trials (RCTs) is entangled in power relations (Bode and Payyapplallimana, 2013: 1), or what Oloyede (2010: 75) calls "the power and superiority of the [RCT's] mode of evaluation of efficacy." It has been argued that clinical trials of traditional medicines are epistemologically problematic: They cannot be evaluated by scientific methods (Mackenzie-Cook, 2006) because science-based medicine is said to be reductionist, while traditional herbal medicine is vitalistic (Coulter & Willis, 2004; Oloyede, 2010).

Although patient's entitlement "to treatments of proven efficacy" (Calapai, 2008: 428) that takes cognizance of their values (Kelly et al., 2015) is germane and a human rights, EBM is pure rhetoric[2] and therefore easy to manipulate because it is an ideal and not a reality. While EBM always requires integration of patient values with 'best' clinical evidence, scientific practices and

---

2 This is a debatable issue because we are unable to explain the perceived efficacy of drugs and therapies developed in this way (see Maxim, 2006). A pragmatic approach is to rather perceive CAM as a domain of treatment which "according to the self-concept of its exponents and opponents is outside science-oriented medicine" (Anlauf et al., 2015: 1). We cannot rule out the fact that "measures attributed today to CAM may tomorrow belong to science-oriented medicine after corresponding proof of efficacy. Such a switch from individual CAM procedures to science-oriented medicine would not however prove the therapeutic efficacy of other CAM procedures, leave lone all CAM procedures" (Ibid.).

discoveries, including those of EBM have been widely recognized to be value-laden (Kelly et al., 2015). Additionally, the criteria for evaluating efficacy and safety are underpinned by "...different point of views and filtered by different opinions according to the clinical or traditional experience in various folk systems of medicine in different European countries" (Calapai, 2008: 428; citing Mahady, 2001). Less than "twenty percent of medical treatments performed in state of the art biomedical hospitals are evidence based" (Bode & Payyapplallimana, 2013: 5). The logic of capitalism (profitability) significantly determines the focus of medical research as well as its outcomes. This implies that diseases of the poor do not get the attention they deserve (Abraham, 1995; Fischer, 2009; cf. Bode & Payyapplallimana, 2013: 5). Furthermore, in the discourse of 'integration,' the form of partnership between traditional medicine and biomedicine remains contentious partly because both systems are based on different philosophies about illness and disease, or different and incompatible ethos (Sobiecki, 2014). Additionally, traditional medicine is a concatenation of diverse medical thoughts and practices (de Roubaix, 2016; Sobiecki, 2014; Van der geest, 1997) and not a monolithic system of healing and practice. The term alternative medicine refers to a huge heterogeneous category defined by what they are not, rather than what they are (WHO, 2002: 8). Calls for the integration of both systems of health care is tantamount to, and suggests the standardization and control of what does not fall under the province of biomedical modality of knowing and knowledge (Oloyede, 2010: 75; Sobiecki, 2014). TCAM is an all-encompassing label for a "genre of health care practices or services that got bounded together as a class through the logic of *reductio ad absurdum*, defined by a criteria of absence from the mainframe of what has come to be known as modern medicine" (Patwardhan, 2005; cf, Payyappallimana, 2010: 58; Oloyede, 2010: 75). In tandem with the recommendations of WHO as translated through various global and regional initiatives including the ALMA ATA Declaration (1978) and the UN MDGs, the Bamako Initiative—Africa's interpretation of the Alma-Ata Declaration and the Partnership for Africa's Development (NEPAD)— that recognize the significant contributions of traditional medical systems to health equity for all, African governments are being told to mobilize the skills and expertise of traditional medical practitioners in the fight against both communicable and non-communicable diseases. This lofty ambition is to be achieved through partnerships that will culminate in the integration of traditional medical and knowledge systems into biomedicine. This attempt to biomedicalize myriad traditional knowledge systems and practices read like the total emasculation of the latter by the former (Flint, 2016; Peltzer, 2008). For instance, as exemplified by the fight against the HIV/AIDS pandemic, while traditional healers are willing to collaborate with biomedical practitioners by referring patients to them, the latter are unwilling to recommend patients to traditional healers. "The result has been the 'education' of traditional healers into the biomedical perspective, rather than a meeting of minds" (Flint, 2016: 4332). The euphoria and push for integration is taking place even when the latter (indigenous medicine) "has unique circumstances and qualities that do not easily render it amenable to integration with modern health services" (Mugisha et al., 2004; cf Mutabazi, 2008: 201).

Furthermore, attempts towards integration are entangled "in a war of semantics" as to the form that the proposed partnership should take. Three competing discourses frame the terms of this debate with enthusiastic advocates on both sides of the divide: 'formalisation,' 'collaboration,' "co-habitation and co-existence." This is the case even when both systems of healthcare have always co-existed (Ibid.) as evidenced by the practice of medical pluralism and the increasingly shuttle therapeutic recourse of HIV/AIDS patients (Wringe et al., 2017; Zuma et al., 2018). Even in South Africa, what passes as African, Indian or European medicine has been subjected to change over time. As Flint (2008: 16–17) maintains, "[i]n other words, there is the potential for leakage- the diffusion, adoption, and appropriation of other cultural ideas, practices, and artifacts. The result is a polycultural amalgam that blends various strands of influence, creating new and sometimes unexpected patterns in the cultural fabric." This suggests the existence of interaction between various knowledge systems as well as the shuttling therapeutic recourse strategy of patients as captured by the term "syncretic auto-medication" (Pemunta et al. 2020). Even the so-called 'co-optation of traditional medicine' and knowledge systems into the dominant biomedical system through research "would not only improve and demystify its therapeutic qualities" (Nyika, 2007: 25), but will provide validated information to traditional healers and patients on "their judicious use of indigenous medicine" (Mills et al., 2005: 1; cf, Oloyede, 2010: 75). The medical epistemology of integration is "an extension of the politics of knowledge domination by the West through the strengthening of the long-standing 'hegemony' of biomedicine" (Oloyede, 2010: 75; Sobiecki, 2014).

This multiple case study explores the role, nature and contribution of traditional practitioners towards the provision of healthcare in Qokolweni-a southern Nguni community of the poor Eastern Cape Province of the Republic of South Africa in an era of HIV/AIDS, democracy and the perpetuation of biomedical hegemony. Framed against the global movement for the integration of traditional healing practices into the dominant biomedical system, this book articulates the challenges inherent in this optimistic vision in the light of ambivalent state policies towards the integration of traditional practitioners into the mainstream healthcare system in the RSA in an era of HIV/AIDS. Alongside segregationist policies, which were instantiated through spatial policies such as the Group Areas Act (1950) and anti-miscegenation laws, traditional medicine was imbricated in the maintenance of cultural boundaries during apartheid, although cultural boundaries are not discrete. The enactment of segregationist policies and the neglect of traditional medical systems as tacit strategies meant to coerce medical pluralism, led to some unfettered effects including the continuous dominance of the biomedical paradigm (Chapter 3).

Beginning in the late 19th century indigenous medical practices in South Africa have been subjected to myriad transformations. The state attempted to regulate traditional medical practice by legalizing the practices of herbalists (*izinyanga*) while simultaneously forbidding the practices of diviners (*izangoma*). In the early 20th century, biomedicine became established, while indigenous medical practices were proscribed (de Roubaix, 2016). Although vigorous campaigns to prohibit indigenous medical practices intensified, these campaigns failed. However, the surging crime wave of the 1980s and 1990s and the collapse of law and order led to recourse to magical solutions in a bid to address threats to life and property (Ashforth, 2005; Flint, 2005; Geschiere, 2008; Pelgrim, 2003; Faure, 2002). This "dark side of traditional medical practice" gave rise to calls for the prohibition of indigenous medical practices, while others vigorously championed their normalization (Faure, 2002: 23) (Chapters 3 and 4).

> In general, [bio]medicine doesn't act on people coercively but through the subtle transformation of everyday knowledge and practice concerning the body… This is how hegemony operates and this is why one encounters such resistance in attempting to challenge notions and relationships that are now part of the shared common sense world. (Scheper-Hughes, 1992: 199)

Nancy Scheper-Hughes' statement quoted above provides a useful and evocative prism into the contentious debate raging on between those in favour of, and those against the integration of TCAM into the hegemonic system of biomedical healthcare worldwide in general and in South Africa in particular. The aim of integration is to biomedicalize traditional medicine and other forms of alternative therapies through standardization and regulation (Fournier, 2013: 55; Sobiecki, 2014). In his systematic overview of traditional healing practices in Australia, Europe, and the United States, Vincent Di Stefano (2006) discusses the increasing popularity of natural and complementary therapies. Exploring the development of the Western biomedical model and explaining the holistic philosophy on which alternative Western medicine is based, he provides a guide to the origins and core principles of natural therapies but also addresses key practice issues such as the role of holistic principles in today's healthcare system and their place in the therapeutic relationship. He poignantly and succinctly states that:

> The cultural dominance of biomedicine and its extraordinary successes have led many to believe it to be the one true medicine, the safe and effective medicine that has evolved out of the ages, superior in every way to everything coming before it and to the many other, lesser known, systems of medicine. Biomedicine has realized its present status through a commitment to what has become known as scientific method, a powerful method of inquiry aimed at generating new knowledge that can be codified, tested and transmitted to a professional community. (Ibid.:145)

Biomedical beliefs and practices are constitutive elements of a dominant and superior medical "science," which has developed out of a specific epistemological paradigm- essentially on the concepts of materialism, mechanism and rationality (Di Stefano, 2006). Today, biomedicine provides the barometer for the measurement of myriad other forms of medicine (Quah, 2003). Some of these other forms of medicine, including African traditional medicine that have been tested over thousands of years, have become erased, devalued and contorted by biomedical hegemony (see King, 2002; Arnold, 1988). Anthropologists who have traditionally been interested in medicine and in indigenous healing practices that were framed as ethnomedicine were complicit in the balkanization of local knowledge systems. Ethnomedicine is the study of medical systems from the native point of view. It involves the study of native categories and explanatory models of illness (aetiologies, symptoms, progression of illness and therapeutic recourse strategies) (Kleinman, 1980; Leslie, 2001).

By designating traditional health practices as ethnomedicine, anthropologists contributed to the bifurcation of knowledge: traditional versus modern, superstition and science, rational and irrational cultures (de Roubaix, 2016), a situation that reinforced the position and hegemony of biomedicine and its truth claims. Are both systems of healthcare different? Why do patients and providers "dip" into both simultaneously?

1.4 Different but Complimentary?

The distinction between biomedicine and traditional medicine is not difficult to solve. Both systems of therapy are underpinned by belief in the supernatural.

This undermines the often-made distinction between biomedicine as based on science and traditional healing practices as based on superstition, and belief in the power of supernatural intercession. This is despite differences in terms of the training and expertise of both categories of practitioners. The premise that biomedicine is based on science and traditional medicine on the supernatural has been questioned (Benson et al., 2002; de Roubaix, 2016; Flint, 2016). According to Adrian Flint: "At the same time, appeals to the healing powers of supernatural forces are not as divorced from a contemporary biomedical perspective as mainly operating within a "rationalist" mindset would like to admit. Chaplains of various faiths are attached to most biomedical hospitals and users of biomedical institutions employ prayer regularly as a complement to treatment. A survey suggests that up to 70 percent of Americans believe that prayer can help to cure sickness" (Benson et al., 2002: 577; cf. Flint, 2016: 4327).

Biomedicine claims to be based on "sound, scientific, evidence."[3] That is to be based on formal studies for diagnosing, treating and curing disease (at least, alleviating and consoling patients) compassionately and respectfully (de Roubaix, 2016). This is contrary to African traditional cosmology that is based on the co-existence and harmony between the physical and metaphysical worlds: "confluent explanations of existence and natural occurrences of life, religion, health, disease, healing and death" (de Roubaix, 2016: 160). The vision of African society is that of a collective. This concept of Ubuntu is eloquently summed up by John Mbiti's aphorism: "I am because we are, and because we are, therefore I am" (Mbiti, 1992: 141; de Roubaix, 2016: 160; Menketi, 2004). This implies that the cause of illness is searched for within the extended relationship of the patient and treatment sometimes entail bringing harmony into this relationship by involving even extended family members. This is for instance, the case when a ritual is offered to the ancestors to assuage their anger and bring good health and luck.

While the world of science and biomedicine are opened to traditional healers, the contrary is not true of biomedical practitioners. The former combine elements of biomedicine with traditional healing practices (de Roubaix, 2016;

---

3 In "science-oriented medicine," "proof of benefit is normally obtained by gathering and evaluating aggregated patient data in clinical studies using suitable biometric methods. Thus, chances of the benefits and risks of harm are identified, strictly speaking. How a therapy works is not supposed to and cannot primarily be answered by such stochastic experiments (e.g., randomised controlled trials), rather only the fact that it does work" (Walter, 1970; cf. Anlauf et al., 2015: 1). Evidence simply means "grounds for belief," any grounds, not merely scientific. This implies that if a faith healer believes in the efficacy of the therapy he dispenses, his evidence may simply be faith. EBM is based on inductive logic. It involves observing to arrive conclusions. On the contrary, deductive logic allows conclusions to be made without observations (Sarker Seshadri, 2014; Maxim, 2006).

Flint, 2015). Some traditional healers in Tanzania have reportedly embraced "modern" approaches including the testing of treatments for efficacy and dosage, the manufacturing of powders and tablets to make the medicine last longer than fresh plant products, as well as large-scale manufacturing and packaging (de Roubaix, 2016). These innovations suggest that traditional medicine is not cast in stone. As Flint (2016: 4326) points out traditional healing is not static. It is not "a body of knowledge and practices sealed in time." Changes in the practice of traditional medicine is partly a result of engagement with healers from other parts of the African continent and beyond (Ibid.).

Traditional medicine is perceived by patients as "culturally appropriate" (Flint, 2016: 4321). This invites the need to develop "forms of treatment that emphasise complementarity rather than adversarial engagement" between the traditional and biomedical systems (Flint, 2016: 4321). The perception of traditional medicine as based on the binary of superstition and irrationality perspective is being gradually challenged (Flint, 2016; de Roubaix, 2016).

Even the distinction based on different methods of diagnosis and treatment between "traditional" and "biomedical" system of healthcare is not unproblematic. Globally, the separation between the perceived differences of approaches to illness, Bradley Stoner points out is less precisely delineated. The main reason is that both patients and practitioners on both sides "dip into" the alternatives available to them. This patient-doctor pattern of medical pluralism suggests that "meaningful engagement can take place when the need arises" (Stoner, 1986: 2013). As Flint and Stoner variously demonstrate, "what people want in respect to healthcare, are options, irrespective of how these may be defined" (Flint, 2016: 4326; Stoner, 1986: 2013). Practitioners of biomedicine also believe in the power of supernatural intercession, particularly in prayers. This is despite the fact that their impact cannot be quantified. Similarly, although there is no ontological space for the supernatural most patients being treated within a biomedical framework also believe in supernatural intervention (Flint, 2016: 4327).

While the biomedical model is pathology-focused, traditional forms of healing rely heavily on aspects of the supernatural with respect to both diagnosis and treatment. "Healer" and "medicine" have a broad meaning than within biomedicine (Flint, 2016; Johnson, 2002). Healers fix disharmony within the family of the patient to bring him back to good health (Mbiti, 1992). "Traditional practitioners treat their patients exclusively within the community setting, often with the direct participation of family members and significant others in the diagnosis and treatment of diseases" (Bruce, 2002: 163).

In terms of training and expertise, we admit that the supernatural dimension of traditional healing systems is difficult to accommodate within the biomedical framework. The healing power of traditional healers is often derived from the strength of their relationship with the "spirit world" and/the ancestors (Flint, 2016; Mbiti, 1992).

There is no doubt about the existence of a wide gulf between biomedical and traditional African cosmologies as well as differences in "approaches to diagnosis, patient care, and treatment, double-blind testing and laboratory-based demonstration of efficacy" (Flint, 2016: 4328). These biomedical parameters are however "inadequate tools for validating diagnoses acquired through communication with the spirit world" (Ibid.). Despite intense debate, biomedicine focuses on treating disease while traditional healing deals with illness as a psychosocial condition (de Roubaix, 2016; Mpofu et al., 2011; WHO, 1978). Traditional healing is often communal, rather than private as is the case with biomedicine. Although treatment and medications are tailored to the needs of the individual, it sometimes involves both the patient and members of his or her extended family through participation in collective rituals. Healers inordinately spend a huge amount of time with their patients: They are involved in "unhurried and deeply personalised" (Flint, 2016: 4328) treatment. Healers even cover great distances, visiting their patients at home (Flint, 2016; Shuster et al., 2009). This is not the case with biomedicine. Biomedical practitioners spend limited time with their patients (Flint, 2016). Home care and visits are often the exception (Shuster et al., 2009) rather than the rule.

Both biomedical and traditional African health practitioners identify what is wrong with their patients. Biomedicine cannot however, explain misfortune. It is underpinned by the view that "diseases are contracted randomly (at least in part) against a background of a largely disinterested universe" (Flint, 2016: 4330). Jealousy-as-causation theory of disease offers solace to patients (Flint, 2016; Farmer, 2006; Sterk & Del Rio, 2008; Wreford, 2005) including those suffering from HIV/AIDS.

Jean-François Sobiecki (2014) highlights the perceived stigmatization of "traditional healing practices as 'irrational' and ungrounded in scientific methods in the academia" as a miscomprehension accruing from the failure to interpret African traditional medicine concepts because they are "often metaphorical descriptions of the biological and psychological effects of plants or combinations of them used in traditional medicine preparations" (2014: 1). When these metaphorical descriptions of medicinal plants are translated into other languages, including English, they seem to erroneously reflect mysticism and/or superstition with no scientific basis. Secondly, the paucity of academic papers that engage with the science of South African traditional medicine in the biological sciences is an indication of the disconnect between humanities studies and biomedical studies of South African traditional medicine. He combines phytopharmacological studies with participant observation to demonstrate the empirical basis for the use of some plants in divination for providing clarity of thought or dreams.

In South Africa, phytopharmacological studies with focus on screening and isolating phytochemicals for specific pharmacological actions have been conducted with the aim of developing new allopatic medicines (Sobiecki, 2014; Light et al., 2005). The result has been the steady validation of traditional medicine claims from scientific studies. This has been the case mostly with plants traditionally used to cure physical ailments and plants with antibiotic properties used for infections (Sobiecki, 2014; Brooks and Katsoulis, 2007).

The use of biomedical parameters (scientific method) to validate the physical and psychological uses of traditional medicine is problematic. In the case of spiritual healing, there is difficulty in testing, assessing and interpreting the psychological effects resulting from the internal administration of psychoactive plants in humans (Sobiecki, 2014: 2). The more pervasive reason is however "the culturally ingrained prejudice against traditional medicine" and healing methods, including "its associated religious or spiritual plant use which is often deemed irrational, non-empirical and unscientific" (Sobiecki, 2014: 2). The physical and spiritual uses of plants are sometimes intertwined, with mutually inclusive physical, psychological and spiritual therapeutic effects that correspond with the African world sense "of the co-existing and interdependent relationship between the physical and spiritual nature of sickness, medicines and existence" (Petrus and Bogopa, 2007; cf. Sobiecki, 2014: 2; Mbiti, 1992).

The prejudicial assessments of African traditional therapies and the disjuncture between cultural and biomedical studies of African traditional medicine fueled by the neglect of indigenous knowledge in ethno/phytopharmacological research outputs often leave the false impression that the traditional use of plants is partly or largely an "incidental, anecdotal and ultimately insignificant phenomenon" (Sobiecki, 2014: 3). This points to the need not only to take account of a plant's phytochemical actions, but also to "incorporate the interacting dynamics of ritual, phytochemical synergy of the plant mixtures used and the psychology of the medicine user" (Sobiecki, 2012; cf. Sobiecki, 2014: 3).

The view of African traditional medicine as "unscientific" or "irrational" (Sobiecki, 2014) is deeply entrenched in the biological sciences. This is due to the lack of research on the cultural and spiritual dimensions of African medicinal plants. According to Taylor et al. (2001: 24):

> The rational use of traditional medicine is also not well-defined, and often relies on ritual, mysticism and intangible forces such as witchcraft,

with some aspects based on spiritual and moral principles which are difficult to rationalize.

This common misperception of traditional medicine as a medley of irrational aspects, we argue is partly the enduring legacy of "the colonial construction of Africa's 'otherness' and essential 'primitiveness'" (Croucamp, 2001: 1). This has resonances with the invalidation, distortion and simultaneous appropriation of the traditional public domain that also involved the denigration and demonization of diviners (Sobiecki, 2014: 3; Bishop, 2012) as 'pillars of Satan's Kingdom' (Croumcamp, 2001: 1). The imposed religion of the colonialists was in the same light, "contrasted with the superstition of southern Africans" (Ibid.).

There are pervasive prejudicial views about traditional medicine in both the media and in the academic literature on the subject in South Africa and other African countries. The first is the view of Western medicine as based on scientific diagnostics and traditional medicine as unscientific as well as the leveling of toxicity issues against traditional medicine. Writing on the differences between Western and traditional approaches, Bruce (2002: 162) states:

> Modern or Western medicine is dominant in Western societies and is firmly rooted in a scientific paradigm; medical science is used to explain the cause of disease using a biomedical practice model. Traditional medicine operates within an indigenous, spiritual realm, which explains the cause of disease as social or psychological conflicts or imbalance.

The extremely polarized view that there is no scientific basis underpinning the practice of traditional medicine is false. According to Jean-François Sobiecki (2014: 4) "Southern Bantu traditional healers typically assess patients by diagnosing medical signs and symptoms based on repeated observations, and prescribe medicinal plants that have replicable effects and results correlating with the presenting symptoms." Such plant therapies have been tested over generations for observable and replicable effects, which therefore demonstrates "the underlying scientific method involved with such medicine practices" (Sobiecki, 2014: 3). Western practitioners and researchers often gloss over this diagnostic aspect, rather focusing on the overt ritual aspects of traditional medicine.

Although it is true that if African traditional medicine has to be manufactured and sold on a large-scale as products, issues of safety and efficacy need to be addressed through standardization, it is however ironic that toxicity concerns are only levelled against traditional medicines. Concurrently, a blind eye is turned on similar concerns when it comes to modern medicine, even when they do genuinely exist (Bruce, 2002: 162; Sobiecki, 2014). In attempting to address commonalities between Western and African traditional healing practices, Alomar (2013) instead illuminated the dangers of toxic plants used in African traditional pharmacopoeia. He illustrated with statistics of African medicine related deaths caused by toxins with no mention of the adverse drug effects associated with the use of biomedicine, whereas there is mounting evidence that "adverse drug reactions (ADRs) from Western pharmaceuticals are one of the leading causes of morbidity and mortality in healthcare" (Alomar, 2013: 2 cf. Sobiecki, 20144). According to Alomar (2013), in 2000 the US Institute of Medicine reported that an estimated 44 000 deaths occurred per annum because of medical errors, with an estimated 7000 of these cases resulting from ADRs (cf. Sobiecki, 2013). Issues of toxicity clearly pertains to both systems of medicine and highlight the need for complementarity.

While biomedicine is characterized by a high degree of regulation, and formalization, opponents of integration point to the non-existence of regulation and formalization of the traditional medicine sector (de Roubaix, 2016; Flint, 2017; Sobiecki, 2014). Although the prescription and administration of traditional medicine recipes in South Africa is currently unregulated with the likelihood of the misadministration of especially toxic plants, are regulatory standards really the mechanism through which toxicity issues are addressed in Western medicine? The reality is that despite the existence of standard regulatory frameworks and practices, evidence indicates a trend of increasing deaths and injury resulting from adverse drug reactions in allopatic medicine. Sobiecki (2014: 4) reports from ethnographic fieldwork that Southern Bantu healers are able to nullify toxins during drug preparation or through the prescription of specific dosages for limited periods to avert toxicity (see Lantum, 1979).

The absence of sophisticated technology is one other prejudicial viewpoint undermining traditional medicine from the perspective of biomedicine. The healer's practice usually involves "herbs, plants and plant products, animal products and spiritual resources that are used to prevent and treat disease" (Bruce, 2002: 162). She however fails to mention the fact that authentic Southern Bantu traditional healers use the phytochemical synergistic actions of traditional medicine preparations in the treatment of various diseases and illness, as well as the complex psychoactive mechanisms that is constitutive of ritual plant therapy in the healing initiation process (Sobiecki, 2014; Sobiecki, 2012). She also fails to discern the fact that traditional medicine is not cast in stone. It is rather, dynamic (Flint, 2016; de Roubaix, 2016). There is clearly the failure to understand the scientific principles that are operational in traditional medicine. The lack of collaboration between biomedical scientists and traditional healers explain why various ethnomedicines have not been scientifically validated for safety and efficacy (Chinsembu, 2009: 1), rather than "because the treatments or processes lack scientifically verifiable mechanisms of action" (Sobiecki, 2014: 5). The lack of interdisciplinary studies of African traditional medicine is due to prejudices and "difficulties in decoding cultural and language based meanings, rather than the underlying scientific validity of these cultural practices" (Sobiecki, 2014: 5). The view of traditional medicine as irrational is due to the failure by biomedical practitioners and botanists to properly interpret the masked culturally defined metaphorical descriptions of plant use. Many African traditional medicines practices therefore have a scientific basis (Ibid.).

A further obstacle to the advancement and professionalisation of African traditional medicine and its eventual integration into modern medicine that calls for the need for regulation is the lack of "common diagnostic nomenclature, therapeutic method, or curriculum, and thus attempts to create accreditation have failed. Traditional healing is still unregulated because there is no established accreditation procedure. This opens the door to charlatans who give traditional healing a bad name" (Peltzer, 2009; cf. Mcfarlane, 2015: 64). In South Africa, the regulatory framework is replete with ambiguities, and raise issues about the intellectual property rights of healers. This is partly because they are required to submit their curriculum to the regulatory authority (see Street, 2016).

Despite concerns about traditional medical practices, we subscribe to a marriage between traditional medicine and biomedicine because of the commonalities and therefore complementarity between the two systems: (1) Prevention and protection against disease or 'problems' (afflictions), (2) Determination of the cause of disease or 'problem,' (3) Eliminating these problems (Bruce, 2002: 163). It is a self-evident fact that there is widespread use of traditional medicine by the South African population, yet biomedicine remains the dominant medical system in the country.

As Di Stefano (2006) rightly maintains, the advent of modern medicine led to the abandonment of already accumulated knowledge from numerous healers over long periods of time. This stock of knowledge was pushed aside once medical science began to unveil its power. However, traditional medical systems and practices did not disappear, they simply went underground. Among other changes, a grain of purified alkaloids replaced plant extracts with curative properties that had been used as therapy (Ibid.). "Humoral diagnosis, based on the four elements of the ancients, was progressively put aside as new knowledge of anatomical pathology began to emerge. And spiritual or metaphysical interpretations of disease were deemed irrelevant after the discovery of disease causing micro-organisms and the development of modern epidemiology" (Di Stefano, 2006: 117). There is a paradigmatic gulf between what has been designated as traditional/ indigenous medicine that partly comprises what is derogatorily referred to as "TCAM" and biomedicine as universal truth. The former is often presumed as being 'irrational' and 'superstitious' in relation to the latter (Sobiecki, 2014; Arnold, 1988), while the latter is often essentialized as Western, rational, scientific and universalistic(de Roubaix, 2016; Flint, 2016). In reality, biomedicine is increasingly co-opting effective non-orthodox approaches to healing through their integration into the medical curriculum in the name of programmes in integrative or alternative medicine (Di Stefano, 2006). Traditional medical systems that have always maintained a complementary and conflictual relationship with biomedicine have also become syncretic and patients and their "therapy seeking group" (Hsu, 2008) as well as healers have always resorted to medical pluralism (Chapter 8).

Despite biomedical attempts to explain and treat disease, an ancient system of healing- traditional medicine- continues to thrive in Africa. The WHO has since recognized and encouraged governments to accept traditional medicine as an alternative healthcare; and to adopt healthcare policies that will promote traditional medicine as well as its integration into the mainstream healthcare system (Mogkobi, 2013; WHO, 1978; WHO, 2002). Despite this clarion call for recognition, most governments are reluctant and ambivalent to officially incorporate traditional healing practices into healthcare policies even when a majority of their population constantly makes recourse to this therapeutic regimen. Compounding the situation is that even countries-including South Africa—which have recognized the relevance of traditional medicine face greater obstacles and challenges on modalities to control and include traditional medicine and their practitioners into mainstream healthcare (Mogkobi, 2013; Campbell-Hall, 2010).

With the various socio-economic, political and cultural transformations that followed the collapse of the apartheid regime and a renewed challenge to provide affordable and accessible healthcare to all South Africans, as well as the challenge posed by the HIV/AIDS pandemic, the role of traditional medicine has once again taken centre stage in the provision of primary healthcare.

Field research for this study was implemented in the Qokolweni Location in the King Sabatha Dalindyebo (KSD) district municipality of the Eastern Cape Province. Information was elicited using questionnaires, in-depth, face-to-face interviews with respondents and participant observation. The study revealed that traditional healers handle and manage complex hospital diagnosed health conditions. It further shows that perceptions on disease aetiology influence health-seeking behaviour and the choice between treatment options ("subaltern health narratives") (King, 2012). It is therefore necessary to understand the efforts of traditional healers in order to formulate healthcare policies that would officially involve them in the mainstream healthcare system in South Africa. It is noticeable that traditional healing is not only limited to the Qokolweni community. It also occurs mutatis mutandis elsewhere in the Eastern Cape and in the whole of South Africa. Interventions to acquaint traditional practitioners with Western approaches and biomedical practitioners with traditional systems of healing for the treatment of illness, orientation of Western practitioners towards a culture-centred and sensitive approach to healthcare, as well as the establishment of fora to facilitate dialogue and the negotiation of respectful collaborative relationships between the two systems of healing are required to promote an equitable collaboration in the interests of improved healthcare in the RSA.

1.5 Layout of This Work

This chapter has set the macroeconomic context within which traditional knowledge systems including TCAM is increasingly used by patients as they seek to make independent decisions about their health in both the developed and less developed world. We partly critique the 'benevolent,' uncritical calls and optimism for the integration of traditional and modern medicine as echoed at various international conferences and by powerful actors including national governments through the aegis of the World Bank and the WHO. The Chapter further highlights the differences between both systems of healthcare. We however, argue for bridging the seemingly unbridgeable differences between both systems of healthcare because there are many points of convergence including the use of both systems of healthcare by patients and healers alike than meets the uncritical eye.

In Chapter 2, we examine the subject matter, method, theoretical perspectives informing this study that seeks to examine the prospects of integrating traditional and modern medicine in the Qokolweni Location of the Republic of South Africa. We point to the need for healthcare policymakers to seriously take the view from below and explore the mechanism through which patients and their therapy-seeking group make decisions between alternative healthcare providers.

Chapter 3 unpacks the interaction between colonialism and apartheid on the one hand, and modern and traditional medicine on the other hand. It discusses how the former two fields of power ensured biomedical hegemony at the expense of traditional medical practices and practitioners who were labelled as "witchdoctors" and their practices, although banned was still surreptitiously practiced underground. It provides insights into health inequalities between blacks and whites that resulted from the "medical apartheid" that was a constitutive component of the unequal development and that led to the rapid deterioration of the health status and socioeconomic wellbeing of the black population who were herded into reserves and their land appropriated.

On its part, Chapter 4 examines how within the context of democracy that was associated with the re-valorization of African culture and tradition, the ANC-government adopted contradictory policies. Keen on asserting their cultural credentials, the ANC leadership promoted traditional medicine partly as a way of giving a sense of belonging to blacks who had suffered cultural erasure and uprootedness under the apartheid system of exclusionary governance. In line with this policy framework, it forwarded traditional medicine as cure for the ravaging HIV/AIDS pandemic. Concurrently, it banned the use of life-saving antiretroviral therapy thereby leaving frustrated HIV/AIDS patients at the mercy of traditional healers. Traditional medicine simultaneously became both a cure and a curse for the pandemic. The multiple social crises of the time—widespread economic hard times, unemployment, lack of marriage opportunities and mounting inequalities between haves and have nuts led to a witchcraft scare that militated in favour of traditional healers who were solicited for both explanations and solutions for these social problems.

On its part, Chapter 5 examines the social context of disease and the resulting low human development index of the Eastern Cape Province (the site of Qokolweni Location) in comparison with the rest of South Africa. We examine the entanglement of individual and community level factors that have conspired and predispose people to the risk of infection with the HIV.

In Chapter 6, we return to the debate between advocates and opponents of the integration of traditional and modern medicine. We highlight various positions in the debate. We point out collaborative initiatives between biomedical practitioners and traditional healers within the context of the HIV/AIDS pandemic and various policy initiatives towards the integration of both systems of medicine in Africa in general and South Africa in particular.

Chapter 7 provides a broad overview of the African concept of health and disease as well as a typology of various healers and their specialties (heterogeneity) and the overlap between them. We demonstrate that medical pluralism is not only practiced by patients and their "therapy seeking group" (Hsu, 2002) but also by healers. We therefore argue for the prospects of integration between biomedical practitioners and traditional healers.

In Chapter 8, we examine health-seeking decision making between traditional and modern medicine among locals in Qokolweni Location and argue for the need by policy-makers to be aware of "subaltern health narratives" (King, 2012: 1179) and patient's simultaneous recourse strategies as they seek to maximize the chances of restoring themselves to good health. As active agents in their own health, they believe that both systems of medicine are complementary.

Chapter 9 summarizes the findings of this study and suggests some recommendations for the effective integration of modern and traditional medicine in Qokolweni Location in particular and in South Africa in general.

CHAPTER 2

Subject Matter, Method and Theoretical Framework

2.1 Introduction

The aim of this study is to explore the prospects of integrating traditional and modern medicine in the Qokolweni Location of the Eastern Cape Region of South Africa within the context of the HIV/AIDS policy debate. Faced with the ravaging pandemic, the ANC-government was caught between promoting African culture including the use of traditional medicine as therapy for HIV/AIDS while refusing the use of antiretroviral therapy on ground of doubts about its effectiveness and toxicity but also as a way of finding "an African solution" to an African problem (Ashford, 2005). How did this contradictory policy framework affect the use of traditional medicine and shape local views about HIV/AIDS?

To achieve the aim of this study, we explore some of the alleged shortcomings of traditional medicine—traditional medicine as in need of perfection from the perspective of healers, nurses and users but also as a cure and a curse for HIV/AIDS patients. What types of illness episodes are managed through traditional healing and why? We then articulate proper ways of improving on these shortcomings to enhance the prospects of incorporating traditional medicine into conventional medicine as a means of bringing healthcare closer to the majority of South Africans. "Medicine is too important to be left to biomedicine" (McKenna, 2012: 112). This quote implies that medicine is more than what the reductionism of biomedicine is forwarding it to be. This is particularly the case with the myriad array of traditional health practices, beliefs and knowledge systems, which have been reduced to TCAM and are being forcefully biomedicalized in the name of integration into the dominant biomedical healthcare system. The simultaneous devaluation, contortion and even the erasure of a multiplicity of age-old health beliefs, practices and health systems through pharmaceutization (Fournier, 2013) puts these health systems at the risk of becoming increasingly biomedicalized and lost as they are "integrated" into biomedical settings. In the process of negating, but simultaneously converting and appropriating indigenous knowledge systems and practices into new drugs (Sobiecki, 2014; Fournier, 2013), differing worldviews about health, and approaches to healthcare, are becoming increasingly homogenized and monolithicized on a global scale (Fournier, 2013). Against this backdrop, how do users of traditional medicine respond to the benevolent capitalist vision of integration being paraded about by powerful international actors such as the WHO and the World Bank through national governments?

The focus of research on the integration of TCAM into the institutional architecture of biomedicine has been dominated by overemphasis on inter-professional dynamics and tensions between biomedical and TCAM practitioners in clinical settings (see Baer & Coulter, 2008; Mizrachi & Shuval, 2005; Hollenberg, 2006), and the epistemological challenges of integrative medicine (see Hollenberg & Muzzin, 2010). Another brand of studies has explored the epistemological challenges of integrative medicine (see Di Stefano, 2006; Hollenberg & Muzzin, 2010). While these studies fail to critically explore the ontological content of TCAM and the challenges it poses to integration, international organizations such as WHO and the World Bank have for decades continued to express an overly optimistic vision on the integration of traditional healing practices and knowledge systems into the dominant biomedical health care model. Fournier (2013) has explored the incorporation of TCAM within biomedical education, as well as the macro-political-market factors influencing this integration process into the biomedical curriculum in Canada. Contrary to these studies, this book explores the myriad perspectives of users of traditional medicine, healers as well as nurses. It contributes to a nuanced critique of what might be styled as the benevolent integration of TCAM in biomedicine in South Africa despite the government's inconsistency and policy ambivalence. It demonstrates the need to take "subaltern health narratives" (King, 2010; King, 2012) seriously in formulating healthcare policy by exploring the sociocultural context of decision making about the use of traditional medicine in local context.

To the African, traditional medicine is intricable from African culture. It is also intricately linked to diverse African perceptions of reality and worldviews. Traditional medicine is intertwined with the life and worldviews of traditional Africans. According to Wessels:

> The worldviews of traditional Africans are not integrated but form a complex system in which beliefs concerning ancestral spirits, magic, sorcery, witches and pollution exist together. This loose association provides a natural way of understanding misfortune and provides understandable answers to the vexing questions of the purpose of life. (cf. Krige, ND: 6)

Among the Nguni, ideas about illness causation are closely associated with the causes of misfortune, including the ancestors, witchcraft or sorcery, and pollution (Cumes, 2010: 6; Der Villiers, 1985: 48). There is, however, "a distinction between supernatural or mystical, or natural or non-mystical causes" (De Villiers, 1985: 48) of illness among the people. This suggests the co-existence of supernatural/personalistic and naturalistic theories of illness causation. The latter may be attributed to God (De Villiers, 1985: 48; Cumes, 2010: 6) or to exposure to harsh environmental conditions or to disease pathogens. The African worldview is of course, anchored on the belief that departed ancestors incessantly "provide protection, guidance and admonition from the spirit realm" (Wallace, 2015: 30), and that maintaining reciprocal relationships and obligations between the worlds of the living and the dead is a conditio sine qua non for social, physical, and psychic health and wellbeing. This makes practices such as divination, sacrifice and the offering of ancestral ritual critical (Wallace, 2015: 30; Mbiti, 1970). This explains why even benevolent ancestors are alleged to inadvertently cause illness "by turning away from their progeny."

> If the ancestors feel that they are being ignored, they may cause harm by omission rather than commission. In feeling neglected, they may abandon their loved ones and no longer afford them protection. Sometimes an ancestor may want a loved one to join him on the other side, which results in sickness. Malevolent ancestors, and especially vindictive foreign spirits who may have been wronged, can also cause illness, misfortune, accidents, and even death for the descendants of those who have wronged them. All possibilities can be counteracted by the right prayers, rituals, muti, and sacrifices. Ancestors who have turned away can be encouraged to return and defend their descendants against malicious or intruding spirits. Illness is therefore frequently connected to human relationships between the living and the dead. However, if these relationships are perfectly functional and healthy, the sangoma will look to witchcraft or sorcery and pollution for the cause of the problem. Diagnoses are made with the help of Femba, trance-channeling, dreams, and the divining bones. There is usually a remedy for any dilemma. (Cumes, 2010: 6)

From an African perspective, "health thus implies being in harmony with cosmic vitality/energy (e.g., ancestors) are involved in the lives of the living [who] have to be honoured, otherwise they can cause ill-fortune." (Krige, ND:6, see also Mbiti, 1966). Let it be mentioned here however, that not all healers draw on ancestral relations in their healing practices. As Chris Low demonstrates, Bushmen trance healers in Namibia communicate with 'spirits' and are reported to travel in the spirit world "on 'strings' or on the backs of animals" (Low, 2004: 128). Dancing is alleged to activate the healing power or potency of trance healers. The power is believed to come from god and from the wider world but resides within the healer. In trance, healers are able to "see dead people outside the dance setting and communicate with supernal entities" (Ibid.).

Treatment is about the restoration of harmony within the body and between the body and the cosmos. Many people in Western societies have overwhelmingly embraced the health-centered paradigm of TCAM. People are interested in maintaining what can be done to maintain their health and the well-being of their families. TCAM is highly personalized giving patients more leverage in matters of health. "The clinical encounter serves not only to provide relief for the patient's symptoms or condition, but also provides an opportunity to explore preventative and restorative strategies that the patient can work with in their own time" (Di Stefano, 2006: 159).

This study explores the usage, opinions and attitudes of Africans towards traditional medicine in the municipality of Eastern Cape Province, South Africa. The study further examines the people's assessment of the strengths and shortcomings of traditional healing system with the aim of uncovering the role and contribution of traditional medicine in an era of HIV/AIDS and biomedical hegemony as well as a 'return to culture and tradition' as part of the wholesale transformation that the ANC-government adopted after 1994. The study identifies areas of complementarity and differences between traditional and conventional medicines. It then discusses how the relationship between the former and the latter systems of medicine can be improved. This study is an attempt to establish a platform for collaboration between conventional medicine and African traditional medicine for the general improvement of healthcare given the changing pattern of disease. In this regard, the study seeks to:
– assess the role of African traditional medicine in an era of conventional medicine.
– identify the users of African traditional medicine.
– explore people's attitudes towards African traditional medicine.
– explore the opinion and perceptions of different sexes and age groups towards the use of, and to create greater awareness on the utility of African traditional medicine.

The HIV/AIDS pandemic has forced public health officials throughout the developing world to reconsider their negative attitudes towards traditional medicine and its practitioners. It is recognized that traditional healers may be instrumental in preventing the spread of the virus as well as caring for the sick, particularly in rural areas with few conventional medical facilities or practitioners. There is also the possibility that medicinal plants may actually hold the key to fighting the virus. Indeed, in vitro studies of the alkaloid michellamine B, isolated from an indigenous Cameroonian plant *Ancistrocladus korupensis* (Cameroon vine), showed that the compound is active against two strains of the HIV virus, although it is at present far too toxic to be used as a therapy (Cragg & Boyd, 1996: 128). It has, however, since advanced into preclinical development. Continuous infusion studies in dogs have shown that in vivo effective anti-HIV concentration could only be achieved at doses close to neurotoxic levels. "Thus, despite in vitro activity against an impressive range of HIV-1 and HIV-2 strains, the difference between the toxic dose level and the anticipated level required for effective antiviral activity (the therapeutic index) was small" (Chibale et al., 2012: 46). Further studies aimed at clinical development have since been discontinued (Ibid.).

Below we make the case for the Qokolweni Location as the study area, discuss the data analysis process, the ethical considerations and the various theoretical perspectives informing this study of the prospects of integrating traditional medicine into the dominant biomedical healthcare system in South Africa.

2.2 Choice of Study Area

Qokolweni is one of the locations under the King Sabatha Dalindyebo (KSD) municipality in the Eastern Cape Province of the RSA. It is situated between latitude -31.1167 and Latitude (DMS) 31° 7'05, longitude 28.5500 and Longitude (DMS) 28° 33'0E. The 2010/2011 Integrated Development Plan (IDP) for the KSD municipality indicated that the Qokolweni Location has an estimated population of 6846 persons per 7 km radius. The average household income for the broad KSD region is estimated between R3000 and R3500 (KSD-IDP Report, 2010/2011). Most of the people are subsistent farmers. The Eastern Cape is regarded as the poorest region in the whole of South Africa (Chapter 5).

Sources: © Open Street Map, (https://www.roadonmap.com/za/where-is/Qokolweni-Umtata,eastern_cape).

Qokolweni was selected for this study for a number of reasons—principally its accessibility and the diversity of its population. Most importantly and to the best of our knowledge, a study of this nature has never been conducted in Qokolweni. Furthermore, one of the researchers lived in Mthatha which is just a few minutes' drive from Qokolweni for close to a decade and undertook extensive reproductive health and sexuality research in the region. He built networks with key stakeholders and community members over time. His familiarity with the area and the people partly provided access into the research sites. Additionally, the area has a mixed ethnic population—largely of Zulu and Sotho ethnicities who had settled earlier as a result of wars, and others who have migrated due to inter-ethnic marriages. Qokolweni also has residents who are foreign nationals. However, a bulk of the population is Xhosa speaking or from various Southern Nguni patrilineal ethnic groups. Lastly, preliminary visits to

MAP 1   Location of Mthatha in the Eastern Cape Region of South Africa
SOURCE: HTTPS://WWW.BRITANNICA.COM/PLACE/EASTERN-CAPE-PROVINCE-SOUTH-AFRICA/MEDIA/1/176933/129602

Qokolweni revealed widespread allegations of witchcraft activities as well as the lynching of several alleged witches and wizards. These allegations equally contributed towards the selection of Qokolweni as a research area. This was in line with the view of Zubane (2001) who noted that in areas where there are many witchcraft accusations more people are likely to use African traditional medicine. The Nguni hold a triple conception of illness: ancestors, witchcraft or sorcery, and pollution, but also maintain that God could be the cause of illness.

2.3   Methodological and Theoretical Framework

This mixed method study combined quantitative and qualitative research methods – survey research, participant observation, complemented by in-depth ethnographic interviews of patients of traditional healers (users) as well as traditional medicine healers and nurses in various locations in and around

SUBJECT MATTER, METHOD AND THEORETICAL FRAMEWORK 33

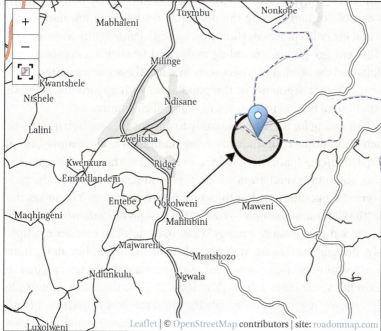

MAP 2　　Position on the map of Qokolweni suburb of Mthatha, Eastern Cape, South Africa
© OPEN STREET MAP, HTTPS://WWW.ROADONMAP.COM/ZA/WHERE-IS/QOKOLWENI-UMTATA,EASTERN_CAPE.

Qokolweni. Apart from patients, through purposive sampling, face-to-face key-informant interviews were conducted with eight knowledgeable persons or sages selected based on their deep knowledge on the domain of traditional medicine. Further in-depth interviews were also conducted with nine traditional healers: five herbalists and traditional birth attendants or midwives, two diviners and two faith healers respectively. In-depth interviews with key informants are indispensable in uncovering information about ways of living that have ceased to exist, or have been sharply modified by the time the fieldworker arrives on the scene (Pelto & Pelto, 1978). Bernard notes that in purposive sampling, the investigator consciously decides which respondents are likely to serve in his study (Bernard, 2006: 465). Similarly, Burns concedes that purposive sampling is useful if it "serves the real purpose and objectives of the researcher by enabling him to discover, gain insight and understanding into a particular phenomenon" (Burns, 2006: 465). In other words, to a limited extent the selection of various custodians of traditional medicine was based on a "sampling logic" with a focus on "those that are representative of the total population of similar cases" (Yin, 1994: 47). We adopted the "extended multiple case study method" (Ibid.). In this method of enquiry, the researcher seeks evidence to describe, understand and explain the case(s) under investigation, rather than to test a hypothesis. As Michael Burawoy rightly notes, this approach is capable of highlighting the discrepancies between normative prescriptions and everyday practices (Burawoy, 1998: 5). Participants were recruited from different age groups, including males and females, teenagers, young adults, adults and the aged. It was necessary to select these participants as they all represent different segments of the population with apparently different views on traditional medicine in an era of biomedical dominance.

Rather than opting for a single case study to answer the research questions, we conducted a multiple case study involving traditional healers, nurses, users of traditional medicine (patients) and members of their "therapy management group" (Hsu, 2008) in several areas within the main research site. In the process, we were still operating within the same research strategy. Yin makes the point that "the single and multiple—case study designs are variants that operate within the same case study strategy" (Yin, 1994: 44). The case for multiple case study designs has been well established: ethnographic data from multiple-case studies is often considered more persuasive and thus argued to make the overall study more robust (Yin, 1994: 141). Furthermore, a multiple case study exposes regularities through the simultaneous inspection of numerous cases (Eckstein, 2000: 137). "All other things being equal, a finding emerging repeatedly in the study of numerous sites ('a multi-site study') would seem to be more likely to be a good working hypothesis about some yet unstudied site than a finding emerging from just one or two sites'" (Schofield, 2000: 79; see also Kennedy, 1979: 662; Burton, 2000; Burt, 1992).

Interview sessions were tape-recorded, transcribed and analyzed thematically in the light of the overall objectives of the study. The actual research was preceded by a pilot study that was conducted to test and strengthen the research instruments. Pilot studies are very important in testing the utility of research instruments (Bailey, 1987; Leedy & Ormrod, 2005). The pilot study consisted of a stratified random sampling of ten traditional healthcare users and six traditional healers. The preliminary data collected during the pilot study was used in designing the final questionnaire that was administered to participants. As a research method, survey research ensures reliability of data collected as well as its analysis. This is relevant in discharging the "burden of proof- objectivity in procedures used in conducting the study and its findings. Proof of objectivity in any study allows for logical organization and presentation of data. Where there is proper presentation of data, valid conclusions can be made" (Miller & Brewer, 2003: 262). A survey can be used for descriptive, explanatory and exploratory purposes. Surveys are chiefly used in studies that have individuals as units of analysis. Surveying is one of the best methods available to social scientists who are interested in collecting original data for describing, measuring attitudes and orientations in a population too large to observe directly (Babbie, 2009: 232). The survey made use of structured, face-to-face interviews, and questionnaires as data collection techniques (see Mathew & Carole, 2004). We used these techniques to ensure flexibility in data collection, reliability and validity of findings.

In the study proper, fifty questionnaires were administered to participants selected from across the different age brackets in the community. Of those who responded to the questionnaire, 6 participants were under 20 years of age; 18 were within the 21–30 age bracket, 10 were within the 31–40 age frame; 6 respondents were within the 41–50 age bracket while 10 others were above the age of 50 years. Overall, 30 female and 20 male respondents completed the questionnaires. The selection of 30 females and 20 males was based on the population ratio of 1: 2 with more females (KSD-IDP, 2010/2011). Apart from the 50 respondents to whom questionnaires were administered, complementary information was adduced from 8 sages and nine traditional medicine practitioners. Additionally, 12 nurses were interviewed on their opinions, experiences and perception of collaboration between traditional healers and biomedical practitioners. Seventy-nine interlocutors participated in the entire study.

Where statistical analysis of materials is secondary to the general descriptive information, questionnaires can be quite useful, and once the schedules have been prepared, very little time is sacrificed in administering them. During the study, questionnaires were administered to save time and because they can, best provide information needed for descriptive purposes (Pelto & Pelto, 1978: 81). The interviews were mostly conducted in the English language. However, and although the second author is fully knowledgeable in isiXhosa, three native speakers—Dotwana Nzona, Dlaba Ncebaka Nzona (graduate students) and Bukindlela Nholosane—a life science teacher at K.T. Mchasa Seniour Secondary School Mhlakulo served as translators and interpreters during seven individual in-depth interviews sessions. The principle of voluntary informed consent, anonymity and confidentiality guided the data collection process. Participants freely granted consent orally or signed a pre-designed consent form. This was in tandem with the Walter Sisulu University's institutional review board guidelines pertaining to human subject research.

Qualitative methods provide rich detail, whereas the quantitative analysis permits extensive statistical analyses (Currall et al., 1999: 5–6). The questionnaires provided socio-economic data about participants and the type of health problems they turn to traditional healers for solution. We collected qualitative field notes on people's experiences with traditional medicine and actor's interaction with traditional healers. The transcripts were quantified by recording counts of different types of verbal behaviours exhibited by participants (Currall et al., 1999).

To further complement the data collection methods mentioned above, observation was used as a tool to ensure that data collected from interviews with key informants, as well as information obtained from the questionnaires was reliable. This was necessary to ensure the basic reality of what was said by informants. Observation, Earl Babbie (2009: 110) concede is the process of watching someone or something carefully, in order to find out or establish something. In this study, the researchers observed the movement of clients in and out of a traditional healer's shrine (*umrhawule/umsamo*). The number of patients going in and out of the traditional healers' consultation lodges (*amagumbi okuxilongela*) were observed and noted. The information obtained was useful in an attempt to establish the percentage of the population using traditional medicine. Furthermore, the study also made use of secondary data collected from the daily registers of some traditional healers. The number of patients they attend to daily was recorded. The intention was to compare this information with the number of patients visiting a local clinic in Qokolweni daily.

2.4 Data Analysis

This study used both qualitative and quantitative data analysis procedures. Quantitative methods are used when data is collected and presented in numerical and statistical values. On the other hand, qualitative methods are used when data is largely in the form of explanations, requiring inductive interpretations. The most elementary distinction between the two approaches lies in the use of statistical inferences in the quantitative approach and explanations in the qualitative approach. Once the phenomena have been quantified and qualified, they are subject to analysis through statistical methods, sometimes facilitated by designated computer packages. These methods are powerful but utterly dependent on receiving numerical data as the input (Descombe, 2003: 232).

The quantitative data collected was coded and is presented in tables in line with the objectives of the study. On the other hand, the qualitative data collected was checked, coded and analyzed thematically. We made use of descriptive statistics to organize, tabulate, depict and describe, summarize and reduce the mass of primary data. Inferential statistics was then applied in drawing conclusions about certain measures and description of the population. The overall data collected has been analyzed and presented in tables and pie charts.

However, the famous English proverb, "...nothing good comes easy..." may be recalled here. In the course of the study, we faced a series of challenges. Among others, some respondents solicited payment for their time. Furthermore, some respondents, especially those who belong to denominations that do not tolerate the use of traditional medicine were reluctant to participate in the study. However, only those respondents who were willing to participate were included in the sample. Additionally, some traditional healers who had initially granted their consent as key respondents later changed their minds. They were apathetic that the study could reveal their secret since they maintain that their knowledge is sacred and must be kept as such. Some traditional healers even suspected that the information would be used for purposes other than research. Their fears are not unfounded: the process of contorting and Balkanizing indigenous ontologies has a long history and involves ongoing processes such as bio-piracy. Furthermore, the majority of varieties of TCAM practiced in the Western world, including Canada are actually offshoots or 'westernized' versions of indigenous medicine/knowledges (Hollenberg & Muzzin, 2010). Various commentators (Kinchloe, 2006; King, 2002; Arnold, 1988) maintain that many of the so-called TCAM practices are based on versions of health practices and beliefs that were devalued, contorted and even erased during the colonial period, in favour of western medical models.

Moreover, the process of distorting and balkanizing indigenous ontologies remains omnipresent. This is evident in the reductionism of local knowledge systems variously as "traditional medicine", "TCAM" as a representation of thousands of years of knowledge, tradition and practices that have been handed over from one generation to the other. Today, new knowledge-often a blend of ancient and contemporary scientific knowledge- is being generated in the West with labels such as phytomedicine, health supplements and macrobiotics and other therapies including reiki or shiatsu which is also a mix of one or more older medicinal knowledge systems (Payyappallimanna, 2010: 59). They are then pigeon-holed and measured against the benchmark of modern western scientific cosmology (Basalla, 1967; Baronov, 2008). This is happening against the backdrop of protests from indigenous communities who rightly believe that Western pharmaceutical companies are benefitting inordinately from the conversion of indigenous herbs into modern pharmaceuticals with neither compensation nor recognition of intellectual property rights. Unfortunately, the new development paradigm that seeks to promote indigenous people's knowledge systems does not seem to reflect ground level reality. The United Nations Commission for Human Rights in the document "Protection of the Heritage of Indigenous People" maintains that industrial property laws are limited to the protection of 'new' knowledge and that time-tested 'old' knowledge systems like herbal remedies may not be perceived as patentable.[1] At the Nairobi Conference, delegates maintained that regional specificity, and the short duration of the patent rights (contrary to those of an individual applicant), and lack of emphasize on the availability and access of local communities to medicinal plant resources (Richter, 2003; Mutabizi, 2008: 208).

Most respondents were black African residents of Qokolweni. Research on a multicultural sample might have resulted in different findings regarding the use, attitude and perceptions of people towards traditional medicine. However, we also exchanged informal views with enthusiastic white South Africans in the research area. Furthermore, this study neither examined the chemical properties of the herbs used as medicines, nor did it look into the overall effectiveness of traditional medicine. It relied exclusively on responses obtained from informants. Lastly, the quality of care, the efficiency and efficacy of treatment regimens were not taken into consideration. These areas remain unexplored and therefore require further research. However, Bode and

---

[1] See also the United Nations Declaration on the Rights of Indigenous Peoples (United Nations, 2007).

Payyappallimana (2013: 2) concede that even the "...scientific validation of treatment efficacy by itself does not guarantee treatment effectiveness for individual patients and local communities especially not for those who have to survive on a few dollars a day." They further concede that:

> ...medical evidence and medical effectiveness are deeply embedded in social relations. When it comes to clinical practice factors like the natural course of disease trajectories, the body's capacity to cure itself, the health benefactions that come with care and attention, the easing of anxieties through diagnosis and treatment, the expectation of relief, the power of the human imagination, and the will and trust of both patient and practitioner at times substantially add to disease management and cure.
> (Bode and Payyappallimana, 2013: 3)

2.5 Ethical Considerations and Reflexivity

Social science research ethics guided our actions all through the research process. After obtaining ethical clearance from the Ethics Committee of the Walter Sisulu University, letters of introduction were obtained from the Head of the Department of Anthropology, and from authorities of the Eastern Cape Department of Traditional Affairs. We further sought and obtained authorizations from the Chief of Qokoloweni Location in whose jurisdiction the research was implemented. The purpose of the study and role of the participants were clearly stated in the letters. These letters were further presented to all participants, created trust and eased interaction between the researchers, the community leaders and the informants. The researchers were further introduced to the community by the chief during a community meeting aimed at addressing issues of land tenure and conflict resolution.

The research was based on the principle of freely informed consent and respondents had the option of terminating their participation at any time. Confidentiality and anonymity of the respondents was ensured. The names of individuals who participated in the study were kept anonymous throughout the study and beyond. Anonymity was also observed through the questionnaires that were administered during the survey. For the interviews conducted, as well as in all published accounts, pseudonyms have been used to protect the identity of the respondents.

We are deeply aware and sensitive of our own positionality as western educated "traditional" African scholars who have either used or been submitted to the use of traditional medicine, knowledge systems and practices at various times in our lives. In our individual and collective 'quest for therapy as quest for relieve' (Hsu, 2002), we have simultaneously been submitted to biomedical treatment regimens depending on the illness episode or on the medically diagnosed health problem. We have also combined and used both systems of medicine simultaneously as most of our interlocutors. We do not therefore romanticize the efficacy or otherwise of one system of medicine over the other. In other words, we are also instrumental human beings and recognize that there are no absolute distinctions between the social and the biological in the every struggle for survival.

The public acknowledgement of the HIV/AIDS pandemic, and the political promises made by the ruling ANC government towards the legalization of traditional healing practices, provided a useful backdrop to interviews with traditional practitioners and nurses. It allowed them to articulate their concerns that included, but were not limited to: "fear of losing their 'tradition' and hence the need to record their history." Further concerns expressed by traditional healers included "a desire to gain academic validation for their craft, uneasiness over the seeming proliferation of witches and witchcraft, awareness of the environmental impact of overharvesting of medicinal plants, and consciousness of the possible consequences involved in the legalization of healers"(Flint, 2008: 32–33).

2.6   Theoretical Framework

This study seeks to establish dialogue between traditional medicine and modern medicine in the Qokolweni Location in the Eastern Cape region of South Africa. The work draws theoretical insights from a wide range of critical theory-what might be called "critical eclecticism" (Fournier, 2013). This "critical eclecticism" (Fournier, 2013) is comprised among others by the overarching political economy of deprivation and underdevelopment framework (Farmer, 2006) that looks at place from a macro and multiscalar perspective in terms of linkage into and out of a place over time (Kalb & Tak, 2005). It further draws on critical medical anthropological approaches (Susser & Baer, 1995) that are underpinned by the notion that increasing the global economic system is the most important social process of this era (Susser & Baer, 1995). From this prism, biomedicine is embedded within dominant ideological assumptions rooted in colonialism and capitalism (Stefano, 2006; Hollenberg & Muzzin, 2010; Arnold, 2004; Baer, 2004).

Furthermore, we draw theoretical support from critical political economy. This form of analysis critiques dominant political economic arrangements and challenges the seeming logic behind the dominant theories and ideologies deployed in its defense (McKenna, 2010, 2011, 2012; Singer and Baer, 1995; Marx, 1983; Navarro, 1976). This paradigm exposes the influence of capitalist ideology on the ontological content of "TCAM" as it is integrated into biomedical settings (Coburn et al., 1983).

Additionally, theoretical insights are drawn from anti-colonial critiques and case studies (Hollenberg & Muzzin, 2010; King, 2003; Rao, 2010; Qadeer, 2011). Accordingly, we argue that "[t]heorising the development of integrative medicine from the perspective of subjugated [or contorted] knowledges [and beliefs] provides an important dimension for examining the emergence of integrative medicine" (Hollenberg & Muzzin, 2010: 35–36). Integrative medicine is based on a good physician-patient relationship where the physician acts as a healer, the preventive maintenance of health that pays close attention to all components of lifestyle, diet, exercise, stress management and emotional wellbeing, natural and minimally invasive management methods (Snyderman and Weil, 2002).

Anti-colonial or postcolonial perspectives is a set of attempts to capture the view point of marginalized peoples, their worldviews, and knowledge systems and to make visible alternative perspectives that have been masked by dominant worldviews (Hollenberg & Muzzin, 2010). This is what Brian King aptly calls "subaltern health narratives" (King, 2012; 2010) that might be quite different from the dominant perspective being imposed on local people. It is an already well-established fact that knowledge is always co-produced. This implies that various knowledge systems interact and are shaped by each other. The so-called dominant European science is nothing else, but an appropriation and alteration of non-European technologies from past and colonized civilizations of India, China, the Americas and other places[2] (Hollenberg & Muzzin, 2010: 38; Deb Roy, 2018; Chakrabarti, 2010). A clear case in point is that of an early 18th century slave who was supposedly found with a "poisonous plant" in a Jamaican plantation. He was executed for fear that he was conspiring to cause disorder. However, out of curiosity, Europeans living on the plantation undertook scientific enquiry and came to discover the slave's "accidental finding" was not poisonous. It was accordingly, appropriated and later became

---

2 We argue that although the colonies had an epistemologically active role, there was also a dynamic interaction between the metropolis and colonies in the exchange of scientific knowledge. Both colonies and peripheries were therefore epistemologically active. Knowledge did not only dynamically circulate among the metropolis and colonies, but also among European centres and peripheries. Subaltern studies have demonstrated that metropolis and centres have imposed a hegemonic historiographical view on colonies and peripheries (Gavroglu, 2008: 158).

known as a cure for worms, warts, ringworm, freckles and cold swelling and was given the name *Apicynum erectum* (Deb Roy, 2018). Following Praktik Chakrabarti (2010), this incidental discovery illuminates how under European political and commercial hegemony, the gathering of knowledge about nature took place concurrently with exploitation (Deb Roy, 2018; Chakrabarti, 2010)

Although indigenous peoples were represented as intellectually inferior, the basis of 19th century British science was "a global repertoire of wisdom, information, and living and material specimens collected from various corners of the colonial world" (Deb Roy, 2018: online, Gavroglu, 2008). The extraction of raw materials from colonial mines and plantations was intertwined with the extraction of scientific information as well as specimens from colonized people. Frontline scientific institutions in imperial Britain including the Royal Botanic Gardens at Kew and the British Museum relied on a global network of colonial collectors and intermediaries (Deb Roy, 2018; Chakrabarti, 2010; Gavroglu, 2008).

"Recent scholars have emphasized that the conceptual shift that accompanied European science was closely linked to colonial endeavours" (Hollenberg & Muzzin, 2010: 38). Technological developments in navigation for instance, orchestrated the connection of more remote places of the world, facilitated the crusades, the propagation of natural law theories of theologians including ST Thomas Aquinas, liberalism (idea of each individual as being capable of reason and self-government) and Empire. Furthermore, the rise of anti-colonial political theory that recognizes the shared humanity of all people was a hallmark of this conceptual shift (Gavroglu, 2008). Similarly, Sandra Harding (1998) suggests that, historically "non-European knowledges and worldviews (e.g. non-biomedical) have been adulterated in the pursuit of one 'true' account of nature" (pg. 165), called biomedicine. In this light, attempts to "integrate" TCAM practices into biomedical settings (medical schools, hospitals) comprises part of an entrenched pattern of knowledge and worldview expropriation, homogenization and even erasure (Harding, 1998).

Additionally, this study is informed by the psycho-socio-environmental paradigm (Gilbert et al., 2002; Ray, 1986; WHO, 2002). The psycho-socio-environmental model focuses on the promotion and maintenance of health through socio-environmental and behavioural changes. It emphasizes the role of people's behaviour, perceptions, what work they do, how and where they live in determining their health status and therapeutic choices. There is the recognition that the above factors are no less significant than the biomedical ones considered by the biomedical model (germ theory). According to the advocates of the germ or mono-causal model, the nature and causes of diseases can be traced to a specific aetiology or pathogen such as a virus, parasite or bacterium. The treatment of diseases therefore requires identification of the pathogen as well as its subsequent destruction (Ray, 1986).

The Psycho-socio-environmental model emphasizes that the prevention, treatment of ailments and comprehensive rehabilitation should be holistic. This means that disease causation, disorders and treatment should be viewed from a more comprehensive point of view.

It is essential to note that the biomedical model essentially limits health to the biological context while the psycho-socio-environmental model places it in the wider social context. As such, the latter paradigm offers a broader perspective, or a "macroscopic" view of disease and health.

Following Gilbert et al. (2002: 5), the biomedical and psycho-socio-environmental models represent different ways of thinking which emphasizes different aspects of health and disease. This study advocates the adoption and use of the psycho-socio-environmental health model by all health professionals because the two models provide complementary explanations rather than alternative or competing ones. They should, therefore, be seen as two extremes on a theoretical and empirical continuum that extends understanding of health and disease in society and the role of health professionals.

This theoretical framework articulates the need to understand and treat health problems from different perspectives, taking into consideration the physical, psychological and even spiritual aspects of disease. Healthcare pluralism involving traditional and biomedicine is a comprehensive and holistic approach to healthcare needs and expectations. It should be emphasized before an attempt is made to embark on treatment. After all, prevention is better than cure.

Lastly, the overall research strategy however consisted of a historico-spatial view of the macro historical political economy of deprivation and underdevelopment (Farmer, 2006) of the Eastern Cape Province during the colonial and apartheid eras and how this has inordinately affected the province's socioeconomic development. The effects of the historic neglect of the province is evidenced by its deeply entrenched poverty, higher rates of HIV/AIDS infection (Lerclec-Madlala et al., 2009), teenage pregnancy, and infant mortality (Aliber et al., 2018; Aliber, 2003) in comparison South Africa's overall human development indicators. The Province topped the chart of grant recipients with 40,8% (more than one-third of individuals) in 2016 (Stats SA, 2017b).

In the words of Paul Farmer, it is the anthropologist's job to bring to light the unseen connections between large-scale forces in small-scale settings (Farmer, 2006: 9; see also Kalb & Tak, 2005) such as the historical and contemporary impact of socio-economic and political marginalization as well as transformations in the RSA on the Eastern Cape region of the country. This explains our choice for a macro-level, multi-scalar and temporal perspective in our analysis of the interaction between the traditional African healing system and the biomedical establishment in the larger Eastern Cape region where the Qokolweni Location of the King Sabata Dalindyebo Local Municipality is located. In line with Don Kalb and Herman Tak, it is about recognizing the effects of the past and present (the past in the present), and how history affects the construction of reality. It is about factoring in our analysis "the connections in space (in and out of a place/in and out of a group), the relations through time, the internal and external relations of power and dependency, and what Eric Wolf has called the "interstitial relations" between apparently separate institutional domains" (Kalb & Tak, 2005: vii). It is about studying social phenomena through "institutionally based" "global ethnography," studying social phenomena "up and outward" (Ibid.). This implies looking at the historic situational properties of the region that includes labour-related migration, their impact on family relationships and poverty as well as the historic marginalization of the region. This emphasizes the need to capture the impact of apartheid era policies on the region's economy and the effects in the post-apartheid era. These historic configurations partly constitute the effects of extra-local forces within South Africa as well as the effects of national policies on the practice of traditional medicine and biomedical initiatives tackling HIV/AIDS in South Africa and in the region. This partly explains our focus on the effects of the advent of antiretroviral drugs since 2004 and the transformative impact on the meaning of HIV/AIDS. How has the revival of cultural practices that had either been banned or became obsolete during the apartheid era affected the transmission of the HIV/AIDS pandemic at both the societal and individual levels? How has the introduction of the lifesaving antiretroviral drugs affected medical pluralism within the community under investigation? Stated otherwise, we should take cognizance of the multiple interconnecting factors that influence the reality of an illness such as HIV/AIDS as well as the choice between traditional and modern medicine by patients. This invites for a holistic approach to the study of illness within a specific geographical and sociocultural context by unpacking the complex sociopolitical, economic and historical context of disease and poverty (Millan, 2011: 84; Winkelman, 2009; Farmer, 2006) within the region.

This book argues that understanding health in local context implies capturing historical and national level factors and their impact over time. This includes the spatial inequalities of the apartheid system that is most accentuated in the Eastern Cape Region. In addition, the impact of the debate on the use of traditional medicine to cure HIV/AIDS in South Africa that followed the collapse of the apartheid system of governance in 1994 and was part of Thabo

Mbeki's policy of "returning to African tradition" is equally significant. The former calls for the need to examine the entanglement between culture, place and health (Gesler & Kearns, 2002; King, 2012; King, 2010). That is how "cultural beliefs and practices structure the sites of health experience and healthcare provision" (Kearn & Geisler, 1998; cf. Gesler & Kearns, 2002: 1). We need to pay direct attention to the rich nuances implicit in places by focusing on "both identity and location" (Eyles, 1985) and the necessity of "putting health into place" (Kearn & Geisler, 1998; cf. Gesler & Kearns, 2002: 1). The sociocultural context of healthcare consumption that is shaped by macro-level politico-economic processes as well as cultural factors such as gender, religion and ethnicity show complexity, diversity in the daily operations of healthcare and health seeking behaviour (Andrews & Evans, 2008). Political economy produces disease and shape health decision making, as well as health discourses and understanding of the ensuing interactions between social and environmental systems. For example, the contradictory policy framework of promoting African traditions concerning HIV/AIDS by encouraging the use of traditional medicine in South Africa has resulted in the decimation of the population (HIV positive patients) because they were refused access to lifesaving antiretroviral drugs on grounds that it was toxic and its efficacy unknown. The pandemic has further shaped demographic patterns, regional and national economies as well as decision making about the choice of healthcare (King, 2012; King, 2010). The witchcraft theory of AIDS (Farmer, 2006; Ashforth, 2005) led to the questioning of biomedicine for its inability to stem the spread of the epidemic and to the patronage of traditional medicine. This contributed to the intractable debates surrounding HIV/AIDS policy by highlighting the specific ways that sociocultural systems including for example, belief in supernatural powers and in the ability of traditional healing systems to do away with bad luck and witchcraft shape perceptions and therapeutic decision making concerning choice of healthcare in a local setting. It further demonstrates the significance of "engaging with subaltern health narratives that conflict with (biomedically based) state discourses and policies that might be based on misunderstandings of local practices and knowledge systems" (King, 2012: 1179; Farmer, 2006).

The research findings reported herein are based on an in-depth qualitative and quantitative analysis of data collected in the field. Analysis is the process of bringing harmony, structure and meaning to the mass of collected data. Analysis is the categorizing, ordering, manipulation and summarizing of data to obtain answers to research questions. The purpose of analysis is to reduce data to an intelligible and interpretable form so that the relations of research problems can be studied, tested and conclusions drawn (Babbie, 2004; Descombe, 2003). Data may be qualitatively or quantitatively analyzed. The opinions, knowledge, beliefs and practices as well as the demographic characteristics of different participants about traditional medicine have been qualitatively and quantitatively analyzed.

2.7 Conclusion

This chapter has discussed the subject matter, research methodology and the theoretical perspectives underpinning this study that seeks to provide knowledge on respondent's attitude towards the prospects of integrating traditional and modern medicine in the Qokolweni Location, Eastern Cape Region of the RSA. Although the gulf between both systems of knowledge/healthcare seems irreconcilable, patient's multiple and simultaneous recourse strategies suggests that integration will enhance the socio-economic well-being of many people, both in the study area, in South Africa and beyond. These therapeutic strategies further underlie the need for a view of health seeking behaviour and healthcare from below by identifying the myriad sociocultural and other factors that shape health decision making and the choice between modern and traditional medicine in the post-apartheid context of democracy and a return to African traditional values and practices. How did apartheid affect traditional healing practices and their practitioners?

CHAPTER 3

Traditional Medicine, Colonialism and Apartheid in South Africa

3.1   Introduction

Traditional medicine is often referred to as indigenous or folk medicine comprising of medical knowledge systems that have been developed and transmitted orally over generations (WHO, 1990). Various societies had indigenous medicinal knowledge systems before colonialism and the advent and subsequent hegemony of biomedicine. African traditional medicine is a lucrative business generating billions of rands to practitioners in South Africa. The profit made by healers has attracted more people, some of whom are self-proclaimed healers into the practice of traditional healing. Okpako (2006) argues that the influx of people into the vocation of traditional healing may contribute to the falsification and counterfeiting of herbs. If this happens, it could lead to irreversible health hazards. Such health hazards may include the prescription and consumption of poisonous substances that are capable of destroying life.

We dedicate this chapter to the interaction between colonialism and apartheid and the impact of these two fields of power on the development of traditional medicine in South Africa. We should state here that in the late 20th century, the health of the black population in South Africa deteriorated. The factors for their dismal health status and their continuous relationship with high burden of poverty-related diseases include(d) low wages, overcrowding, inadequate sanitation, malnutrition and stress. Today like in the past, income inequalities and inequities in medical care resulting from apartheid have also influenced problems of crime and violence (Schellack et al., 2011: 559). It was however, at the outset of the twentieth century that the competition between African traditional practices, indigenous experts, and natural materials on the one hand and on the other hand, modern biomedical medicine practiced by doctors with scientific training became accentuated. This competition between the two systems led to the reconfiguration of what counted as authentic and effective medicine, and struggles all over the colonies over the status of indigenous medicine. Concurrently, concepts of the indigenous and modernity became entangled and disputed through sites such as complex configurations of laws and discourses (Flint, 2008) including laws that banned traditional medicine in South Africa through the Suppression of Witchcraft Act (enacted in 1895; amended in 1957). This act banned the spiritual side of traditional healing practices because it was perceived as witchcraft (Ashforth, 2005) and by implication, the use of herbs as medicines, since both are vital to the practice of traditional medicine (Bishop, 2012).

The chapter opens with an examination of the intertwinement of biomedicine and capitalism on the one hand and capitalism and apartheid as a system of racial segregation and domination on the other hand. The colonial medical apartheid paradigm denigrated traditional systems of knowledge and practices in favour of biomedicine while the racial segregation of the apartheid system was concretized through urban spatial policies that were meant to create healthy environment, void of noise and disease for Europeans through the herding of Africans into reserves and the appropriation of their fertile lands. This policy of segregation inordinately affected the health status of blacks and alongside underdevelopment of healthcare infrastructure partly accounts for their low health status and for poor development indicators in South Africa's Eastern Cape Province.

3.2   Biomedical Capitalism

By the twentieth century biomedicine had become a huge "profit making venture" with a firmly established "self-confident worldview" in Western society (Baronov, 2008: 236), as the "only reliable and proven form of medicine" (Baronov, 2008: 245). Additionally, it has become the benchmark by which all other forms of medicine and knowledge systems were to be evaluated (Baer et al., 1997; Baer, 2004; Di Stefano, 2006; Baronov, 2008). Biomedicine's cultural hegemony and its wonderful success erroneously gave the impression that it was the only true, safe and effective medicine in relation to other systems of knowledge that were subjugated and negated as being inferior since they were not based on "the scientific method" (Di Stefano, 2006: 145; de Roubaix, 2016) and therefore were void of any truth claims. "Biomedicine has realized its present status through a commitment to what has become known as scientific method, a powerful method of inquiry aimed at generating new knowledge that can be codified, tested and transmitted to a professional community" (Di Stefano, 2006: 145). This is the case even when there are multiple truth claims, multiple rationalities and modernities, and not one single, universal one. Both patients and doctors have similar understandings of the clinical reality and similar ideas about what successful treatment consists of (Hemmings, 2005: 93). According to Max Weber "there is no single Reason or universal standard by which to judge all forms of thought and …what we call Reason, is only the specific and peculiar rationalism of the West" (Ibid.). Foucault also give us to understand that even within western rationalism, "there is a multiplicity of rationalities, of different ways of thinking in a fairly systematic manner, of making calculations, of defining purposes and employing knowledge" (Dean: Ibid.). The prestige and structural power of modern biology and biomedicine has led to the negation of alternative rationalities. Although reliance on Randomized Control Trials (RCTs) as the basis of valid medical knowledge, has "led to the dissection of the approaches of traditional medicine into researchable components, (there has been) the use of biomedical parameters to measure outcomes, and to focus on material medica at the expense of non-material treatment aspects" (Bode and Payyappallimana, 2013: 4; FØnnebo al., 2007).

Biomedicine's profit making potential, alongside its focus on microscopic pathogens as the cause of disease was in tune with capitalism, as it dismissed socio-economic disparities as a health determinant (Baer et al., 1997; Baer, 2004). The pervasiveness of western medical assumptions obscures the influence of social, political and economic factors, including capitalist ideology, but also "serves other identifiable politico-economic functions for the capitalist world system, including profit-making" (Singer and Baer, 1995: 65). This was and remains the case even when all over the global South, the colonial masters instituted "medical apartheid" in favour of colonial civil servants and other contributors to the colonial enterprise at the detriment of women and children. In South Africa, where employers deliberately decided for their selfish interests to keep migrant workers' wages low "and almost static in real terms from 1897 to 1970" (Delius, 2017: online), some factory workers and miners were children. As industries struggled to secure vast numbers of low paid workers, migrant labour—initially not cheap labour—was transformed in the gold mines into low wage labour. The reason is that migrant labourers had lost their economic and political autonomy and therefore much of the room for maneuvre. They became a cheap pool of labour with diminished rights in industrial centres (Delius, 2017; Njoh, 2008). The social class apartheid that limited minimum healthcare only for the colonial labour force (colonial agents and factory workers) reflected the priorities of the political economy of colonialism. Women, children and the general masses who were considered unproductive to the colonial enterprise, sometimes, however, benefited from vaccination campaigns (Njoh, 2008). The entanglement of biomedicine and capitalism has been more clearly articulated by David Baronov (2008): the "scientific content of biomedicine is linked to the interests of industrial capitalism" (pg. 246). Furthermore, many metaphors in biomedicine are reflective of industrialism and economic organization (Martin, 2001). This demonstrates the different ways in which biomedicine resonates with capitalist and neoliberal ideologies; for example, the machine metaphor of the human body which implies that when the body is sick, it needs fixing (Martin, 2001), or medication, in order for 'it' to 'get back to work.' Brian McKenna uses the analogy of "the drama of [bio] medicine" thereby suggesting that the doctor helps perform the hard work of a neoliberal [and capitalist] culture by reproducing the conditions for "wage slavery of the worker/citizen..." (McKenna, 2012: 98). Yet, this mechanistic view of the body deprives it of its meaning giving capacity. "The dismissal of the placebo is an intentional act and part of biomedicines' quest to identify those aspects of human experience over which it can claim authority and therefore assert control" (Waldram, 2000: 32). Furthermore, good health is measured in terms of productivity, as well as the ability to work. As Nancy Scheper-Hughes maintains, symptoms of poverty and hunger get reconceptualized and packaged as medical conditions, that are then treated with biomedicine, rather than ensuring equity in the distribution of wealth and access to resources (Scheper-Hughes, 1992). This serves to perpetuate the socio-economic inequalities fostered in capitalist societies, at the expense of human dignity, human security and suffering.

Additionally, biomedicine's association with science, or with what could be more poignantly described as "science under capitalism" (McKenna, 2010; Panitch & Leys, 2009; Nanda, 2001; Navarro, 1976, 2007) limits "the ontological world of health and healing to observable and measurable physical phenomena" (Baronov, 2008: 241). This may influence the ontological content of TCAM as it is integrated into biomedicine. As TCAM is increasingly "integrated" into biomedical settings, including medical education, TCAM practices may be increasingly diluted into biomedicine's dominant "ontological world of health and healing" (Barnonov, 2008: 241) in order for TCAM knowledge and approaches to health to be more in tune with capitalist ideologies. To illustrate, how can traditional medicine with its holistic worldview of health or Ayurvedic medicine, which views humans as intricately intertwined with nature and sees one's environment as having a "direct role in individual health and disease" (Nayak, 2012: 19) maintain its integrity within biomedicine's reductionist framework?

A crucial feature of critical ontology in the context of integrating "TCAM" into biomedicine includes recognizing and disentangling the "machine metaphors of Cartesianism" (Kincheloe, 2006: 182) which is the bedrock of biomedicine. This ontological position acknowledges the reductionism inherent in biomedicine, which sharply contradicts the holistic worldview of the person on which traditional medicine is based. For example, the machine metaphor of the body conceptualizes the human body as a machine made up of fragmented and breakable parts, and the physician as a "tinkering mechanic" (Baronov, 2008: 242; see also Hemmings, 2005: 92) charged with repairing it.

Galileo called attention to the need to dispense with theocentrism [faith] as a source of knowledge and to concentrate on reason through the dual processes of "experimentation and observation." According to him, "human reason and the senses were the sole reliable sources of knowledge; demonstrable, verifiable, and [that only] quantifiable phenomena alone should be accepted as true knowledge" (Nayak, 2012: 18). Biomedical ontology is considered post-Galilean (Nayak, 2012). Galileo is credited with having introduced experimentation and observation into science (Nayak, 2012: 18). Ontology is a reference to the fundamental concepts/substances, as well as the nature of its existence (Kaipayil, 2002). Ontologically, biomedicine is further associated with rationality and modernity (King, 2002), and the notion of a superior, Eurocentric science (Hollenberg & Muzzin, 2010; Gordon, 1988; Basalla, 1967; Di Stefano, 2006).

Various definitions of traditional medicine (Marlise, 2003: 17; WHO, 1990: 65) (see Chapter 1) underscore the fact that traditional medicine is indigenous, anchored in people's indigenous knowledge, and have been orally transmitted from one generation to another. This knowledge is used for disease prevention, diagnosis and treatment. African traditional medicine is holistic in nature: it encompasses both physical and spiritual characteristics for the management of so-called "African diseases." These so-called "African diseases" are what anthropologists have described as culture-bound syndromes, which are not generally shared by different culture groups. Under the influence of Eurocentric and colonial categories, early anthropologists characterized African traditional medicine as "ethnomedicine" encapsulating "... a full range of [the] distribution of health related experiences, discourse, knowledge, and practice among different strata of a given population" (Nichter, 1992: 416). From Nichter's perspective, as a medical system, ethnomedicine provides the members of a given community with a popular approach to the explanation and subsequent resolution of health problems which are concomitant with social change, social relations of health related ideas, behaviours and practices. But even this medical knowledge is unevenly distributed within a given society. Colonialism negatively influenced the development of African traditional medicine. It was denigrated as superstition and a symbol of the African's primitivity and subsequently banned, thereby forcing practitioners underground. According to local history told in African communities, all persons suspected of using or practicing traditional medicine were subjected to torture and fines. This affected the practice and local mode of knowledge transmission since practitioners went underground. At schools in the Cape through to Natal, pupils were taught to dismiss traditional medicine as fake and its practitioners as witches and wizards (Wallace, 2015). The aim was to oblige Africans to make recourse to modern medicine under the pretext of civilizing them.

3.3 Colonialism, Biomedical Hegemony and Alternative Healthcare

The history of traditional medicine is important for understanding biomedical hegemony in South Africa because it shows the role of traditional medicine before the advent of colonialism and modern medicine as well as during the apartheid era. It also reveals that modern medicine despite its ascendancy and global hegemony actually developed from traditional medicine. This suggests that biomedicine needs to be seen as part of a broader cycle of historical and cultural transformations (Di Stefano, 2006). External, socio-political and economic influences have a bearing on biomedicine and biomedicine is subset of a "larger social formation- society" (Navarro, 1976: vii) which is largely controlled by social class and "contemporary capitalism" (Ibid.: viii). Most of the so-called TCAM modalities in practice in Canada are "westernized" versions of indigenous medicine/ local knowledge systems (Hollenberg and Muzzin, 2010). They are based on devalued and demonized versions of local health beliefs and practices that were summarily packaged and characterized as "superstitions" and "paganism" during the colonial conquest in favour of western medical paradigms (Fournier, 2013: 13; Kinchloe, 2006; Arnold, 1988; King, 2002). During the colonial period, Euro-American colonialists waged an unrelenting war in favour of "rational western medicine and [against] primitive traditional therapeutics," with the aim of chasing away traditional health beliefs and practices that were perceived as "suspicious and primitive" (King, 2002: 780). This mission civilizatrice that targeted indigenous peoples, their sociocultural institutions and knowledge systems formed part of the complex "ideology of colonial" [conquest] paradigm that was aimed at a process of conversion from traditional medical beliefs and paganism to "modern ways of knowing and doing" (King, 2002: 780; Sobiecki, 2014). This pattern of the conversion of traditional medicine as a form of erasure is evident in the movement underpinning the integration of traditional medicine into modern medicine. Stated otherwise, this might be read as a form of "colonization" of alternative worldviews, and approaches to health and healing by the Western imagination (King, 2002) now packaged as a 'humanitarianism' to ensure public health and safety through pharmaceuticalization (Fournier, 2013). This 'humanitarianism' underpins WHO's motivation to ensure the "rationality" and worldwide 'safety' of TCAM for the improvement of global health through the standardization and regulation of TCAM globally, the adoption of a biomedically defined 'evidence' base and 'real science' to support its validity (WHO, 2004). This implies that biomedicine has been naturalized and provides a yardstick for any other type of medicine.

The use of plants for medicinal purposes predates recorded history. Ancient Chinese and Egyptian papyrus writings document medicinal uses for plants as early as 3,000 BC. Indigenous cultures (such as African and Native American) used herbs in their healing rituals, while others developed traditional medical systems (such as Ayurveda and Traditional Chinese Medicine) in which herbal therapies were used (Taylor, 2013). The origin of traditional medicine can be traced back to the old testament of the Christian Bible. Ezekiel 47: 12 refers to the use of leaves for medicinal purposes thus: '...*their leaves will be used for healing people.*' It is alleged that during the creation of the earth, God himself created everything in the universe, including some of the plants and animals that are currently used as medicines (Zubane, 2001; Fyhrquist, 2007). The Egyptians are reported as being the first people to have developed and documented the use of traditional medicine in their papyri for curative reasons (Abou El-Soud, 2010; Gumede, 1990). A few surviving papyri include the Edwin Smith Papyrus describing surgical diagnosis and treatments, the Ebers Papyrus on ophthalmology, diseases of the digestive system, the head, the skin and specific maladies. This compilation of earlier works contains a large number of prescriptions and recipes. The other surviving papyri are—the Kahun Gynaecological Papyrus, the Berlin Medical Papyrus, the London Medical Papyrus, the Hearst Medical Papyrus repeats many of the recipes found in the Ebers Papyrus (Abou El-Soud, 2010: 82). The early Egyptians allegedly used various parts of plants and the carcasses of dead animals to make medicine. Their medicine has today become a source of the art for healing (Gumede, 1990: 1). Most of the complementary medicine modalities including herbal medicine originated from the ancient Egyptians. Through the process of diffusion, various Egyptian inventions including traditional medicine subsequently spread into other parts of Africa and even beyond.

The ancient Greeks developed modern medical practices by making use of the foundation laid down by the Egyptians (Singer, 1928: 7). There is therefore no denial judging from history that traditional medicine has contributed greatly towards the advent and development of modern medicine. According to Leslie Taylor, ethnobotanists have found that cross culturally, people tend to use the same or similar plants for the treatment of the same diseases and conditions. This implies the existence of "a specific reason the same plant was used for the treatment of the same disease continents away from each other" (Taylor, 2013: online). This explains why pharmaceutical companies have bankrolled a good number of educated and trained ethnobotanists who identify plants that people use effectively for various diseases and conditions and turn them over to their in-house researchers in charge of new drug discovery (Taylor, 2013). The novel and active plant chemicals identified by ethnobotanists alongside their biological activities are then turned into pharmaceutical drugs. Although traditional medicine is timeless and has no birth certificate, written reports on the use of indigenous medicine first appeared in Egypt. Ancient Egyptian priest-doctors, Di Stefano reports, emphasized the importance of preventive medicine by encouraging the use of hygienic practices to preserve the health of their patients. The people of the Nile delta regularly involved themselves in ritual cleansing of their bodies using purgatives, enemas, and dietary prohibitions. Di Stefano quotes Egyptian medical historian Paul Galioungou as reporting that the Greeks felt the Egyptians paid excessive attention to their bodies. This was a reference to the Egyptian customs of washing the hands and the crockery, the monthly taking of purgatives and emetics in line with the teachings of the priests. This was obviously a coping strategy against innumerable water borne diseases and parasites that resulted from the early flooding of their rivers and waterways. Additionally, they took advantages of the benefits of metabolic renewal resulting from short periods of fasting and cleansing (Di Stefano, 2006: 158).

Through migration, culture contact and diffusion, traditional medicine that was commonly practiced by the Egyptians and their other health enhancing practices eventually spread into other parts of Africa. African traditional medicine is the oldest and perhaps the most diverse of all medical systems. Africa itself is considered as the cradle of humankind with a rich biological and cultural diversity. Modern paleontological and archaeological studies provide evidence in this regard (Gurib-Fakim, 2006).

There are differences between different regions in the African continent when it comes to healing practices. Medicinal and poisonous plants, including a variety of woody plants have always played an important role in people's lives in Africa. The social practice of collecting plants as well as processing herbal remedies and applying them has been passed on from generation to generation (von Maydell, 1990). Most African cultures have oral traditions. However, written information on cultural features is often not readily available. This is in contrast with other parts of the world. The first documents on African traditional medicine were written by the famous Arab doctor and polymath, Avicenna who lived from 980–1037 A.D. His most famous works are *The Book of Healing*- a vast philosophical and scientific encyclopedia- and *The Canon of Medicine* which was a standard medical text at many medieval universities. *The Canon of Medicine* was used as a text-book in the universities of Montpellier

(France) and Leuven (Belgium) as late as 1650. Ibn Sīnā's *Canon of Medicine* provides a complete system of medicine according to the principles of Galen and Hippocrates (Nasr, 2007). With the colonization of Africa, European botanists started to explore the flora of various parts of the African continent. The ethno-botanical information on the uses of plants was sometimes documented on herbarium labels. In this way, ethno-botanical information on a number of plants began to accumulate (Hedberg & Staugård, 1989).

Systematic accounts in written form, dealing with medicinal plants in Africa, are a recent feature and reports dealing with ethno-pharmacological aspects are even far more recent. A Nigerian ethno-pharmacologist has provided an extensive review of the use of plants for medicine in Africa (Iwu, 1993).

The practice of modern medicine followed the colonization of Africa. Despite the proscription of indigenous medical practices, economic constraints in Africa made it difficult for most Africans to access the use of the urban-based modern healthcare system introduced by the colonial authorities. The medical apartheid of colonial society further left most Africans with no choice than to resort to herbal medicine and other traditional healthcare practices. Despite the blanket ban on traditional medicine and analogous cultural practices as part of 'civilization' including- widow inheritance, polygyny and female circumcision among others- traditional medicine continued to thrive illegally amongst most black African communities (Gumede, 1990). "Prior to the introduction of the cosmopolitan medicine, TM used to be the dominant medical system available to millions of people in Africa in both rural and urban communities." (Abdullahi, 2011: 115; McFarlane, 2015). During colonialism, traditional healers were accused of practicing witchcraft by many colonists (McFarlane, 2015: 60), as "being nugatory by Europeans," and as "bearing many social stigmas" (McFarlane, 2015: 61), "which led to the prohibition of the practice across various regions in Africa" (including in South African society) (McFarlane, 2015: 60). Africans identified themselves with this healing system, which they considered part and parcel of their cultural heritage (Gumede, 1990) and identity. The development of African traditional medicine was characterized by three distinct periods (Bannerman, 1983: 310–311).

3.4 The Pre-Colonial Era

During this period traditional healers practiced their trade freely and were the sole guardians of people's health in Africa. Their knowledge and practices were not documented but passed down to members of the same family or clan. The techniques of diagnosis and treatment were kept secret. Today the only written sources available on the early use of traditional medicine comes from reports of the early missionaries, explorers, travelers, traders, reporters, fortune seekers and survivors of wrecked ship crews. Since the fifteenth century, European naturalists have shown an unflinching interest in local biological knowledge, a stock of knowledge that informed biological science as evident in Karl Linnaeus' research, which was partly undertaken through correspondence with people around the globe and through exploration. It might be stated that European colonialism was not only about "understanding the new regions they invaded but also were on the lookout for resources that they might profitably exploit engaging practices that today we should consider tantamount to biopiracy.... Those who engage in bio-prospecting, hoping for example, to find elsewhere plants with unknown medicinal or cosmetic properties, are also current-day descendants of this tradition, although from a humanistic perspective such work gives rise to worries about theft of other's knowledge" (Silitoe, 2006; cf Oloyede, 2010: 78). Early European travellers such as Henry Meredith intimate that Africans developed medicinal remedies for fighting against endemic diseases. For example, a cocktail from the bark of a tree, *Crossopteryx febriguga* (colloquially referred as the 'African quinine') was used both as a cure for and a prophylaxis against malaria. Europeans took full advantage of the medicinal expertise of Africans at the time of the colonial conquest while simultaneously denigrating this knowledge and local peoples as 'ignoramuses' (Njoh, 2006). As Geri Augusto (2008) makes it eloquently clear on the case of the Cape colony, both settlers and travelling botanists and physicians acquired knowledge of medicinal plants through their acquaintance with indigenous people's knowledge of those plants. Additionally, the knowledge of slaves (those in "various degrees of 'unfreedom'") at the Cape made tremendous contribution to the understanding and use of both local and imported medicinal plants and plant products (Augusto, 2008: 138). In fact, the colonialists denigrated the medicinal accomplishments of Africa[1] (Njoh, 2006).

> The green herbs, the principal remedy in use among the Negroes, are of such wonderful efficacy, that 'tis much to be deplored that no European physician has yet applied himself to the discovery of their nature and virtue.
>
> (quoted in Maier, 1979; cf, Njoh, 2009: 15)

---

1 Africa is not a single cultural complex. The continent exhibits diversityboth within ethnic groups and within various cultures. It is pluralistic. There is no suggestion here that widespread, cultural historical complexes represent the whole of the continent prior to, and after the European conquest.

In assessing the works of Edward E. Evans-Pritchard, Huges, John S. Mbiti, K. Thairu and Raimo Harjula on the theme of healing and medicine in Africa, Alembi cites K. Thairu as arguing that Africa had doctors and surgeons before the advent of colonialism and modern medicine. These surgeons treated among others, fractures and wounds. They even performed major operations such as complicated births through Caesarian section in West Uganda, including "the opening of the skull to relieve pressure causing headaches with brain tumours etc." (Thairu, 1985: 86; cf Alembi, 2003).

At the community level, public health systems were an integral part of governance structures. According to Njoh (2009b: 10), precolonial flourishing towns and cities including, but not limited to Menroe, Axum, Kumbi-saleh, Timbuktu, Djenne, Ife and Goa, Great Zimbabwe, Kilwa, Sofala, Mombasa and Zanzibar had public health departments. Some, such as the ancient city of Kahun (2100–1700 BC) were endowed with a complex drainage network and an excellent potable water supply system (Rossen, 1993; cf, Njoh, 2009b: 10). They also prevented urban sprawl as well as the health and safety of their inhabitants. Furthermore, human settlements were located along, or close to rivers with the aim of accomplishing public health goals. Rivers and other bodies of waters were used for hydrotherapy- as a public health measure (Njoh, 2007). In the kingdoms, the ruling elites were charged with the responsibility of "dealing with ill-health conditions and illnesses beyond the scope of the household fell under the jurisdiction of [the indigenous] ruling elites who were typically priests, chiefs or kings." They dealt with

> hygiene and sanitation, epidemics, environmental degradation, draughts, food shortages, and sorcery-induced ailments. Keeping market squares, the chief's/king's courtyard, springs, rivers and other water sources, clean was the responsibility for all members of the community. The ruling class was responsible for distributing sanitation tasks to different communal groups and scheduling communal clean-up campaigns.
> (Njoh, 2009b: 10)

Traditional Africans hold a personalistic and naturalistic view of disease as caused by spirits, or God (The Supreme Being), requiring the appeasement of ancestral spirits or God. The former perspective is tied to the world view that the "living dead" (Mbiti, 1966) influence the daily life of their relatives in both a positive and a negative way. Draught and the resultant food shortages were seen as acts of God and priests, kings, rainmakers and other community leaders were called upon to invoke the ancestral spirits and through their intermediary role to ask God to intercede on behalf of the community (see also Njoh, 2009b: 10).

Epidemic outbreaks often led to the limiting of the movement of people, the prohibition of conjugal relationships, congregation in public places as well as activity involving direct human contact (Waite, 1987; cf, Njoh, 2009b: 10). People were prohibited from defecating or dumping in lakes, rivers and other bodies of water, while environmental pollution was treated as criminal behaviour. As Njoh (2009b) intimates, the attribution of disease causation to acts of God actually worked against efforts to find out the actual causes of public health problems. This, we maintain, laid the foundation for the colonial conquest in the name of "civilization" which was meant to do away with "superstition" and instill a sense of "reason" into the psyche of the African. Europeans accordingly, rejected taboos, norms and beliefs relating to environmental pollution, hygiene and sanitation as "superstition" and the mark of the African's primitivity. Traditional healers who were, without distinction called "witchdoctors" encapsulated African primitivity. They were used as "a trope of African superstition" [and] were blamed for all troubles, "from low rates of Christian conversion to the inability of the state to secure a stable African work force" (Flint, 2008: 36).

3.5 The Colonial Era

The second phase in the development of African traditional medicine took place during the colonial era and was characterized and influenced by the introduction of Christianity as a foreign religion, formal western education, medicine and technology. The colonial authorities introduced western medicine to look after the interest of the colonial agents, most of who lived in urban areas and worked in the colonial civil service. During this period the colonial authorities vigorously repressed indigenous cultural practices in general and traditional medicine in particular. As of the 1860s, a blanket ban was imposed on all healers, but in 1891(Natal Native Code), the white legislators decided to license African midwives and *inyangas*. Simultaneously, white administrators, doctors and chemists held the view that "native medicines" were static and unchanging and was accordingly defined as "what was considered 'white' that is, exclusive rights to biomedical ingredients, titles, tools, practices, scientific methods, and white patients" (Flint, 2008: 2). The *inyangas* were however forbidden from the sale of love philtres or charms. In 1932, administrators amended the code so as to clearly delineate the two medical cultures when they stated that *inyangas* "may prescribe, deal in and sell native medicines only" (Ibid.). Because of these bans, traditional health and cultural practices however went underground. The reason is that "the missionary version of Christianity accepted by Africans can be described as hypocritical because many African Christians still patronize [African Indigenous Religion (AIR)], especially in times of emergency. This means that the influence of AIR is still strong, especially in moments of crises" (Mercado, 2005: 104; cf Adamo, 2011: 285). During the Apartheid era in South Africa, AIR was widely practiced in secrecy because by the 19th century, "the missionaries whether... Congregational, Methodist, Anglican and Lutheran, or Catholic, were aggressively opposed to traditional African practices that they considered barbaric and based on superstition" (Denis, 2006: 310323; Mills, 1995: 153–172). As Gort (2008: 748) concedes "the religions of other cultures were viewed as 'non-Christian,'" "expressions of 'heathen unbelief' and evil superstition" and the world outside the church was seen as "the kingdom of darkness" (Ibid., 2008: 748). Apart from banning traditional medical practices, the colonial masters even attempted to control the sale of herbal medicines because it competed with their economic interests. In 1920 for instance, the Durban Corporation closed the market for the sale of indigenous medicine at Victoria Street beer hall, eMatsheni following complaints from doctors, pharmacists and *amakhosi* (traditional leaders) (Faure, 2002: 37). While the Natal Code of Native law (No. 19 of 1891) legalized the practices of the *izinyanga*, it proscribed the practices of *izangoma*. Until date, the practices of *izangoma* are accepted, while those of the *abathandazi* are banned. These two categories of healers however, continue to resolve psychiatric disorders and the treatment of mental illness (Chavunduka, 1986: 70–71; Faure, 2002). This legal ambiguity and double standard gives the lee-way for impersonation and quackery and poses significant risks to the health of patients. In the colonial era, this legal ambiguity and double standard is encapsulated by Ngcobo, a licensed African *inyanga* or "traditional herbalist" who combined traditional herbs and modern medicine and thereby posed a challenge to the biomedical enterprise by competing for patients with western-trained biomedics. He further appropriated the title of "doctor," and advertised himself as a "native medical scientist." This "not-so-traditional" healer who was proprietor of five muthi (African medicine shops) that sold bottled medicinal remedies labeled in both Zulu and English was put on trial for "carrying on the business of chemist or druggist," that is, for "not acting within the rights conferred upon him by his license as a native medicine man and herbalist." His innovative blending of traditional medicine (local herbs, some Indian remedies, chemist drugs and patent medicines) exposed the duplicity of the law that allowed for innovation among white biomedical practitioners while refusing it to Africans. It provides evidence of medical syncretism (medical cultural exchange), and exposed the economic and ideological competition between African and white medical practitioners as a site of larger colonial struggles over political and cultural hegemony (Flint, 2008: 1, 4–5). The building of general hospitals by the colonial authorities followed the expansion of colonialism and the spread of Christianity. Christian missionaries built private hospitals to combat widespread diseases. Both however failed to find out the legitimacy of local cultural and health practices. They simply believed that local cultural medical beliefs and practices were pagan and superstitions-calling for the need to oblige the natives to adopt western methods (Helwig, 2010; Onwuanibe, 1979: 27). Colonial imperatives couched in the language of benevolence informed the exportation of biomedicine to most parts of the world. Western medicine was one of the weapons for exploitation and civilization, a cultural artefact meant to showcase European cultural superiority and to ensure colonial governmentality. Although characterized by social class apartheid, that was reflexive of the priorities of the political economy of colonialism, the miracle of scientific achievements symbolized by the Pastorian revolution and the invention of the practice of vaccination was diffused to the entire colonial society to demonstrate the benevolence of colonialism. Biomedicine's ascendancy and hegemony has been traced to its supposed political conquest over other competing epistemologies in medical practice and its claim to scientific rationality unlike other competing medical systems (Oguamanam, 2006). Reminiscent of public health campaigns in Europe, the initial focus was on 'magic bullets'- curative care rather than prevention, vertical disease campaigns to eliminate single diseases such as sleeping sickness, yaws, tuberculosis among others. This is reflected by the following statement made in 1911 by Ludwig Kolz, physician to the German imperial government to Togo and Cameroon: "[The] colonial economy should make the negroes' strong arms subject to its purposes, hygiene should preserve their strength and increase their number" (quoted in Thomas, 2001: 59).

Zubane (2001) argues that during this period, traditional healers and users of traditional medicine went underground making sure that the authorities did not detect their activities. Thus, two parallel healthcare systems developed. One was official but only a small fraction of the population had access to it. The vast majority of the population in rural and remote areas used the other, though, unofficial system. Missionaries also served as agents of colonialism and combined both medicine and the salvation of souls despite the ambivalence between secular and mission medicine. Both emphasized the monocausality of social pathology. Nevertheless, unlike mission medicine, secular medicine indicted modernity and the disintegration of 'traditional societies' as fundamental causes of disease. On the other hand, missionary medicine took the view that disease would only be conquered through conformity with and the advancement of Christian morality, "a sanitized modernity and family life"

(Vaughan, 1991: 57). Furthermore, secular medicine was based on an ethnic paradigm of collective pathology, whereas mission medicine focused on individual Africans and individual responsibility for sin and disease, aimed at creating particular subjectivities through its practice (Vaughan, 1991: 57). There were however differences in medical practices between various religious congregations based on ideology although healing was generally seen as part of salvation and a mechanism for conversion and all were simultaneously faced with the dilemma of serving souls.

German, French and British colonialism all adopted a "civilizing" health policy meant to showcase, foster and market colonial encroachment and imperatives. As Vaughan (1991: 65) readily observes:

> Medical missionary memoirs abound with stories of the early African dispensers, and the value of their work was readily recognized. In particular, they were the vanguards of the 'battle against superstition and witchcraft,' persuading recalcitrant patients and skeptics of the superiority of western medicine. (Vaughan, 1991: 65)

Disease was constructed as embedded in indigenous cultural practices and the fight against disease became a smokescreen for the fight against local cultural practices with the aim of doing away with these cultural practices and bringing 'civilization' to the natives. In India for instance, the British attributed the outbreak of cholera to various aspects of Hindu culture (Arnold, 1998), even when the toilet project meant to curtail the spread of the disease backfired due to the British failure to understand that various lower castes in charge of collecting bodily wastes were functional entities to the hierarchical religious power structure of Indian society. The toilets remained as clean as they had been constructed and left behind. In fact, colonial public health campaigns including but not limited to the plague in India in 1890, sleeping sickness in Uganda in 1901 or malaria in Malawi in 1912- served as disguised smokescreens and launching pads for attacks on indigenous customs and lifestyles (Marks, 1997). In Nigeria, the British outlawed the Sopona small pox cult in 1917 before instituting sweeping anti-witchcraft ordinances across all their African colonies in the 1920s and 1930s (Arnold, 1993; Porter, 1997). Tropical medicine became a counterforce for suppressing indigenous medical practices.

It might be stated here that disease finds its origins in people's living and working conditions. Colonial policies for instance, often entailed the herding of native populations into reserves so as to acquire land for the setting up of colonial administrative and development structures without any care for the health and well-being of the local population. This was the case with the implantation of German colonial plantations in Southwest Cameroon (see Fonmboh, 2008; Pemunta and Fonmboh, 2010) and elsewhere in Africa such as in the setting up of the mines in South Africa where blacks were confined to 'black townships.'

Furthermore, as Njoh (2009) intimates, urban planning was used as a tool of power and social control in colonial Africa. Europeans and Africans were spatially segregated through the location of colonial towns. "These towns were/ are typically located on the highest elevation and separated by considerable distance from the residential areas of the indigenous population" and "… contained structures that adhered strictly to European architectural and construction standards. In some cases, the structures, were of elements prefabricated in Europe and only assembled in the colonial territories" (Njoh, 2009: 304). In fact, racial segregation of cities in colonial Africa was the norm independent of the colonizing authority through town planning schemes. While the British colonial authorities adhered to a philosophy of racial segregation, their French counterparts segregated on the basis of socio-economic and cultural grounds (cultural spatial segregation, a euphemism for racial segregation) using subtle measures including building and subdivision codes at the expense of the nonwhite population. French colonial Madagascar is illustrative of this spatial and racial segregation policy. This was despite misgivings by the French public at home. Although there were differences in racial philosophies, both the French and the British colonial authorities, however shared similar cultural, psychological, political, social, and ideological objectives that were concretized through racially segregated space (Njoh, 2008b). Segregation was meant to create living conditions in the colonies that paralleled those of Europe, "…to establish enclaves of European social and physical infrastructure that dwarfed and stood in sharp contrast to their traditional African equivalents, and to contain African urban residents in specific and well-delineated districts where they would be under the constant gaze of European colonial authorities." Furthermore, racial segregation was also an outcome of indirect measures to promote "functional spatial structures, a healthy physical environment and socioeconomic Development" (Njoh, 2008: 87) as well as the regulation of land use activities. Accordingly, colonial urban spatial policies were underpinned by segregationist ideologies or residential sectorialisation as evident in the duplication through the enactment of the "municipal codes that were already in force in Europe" (Njoh, 2009a: 304). They were firmly embedded in contemporary racial prejudices and assumptions concerning sanitation in Africa. Writing on the Cape Colony of South Africa, Maynard Swanson coined the notion of "sanitation syndrome" as a reflection of these prejudices. Similarly, Njoh (2009a) refers to the concoction of "pseudo-scientific rationales for implementing such policies in British colonial Africa" (p. 311), "dubious scientific work...designed to afford scientific cover to what were purely racist policies" (Njoh, 2009b: 11) as well as the perception of Africans as vectors of disease, an ideology that tremendously influenced colonial health and spatial policies (Njoh, 2009b: 10).

Equally important was the view held by the French of Africans as "noisy, disorderly and... inclined to criminal behaviour" (Njoh, 2009b: 11). This necessitated the enactment and implementation of curfew laws. For example, the draconian law of 15 December 1926 by the French in Brazzaville (present-day, Kinshasa) forbade the movement of Africans beyond 9 pm (Ibid.). Following Swanson, before the institutionalisation of apartheid by the Afrikaner party in 1949, the African population of Cape Town was pushed out of the urban sphere into the hinterlands. Africans were discouraged from migration into towns and only those with jobs were allowed there. Furthermore, interracial marriages and sexual intercourse were forbidden (miscegenation). In South Africa, this policy of the spatial exclusion of the native population away from urban areas was achieved through the enactment of the so-called "pass laws" (Njoh, 2009a: 305; Njoh, 2009b). This spatial reorganisation achieved through the uprooting of the local population (segregationist policy) was a result of the bubonic plague that originated from Southern China and spread into South Africa through the maritime routes. Though the contamination rate among the coloured or white population was higher, the plague was identified with the black population and vice versa-an incarnation of both biological fact and social metaphor (Swanson, 1977; Maylam, 1995; Bigon, 2012: 2). This same policy of racial segregation was also replicated by the British in the wake of the outbreak of the bubonic plague in Lagos in the early part of the twentieth century and it turned the area into an exclusive European settlement (Njoh, 2008: 93). The labelling of non-whites as a threat to the health of whites led to the unsettlement and intimidation of African subjects. The colonial preoccupation with sanitation was to create major settlements for Europeans since disease posed a threat to the entire colonial project. While ill health was associated with crowded and filthy environments, racial segregation offered health benefits only to a selected few: "Reflecting the particular concerns of Europeans living in Africa," colonial cities "were deliberately and rigidly segregated on racial grounds. Europeans, Asian and African living and working were placed in separate parts of the city. In this pecking order anchored in European racial discourse, whites came first, blacks came last while the rest fell in between. In Tanzania, Kenya and South Africa with a mixed population of 'Whites,'" 'Coloureds,' and 'Blacks,' Whites were given the most desirable areas with amenities, followed by the 'Coloureds' and 'Blacks' got the least preferred and disease infested (Njoh, 2008a: 94; 2008b: 591). The Ndola municipality of Rhodesia which in the mid-1930s had 'a population of 4,000 living in 1,700 mud huts 12 feet apart, infested with vermin and provided only with fifty communal pit latrines' in contrast to the low population density and well-equipped European quarter (Rakodi, 1996: 198). "Segregation was justified on grounds of security and public health" (Stock, 2013: 402) whereas it was actually an instantiation of White racial superiority that considered Africans as inferior and sub-human. White superiority and occupation of the world was seen as an act of benevolence. In Free Town, Sierra Leone in 1898 for instance, when it was discovered that the Anopheles mosquitoes spread malaria, the British decided to segregate European and African residents to protect the health of colonial officers by constructing the Hill Station overlooking the city (Stock, 2013: 408; see also Swanson, 1977; Njoh, 2009a; Njoh, 2009b; Njoh, 2008). From 1898 to 1900, a team of experts led by Dr Ronald Ross of the Liverpool School of Tropical Medicine pointed out that the anopheles mosquito was the vector for malaria and "recommended the nocturnal separation of the native from the European population as a means of protecting the latter against malarial infection" since infection was alleged to take place only at night (Njoh, 2009b: 11). One key "revelation of Dr Ross' study was that the anopheles mosquito could not cover a distance more than 430 yards" (Ibid.). This finding became the benchmark "for the colonial spatial policy requiring that European districts be separated by a distance of at least 430 yards from the residential areas of members of the indigenous population" (Ibid.). However, the enactment and subsequent implementation of racial segregation policies in India dates back to 1819 and therefore predates their activities (Njoh, 2009a: 311–112; Njoh, 2009b: 11). Racial segregation policies were a covert strategy to guarantee Europeans access to easily accessible arable parcels of land at the expense of the native population who were pushed onto marginal and unproductive lands (Pemunta and Fonmboh, 2010; Njoh, 2009a). As Frantz Fanon maintains, racially segregated spaces in colonized territories were psychologically oppressive and was tantamount to a form of violence against members of the indigenous population (Fanon, 1963).

In the 1990s, apartheid that mandated hierarchical forms of relationships that existed between blacks and whites collapsed in South Africa, but deeply entrenched inequalities created by this system of exclusionary governance mostly by the rich continued. The coming of democracy coincided with "a return to tradition and culture" (Ashford, 2005) as part of wider transformations within the South African polity. It also coincided with the outset of the HIV/AIDS pandemic that has continued to decimate the population. Most blacks who are in the majority continued to rely on traditional medicine for their health care needs. Veronique Faure (2002: 23) argues that between the mid-1980s and mid-1990s prevailing socio-economic and political conditions in South Africa (characterized by 'high levels of political violence ... violent crimes' and an economic recession) tremendously transformed the economic, political, social and personal security of Africans and that faced with state failure to effectively respond to their security and socio-economic needs, people found refuge in the protective power of traditional medicine as well as a solution to their economic woes, including high rates of unemployment that was accentuated by rural-urban migration due to drought. These new conditions led to the continuous transformation of indigenous medicines[2] so as to effectively respond to such needs. In response to the new socio-political situation of Africa, traditional medicine witnessed changes, as practitioners improved upon their practices and medicines such as those meant "to make men likeable to women, were modified to make people both to get and keep employment" (2002: 27). In desperation, many people increasingly made recourse to magical cures, amulets and solutions. Charlatans took advantage of this general atmosphere of desolation to prey on desperate people (Faure, 2002: 23). "Among some of the 'cures' produced were concoctions, which were mixed with human body parts. The emergence of charlatans, the discovery of the use of human body parts, coupled with the lack of the appreciation of the differences between them and authentic indigenous healers, resulted in calls for the proscription of the practice of indigenous medicines. Another better-informed response was the suggestion for the normalisation of indigenous medical practice" (Ibid.: 23–24).

Following the dismantling of apartheid, a sea change in residential segregation has occurred in South Africa, but deeply racialized poverty remains. During the apartheid era, even the poorest of whites were socially and racially, set apart from, and above blacks. Since the mid-1990s, this hierarchical social and racial system has been systematically transformed through social equality policies. Although the old racial dimensions have persisted, "a new set of class divisions-both overall and within each of the racial groups-was superimposed on them" (Stock, 2013: 410). Some well-to-do and middle class Africans moved to former white reservations. However, the vast majority are unable to afford decent housing outside the townships or in the mushrooming squatter settlements of recent years. "Almost two decades after the demise of apartheid,

---

2   Indigenous medical practice is an umbrella concept referring "to the practices that izinyanga, izangoma and abathandazi (Christian spiritual healers) engage in when they treat people who come to them with physical, social and psychological problems. These practices are considered indigenous not because they can be dated in the distant past, but because the practitioner relies on the invocation of African conceptions of cosmology and cosmogony" (Faure, 2002: 24).

Johannesburg remains the most highly segregated major city-by race and by wealth anywhere in the world" (Ibid.).

Historically, anthropologists have shown an unflinching interest in medicine and in indigenous healing practices. As a Western product, medical anthropology developed in the wake of Western medicine's colonization of the world from the early 19th century onwards. Initially, biomedicine was considered to be the only type of health service available, and was bestowed enormous power, hegemony and cultural legitimacy while all other forms of healing knowledge and practices were classified as ethnomedicine, alternative therapy, superstition, "illegal" or "deviant" and were vigorously suppressed (Connor, 2001; Flint, 2001). Ethnomedicine is the study of medical systems from the emic perspective (native's point of view). Native categories and explanatory models of illness, including aetiologies, symptoms, courses of sickness, and treatments are investigated (Kleinman, 1978; Kleinman, 1980).

In the 1950s and 1960s, anthropologists entered the field of international development programmes as consultants. Their new role in international healthcare delivery programmes stimulated the emergence of medical anthropology as a specialised field of research and practice. The benevolence of international healthcare programmes was, however, undermined by resistance from the target populations (Leslie, 2001: 430). Physicians and public health experts who directed these programmes saw the problem from the prism of a chasm between modernity and tradition, superstition and science, and rational and irrational cultures (Leslie, 2001: 430).

The 1980s and 1990s witnessed a dramatic shift, as well as a distinctive and in-depth analysis of illness and medicine. The hegemonic claims of biomedicine and the dichotomy between tradition and modernity were readily challenged, alongside a cultural critique of biomedicine as well as its truth claims. The comparative analysis of biomedicine revealed that it was merely one among many systems and that the rapid spread of biomedicine had neither eclipsed nor led to the disappearance of so-called traditional medical systems and practices. Leslie (1992) avers that all medical systems-modern as well as traditional, are inherently dynamic and responsive to socio-political changes. The spread of biomedicine did not result in the complete integration of traditional medical systems into a dominant modern system on the principle of scientific rationality. Biomedicine is confronted among others with the mind-body dichotomy, a paradigmatic problem that reflects a fundamental inadequacy in the core elements underpinning the practice of biomedicine. While non-orthodox approaches to healing are seen as presenting a challenge to biomedicine's cultural dominance, biomedicine is increasingly co-opting non-orthodox medical approaches that have been shown to be effective "into the medical curriculum as units or programs in complementary or integrative medicine" (Di Stefano, 2006: 171). In Southeast Asia for instance, the revitalisation of Aryuveda led to the development of a syncretic Aryuvedic medical tradition that co-existed in a complementary and conflictual relationship, with ritual curing and cosmopolitan medicine (Leslie, 1992: 204). Similarly, practitioners in Africa and Latin America integrated antibiotic injections into ritual curing and herbal medicine (Leslie, 2001: 431). Medical pluralism and syncretism were thus finally acknowledged paving the way for medical pluralism as a central concept in medical anthropology.

It was only by the late 1950s that anthropologists began engaging with indigenous forms of healing practices in different cultures under the banner of ethnomedicine- the study of folk illness categories, traditional medical systems and herbal remedies (Kleinman, 1980; Van der Geest, 1988). Despite this growing interest in the healthcare services used by different communities, it was however Janzen's (1981) seminal study that provided a "holistic picture" of a pluralistic medical system, offering perceptive insights into the simultaneous use of biomedicine and traditional medicine. Since then anthropologists including Arthur Kleinman and Cecil Helman (Kleinman, 1980; Helman, 1984) have embraced medical pluralism. Nevertheless, anthropologists have been preoccupied with defining different existing medical systems, basically the co-existence of traditional and biomedical systems, thereby excluding healthcare systems and practitioners who do not fall wholly or partly within the provinces of these systems. Minocha (1980) points out that few studies acknowledged medical syncretism- traditional healers who use or incorporate biomedical techniques such as laboratory tests within their practice. Early studies informed by the concept of medical pluralism showed that patients are pragmatic and see nothing inconsistent about liberally combining different forms of therapy in their quest to restore health (Nichter and Lock, 2001: 4). Janzen examined 'the quest for therapy'- on the ways in which people use and evaluate the different therapies available to them. Janzen also introduces the 'lay therapy managing group,' consisting mainly of close kins, as important actors in the quest for therapy (Janzen, 1978: 3–4).

The failure to recognize the intersection between different medical systems has prevented the definition of various medical services even within the same locale. These setbacks have for instance, prevented the investigation of the utilization of the "African pharmacy" since this informal institution cannot be categorized under existing healthcare typologies. Additionally, medical anthropological studies have focused on the later stages of the referral system of therapeutic recourse, with less focus on self-administered healthcare (Kleinman, 1979; Ryan, 1998). Self-medication entails seeking and obtaining access to various medicines for oneself and one's family members, including over the counter drugs and herbal medicines. Herbal therapies are readily available in the immediate environment for harvesting, at street corners and markets, and in the African pharmacy for sale.

3.6 The Post-Colonial Era

During this period, traditional medicine recovered its former glorious status in many countries and there were several attempts to revive its recognition, status and eventual collaboration with modern medicine. There is hope that many countries will realize the role of traditional medicine and the need for its formal recognition and subsequent integration into the mainstream health care delivery system. WHO championed this movement for the integration of both modern and traditional medicine through several global and regional initiatives.

The rise of African nationalism saw the birth of a regional committee in Africa aimed at promoting traditional medicine. The committee did not only invite member states but it also encouraged the WHO to take appropriate steps to ensure the use of essential drugs and medicinal plants from the African pharmacopoeia. This step was necessary to meet the basic health care needs of communities and to ensure the development of the African pharmaceutical industry. The regional committee for Africa supported programmes at both local and regional levels. It is reported that today member states are setting up a mechanism for traditional and conventional medical systems to work in collaboration (Bannerman et al., 1983: 209). A number of national pharmacopoeias starting with Madagascar in 1957 have appeared. Research in the field of ethno-botany and ethno-pharmacology has developed rapidly in many African countries (Hedberg & Staugård, 1989). The Scientific and Technical Research Commission of the Organization of African Unity (OAU) have, beginning in 1985 published, a series of compendiums covering the traditional medical system of many African countries. Other independent research publications are on the rise.

The Scientific Council for Africa and The African Union (replacing the OAU) is currently working towards the promotion of systematic research on traditional medicine in different African countries (Ibid.). The rising cost of Western medicine has created a situation where most Africans are increasingly turning to traditional medicine as an affordable healthcare alternative. There is, however, need for African countries to develop policies that would incorporate traditional medicine into the formal healthcare sector (Tsey, 1997). In some African countries, there is an increasing feeling that traditional medicine should be taught and practiced as part of formal healthcare (Tamalaoke, 1995). Gradually, traditional healers are being officially accepted as part of African health service providers and their medicinal knowledge is gradually being accepted in hospitals and clinics (Neuwinger, 2000). In South Africa for example, traditional medical practices have since the early 1990s been officially recognized as a legitimate form of healthcare due to its social acceptability and the scourge of the HIV/AIDS pandemic to which biomedicine does not yet have a solution. Traditional medicine and indigenous knowledge are now being integrated in the official healthcare system under the Reconstruction and Development Plan (RDP) (Neuwinger, 2000).

Since the 1978 landmark ALMA ATA resolution which pointed out that traditional healers were an important human resource worthy of mobilization for achieving the goal of "health for All by the year 2000," WHO governing bodies have adopted a number of resolutions at both the regional and global scale (WHO, 1998). Despite its ambivalence, the South African government has been part of these regional and global initiatives. Resolution AFR/RC49/R5 on Essential Drugs in the WHO African Region called on Member States to conduct research on medicinal plants and to promote their use in healthcare delivery (WHO: 2000). In adopting Resolution AFR/RC49/R5, the Regional Committee called on WHO to put in place a comprehensive strategy on African traditional medicine (Kasilo et al., 2010).

In 2000, the fiftieth session of the WHO Regional Committee for Africa held in Ouagadougou, Burkina Faso adopted the regional strategy through resolution AFR/RC50/R3 on the promotion of the role of traditional medicine in healthcare (WHO, 2001) under the theme: "Promoting the role of traditional medicine in health Systems: A Strategy for the African Region." The Regional Strategy sought to contribute to the achievement of health for all in the African region by fostering the use of traditional medicine through the promotion of its integration into national health systems on grounds that there is evidence on safety, efficacy and quality as well as the generation of such evidence wherever it is unavailable. The Regional Strategy focused on policy formulation, capacity building, the promotion of research, the development of local production-including the cultivation of medicinal plants, the protection of intellectual property rights and indigenous knowledge systems (Kasilo et al., 2010: 8).

South Africa is one of 36 African countries with national policies on traditional medicine out of 46 countries in the Region. Furthermore, in an effort to regulate, promote, develop and standardize African traditional healing practices, 21 countries have adopted legal frameworks for traditional medicine. South Africa put in place the National Traditional Health Practitioners (THPs) Act, 2004 (Traditional Health Practitioners Act. No. 35, 2004).

In 2003, South Africa hosted inaugural activities marking the African Traditional Medicine Day which is celebrated on 31st August annually. This was in conjunction with the Fifty-third Session of the WHO Regional Committee for Africa celebrated under the theme: "African TM, Our Culture, Our Future." Events such as these have created an enabling atmosphere for training, collaboration, networking and the exchange of information between traditional healers and allopathic medicine practitioners (Kasilo et al., 2010: 10).

Furthermore, South Africa, Benin, Burkina Faso, Cameroon, Cote d'Ivoire, Guinea, Madagascar, Mali, Senegal are among African countries that have developed inventories and monographs on medicinal, aromatic plants and herbal pharmacopoeias.

Additionally, between 2001 and 2005, South Africa was one of the beneficiaries of WHO's support for feasibility studies and needs assessment on the local production of traditional medicines in collaboration with the African Union's Scientific and Technical Research Commission. Other countries that benefited from this initiative included Benin, Burkina Faso, Cote d'Ivoire, Democratic Republic of Congo, Ghana, Kenya, Madagascar, Nigeria, the United Republic of Tanzania and Egypt (2004–2006). This was part of WHO's overall strategy aimed at strengthening capacities for the local production of traditional medicine (WHO, 2004). WHO further developed guidelines for the protection of cultural rights and intellectual property rights for countries to adapt to their particular situations (WHO, 2011), as well as a regulatory framework for the protection of traditional healing knowledge. These are complementary to the OAU Model Law (Ekpere, 2000; Kasilo et al., 2010).

In many African countries, traditional methods of healing are currently being used for the management of HIV opportunistic infections (Morris, 2002) and malaria (Njoroge & Bussman, 2006). Medicinal plants are being used as immune boosters to suppress and treat "opportunistic" infections. These methods are sometimes claimed to give fewer side effects than conventional antiretroviral and antimalarial therapy (Morris, 2002). However, the high cost associated with life-long antiretroviral therapy has dogged the South African government's efforts to make it available to its citizens as part of comprehensive health care (Summerton, 2006). In South Africa, there is ambivalence and the lack of concerted political commitment towards the integration of traditional medicine into the official health care system. This is despite the huge following and the revenue traditional medicine and healing practices generate. The lack of the enforcement of regulation in the sector might be read as a tacit government mechanism to pacify the people and avoid social unrest and as a mechanism for settling the inherent contradictions of capitalist societies as evident in inequality to quality health care by appeasing "alternative health practitioners and their clients" (Singer and Baer, 1997: 182; Fournier, 2013: 23). Traditional medicine is a cost-effective therapeutic option when compared to the dominant biomedical system (Singer and Baer, 1995). This partly explains why the South African government is keen to integrate alternative healers into the health care system, but has unfortunately adopted a fragmentary policy framework.

In the countdown to the democratic elections in South Africa in 1994, the ANC proposed to include traditional health practitioners as an integral part of health care delivery in the country, and consumers were to have the right to consult a practitioner of their choice. They further proposed changes in legislation to ensure the controlled use of traditional medicines (ANC, 1994: 33). In 1997, it issued *The White Paper for the Transformation of Health System in South Africa* as a follow up. It stated that "the regulation ... and control of traditional healers should be investigated for their legal empowerment. Criteria outlining standards of practice and an ethical code of conduct for traditional practitioners should be developed to facilitate their registration" (Ministry of Health, 1997: 34). In 2004, the Traditional Health Practitioners Bill for South Africa was approved and unanimously adopted in parliament. It was later enacted in February 2005 (Republic of South Africa, 2005; cf, Summerton, 2006: 16). The Interim Traditional Health Practitioners Council was charged to "provide for a regulatory framework to ensure the efficacy, safety and quality of traditional health care services, to provide for the management and control over the registration, training, and conduct of practitioners, students and specified categories in the traditional health practitioners profession, and to provide for matters connected therewith" (Flint, 2008: 5-6). Despite its broader outlook, the recently adopted Traditional Health Practitioners Bill is replete with ambiguities. The 2004 Bill defines traditional medicine and practitioners "by the absence of biomedical substances and practices and assumes them to be self-evident" (Ibid.). According to the law, the basis of "traditional health practices" is "traditional philosophy"-indigenous African techniques, principles, theories, ideologies, beliefs, opinions and customs, and uses of traditional medicines... which are generally used in traditional health practice. This definition sees traditional medicine as unchanging, bounded and separate from other systems of medicine even when medical syncretism is, and has always been, a worldwide phenomenon. In South Africa, African healers and Indian practitioners modernized and professionalized their practices "by winning the confidence of a multiracial urban ethnic clientele while also seeking to circumvent the legal restrictions imposed upon them" (Flint, 2008: 7-9).

The AU declared the timespan 2001–2010 as the Decade of Traditional Medicine. The NEPAD has recognized traditional medicine as a significant strategy in its plan of action to achieve the goal of health for all (African Union, 2001: 2; NEPAD, 2001: 31).

There are a variety of views about traditional healers in South Africa. The Health Act of 1971 officially banned traditional healers though many organizations still had them registered. Such organizations included: the Southern African Traditional Healers Council, the Association of Traditional Healers of Southern Africa, the Congress of Traditional Healers of South Africa, the African Dingaka Association, or the African Skilled Herbalists Association.

In the wake of the recession of the mid-1980s and mid-1990s, indigenous medical practices enjoyed a high following as law and order break down, and generalized insecurity became the order of the day, unemployment skyrocketed[3] (see Chapter 4). The unprecedentedly huge following enjoyed by traditional healers who claimed to have a ready solution to various socio-economic and political problems including political violence led to the proliferation of 'self-styled healers' (charlatans). This was the case as healers migrated from their rural enclaves where they used to harvest medicines from traditional health shrines to the urban milieu where they have set up traditional medicine clinics and health centres (Pemunta, 1999; Pemunta, 2000; Muweh, 2011). This subsequently led to an unprecedented "increase in fake traditional health products in urban markets and a multiplicity of individuals without the requisite skills who paraded the streets with the sole aim of duping and extorting money from their victims" (Muweh, 2011: 2). Similarly, in her discussion of "pretending ukuthwasa," Joanne Wreford points out that some HIV patients are able to "portray their illness as a calling rather than as symptoms of HIV" (Wreford, 2008: 2). This partly accounts for the tarnished image of traditional medicine and the contentious relationship between THPs and biomedical practitioners. As Chaudhury (1997) rightly maintains, the regulation of traditional systems of medicine, the products used in the system, and the practitioners of the systems, are weak in most countries. This weakness of the regulation of traditional medicine as in South Africa often leads to the misuse of the products used in the system by unqualified practitioners and loss in the credibility of the system. In South Africa, the use of body parts fuelled calls for the proscription of traditional healing. The failure of some people to distinguish between witchcraft and indigenous medical practice reinvigorated calls for a ban on indigenous medical practices. Various responses followed this call:

---

3 Except otherwise stated, this section draws heavily from Faure (2002: 34–37).

In 1996 the Northern Province government set up a Commission under the auspices of Prof. NV Ralushai to probe into the reasons underpinning the widespread "witch killings" (muti killing). The report of the Ralushai Commission published the same year maintained that the government should institute: (1) A code of conduct for traditional healers (2) Different penalties for witches as well as those who sniff them out (3) A blanket ban on the forced collection of money required to compensate *izangoma*, and (4) Carry out mass sensitization so as to dissuade people from believing in witchcraft or muti.

The Institute for Multi-party Democracy (IMPD) undertook a review of the Anti-Witchcraft Act of 1957. After consultations with stakeholders in various communities, the IMPD issued a document as the basis for discussion at the *Witchcraft Summit, Towards New Legislation*. The summit drafted a witchcraft Control Act with the aim of replacing the 1957 Witchcraft Suppression Act. Among other recommendations, there was a call for the creation of special witchcraft tribunals: "special witchcraft courts as appendages to the formal court system" that will in collaboration with the Departments of Health and Justice have the power to lay down fines for people "making reckless or self-serving witchcraft accusations and on those found actually practicing witchcraft."

In 1999, the Commission on Gender Equality (CGE) waded into the debate through a Conference with the aim of making recommendations for the reform of the Witchcraft Suppression Act (1957). In a key note presentation, Dr. Njiro (1999), then Director of the University of Venda Centre for Gender Studies argued against the 'smelling' of witches (mostly females) by males (mostly youths) as a form of gender-based violence. Nthai (1999) admonished the government against addressing its relationship with "traditional healers" in the same manner like the former regime.

On the other hand, those who advocated for the 'normalisation' of indigenous healing practices maintained that the benefits of traditional healing methods and practices far outweighed the perceived shortcomings. They therefore stood for the decriminalization of such practices. A triple response followed suit:

1) Government instituted its own review of existing legislation including the Anti-Witchcraft Act of 1957. The Select Committee on Social Services recommended among other measures, the creation of a statutory national traditional medicine council.

2) The establishment of research centres for the identification of the biological properties and medicinal advantages of various indigenous medicines. Most notably, a Medical Research Council funded collaborative project bringing together the Pharmacology departments of the

Universities of Cape Town and Western Cape was put in place to test plants brought to them by indigenous healers for their medicinal qualities.

On the other hand, indigenous health practitioners made attempts towards the institutionalization of their practice through:

1) The establishment of indigenous medical hospitals. Between 1994 and 1998, Durban witnessed the establishment of five of these hospitals. However, state subsidies were never provided to these institutions. They relied on fees paid by patients that were inadequate and they eventually shut down.

2) A few employers and medical aid funds recognized indigenous medical practice and accepted to allow indigenous medical practitioners to claim against medical aid funds. The electricity parastatal (Eskom) was one company that was allegedly recognizing medical certificates issued by indigenous medical practitioners.

3) The KwaZulu-Natal Traditional Healer's Council (KZNTHC) was established as a conglomerate of various Traditional Healer's Associations from the area. One of its aims was to provide certification of members so that they could be issued with the Health Ministry's recognized certificate of competence and membership cards to keep away charlatans. (see also Chavunduka, 1986: 70)

Faure (2002: 37) rightly maintains that the 'normalisation' of indigenous medical practices may tremendously transform this concatenation of healing practices. While it might imply that indigenous practitioners benefit from the advantages of 'modern medicine,' 'normalisation' is however "based on an old understanding of indigenous medical practice" that fails to take account of its transformations and commodification over time. The result is that it might not provide practical solutions to people's problems. Moreover, indigenous medicine will be forced to adopt the 'scientific' procedures of biomedicine- a situation that will turn indigenous practitioners into "junior partners" given the hierarchies between various knowledge systems. As demonstrated for Tanzania, there is conflict between biomedicine and other systems of medicine including traditional Chinese medicine (TCM). Biomedical doctors vigorously lobby against traditional practitioners for allegedly combining biomedical knowledge with traditional Chinese medicine, a self-interest polemic that arises from the biomedical profession, "rather than from an engagement with a viable health policy for the improved well-being of ordinary people". (Hsu, 2002: 297)

Despite South Africa's active participation in global and regional initiatives for the promotion of traditional medicine, there is a clear lack of policy dialogue between policy makers, consumers and informal providers of traditional medicine. This is the case like in Uganda where although "the latter [traditional practitioners] constitute a significant source of care for both the urban and rural poor…while communities recognize and consult with this category of provider, the integration policy seems not to be interacting, or catching up, with some of the realities of the… health care system" (Birungi et al., 2001; cf. Mutabazi, 2008: 209). The starting point for collaboration between traditional and modern medicine should be a prior evaluation of the potential benefits and obstacles, an assessment of the medical service utilization pattern of communities, as well as a consideration of the specific role of the traditional healer. Healer's ideas about collaboration should also be taken on board (Boerma and Baya, 1990).

3.7 Conclusion

This chapter has examined the encounter between colonialism and traditional medicine on the one hand and on the other hand, between colonialism and apartheid as systems of racial domination. The colonial "medical apartheid" paradigm was appropriated by the apartheid regime and deployed through spatial and social segregation policies that were meant to separate the races and protect the health of whites. Prior to colonialism, traditional medicine which was the only therapeutic recourse strategy had made great strides in the diagnosis and treatment of diseases. Colonialism and later apartheid, enforced biomedical hegemony, while simultaneously disparaging alternative knowledge systems that were not only treated with contempt and ridicule, but also summarily proscribed. Bans were even instituted against the sale of traditional medicine, but the practice of traditional medicine went underground and continued to serve the health needs of the majority since the medical segregation of the colonial era reserved biomedical care only to colonial agents and reproducers of the colonial system such as labourers. The postcolonial period and the end of apartheid has witnessed ambivalence and a lack of political will from the South African government which has continued to sign on to regional initiatives for the promotion of traditional medicine, but has implemented some at a rather slow pace thereby making the integration of both traditional healing practices and allopathic medicine a far-fetched dream. Patients however continue to shuttle across both medical systems to maximize their health care needs, to seek explanations for the witchcraft scare that gripped South Africa in the post-apartheid period. Simultaneously and against this backdrop, traditional healing practices, though on the margins of the official biomedical health care system, became a cure and a curse for HIV/AIDS patients. The ANC government was caught between promoting African cultural values as part of the democratic transition process but simultaneously refusing patients from accessing life-saving antiretroviral therapy on grounds of its alleged toxicity and its unknown effects.

CHAPTER 4

Democracy, Witchcraft and Traditional Medicine

> The year 1994 marked the beginning of a journey towards reclaiming human dignity for all in South Africa—a societal reconstruction towards ubuntu and its respect for all life, its recognition of the past, its care for present and future well-being, its consciousness of human interdependency, and its philosophy of equality, and social and economic justice.
> (Eastern Cape Vision Planning Commission, 2014: iv)

4.1 Introduction

The aim of this ethnographic study is to initiate a dialogue between modern and traditional medicine within the context of the escalating HIV/AIDS pandemic in the democratic Republic of South Africa. The dual legacies of colonialism and apartheid tarnished the image of traditional medical practices and their practitioners in the country. These myriad practices were lumped together and associated with witchcraft. The false and lingering image left behind by this conflation of traditional medicine with witchcraft is that traditional healers are engaged in harming rather than healing people (Bishop, 2012). The conjuncture between the end of apartheid, the outbreak of the HIV/AIDS social crises and the wholesale sociocultural transformations associated with democratization serve as a useful background for understanding the HIV/AIDS policy debate that partly led to heightened interest in revitalizing and regulating traditional medicine. By initially endorsing traditional medicine as therapy against the epidemic, South African leaders perpetuated the witchcraft theory of the disease thereby paradoxically hindering HIV-positive patients from accessing lifesaving antiretroviral drugs. How do competing state policies affect the choice between traditional and modern medicine in an era of HIV/AIDS? Can we really talk of biomedical hegemony?

First, this chapter sets out the conflicting policy context within which traditional medicine became imbricated in the HIV/AIDS policy debate in South Africa thereby making it both a cure and a curse for patients. Secondly, it highlights the political incentives of the ANC-government's policy of a "return to tradition" as well as its simultaneous official denial of the existence of HIV/AIDS pandemic that partly delayed the uptake of life-saving antiretroviral therapy and sent desperate patients to traditional health practitioners. Thirdly, it examines the reasons for the preference of traditional healers by HIV/AIDS patients within this contentious policy framework.

4.2 The HIV/AIDS Policy Context, Traditional Medicine and Democracy

The various incentives for an "official" return to traditional medicine in the post-apartheid period in South Africa include the lingering socioeconomic inequalities of the apartheid era, the spiraling HIV/AIDS pandemic that was accentuating deficiencies in the healthcare system, the political desire to return to African culture within the context of democracy. It was a mechanism of obliterating the cultural deracination caused by the apartheid system. In addition, to give the majority black South African population a sense of belonging in a democratic South Africa. In other words, the aim was to redress aspects of the injustices of apartheid. In a sense, the new South African leadership was thus, keen on highlighting their cultural credentials by revalorizing African cultural values and practices. Paradoxically, some of these cultural practices including belief in witchcraft, virginity testing, male circumcision in unsterilized environments and the use of the same instrument on a group of initiates are antithetical to the fight against the HIV/AIDS pandemic. The belief in the witchcraft theory of AIDS (Farmer, 2006; Nattrass, 2008) alongside denial of the existence of the epidemic by the political class led to confusion, the denial of the existence of the epidemic among the masses and recourse to traditional healers by patients.

The Jacob Zuma's tenure (2009–2014) however, marked a dramatic break away from the ultra-conservative and AIDS denialist policies of the Thabo Mbeki administration. It witnessed the scaling up of ART and increased health promotion (Zuma et al., 2016). Zuma stated in a speech on World AIDS Day (December 1, 2009) at a ceremony in Pretoria that:

> Let today be the dawn of a new era. Let there be no more shame, no more blame, no more discrimination and no more stigma. Let the politicization and endless debates about HIV and AIDS stop. Let this be the start of an era of openness, of taking personal responsibility, and of working together in unity to prevent HIV infections and to deal with its impact.
>
> (Grünkemeier, 2013: 41)

He passionately implored his audience to cooperate and to synergize with government efforts to curb the spread of the epidemic. Using the rhetorical strategies—particularly the anaphoria 'let' and the 'dawn' metaphor, he prescribed how the epidemic should be addressed moving forward (Grünkemeier, 2013: 41). In his determination to "improve the health profile of all South Africans" (Govender, 2009: online), his government scaled up its interventions in combating tuberculosis, HIV and AIDS, ARV treatment programme and launched the National HIV Counselling and Testing Campaign. This resulted in the largest ARV programme in the world. The DoH stepped up the number of public facilities providing ARVs from 490 in February 2010 to 3540 (2014) (Ibid.). Some 2.4 million individuals were benefitting from ARV treatment compared with 923,000 in February 2010. The president's 2012–13 Annual Report spoke of a positive impact on childhood mortality resulting from the turnaround in HIV management (Oldenburg, 2016; Iwuji, 2013; Govender, 2009). There was a noticeable reduction in mother-child- transmission of HIV from 8% in 2008 to 2.5% in 2012. This resulted in the protection of more than 100,000 babies from HIV infection. The government further reduced the daily ARV cocktail of three pills to one tablet. The new single dose ARV was not only revolutionary, but also extremely affordable at a monthly cost of R89.39. In a bid to foster and promote openness and to eradicate the silence and stigma associated with this pandemic, Zuma told South Africans he had tested HIV negative (Govender, 2009).

All babies with HIV received treatment at public facilities while women began receiving care earlier in their pregnancies in a bid to prevent transmission to new borns. On April 26, 2010 at the Natalspruit hospital in Ekurhuleni, Gauteng, Zuma launched the world's biggest HIV testing programme with the ambitious target of persuading 15-million people to voluntarily take HIV test and get treatment. This culminated in a six-fold increase on the 2,5-million tested in 2009 (Govender, 2009).

In line with the recommendations by the WHO, beginning in 2016, South Africa initiated ART with all patients testing HIV positive regardless of CD4 count (Moodley et al., 2016; Oldenburg, 2016). The guidelines recommends that ART should first, be initiated in everyone living with HIV at any CD4 cell count. Second, it recommended the use of daily oral pre-exposure prophylaxis (PrEP) as a prevention choice for people at substantial risk of HIV infection. This was part of a combination of prevention approaches (WHO, 2015). The adoption of the WHO guidelines marked a milestone and has significantly contributed to the positive developments in the anti-HIV/AIDS fight in South Africa (Cohen et al., 2016; Moodley et al., 2016; Oldenburg, 2016; Iwuji, 2013; Johnson, 2012; Dabis et al., 2010).

4.3 The Lingering Socioeconomic Inequalities of the Apartheid Era

Since 1994, various democratically elected ANC governments have faced many intractable problems including the widening gap between rich and poor, low level of education that is accentuated among women, a sluggish economy and lack of access to basic services such as healthcare. The expansion of access to livelihood resources have been excruciatingly slowed by the fight against HIV/AIDS as well as an upsurge in fears of witchcraft accusation scares and related ritual killings (Ashforth, 2005). Amidst these social and economic problems, witches and their familiars are strongly held to slow people's progress, cause misfortune and disease including HIV/AIDS (Ashforth, 2005; Flint, 2005; Geschiere, 2008). In the post-apartheid period, witchcraft-related violence flared up: In the Northern Limpopo Province for instance, the number of witchcraft-related violent assaults on individuals or groups believed to be practicing witchcraft rose from 115 cases per annum in 1994 and 1995 to 1,093 in 1996 and 1, 293 in 2001 (Pelgrim, 2003: 87; Ashforth, 2005). There is a consensus that more evil spirits evidenced by pollution and the seamless entanglement between visible and invisible worlds (spirits of the ancestors) that is reminiscent of other parts of Africa were at work and the cause of HIV/AIDS. This feeling of spiritual insecurity, helplessness and uncertainty in the face of the legal, social and policing dilemma posed by the problem of witchcraft drove masses of people to traditional practitioners such as *sangomas* and *inyangas* leading to an uneasy atmosphere of insecurity, crime and distrust (Ashforth, 2005; Pelgrim, 2003; Roxburg, 2014; Parker, 2010). In the face of extreme and widespread poverty, and the desperation to break out of it, make sense of it, and the need to find a sense of comfort amidst turmoil, most of the rural masses turn to sorcery to combat the unequal distribution of wealth and resources (Farmer, 2006: 204; Ashforth, 2005; Geschiere, 2008; Geschiere, 1997). The state and other stakeholders including religious bodies, NGOs and traditional authorities have proven unable to address the spiritual insecurity associated with violence resulting from logical constraints (Roxburgh, 2014; Pelgrim, 2003). While belief in witchcraft led to the effervescence of traditional healing practices, including for the 'strange,' 'mystical' and 'new' disease of HIV/AIDS by desperate patients, it has had a deleterious effects on efforts to roll back the spread of the pandemic. It slowed the uptake of antiretroviral therapy.

4.4 The "Return to Tradition" Policy

The official end of apartheid as a system of institutionalized discrimination coincided with the beginning of the HIV/AIDS pandemic that has continued to decimate South Africa's population. The end of apartheid ushered in a period of tremendous changes in all aspects of life in the country. The democratically elected leadership of the ANC that came to power was determined to implement changes including the re-valorization of traditional values and practices and to create an inclusive society with equal opportunities for all citizens. South Africa's first Bill of Rights was contained in Chapter 3 of the transitional Constitution of 1993, which was drawn up as part of the negotiations to end apartheid. This "interim Bill of Rights," which came into force on 27 April 1994 (the date of the first non-racial election), was largely limited to civil and political rights (negative rights) (Cockrell, 1997). The current Bill of Rights, which replaced it on 4 February 1997 (the commencement date of the final Constitution), retained all of these rights and added a number of new positive economic, social and cultural rights (Cockrell, 1997). The return to culture and the customary included the adoption of the Traditional Courts Bill as well as the formal regulation and integration of traditional medicine into the mainstream biomedical health system. During the colonial and apartheid eras, traditional healing practices were lumped together with witchcraft and banned through the Suppression of Witchcraft Act (1957) (Ashforth, 2005; Bishop, 2012).

The Witchcraft Suppression Act 3 of 1957 (amended 1970) had declared TM as unlawful. When the authorities were, however, confronted with the intractable problem of HIV/AIDS, and under immense pressure to do something to alleviate the pains and suffering of South Africans by delivering healthcare to them, they saw the need for collaboration between the biomedical and traditional healing systems. This partly explains the institutionalization and regulation of the latter through the promulgation of the South African Traditional Health Practitioners Act 22 of 2007. Practitioners of traditional medicine outnumber biomedical practitioners in the country.

In the immediate post-apartheid era, South Africa also witnessed the revival of male and female coming-of-age rituals, virginity testing (initiation and *umemulo*), *ukuthwala* (a form of irregular marriage), mourning obligations and widowhood rites and practices (*ukuzila*) (Thonberry, 2015). Many organisations including 'the prominent AIDS Activist Group, Treatment Action Campaign (TAC)[1]' (Watson, 2005) and the Traditional Healers Organization (THO) (McFarlane, 2015: 62) championed the cause of integrating traditional medicine within South African society (McFarlane, 2015: 62). They were supported by government leaders and South African activists such as Zackie Achmat, Phepsile Maseko and the most prominent, Manto Tshabalala-Msimang. These

---

1 "The vociferous campaigns by the Treatment Action Campaign and other activists in South Africa demonstrate that ARVs can serve to lessen stigmatisation by presenting healthier images of people living with the disease" (Wreford, 2008: 6).

individuals have all helped to outline and shape African traditional medicine into a legitimised form of medical practice, which celebrates African culture (McFarlane, 2015: 63). The aim of this political agenda was to give a sense of belonging and identity to the majority black population that had inordinately suffered from marginalization in all spheres of national life with debilitating effects on their health and living conditions under the apartheid system of rule.

4.5 Shortages of Human Resources for Health

Faced with the HIV/AIDS policy debate and the virtual collapse of the healthcare system inherited from the apartheid era, the South African government was willing to coopt traditional healers with their numerical strength into the healthcare system in the fight against the pandemic. The spiraling HIV/AIDS pandemic that was decimating the population had accentuated deficiencies in the healthcare system. South Africa has a 50:100,000 ratio of doctors per population (George et al., 2013) with rural areas particularly poorly served (understaffed) and underfunded (Flint, 2016). According to WHO guidelines, the minimum requirement for a middle-income country like South Africa is 180:100,000 (George et al., 2013). The number of traditional health practitioners (THPs) in South Africa is estimated at ~300,000 (Flint & Payne, 2013), a ratio of more than 1:70 (de Roubaix, 2016; George et al., 2013). Estimates have it that some 80% of South Africans may rely on THPs for their healthcare needs (de Roubaix, 2016; George et al., 2013; Flint & Payne, 2013). An estimated 72% of the Black African population in South Africa rely on traditional medicine, and account for an estimated 26.6 million consumers (Mander et al., 2007). THPs far surmount biomedical practitioners by almost 10:1 (Flint & Payne, 2013). In 2007, the traditional medicine trade in South Africa was estimated at ZAR 2.9 billion (Mander et al., 2007). Some 5100 full-time THPs practice in the townships of Cape Town and trade an estimated 1 300 tons of plant products annually (de Roubaix, 2016: 159).

The government initially refused the existence of the HIV/AIDS pandemic and accordingly resisted antiretroviral thereby leaving HIV-positive patients at the mercy of traditional healers. Persuaded by most of the denialist "science" on the subject, Thabo Mbeki expressed "scepticism" about the link between HIV and AIDS. He presented his position as "being one based on resistance to imperialist values," (and there) was an increased focus on traditional medicine as a potential "African solution to an African problem" (Flint, 2016: 4332). Against this backdrop of official denial of the existence of the epidemic at its very onset and in the absence of a biomedical response such as antiretroviral

(ARV), there was widespread confusion among HIV positive patients who in desperation sought alternative treatment regimens, including forms of traditional African healing (Flint, 2016; Nattrass, 2008; Beck, 2003).

Thabo Mbeki's aggressive public policy campaign promoting traditional medicine for the cure of HIV/AIDS while deeming antiretroviral (ARVs) drugs toxic or poisonous instilled a general fear of biomedicine within the HIV-positive population in South Africa. The government under his leadership further stated that the cost of the medicines (ARVs) is too high, and their effectiveness is unknown (Bishop, 2012; Nattrass, 2008). It is estimated that between 2000–2005 about 330,000 people lost lives because of this policy (Chigwedere et al., 2008). While it is widely accepted that this policy was detrimental to the lives of HIV-positive individuals (Nattrass, 2008; Chigwedere et al., 2008), Kristina Monroe Bishop maintains that it was a reflection of "an ongoing struggle between indigenous and colonial practices that have dominated South Africa's social, cultural, and economic landscape for over a century" (Bishop, 2012: 572). In other words, the neglect of the pandemic that has continually ravaged the country (with a higher infection rate among the Black population) and created a health crisis of unprecedented proportions. It is a reflection of the colonial context of South Africa's political struggle over medicine that is usually captured using colonial images of indigenous use and understanding of medicine "as exotic, dangerous, and quaint" (Bishop, 2012: 754).

The later adoption of life-saving AVR only came to transform the meaning of AIDS from a jealousy-as-causation (witchcraft) to a disease associated with life style and sexual morality (Chopra et al., 2006) and led to the "whittling away of public denial of AIDS" in some rural areas in the Eastern Cape (Steinberg, 2007: 9). Traditional healers have however, frequently continued to prescribe traditional remedies as ART alternatives (Flint, 2016: 4334) thereby leading to low ART uptake and the continuous spread of the disease. By failing to engage with biomedical HIV/AIDS treatment regimens at the beginning of the epidemic, the human cost in South Africa escalated. For instance, the Harvard School of Public Health suggests that between 2000 and 2005, "more than 330,000 lives or approximately 2.2 million person years were lost" (Chopra et al., 2006: 1977). According to the same study, 35,000 babies acquired HIV via mother-to-child transmission, a situation that could have been averted by the government through the rolling out of ART. The authors of the study emphatically concede that *"if antiretroviral agents are to compete more successfully in the therapeutic continuum, there needs to be explicit recognition of, and further strategies to counter, the attraction of alternative therapies for patients and the systematic promotion these treatments receive"* (Chopra et al., 2006: 1977). Many South Africans, Flint (2016) argues, simply saw ART as one of several alternative treatment options, showing the persistence of confusion concerning the epidemic. The epidemic thus continues to ravage South Africa, twenty years and counting since the democratic transition. A 2014 report showed that there were an estimated 469 000 infections in 2012 alone (Shisana et al., 2014: xxxix, Flint, 2016), with 11.6% of the national prevalence rate found in the Eastern Cape (Stats SA, 2014). The number of people living with AIDS and receiving ARV in South Africa in 2016 was 3,900,000 (a meagre 53% of those eligible for treatment) (Stats SA, 2018).

4.6 The Adoption of Democracy and the Promotion of Cultural Rights

The adoption of democratic values entailed the upholding of cultural, women's and children's rights. Chapter 2 of the Constitution of South Africa for instance, contains the Bill of Rights, a human rights charter that protects the civil, political and socio-economic rights of all people in the country. The rights in the bill apply to all laws, including the common law, and bind all branches of the government, including the national executive, Parliament, the judiciary, provincial governments and municipal councils (Cockrell, 1997). Some provisions, such as those prohibiting unfair discrimination, also apply to the actions of private persons (Cockrell, 1997).

In South Africa, two camps are pitted against each other in the ensuing debate between the preservation of cultural/community rights and democracy. There are advocates of custom and tradition on the one hand and on the other hand, women's and children's rights advocates. The Council of Traditional Leaders of South Africa and the current Zulu king, Goodwill Zwelithini, are champions of traditional values (traditional authority). Advocates of women's equality are made up of myriad civil society organizations—"including, at times, the Women's League of the ruling African National Congress—for whom gender equality forms a core part of the nation's democratic transformation" (Thonberry, 2015: 130). Some of the latter organizations vigorously opposed the Traditional Courts Bill for its apparent male bias.[2] However, some

---

[2] The bill, proponents concede, is a means of protecting African culture. Opponents point out that the bill entrenches gender inequality between men and women in traditional courts. For instance, women can only address the court by proxy, in the presence of a male representative. Widows, unlike widowers are refused the right to inherit marital property. These objections, particularly the refusal of women's constitutionally guaranteed property rights expose them to gender based violence and HIV/AIDS infection. They further perpetuate an assumed chasm between the idea of tradition and women's human rights (see Thonberry, 2015; Hassim, 2002; Thipe, 2013).

organizations such as the Rural Women's Movement, that was vigorously opposed to the bill "also voiced support for a nondiscriminatory regime of customary law" (Thonberry, 2015: 130). According to Sizani Ngubani, leader of the Rural Women's Movement: "what we need ... is a law that protects real custom and protects women" (Alliance For Rural Democracy, 2014; cf. Thonberry, 2015: 130). Through claims to support "'real custom,' gender activists inoculate themselves against charges that they are 'un-African.' The invocation of 'real custom,' however, is also a reminder that colonialism and apartheid reshaped customary law, often to the detriment of women" (Thonberry, 2015: 130). The protection of custom and tradition has become associated with "the regulation of gender and sexuality" (Ibid.). Arguments in support of the opposition between women's and children's rights and custom and tradition reflect the mantra of justifications for cherry picking in the implementation of the Convention on the Elimination of All Forms of Discrimination against Women (CEDAW) (Thonberry, 2015; Pemunta, 2011) and the Child Rights Convention (Pemunta, 2011; Pemunta & Fubah, 2016). Attempts by the South African political class to simultaneously revalorize culture and tradition as well as to promote gender equality led to ambivalent policies and a backlash. They were keen on highlighting their cultural credentials as real representatives of the people but also to show to the international community that they are upholding human rights in general and women's and children's rights in particular.[3]

In South Africa, the Children's Act was widely perceived among the Zulu as an affront on parental authority and African custom or tradition and led to resistance. Although the bill forbids virginity testing on girls under sixteen, that was not the most controversial aspect of the bill. It however, significantly framed the tune of the debate in which the "rights of the child" stood in stark opposition to cultural rights (de Robillard, 2009; Thonberry, 2015). Resistance against the bill has produced a counteraction as girls under sixteen are being tested contrary to the spirit of the bill. Young women are victimized and accused of being responsible for the HIV/AIDS pandemic while male sexual partners are exonerated. Other consequences of the backlash include the commodification of female sexuality, and the blaming and shaming of young women victims of rape (Thonberry, 2015; Leclerc-Madlala, 2003). We argue that the appeal to the idea of a pure "custom rooted in nostalgia for a precolonial past" (Thonberry, 2015: 135; Pemunta, 2011) is a patriarchal mechanism used by cultural

---

3 On this, and similar debates, such as on the perceived "UnAfrican" practice of homosexuality in Africa (see Pemunta, 2018 and on women's human rights and culture in Sierra Leone, see Pemunta & Obara, (2011). On the chasm between culture and women's human rights in international perspective, see Griffiths, 2001 Cowan et al., 2001).

entrepreneurs to maintain their power. The glorification of an ideal past that underpins the revival of ancient cultural practices including virginity testing as a bulwark and "native antidote" against the HIV/AIDS pandemic (Pemunta, 2016) constitutes part of the antiapartheid struggle associated with democratization. The return to tradition (virginity testing) ironically continues to perpetuate the inequalities of the apartheid system as well as to expose women to the risk of contracting the virus because their "certification" as virgins instead expose them to HIV infected men who believe that having sex with a virgin serves as therapy.

4.7 Traditional Medicine as Cure and a Curse for HIV/AIDS

In South Africa, there is a high preference for traditional medicine by HIV/AIDS patients partly because of the belief in the witchcraft theory of the disease. Is this preference for traditional medicine a double-edged sword in the fight against HIV/AIDS in the country? What factors are responsible for this apparently gendered preference? Men are especially more likely to consult traditional healers for HIV/AIDS-related sicknesses. This seems to suggest that although both genders navigate multiple sources of treatment for HIV/AIDS, men are more liable to belief in witchcraft as the causative agent of the disease, and as heads of households, are the ones charged with meeting up with family expectations (Zuma et al., 2018).

At the outset of the HIV/AIDS pandemic, the political leadership under Thabo Mbeki refused the existence of HIV as causing AIDS. Mbeki contended that ARVs may be "toxic," expensive and their efficacy unknown. He instead recommended the use of traditional medicine and nutrition. This political stance left desperate HIV positive patients confused and traditional medicine became "a cure and a curse for those sick with AIDS" (Bishop, 2012: 578). Alongside witchcraft-related violence, spiritual insecurity, helplessness and uncertainty in the face of the legal, social and policing dilemma posed by the problem of witchcraft, the masses consulted traditional practitioners such as *sangomas* and *inyangas* (Ashforth, 2005; Pelgrim, 2003; Roxburg, 2014; Parker, 2010). This paradoxical situation led to an uneasy atmosphere of insecurity, crime and distrust. Some individuals sought explanations, but also protection against bewitchment from traditional healers. Although belief in witchcraft led to the effervescence of traditional healing practices, including against the 'strange,' 'mystical' and 'new' disease of HIV/AIDS by desperate patients, it has a paradoxical effect on traditional medicine since healers are alleged to be involved in ritual killings (*muthi*) and of consequently barring efforts to roll back the spread of the pandemic(Bishop, 2012; Peltzer & Mngqundaniso, 2008). Similarly, the self-contradictory effects of casting doubts on the existence of AIDS and representation of ARVs as toxic and harmful by the Mbeki administration included (1) fears of ARVs (withholding of the drug from HIV positive people) and a turn to traditional healers, (2) the use of unreliable traditional remedies, (3) the need for the regulation and control of traditional healers as well as their enrollment in AIDS management (Bishop, 2012: 755). In their desperation, some patients simultaneously used traditional medicine and ART or dropped out of ART treatment regimens because of side effects and continued using traditional medicine for HIV (Peltzer & Mngqundaniso, 2008). Concurrently, THs were accused of prescribing "harsh traditional cleansing remedies for patients on ARVs" (Wreford, 2008: 14). Nevertheless, why do HIV/AIDS patients prefer traditional healers when biomedicine remains the dominant healthcare system and what could be the effects on patient care?

4.8   The Preference for Traditional Healers

An estimated 70–80% of HIV/AIDS patients in South Africa seeking therapy from traditional healing systems is partly the result of the fear, stigma and discrimination associated with the disease that prevent people from getting tested and accessing appropriate care (Ross, 2010; Ramgoon, 2011; Latiff, 2010). The association of symptoms of the disease, most especially wasting, skin conditions and diarrhea with witchcraft fuel the recourse to traditional healers but ironically compounds the situation of HIV/AIDS patients (Nattrass, 2008: 25; Ashforth, 2005; Hunter, 2005; Farmer, 2006). It further strengthened men's propensity and likelihood of consulting THPs in preference of biomedical practitioners (Nattrass, 2008: 25) since they are in charge of decision-making within households. The introduction and increased accessibility of ART led to the whittling away of public denial of AIDS in some rural localities including Lusikiski in the Eastern Cape. HIV/AIDS infections previously considered the work of witchcraft is being identified with the disease (Steinberg, 2007). Intense stigma about HIV/AIDS and deaths resulting from infection with the disease ('shameful deaths')[4] however remain widespread and thereby pushing infected individuals to remain at home and get sicker, while others try to initiate treatment secretly with traditional and lay-healers

---

4   Such deaths are believed to be caused by infidelity, the inability to control one's sexual appetite and to be transmitted to one's partner. An infected individual is also seen as consciously infecting others so as not to die alone (See also Steinberg, 2007).

(Steinberg, 2007; Nattrass, 2008; Farmer, 2006). Symptoms including chronic diarrhea that is unresponsive to treatment as well as growing very thin and death are defined as AIDS while other symptoms of the disease are not considered: "A person who contracted cryptoccal meningitis, for instance or AIDS dementia, was said to have had a demon sent to him by an enemy. A person suffering from shingles-a common opportunistic infection triggered by immunodeficiency-was said to have had witch's snake crawl over her skin while she slept" (Steinberg, 2007: 11). In this disguising narrative, the cause of sudden, serious debilitating disease is attributed to bewitchment (Wreford, 2008: 7; Green, 1996: 93–94). Stigma reinforces a persistent and powerful resistance to HIV/AIDS disclosure (Maughan-Brown, 2007).

Discourses of bewitchment are used to escape from embarrassment and distress of an unwelcomed reality (Ashforth, 2005: 135). Patients are known to conceal rapid onset of symptoms, loss of energy and vitality of HIV/AIDS. Above all, witchcraft is used to shield family from 'blackmail' (Ashforth, 2005: 67–71). At funerals of victims of HIV/AIDS, family members often conspire and conceal the cause of death by announcing it as "witchcraft." They do so to protect the family's image from embarrassment because of the association of the disease with sexual immorality.

Like in Haiti, accusation narratives were also mounted by HIV/AIDS patients (the accused) in relation to magic and/or witchcraft, which represent AIDS as "jealousy sickness" (Farmer, 2006). "Witchcraft is understood to bring about general misfortune, financial problems, alcohol and/or substance abuse, relationship and personal issues, and, critically, ill health" (Flint, 2015: 4328; Nattrass, 2008: 25; Ashforth, 2005; Hunter, 2005). In the words of Paul Farmer "a sickness emblematic of a (community) of poor people distracted from the 'real struggle' by the hurts they inflict on one another (Farmer, 2006: 109)." The witchcraft theory of AIDS purports that the disease is unleashed by an individual who "out of jealousy or spite through means of sorcery, often by one poor person to another when someone becomes socially or economically successful at the expense of others or without redistributing their accumulated wealth to the desperately poor" (Farmer, 2006: 106; Geschiere, 2008). The second counter-blame theory as elaborated by Farmer that could be labelled as a "conspiracy theory" is that HIV/AIDS is an American invention meant to discourage sex and to curb population growth (Ibid.). A respondent articulated this view thus: "Throwing away sperms by using a condom is like killing children whose future we do not know. To me the story about AIDS and the need to wear a condom when having sex is a whiteman's invention to discourage childbirth and control population." The belief in the witchcraft theory of HIV/AIDS as the causative agent of the disease led to the cultural preference for *sangomas*[5] (Henderson, 2005; Natrass, 2008; Geschiere, 2008; 1997). This is a barrier to the uptake of HAART and other retrovirals. Another male respondent stated that: "Like my grandfather, I believe in the sangoma and not in drugs. I think that drugs will instead lead to a deterioration of my health condition. So, I prefer herbal medicine because it decreases the viral load in my blood." A similar study among miners showed that they were skeptical of western biomedical claims about AIDS and held the view that traditional healers could manage it (Macheke and Campbel, 1998). According to WHO, there are possibilities for linking traditional and biomedical systems of healthcare through incorporation, collaboration and integration of both systems as components of a primary healthcare approach (WHO, 1978; WHO, 2002). As Paul Farmer's ethnographic study of AIDS in Haiti illustrates, biomedicine is conceptually inadequate because of its failure to address the social dimension of debilitating illnesses including AIDS that are intimately intertwined with the socioeconomic conditions of poverty and problematic social relationships (1992: 205). Today's cross-cultural environment calls for the need to incorporate and integrate the perspectives of both folk healers and biomedical practitioners into contemporary healthcare (Millman, 2011; Wing, 1998: 144; Kleinman, 1984) for HIV/AIDS. The pluralistic management of AIDS in Haiti illustrates that treatments of the same conditions vary significantly transnationally, as well as the inclusion of cultural etiologies along with scientific explanations (Farmer, 1992; Sharma, 1993; Kleinman, 1984). As one traditional healer stated:

> HIV/AIDS is like a death sentence. However, if you believe (as some patients do), it is caused by witchcraft and consult amagqirha for instance, you certainly nurse hope of treatment and healing. The witchcraft attack must first be treated before any treatment of the disease can be effective.

The above interview excerpt suggests that HIV is the proximate cause of symptoms but that witchcraft is the ultimate cause. This invites the need for cleansing rituals and practices in HIV/AIDS interventions (Wreford, 2008). If biomedical practitioners adopt this view, and pursue collaboration—by accepting the patient's belief in witchcraft, they could still work alongside traditional healers in improving the health of HIV positive people (Kayombo et al., 2007: 6). While

---

5 They are healers who summon the powers of the ancestors in divining and the healing illness.

traditional cleansing rituals do not cure, they could serve as a medical placebo (Wreford, 2008: 10).

For many patients, meaning, spirituality and trust are core elements to the successful management of illness and calls for an acknowledgement of forms of ritual and their utilization in biomedicine (Millman, 2011; Welch, 2003; Sharma, 1992) with the aim of increasing accessibility to medical treatment (Coe, 1997: 6). This can be achieved by consciously including cultural context within health assessments and therapies to meet the cultural needs of patients and expand treatment (Metzger, 2006: 131–132; Millman, 2011: 96; Kleinman, 1984; Sharma, 1993; Farmer, 2006). The importance of meticulously examining the social, historical, and political context when attempting to understand and treat infectious disease in impoverished nations—is in fact, the crux of Farmer's work on HIV/AIDS in Haiti (Farmer, 2006).

The simultaneous or concurrent use of traditional and biomedical systems (medical pluralism) that manifests across traditional, faith-based and biomedical worlds (Zuma et al., 2018) speaks to the inapplicability and failure of biomedical treatment regimens to correspond with other cultural beliefs and practices (Millman, 2011: 81; Kleinman, 1984; Coe, 1997). The Haitian AIDS pandemic of the 1980s illustrates the interaction of traditional medical practices with biomedicine (Farmer, 1992). In other words, biomedicine is not as objective and acultural as it is forwarded to be (Millman, 2011). This suggests patients believe that different causative agents may be at work. Since AIDS is perceived as resulting from sorcery (Farmer, 2006: 204), it also demonstrates patient's needs to combat external forces with the help of a *sangoma* before taking up HAART.

Medical pluralism is however, alleged to delay HIV-related care and the interruption of care for people living with AIDS (PLHIV) (Puoane et al., 2012; Mngqundaniso et al., 2008; Leclerc-Madlala et al., 2009). Medical pluralism contributes to the simmering tensions between traditional and biomedical systems that are driven by the fear of drug-to-drug interactions and mistrust between providers (Wringe et al., 2017). Zuma and associates (2018: 10) found that patients use THPs "to meet expectations of their social networks, particularly expectations of family members who held authority as heads of households such as parents or grandparents." Although THPs are perceived as incompetent in treating HIV (Zuma et al., 2018), proponents however point to the holistic nature of traditional African therapies. Germond and Cochrane (2010) have for instance, outlined six dimensions of holistic health and wellbeing: the person (as an individual), the family, the village, the nation, religion and the earth (Ibid.). The concept of health-worlds (Germond and Cochrane, 2010) is used to explain the complexity of health beliefs and behaviours. This includes both social and religious dimensions (Dabis et al., 2010; Granich, 2010). It explains interactions between traditional and biomedical healing systems with reference to HIV/AIDS. While biomedicine essentially targets the physical wellbeing of the body by recognizing and treating disease, THPs seek to provide meaningful, in-depth explanations for illness as well as provide responses to personal, family and community issues surrounding an episode of illness (Germond and Cochrane, 2010). They provide responses to different healthcare needs, not as an alternative to ART but sometimes as complementary (Zuma et al., 2018). Some people hold the view that traditional healing does not interfere with accessing HAART (Nattrass, 2008) and other antiretrovirals (Zuma et al., 2018). The encounter between traditional medical systems and modern medicine is far more complex. As uncovered among healers and patients in the Eastern Cape region, it sometimes takes neither a pluralistic nor dichotomous form but rather, a syncretism, imbricated in local health systems. This has reminiscences to what obtains among the Maya community of the Western Highlands, Conception Huista where Elizabeth Hoyler and associates found a "significant overlap and interpenetration between biomedical and traditional medical models, described as a framework where practitioners in both settings employ elements of the other in order to best meet community needs" (Hoyler et al., 2016: 505) . The emphasizes on "practitioner's perspective illustrates the fact that apart from patient's willingness to seek care across health systems, practitioners converse across seemingly distinct systems via the incorporation of certain elements of the 'other'"(Ibid.).

Women are socially and biologically more vulnerable to HIV infection than men, and they disproportionately access HAART in large numbers. Men generally access health services less readily than women (Nattrass, 2008; Department of Health/ South Africa and Micro International, 2002). One reason for the choice of traditional medicine by PLWA is the quest for independence over treatment instead of surrendering to an "infantile state." For instance, 'Khabzela' a black radio personality in South Africa reportedly refused antiretroviral and opted for traditional therapy as a matter of choice and to have independence over the treatment instead of surrendering himself to the biomedical institution. Simultaneously, top medical authorities in South Africa endorsed traditional medicine for HIV/AIDS care as was the case of 'Khabzela' who was allegedly sent "a purveyor of untested alternative remedies" (Nattrass, 2008: 31) by the South African Health Minister.

Also undermining the fight against HIV/AIDS are local notions of sexual intercourse. Former South African president Jacob Zuma, a Zulu allegedly had unprotected sex with an HIV-positive woman and thereafter, immediately took a shower because it is contrary to Zulu custom "to leave a woman in a state of arousal" (Nattrass, 2008: 32; see also Gordin, 2006). Similarly, Zeblon Gwala and his uBhejane (rhino) herbal "cure" for AIDS was actively supported, amongst others, by president Thabo Mbeki's Minister of Health, Mantombazana Tshabalala-Msimang and other political elites. According to Manto Shabala "African traditional medicine is a science in its own right" (New African, July 2004; cf. McFarlane, 2015: 61). In 2005 when the Medical University of South Africa subjected the drug to clinical trials, it was however found to have no positive effect on the treatment of HIV/AIDS (Flint, 2015). Such official support for uBhejane, AIDS activists argued (along with other traditional treatments), created confusion in the minds of South Africans as to the value of ART (Flint, 2015; Nattrass, 2008).

Another reason explaining the low uptake of ART is the purported "ethnomedical inconsistencies existing between traditional and biomedical health paradigms" (Moshabela et al., 2017: 84; Sterk & Del Rio, 2008; de Roubaix, 2016). Practitioners of the former system simultaneously address the physical causes of illness ("proximal cause") and the reason for that illness ("ultimate cause"). As articulated by Malcolm de Roubaix (2016: 160):

> In traditional African thinking, disease may have more direct immediate causes, but often has an ultimate cause, e.g. to be found in some relational disharmony (between individuals in a community, between the patient and some animate or inanimate entity, nature or the ancestors). The diviner (sangoma) determines the nature of disharmony and prescribes corrective measures.

The ultimate cause usually associate HIV and other STDs with witchcraft "a malevolent force understood to be the product of jealousy or anger" (Sterk & Del Rio, 2008: 17; Wreford, 2005; Farmer, 2006). Biomedical interventions is assumed to treat the proximal, rather than the ultimate cause of witchcraft. Many traditional healers are of the opinion that these interventions are unable to provide holistic care for HIV/AIDS (Sterk & Del Rio, 2008; Wreford, 2005). We subscribe to the view put forward by Mosa Moshabela, Thembilehle Zuma and Bernhard Gaede according to which "the merging of biomedical and traditional healing paradigms provides for a complementary system of plural health care, which could offer patients a truly holistic and comprehensive form of care" (2017: 18).

The HIV situation in South Africa is further compounded by the failure to believe in the existence of AIDS and fear that antiretrovirals could lead to harmful effects and eventually death. Whereas one quarter of survey respondents held this view, 15% were of the opinion that traditional medicine was capable of reducing the amount of HIV in the blood (Nattrass, 2008: 23). Although the survey data were however, not desegregated for gender, it is clear that if most South African men hold such beliefs, this is a plausible reason for their relatively low uptake of HAART (Nattrass, 2008: 23; Nattrass, 2005; Beck, 2004).

Masculinity factors mostly accounts for differences between men and women when it comes to accessing HAART. Gendered norms makes it difficult for men to admit weakness and seek medical attention for all illnesses including HIV/AIDS-related or otherwise for as long as possible than women. This seems to explain the low uptake of HAART in both the public and private healthcare sectors in South Africa. Although 43% of people requiring HAART were estimated to be men, men comprised only 30% of life-prolonging HAART patients (Western Cape Department of Health, 2006: 11–12; Nattrass, 2008: 19). Men are more likely to consult THPs than women but this is however "complementary to, rather than a substitute for, accessing HAART" (Nattrass, 2008: 19). One reason offered for the low uptake of HAART was the fact that the facilities were linked to mother-to-child-transmission-prevention (MTCTP) programmes and therefore skewed towards women who are better connected to community networks and dispose of better healthcare information and are thus better placed to access public health facilities than men (Ibid.).

Apart from this construction of the clinic as part of the feminine world, contrary to standard economic logic (cost-benefit analysis) according to which men typically boast of greater financial and human capital than women, health-seeking behaviour is underpinned by cultural and contextual factors. It is thus, socially constructed and constitutive of masculinity (Nattrass, 2008: 22; Hunter, 2005). With reference to the United States, Will Courtenary observes that "men reinforce strongly held cultural beliefs that men are more powerful and less vulnerable than women, that men's bodies are structurally more efficient and superior to women's bodies, that asking for help and caring for one's health are feminine, and that the most powerful men among men are those for whom health and safety are irrelevant" (Courtenary, 2000: 1389; Nattrass, 2008: 22; Hunter, 2005). A 2004 survey found unanimity among two-thirds of South African residents with the statement that "men think of ill-health as a sign of weakness which is why they go to a doctor less often than women" (Magruder and Nattrass, 2006; cf. Nattrass, 2008: 22). Contrary to men, women's preference for biomedicine has been explained in terms of their contact with birth control technology and medical services associated with pregnancy and birth (Beck, 2004: 11–12).

The HIV/AIDS epidemic has a gendered character in South Africa. The "feminisation" of the epidemic is partly the consequence of women's low socioeconomic status. According to the joint United Nations Programme on HIV/AIDS (UNIAIDS): "Gender inequalities as well as gender norms and relations, including practices around sexuality, marriage and reproduction, harmful traditional practices, barriers to women's and girl's education, lack of access for women to health information and care, and inadequate access to economic, social, legal and political empowerment are major contextual barriers to effective HIV prevention" (2005: 25–26). While HIV prevention obviously "requires myriad strategies to empower women" (Global Partnership on Women and AIDS, 2005), the widespread association of male identity with unwillingness to negotiate safe sex poses danger to both genders. Men in the study area have a soft spot for "skin-on-skin" penetrative intercourse and simultaneously maintain sexual relationships with multiple partners. Risky sexual behaviours are reinforced by socioeconomic factors including dangerous working environments, such as mining in South Africa (Nattrass, 2008; Hunter, 2005). This harsh socioeconomic environment leads to physical and psychological stress and men find leisure in alcohol and transactional sex with prostitutes while working in the mines (Hunter, 2005; Crush et al., 2005; Corbett et al., 2004; Williams et al., 2000). The harsh working environment is accentuated by men's aversion to engage in risky sexual behaviour ('dangerous masculinity'). In conjunction with a fatalistic approach to life, it fuels the spread of the epidemic. This fatalistic attitude to life and HIV/AIDS is evident in the following statement: "whether you have sex with a condom or not, everyone will eventually die. It is better to enjoy full sexual pleasure before death comes. May be that is how God had designed it and no one can change it." Despite the malleability, contestation and responsiveness of the concept of culture, risky sexual behaviours persists in the wake of the burgeoning HIV/AIDS pandemic. Most men gave us to understand that "If AIDS does not kill you, then you are not a man." This suggests that rather than catalyzing behaviour change, AIDS seems to be an extension of what manhood symbolizes (Nattrass, 2008: 20; Hunter, 2005; Brown et al., 2005: 594) and masculinity remains deeply intertwined with control over gender relations and leverage in sexual relationships (Harrison et al., 2006; Nattrass, 2008).

In our view, the ping-pong between traditional healers and allopatic providers and HIV+ patients about the disease is a recognition of the complementarity between both systems of healthcare. Collaboration between traditional and modern healthcare providers is seen as a way of scaling up the provision of ART (Audet et al., 2017; Audet al., 2014). The factors for the acceptance and support of ART among THPs include cultural consistencies between traditional and allopatic medicine, education as well as legal and financial incentives to collaborate. A study conducted in South Africa's Northern Cape region found that 75 (70%) of healers who had received previous HIV/AIDS training were willing to refer HIV/AIDS patients to biomedical healthcare facilities whilst 33 (30%) did not. Of those who had not received any previous HIV and AIDS training, 57 (83%) responded in the affirmative (meaning they were willing to refer patients) whilst 12 (17%) were unwilling to refer their patients to clinics/hospitals for HIV treatment (George et al., 2013).

As a group of community health workers, traditional healers are perceived by HIV patients as capable of assisting with patient adherence and retention to ART (Audet et al., 2017; Audet al., 2014; Audet et al., 2012; Bishop, 2012). They are also willing to engage local formal health providers (Hoyler et al., 2016). This speaks to a productive way forward. On the other hand, traditional healers are perceived as delaying ART among patients who first seek care from them (Audet et al., 2014; Audet et al., 2012). Some HIV-related practices of traditional healers including delayed care and the reuse of razors are likely to increase risk for both HIV infected persons and healers. Some healers routinely use razor cutting to rub herbs into blooded skin. Some studies have also pointed to the continuation of other HIV/AIDS risk-associated practices, including the use of unsterilized equipment for the administering of enemas and the use of single blades for the scarification of multiple patients (Flint, 2015; Audet et al., 2014; Peltzer et al., 2006). Some are incapable of recognizing HIV symptoms/signs, while some believe they can treat the disease (Flint, 2015). Most healers are far more likely to believe in spiritual rather than an infectious origin of HIV disease (Audet et al., 2017; Wanyama et al., 2017; Audet et al., 2017; Audet al., 2014; Flint, 2015; Audet et al., 2012). A three country (Tanzania, Zambia and Uganda) comparative study undertaken among patients at HIV treatment centres showed that "consulting a traditional healer/herbalist because of HIV" (Wanyama et al., 2017: 1018) was an independent risk factor for incomplete ART adherence. Patients with fewer HIV symptoms, those who have been on ART for five or more years and patients attending ART centres close to famous traditional healers, the study further demonstrated, are likely to consult traditional healers, and therefore poor adherence to ART(Wanyama et al., 2017). Furthermore, non-disclosure of HIV/AIDS status to a family member has been identified as one of the independent predictors of non-adherence to ART. Other factors for non-adherence to ART include the fear of drug-related side-effects, being away from home, forgetfulness, stigma and work-related demand (Adeyini et al., 2018).

Traditional healer's desire to align themselves with the formal biomedical system spurred them to support and advocate ART (Shuster et al., 2009; Peltzer et al., 2006; George et al., 2013; Bateman, 2004). They are also increasingly willing to promote condom use and to stress the dangers of unprotected sex with multiple partners (Flint, 2015; Peltzer et al., 2006; Bateman, 2004). THs are very suitable in providing culturally appropriate health services within communities including HIV prevention and treatment referral services (Flint, 2015; Bateman, 2004). Although they could support the biomedical system and mitigate the impact of HIV and AIDS, they are however, an under-utilized human resource for health. They are enthusiastic about the possibility of collaborating with bio-medical practitioners in the prevention and care of HIV and AIDS patients (George et al., 2013; Flint, 2015; Bateman, 2004). Does the willingness of THs to collaborate in the delivery of healthcare still make biomedicine the alpha and omega of healthcare?

4.9 Biomedical Hegemony?

Hegemony is "the means [the cement] employed to establish and reproduce relations that cohere the organised dominant social group (a ruling class) and impose effective control over the subaltern classes—hegemony organises leaders and lead" (Wells, 2005: 2). Through both consent and coercion, the subaltern class is made to interiorize the values, beliefs and practices of the dominant class as a given (Benedetto, 2008; Wells, 2005) in their health-seeking behaviour. Although there are no comparative data on official research expenditure on traditional medicine in South Africa, expenditure on research in the biomedical sector suggests that it is the dominant healthcare system. It is also responsible for making healthcare legislation through the DoH. This partly explains the enthusiasm of traditional healers to ally themselves with the official biomedical healthcare system and to collaborate with biomedical practitioners in patient care. The failure of the biomedical establishment to accommodate traditional epistemologies and the dual legacies of colonialism and apartheid are some of the obstacle standing on the way of the legalization of traditional medicine in South Africa.

A 2009 systematic review of published and unpublished research investigating the prevalence of TMCAM use in the general population of South Africa found that the use of a traditional and/or faith healer seemed to have decreased over the past 13 years (from a range of 3.6–12.7% to 0.1%). Among the African Black racial group, the prevalence of traditional male circumcision was found to be 24.8% generally and 31.9%. The range of use of alternative and complementary medicine was from 0% to 2.2%. Local utilization surveys of TMCAM for the last illness episode or in the past year however showed a variation in use of 6.1% to 38.5%. The prevalence of conditions treated at different

TCAM out-patients settings ranged from chronic conditions, a complex of supernatural or psychosocial problems, mental illness, acute conditions, generalized pain, HIV and other sexually transmitted infections. Substantial proportions of the South African general population use TM and probably CAM, but differences in study design and methodological limitations make it difficult to compare prevalence estimates (Peltzer, 2009). Compared to its immediate neighbours (Botswana, Mozambique and Rwanda, but spending less than Lesotho and Malawi), South Africa, "official government expenditure as a percentage of the country's GDP ranges from 3.9% in 2017/18 (for official health departments' spending only) to 4.3% (inclusive of all government health expenditures), which identifies South Africa as a high-spending country in the region" (UNICEF, 2017: 7).

Despite recommendations at various international gatherings—the Mexico (2004), Bamako (2008) and Algiers (2008) declarations as well as the South African Ministry of Health that the South African government spends 2% of total public sector health budget on health research, the overall expenditure on health research in the RSA aggregated across the public and private sectors, was R3.5 billion in 2009/10. This equates to 16.7% of gross expenditure on research and development (GERD). However, the total government plus science council spend on health research that year was only R729 million, an equivalence of 3.5% of GERD (0.03% of the GDP) or 0.80% of the R91.4 billion consolidated government expenditure on health. The study further found that R418 million was spent through the 2009/2010 Health Vote on health research, equating to 0.46% of the consolidated government expenditure on health or 0.9% of the R45.2 billion Health Vote (Paruk et al., 2014).

According to Shuster and associates (2009), a number of practical reasons have led to deeper ideological acceptance of biomedicine by traditional healers. First, against the backdrop of new legal restrictions on the practice of traditional medicine in South Africa, they saw the potential for attracting potential clients by aligning themselves with the formal healthcare system and biomedical therapies that are believed to be efficacious. Legal restrictions forbid the treatment of terminal diseases by traditional healers and require practitioners to be certified by the DoH. This restriction led to the referral of terminally ill patients to clinics or hospitals as a quest for certification by the DoH (de Roubaix, 2016; Shuster et al., 2009). Furthermore, certification is perceived as a means of ensuring financial security by making themselves more marketable to potential clients if they supplemented their expertise in traditional medicine with biomedical knowledge of disease and treatment. They are therefore eager to acquire knowledge about the disease. In other words, HIV/AIDS knowledge and education will enhance their skills. Their recognition of the function of ART in controlling HIV/AIDS was influential in the reduction of misconceptions concerning "the toxicity of the drugs as well as increasing the participant's confidence in performing task related to ART treatment support and advocacy" (Shuster et al., 2009: 9121). Furthermore, personal experience in treating HIV/AIDS patients tend to facilitate support for ART as participants failed to save the lives of community members suffering from AIDS but simultaneously witnessed friends revitalized by ART received from hospitals. A further motivation for collaboration is the consistency between traditional and biomedical practitioners (Flint, 2015; Shuster et al., 2009; Kayombo et al., 2007). Therapeutic practices including home visits, private consultations, and dissemination of educational information, attention to nutrition and the treatment of opportunistic infections were found to be consistent between both systems and practitioners (Shuster et al., 2009). This suggests the need for "culturally appropriate forms of treatment that emphasise complementary rather than adversarial engagement between the traditional and biomedical systems" (Flint, 2015: 4321; Kayombo et al., 2007). Additionally, there is consistency of beliefs about illness causation between the two systems. Both believe in the dual causation of disease as found in the African traditional illness paradigm (Flint, 2015; Shuster et al., 2009; Kayombo et al., 2007). The proximate cause of disease explain how an illness occurs physically. Since traditional medicine is believed to physically address illness, healers are able to understand the role of ARVs in the management of AIDS. Like biomedicine, traditional medicine is also believed to boost the immune system (Flint, 2015; Shuster et al., 2009; Kayombo et al., 2007). The ultimate cause of AIDS is the belief that witchcraft is the ultimate reason for the transmission of HIV in local communities. Biomedicine was perceived as incapable of addressing the ultimate spiritual cause of HIV/AIDS. In this collaborative model, there is the recognition of the importance of biomedicine as well as the need for the healer to address the ultimate cause of witchcraft in tandem with traditional illness paradigm (Shuster et al., 2009; Kayombo, 2007). Rituals are essential for healing witchcraft because they can significantly transform emotional effects of stigma associated with HIV/AIDS (Wreford, 2008).

Efforts at formalizing and regulating traditional medicine provided the South African government with a counter-narrative against the HIV/AIDS pandemic and was considered as part of Mbeki's "African Renaissance" project (Ndaki, 2009: 65; Nattrass, 2008; Nattrass, 2005; Flint, 2016) which implied a return to traditional African values and practices in all spheres of life. His predecessor Jacob Zuma had opted for the continued mainstreaming of traditional healing practices: "Our commitment as a government is to bring traditional medicine into the mainstream of health care appropriately, effectively and above all safely" (Makhubu ND, cf. Flint, 2016: 4332). Despite overtures for the accommodation of traditional healing practices within biomedical healthcare within the context of HIV/AIDS, the form of accommodation concerning the treatment of the disease has remained contentious (Flint, 2016; de Roubaix, 2016). Biomedical practitioners "have been accused of conducting what amounts to medical missionary work, rather than attempting to truly accommodate traditional cosmologies" (Flint, 2016:4322 citing Flint and Payne, 2013). While traditional healers are being encouraged to push suspected HIV/AIDS patients to show up for testing, many have expressed their willingness to do so (Flint, 2016; Campbell-Hall et al., 2010; Peltzer, 2008). On the contrary, biomedical practitioners are unwilling to recommend traditional healers to patients (Flint, 2016). As demonstrated by Campbell-Hall et al.(2010) in their study of community mental health services, while the majority of service users hold traditional explanatory models of illness and use dual systems of care, shifting between treatment modalities reportedly cause problems with treatment adherence. Although traditional healers are open to training in Western biomedical approaches and establishing a collaborative relationship in the interests of improving patient care, they expressed a lack of appreciation from Western health care practitioners. In other words, Western biomedically trained practitioners were less interested in such an arrangement. The consequence is that: "South African interactions is, in effect, the 'education' of traditional healers into the biomedical perspective, rather than a meeting of minds" (Flint, 2016: 4332). Science intersects and constitutes the basis of most, though not all cultural healing practices. One way of bridging the hierarchical relationship between traditional medicine and biomedicine is for practitioners of the latter system to "effectively translate and interpret cultural and language based descriptions of spiritual medicinal plant use made by indigenous peoples" (Sobiecki, 2014: 1). This implies that they should recognize and discard "cultural prejudices that prevent a more comprehensive and integrated understanding of the science that intersects and forms the basis of many, though not all, cultural healing practices" (Ibid.).

The dual legacies of colonialism and apartheid as systems of exclusion of traditional African cultural values and practices continue to undermine the discourse about collaboration between biomedical practitioners and traditional healers in the country. The apartheid system of governance made biomedicine the only official system of health care in South Africa. Consequently, an adversarial tone continues to frame the debate. "The HIV/AIDS pandemic in particular, and the policitised narrative that emerged from it, has served to entrench yet further the distance between the two systems" (Flint, 2016: 4332). In fact, both systems continue to be presented despite the political rhetoric of collaboration as an "either or scenario" (Ibid.).

4.10 Conclusion

This chapter has examined the ANC-government's conflicting policy framework that vacillated between the promotion/return to African traditional values and practices and the refusal of ART to HIV/AIDS patients on grounds that it was toxic and its efficacy unknown. It argues that it was partly the desire to stem the tides of the burgeoning HIV/AIDS pandemic by doing away with acute human resource shortages in the healthcare system that led to the cooptation of THs in the fight against the pandemic. Simultaneously, the South African government was obliged to promote traditional medicine as a way of revalorizing African cultural values and practices and giving blacks a sense of identity and belonging in the new democratic South Africa.

The denial of the existence of AIDS and representation of ARVs as toxic and harmful by the Mbeki administration led to paradoxical effects. These included (1) fears of ARVs (withholding of the drug from HIV positive people) and a turn to traditional healers (2) the use of unreliable traditional remedies and (3) the need for the regulation and control of traditional healers as well as their enrollment in AIDS management (Bishop, 2012: 755). This was despite concerns about some traditional medical practices involving bloodletting that is likely to increase the risk of infection for both healers and patients.

> Such ideas [the government policies] are dissuading many profoundly sick people from seeking powerful remedies only now becoming available on a wide scale… "I'm an African," said Tshabalala, 26, who has three children and favors stylish jeans and a short, spiky hairstyle. "I don't believe in anti-retrovirals. I believe in traditional healers.
> (Timberg, 2004)

Besides relying on the traditional medicine sector to offset deficiencies in public healthcare system by the political class, the institutionalization and regulation of the traditional medicine sector was part of the larger process of transformation within the South African polity. After 1994, the country witnessed transformation in social and political life to "an alternative way of believing, thinking and doing: in short, being decolonised" (de Roubaix, 2016: 159). This decolonization process included medicine and biomedical healthcare delivery as well as a return to traditional ways of healing and traditional ritual practices. We argue that the re-emergence in the public sphere of traditional notions of sexuality, masculinity, femininity, virginity testing, male initiation often using the same instruments on initiates have instead undermined the fight against HIV/AIDS and fueled the spread of the epidemic. Despite the various driving forces militating in favour of traditional medicine, "biomedical hegemony has resulted in traditional healing being, at best, tolerated rather than embraced by those within the [biomedical] establishment. Healthcare practitioners and policymakers continue to categorise [traditional medicine and healers] as "alternative" or "supplementary" "(Flint, 2016: 4322). Biomedical personnel should be conversant with folk theories or popular narratives so as to appreciate the local context in which HIV/AIDS causation is associated with witchcraft and why patients seek the services of THPs. The aim is to encourage collaborative initiatives between both groups of practitioners in order to strengthen HIV/AIDS interventions. Biomedical doctors have failed to connect intellectually and respectfully with ideas underlining traditional medical practices (Wreford, 2008). They need to adopt a "bridging strategy" by 'accepting' the validity of popular beliefs including witchcraft as a way of satisfying the cultural and psychological needs of patients who go for cleansing rituals and then convincing them to combine it with ARVs.

CHAPTER 5

The Sociocultural Context of HIV/AIDS in the Eastern Cape Region

5.1 Introduction

With the possible exception of India, South(ern) Africa continues to top the chart of HIV-positive people globally[1](Nattrass, 2008). Among the South African population, the estimated overall HIV prevalence rate was 12, 6%, with an estimated 7, 06 million people living with HIV in 2017. An estimated 8, 0% of the adult population (15–49 years) was HIV positive. There was an increase in the number of people living with HIV from approximately 4, 94 million in 2002 to 7, 06 million in 2017 (Stats SA, 2017a). South Africa has benefited from a wide range of initiatives to roll back the HIV/AIDS pandemic. These programmes include the Global Fund to Fight AIDS, Tuberculosis, and Malaria (2002), the United States president's Emergency Plan for AIDS Relief (PEPFAR), as well as the mobilization of resources by the WHO such as through the provision of HAART to HIV infected individuals (Zuma et al., 2018). The country rolled out the world's largest antiretroviral programme in 2004 to stem the spread of the pandemic. This development resulted in significant improvements in mortality and morbidity as well as improvements in the quality of life of HIV infected individuals (Zuma et al., 2018; Bor et al., 2013; Nattrass, 2008). ART is associated with a reduction in the viral load and in the incidence of HIV transmission, significant reduction in adult mortality, especially when it is initiated early (Bor et al., 2013). An estimated 31,157 HIV-positive individuals were initiated in the launch month of the South African Department of Health's (DoH) Universal Treatment as Prevention (Tasp) strategy, doubling the standard monthly ART initiations (Department of Health KwaZulu-Natal., 2017).

As part of its overall strategy that includes biomedical and behavioural interventions, the DoH recognizes the significant/frontline role of traditional health practitioners (THPs) in improving the fight against the pandemic (de

---

1 Swaziland comes first with the highest rate of HIV/AIDS infection globally, with 27.20% of the population living with the disease. Botswana follows suit with 21.90% of the population, 25.00% of Lesotho's population is infected, making the country the third highest worldwide. South Africa has the fourth highest HIV/AIDS prevalence rate with 18.90% of its population living with HIV/AIDS (see www. worldatlas.com).

Roubaix, 2016; Mpofu et al., 2011). Outlawed during the apartheid era by the Medical Association for allegedly being unscientific, traditional medical practices witnessed a revival following the signing into law by the democratically elected government of South Africa of the Traditional Health Practitioners Act (The South African Traditional Health Practitioners Act 22 of 2007). The Act acknowledges African traditional healing systems as providing a holistic approach that is consonant with cultural beliefs, and as working in tandem to positively influence health, wellbeing and misfortune (de Roubaix, 2016; Mpofu et al., 2011; WHO, 1978).

The aim of this chapter is to examine the social context of HIV/AIDS in South Africa with specific reference to the study area where HIV/AIDS patients are concurrently using both traditional and modern medicine (ART) in their quest for therapy and relief against the pandemic. We argue that the simultaneous use of both the traditional and biomedical health systems by HIV/AIDS patients should be seen as a welcome solution because of the deep embeddedness of illness in sociocultural relationships and ontological frameworks as well as the social nature of the healing experience (Millman, 2011; Coe, 1997; Sharma, 1993). The chapter is organized into two parts. First, we set the sociocultural context of HIV/AIDS in the Eastern Cape region. Secondly, we illuminate the paradoxical reasons for the preference of the traditional African healing systems against the biomedical system for the management of the epidemic.

5.2 The Eastern Cape Region and the Legacy of Apartheid Era Policies

This section provides understanding of the complex social context of disease and deprivation. It begins with a brief historical overview of the political economy of deprivation and underdevelopment (Farmer, 2006) in the Eastern Cape region during the colonial and apartheid eras. Secondly, we unpack their impact on the region's socioeconomic development as evidenced by deeply entrenched poverty in comparison to national level human development indicators in the country.

The Eastern Cape Province (the former Transkei) is located on the east coast of South Africa between the Western Cape and KwaZulu-Natal provinces. Inland, it borders the Northern Cape and Free State provinces, as well as Lesotho. It has an estimated population of 6,498,700 (11.5%) of South Africa's total population of 56, 521900 (Stats SA, 2017). It is the second largest province after the Northern Cape. It covers an estimated 169 000 sq km (13.9%) of South Africa's area. It is comprised of 2 metropolitan municipalities (Buffalo City Metropolitan

Municipality and Nelson Mandela Bay Metropolitan Municipality), 6 district municipalities, and 38 local municipalities (Hamann & Tuinder, 2012: 13). In terms of population groups, black Africans constitute 99.04% (1,351,789), Coloured 0.47% (6,434), White 0.19% (2, 6421), Indian/Asian, 0.19% (2,654) and other groups (1,425) accounting for 0.10% of the region's population (South African Census, 2011). Population density, suggesting overcrowding is higher in the former homelands (30% of the province's surface area), where 67% of the people live in abject poverty (Hamann & Tuinder, 2012).

The Eastern Cape region where Mthatha, the seat of the King Sabata Dalindyebo Local Municipality is reputed for having mounted the most vigorous resistance against both colonialism and apartheid in South Africa. Two decades and counting after the collapse of apartheid, the discriminatory legacy of that system of racial discrimination and inequality however lingers on in the province. It suffered from apartheid policies, economic failure and corruption. This suggests that the homelands witnessed little economic and infrastructural development. The result is a landscape of spatial dualities and inequalities within the region. This includes urban industrial areas versus marginal rural areas that are "often locked on social grants and remittances from migrant labour" (Hamann & Tuinder, 2012: 11; Eastern Cape Planning Commission, 2014) and the better developed commercial farming sector in contrast to struggling subsistence farming (Hamann & Tuinder, 2012). We should emphasis on the existence and effects of multiple forms of economic and political violence orchestrated by colonialism, the apartheid and post-apartheid state among the most marginalized strata of society (see Farmer, 2006). According to a 2008 report put together by the Social Sciences Research Council (HSRC) and the Africa Strategic Research Corporation on behalf of the Eastern Cape provincial Department of Social Development, "poverty in the Eastern Cape is a national disaster."[2] For instance, its human development indicators have consistently been among the lowest in the country. Data deduced from the 2007 Community Survey indicated that the province had one of the highest number of under-5 mortality (105 per 1000 live birth births) (Rademeyer, 2017: 20). The region had an infant mortality rate of 57.1% per 1000 live births in 2010. A child living in the region "is more than twice more likely to die in the first year of life than a child from the Western Cape" (Gaedeim & Versteeg, 2011: 101). An analysis of under-five deaths in 2015 showed that the province recorded the fourth highest number of deaths (3, 240), coming after Gauteng (7,348), KwaZulu-Natal (5,372) and Limpopo (4,426) (Bamford et al., 2018). According to the 2011

---

2 http://www.ngopulse.org/press-release/state-eastern-cape-population-dynamics-and-poverty-trap.

THE SOCIOCULTURAL CONTEXT OF HIV

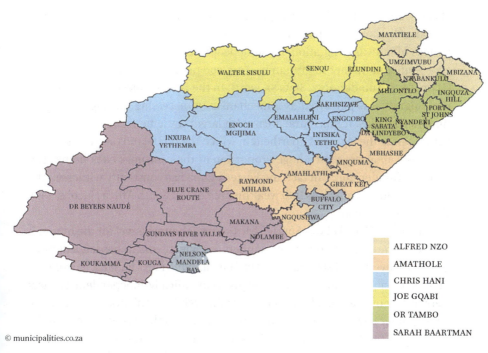

MAP 3 Map of the Eastern Cape Region
SOURCE: HTTPS://MUNICIPALITIES.CO.ZA/PROVINCES/VIEW/1/EASTERN-CAPE

Census data, although the majority of children (2 040 311) aged between 4 and 25 were attending school, some 588 802 (most of whom were girls and women) were not in school. Similarly, 1 861 071 were attending public schools and only 85 309 were in private schools (Statistics SA, 2014). It came third in terms of the highest number of deaths in 2016 with (14, 5%) after Gauteng province (21,3%) and KwaZulu-Natal (18,6%) (Stats SA, 2018b: 17).

Women make up 53% of the province's population (Stats SA, 2011). This gender imbalance is the result of patterns of migration in the active population bracket, gender differences in mortality rates in older population (Hamann & Tuinder, 2012), HIV/AIDS-related deaths and high rates of infant mortality. The gender imbalance is exacerbated by disproportionate economic burden as well as subtle forms of gender imbalances in other spheres of economic, social and cultural experiences on women who are predominantly found in low paying insecure jobs. They are mostly employed in the private household services sector. Men mostly occupy senior government and private positions (Jacobs, 2014). There is widespread unemployment and abject poverty in the province, leading to migration of the active population and the disruption of family life

(Jacobs, 2014). Family life in the province has been negatively affected by historical policies and patterns of economic activities including a sex-selective pattern of outward migration of young people. Estimates have it that between 2006 and 2011, the net migration was 215 000 people out of the Eastern Cape (Hamann & Tuinder, 2012; Stats SA, 2011). In the face of abject poverty, temporary migration is perceived as a mechanism of accessing income to support rural households. It links rural areas with larger settlements and continues in perpetuating the legacy of apartheid in which the homelands served as labour reserves. Labourers send a huge proportion of their incomes back home (Hamann & Tuinder, 2012). In fact, the Eastern Cape has constantly witnessed the largest outflow of migrants into wealthier regions of South Africa (Jacobs, 2014; Williams et al., 2000).

The former Transkei was South Africa's first "labour reserve" for the mines. It still bears the scars of "long-term, deliberate neglect [which] has left a durable legacy of poverty and stagnation" (Aliber et al., 2018: 1). As far back as from the time of Cecil John Rhodes in the 1890s, economically independent farmers were driven off their land into the mines through a combination of hut taxes, anti-squatter laws and labour taxes (Aliber, 2003). In the past decade with the faltering of the fortunes of the mines, ex-miners with tuberculosis and HIV, dying of silicosis, have been sent back to their rural homes. They are further draining the health services while awaiting death (Health-e News, 2008; Crush et al., 2005). An estimated half of all households are female-headed with many children and young people living in single parent families (Aliber, 2003). This resonates with the view that "family forms other than two-parented marriages and communities with high levels of family disruption increase the likelihood of teenage pregnancy. Similarly, increasing household service delivery inaccessibility predisposes teenage females to higher odds of pregnancy, as expected" (Mkwananzi, 2017: 1). Care has been devolved to older persons in multigenerational families who are increasingly using their old age grants to support younger family members (Williams, 2000; Stats SA, 2014). The migration of young people in their active working life (between 25 and 39 years) negatively affects the socioeconomic development of the province. They are migrating in droves to the more affluent provinces—(mostly Gauteng and the Western Cape) and the city of Johannesburg, for economic opportunities, and better living standards (Jacobs, 2014; Williams et al., 2000). As young men migrate, they are most likely exposed to sexually transmissible diseases including HIV/AIDS in the new destination. They also leave behind a large proportion of females. This outward migration is a reflection of the general trend in South Africa where there is a higher proportion of women in poorer provinces. This allies with Farmer's (2006) view that economic and political relations in favour of wealthy regions have led to widespread gendered poverty and unemployment, thereby facilitating an industry of transactional sex and institutionalized prostitution as a survival strategy among women (see also Pemunta & Tabenyang, 2016; Hunter, 2005; Williams et al., 2000).

A recent desk review of existing literature and small-scale studies on the Eastern Cape that included a review of the National Department of Health Antenatal Survey Data (2006–2008) and a secondary analysis of the Human Sciences Research Council (HSRC) National HIV Survey (SABSSM) data (2002; 2005; 2008) among other findings showed that the rate of HIV/AIDS prevalence among antenatal clinic attendees was 28.6%, 28.8%, and 27.6% respectively (Phaswana-Mafuya et al., 2017). Another study from the region suggests very low uptake of Voluntary Counseling and Testing (VCT) services and that most individuals only submit to testing if they are compelled by other factors, including illness and pregnancy (Hutchinson & Mahlalela, 2006; Ephraim, 2013). The study however illuminated a positive association between age, education and socioeconomic status, proximity to clinics, availability of rapid testing and outreach services and lower levels of HIV/AIDS stigma to the utilization of VCT (Hutchinson & Mahlalela, 2006). In the Eastern Cape, the rate of HIV infection among 15–24 year olds was 9.2% (2002), 11.7% (2005) and 6.6% in 2008. Concurrently, the average national prevalence rate was 29.1%, 29.4% and 29.3% respectively (Department of Health, 2009 cf. Phaswana-Mafuya et al., 2017). The above figures suggest that the Eastern Cape is inordinately affected by the spiraling HIV/AIDS pandemic.

Since 1996; the province is witnessing declining fertility rates and a noticeable decline in the prevalence of marriage among women in the reproductive age bracket (15–49) (Harrison, 2009). Only an estimated 30.2% of all people aged 15 years or older were married as of 2007 (Harrison, 2009; Hamann & Tuinder, 2012). High fertility rates are however, still widespread among black Africans, rural women and those with no formal education. Teenage pregnancy remains widespread among Coloureds and Africans than among Indians and Whites (Harrison, 2009).

The post-apartheid period bequeathed the province with dysfunctional and under-resourced apartheid and Bantustan institutions. It further witnessed the deliberate disruption of its health system by white health professionals. Furthermore, the healthcare system is bedeviled by mismanagement within the Department of Health, and funding shortfalls (Harrison, 2009; Hamann & Tuinder, 2012). Like elsewhere in South Africa, the weak healthcare infrastructure in the region has been greatly impacted by the "increased burden of disease related to HIV/AIDS, generally weak health systems management and low staff morale" (Harrison, 2009: 2). Despite progress since 1994, the province still lags behind in the provision of basic services and housing by the South African government and on other development indicators. It has for instance, some of the highest levels of poverty and unemployment. In 2004, the population of the province living below the poverty line was 72%. The unemployment rate among whites was 4%, compared to 30% and 31% respectively for Africans and Coloureds (Hamann & Tuinder, 2012). Although having 13.5% of the national population in 2010, it received approximately 17.5% of the national total of both Child and Old Age Support grants doled out by the beginning of 2010 (Hamann & Tuinder, 2012). According to data from the 2016 General Household Survey (GHS), the province topped the chart of grant recipients with 40,8% (more than one-third of individuals) (Stats SA, 2017). This suggests a tremendous increase in the rate of poverty in the region. Other top grant recipient provinces were Limpopo (37,6%), Northern Cape (37,1%) and KwaZulu-Natal (36,0%). This was in contrast to 16, 9% in Gauteng, and 22,0% in the Western Cape (Stats SA, 2017). Citing the South African National Treasury's 894-page Estimate of National Expenditure (ENE), Crotty (2019: online) maintains that grants are meant to "improve the living conditions of life for all South Africans, especially the poor." It further states that "Social assistance protects against inequality, and poverty, and promotes the social and financial inclusion of the population" (Ibid.). Grant recipients however, remain exposed to the economic schock of inflation and therefore, deeply entrenched poverty and inequality. In 2017 for instance, the nominal increase in the old-age pension was insufficient to cover inflation. It instead amounted to a slight decline in real terms (Ibid.). It has similarly been pointed out that: "In South Africa, social grants to the poor as an external motivator could foster dependency and undermine responsible, self-regulated behavior. Having more children may be interpreted as having more money without having to put in any effort" (Henning & Akoob, 2017: 2).

Partly challenged by low levels of centralization and the dispersed nature of homesteads that inhibit service delivery, the province has the lowest percentage of households with access to piped water. Only 37% of people receive piped water to their dwelling, only 20% of this water is safe for drinking, and 31% of the population relies on natural sources of water, which is of doubtful quality. Up to 30% of households are without sanitation and only 40% of households have flush toilets. On average, only 49% of the province is electrified while only 45% of households have electricity (PGDP, 2004; cf. Hamann & Tuinder, 2012; Harrison, 2009). Lack of electricity is accentuated among most of the inhabitants who live in informal settlements—a site associated with the highest rate of HIV infection—partly "a result of the socially fragmenting effects of urban transition" (Harrison, 2009: 10). In comparison to urban district municipalities, people in most rural municipalities are unemployed and poor. There is also a higher rate of sexual frequency in rural and informal areas than in formal housing areas and among adolescents living in poorer socio-economic circumstances in the Eastern Cape (Kelly, 2005; Swaartbooi-Xabadiya, 2010). The skewed distribution of social services, especially the distribution of health resources is a key contributory factor in the multiplicity of social and environmental conditions affecting quality of life (Winkelman, 2009: 16; Farmer, 2006) in the region.

The King Sabata Dalindyebo Local Municipality where the Qokolweni is located is made up of Mthatha and Mqanduli villages. The vast majority (94%) of the municipality's 1,364,943 people speak Xhosa (2011 Census). It is one of seven local municipalities within the Oliver Reginald Tambo (OR Tambo) District Municipality. Mthatha is the seat of OR Tambo District Municipality, the poorest district in the Eastern Cape Province in terms of all poverty measures. It has the lowest human development index (HDI) (0.45) and the highest poverty gap (2 231 million) in the region (Olive Leaf Foundation, 2017).

The number of people living in poverty is also high in this district (64.6%), unemployment is at 65.5% and the literacy rate is 42.2% (Olive Leaf Foundation, 2017). The poverty of the municipality reflects that of the province as a whole. The Eastern Cape has the highest Multidimensional Poverty Index (MDI) score, alongside Limpopo. This relatively high MDI is driven by relatively high multidimensional poverty head count ratios (World Bank, 2018: 31). The province had 13 private hospitals in 2011(Gaede & Versteeg, 2011: 101). Mthatha has three hospitals—Life St Mary's Hospital, Mthatha Private Hospital and Nelson Mandela Academic Hospital, and a clinic- Ngangelizwe Clinic. The Mthatha Hospital is the main referral hospital for district hospitals in both OR Tambo and Alfred Nzo District municipalities. An estimated 95% of residents have no medical aid (Health-e News, 2008).

Like for most of the Eastern Cape, the poverty of both the King Sabata Dalindyebo Local Municipality and the OR Tambo district is directly intertwined with the wealth of the gold mines (Aliber et al., 2018; Aliber, 2003). Gold mining triggered patterns of labour-related migration with unfettered effects including poverty, the breaking up of families, one-parent families and the transmission of diseases including STDs such as HIV/AIDS. The province therefore remains trapped in a vicious cycle of structural poverty that negatively affects its health and socioeconomic profile. It is one of the worst performing provinces in terms of health outcomes in rural areas, where 62% of its population live (Gaede & Versteeg, 2011: 101). Because of poor health services in the Eastern Cape, a significant number of patients migrate to urban provinces such as the Western Cape in search of better healthcare.

This is despite having a larger number of hospitals, suggesting that the number of resources may not always be a reflection of acceptable levels of care. On the contrary, provinces with fewer hospitals may have higher patient volumes (Dell & Kahn, 2017). This paradoxical situation is happening against the backdrop of the HIV/AIDS social crises that has inordinately taxed healthcare services.

5.3 The Sociocultural Context of HIV/AIDS

Most people in the Eastern Cape are syncretic Christians. Although they profess Christianity and participate in Christian rituals, they simultaneously participate in traditional rituals to honour dead ancestors and to seek protection from them against misfortune and ill-health (Mokhoathi, 2017; Sobiecki, 2014; Ashforth, 2005; Mbiti, 1992; Orubuloye et al., 1994; Hammond-Tooke, 1974; Caldwell et al., 1994). The ancestors are believed to intervene in the daily lives of the people (Sobiecki, 2014; Mbiti, 1992). Apart from the formal Christian denominations, African independent Churches blend aspects of Christian rituals with aspects of traditional culture and religion. In addition, an emerging charismatic movement is extending across the southern African region (Leclerc-Madlala et al., 2009). The amalgamation of Christianity and African Traditional Religion has been dubbed African Christianity (Mokhoathi, 2017: 1; Jarvis, 2009). The dualistic religious belief (contextual Christianity in Africa), (Mokhoathi, 2017: 1) that is also reflected in people's health-seeking behaviours is happening against the backdrop of widespread belief in witchcraft that is independent of the level of formal education and socioeconomic status (Leclerc-Madlala et al., 2009). This seems to be partly a protest against Jarvis's (2009: 43), position that the only possibility of Africans becoming real Christians is by renouncing their cultural and religious beliefs, which are contrary to the revelation of God as found in the Bible. In attempting to cope with HIV/AIDS, people therefore see nothing wrong with consulting traditional healers (Leclerc-Madlala et al., 2009) who could deal with the supernatural dimension of the disease while biomedicine takes care of the virus. This is independent of the logical inconsistencies of both systems of healthcare (Flint, 2015; Shuster et al., 2009; Kayombo et al., 2007). In the same light, the two religious systems are incompatible with the values people espouse in regards to marriage with Christianity preaching monogamy whereas, most African groups are polygynous and men are allowed to pursue and seek wives after marriage as well as to indulge in extramarital sexual intercourse with no rebuke from society (Leclerc-Madlala et al., 2009; Caldwell et al., 1994). This is contrary to the tenets of Christianity in which many men are in monogamous unions but continue to have concubines (informal polygyny) through extramarital concurrent partnering (Leclerc-Madlala et al., 2009) as a form of masculinity. They therefore live double lives (Mokhoathi, 2017), a 'mixed' religious heritage (Mbiti, 1990). As several men stated "Man is a polygamous animal and cannot eat the same soup everyday." This statement suggests that men have a propensity to have sex with multiple partners concurrently. Opposition from their spouses to this patriarchal pattern of behaviour that is capable of spreading HIV is most often met with violence.

Despite transformations owing to pressures on the institution of marriage orchestrated by factors including urbanization, poverty, the migrant labour system that have tremendously destabilized the institution of marriage, polygyny, patrilocality and patriny still strongly influence the nature of matrimonial and by extension, social relations (Leclerc-Madlala et al., 2009; Caldwell et al., 1994; Orubuloye et al., 1994). Although changes have taken place over time, wives are still expected to be subservient to their husbands and in-laws. They conform to expectations about women's culturally subservient roles to husbands, polygyny, bridewealth exchange (lobola) and the patrilocally derived social order in place. They cannot for instance, refuse a husband sex or ask him to wear a condom during sexual intercourse (Leclerc-Madlala et al., 2009). The inability to negotiate safe sex because of power differentials expose women to the risk of infection from sexually transmissible diseases and HIV/AIDS. A young wife's status changed upon the conception and birth of her first child (especially if it was a male child). "She became mother-of-so-and-so" (Leclerc-Madlala et al., 2009: 15; Orubuloye et al., 1994). Apart from the transformation of her identity, childbirth led to her full incorporation and acceptance into her husband's lineage. "These prescriptions continue to inform ways of thinking about marriage, motherhood and the role of fertility in society" (Leclerc-Madlala et al., 2009: 15; Caldwell et al., 1994; Hammond-Tooke, 1974). The same pattern of behaviour (gender identity) seems to explain the high rate of teenage pregnancies in the Eastern Cape region. Young girls are keen on proving their fertility to their boyfriends by conceiving and giving birth to children with the hope of security marriage opportunities.

Myriad cultural practices including beliefs and values regarding courtship, sexual networking (multiple partnering), contraceptive use, ideas about sexual orientation, explanatory models for disease and misfortune, gendered norms and matrimonial relations have been shown to be imbricated in various ways that HIV/AIDS has affected African communities (UNESCO, 2002; Leclerc-Madlala et al., 2009). Polygyny, patrilocality and patrilineality with bridewealth are constitutive elements of a system and the anchor shaping traditional life in the region with implications for HIV/AIDS infection (Leclerc-Madlala et al., 2009; Orubuloye et al., 1994). Apart from labour-related migration resulting from poverty, sexual practices including unprotected sex, multiple partnering and intergenerational relationships, gender inequality and gender-based violence, teenage pregnancies, substance abuse, and cultural factor especially initiation rituals, predispose men and women to infection and the spread of the virus. Stated otherwise, both community level, individual and extra-local factors owing to poverty are responsible for the spread of HIV/AIDS in the Eastern Cape region.

5.3.1 Labour-related Migration

Extreme poverty and lack of employment opportunities in the Eastern Cape region has led to the massive exodus of mostly young men and the active population (20–50 years) to more wealthier regions of South Africa in general, but mostly to Gauteng and the Free State as migrant mine workers (Crush et al., 2005). Strong migration patterns have also been identified between municipalities in the Eastern Cape and the city of Cape Town and coastal intermediate-sized municipalities in the Western Cape (Jacobs, 2014). Trends in inter-provincial migration in South Africa in 2011 showed that of all provinces, Gauteng was the largest (953,024) receiving province, followed by Western Cape (318,917) and North West (196,780). On the other hand, the Eastern Cape was the largest sending province (436,466), followed by Gauteng (402,271) people (Stats SA, 2014: 45). In 2017, the Eastern Cape and Gauteng experienced the largest number of outflow of migrants (Stats SA, 2018a). Migrant men often leave behind their wives and families when they migrate. The men often have sexual contacts with infected women during their seasonal migration and upon return home, infect their wives or partners with STDs and HIV/AIDS (Lerclec-Madlala et al., 2009). Some migrant men have casual sexual partners and engage with sex workers, most of whom are themselves migrants (Crush et al., 2005; Corbett et al., 2004; Williams et al., 2000). Gauteng is one area with "a high prevalence of HIV/AIDS but also a very high proportion of people between the ages of 20 and 40 years, precisely those most likely to be infected and subsequently to die" (Crush et al., 2005: 302).

Most of the active men from the Eastern Cape go to work in the mines in Carletonville (Western Gauteng) and in the Witwatersrand gold mining industry. With little or no social and emotional support, they entertain themselves with alcohol and sexual intercourse with sex workers as a way of coping with the physical and emotional trauma associated with work in the mine. They are further exposed to high-risk rates of silicosis that coupled with HIV leads to higher rates of tuberculosis (Corbett et al., 2004; Booysen, 2003). Faced with the faltering of the fortunes of the mines, ex-miners with tuberculosis and HIV, dying of silicosis, have been sent back to their rural homes. They are further draining the health services while awaiting death (Health-e News, 2008).

5.3.2 Gender Identity and Unprotected Sex

Although waning all over Africa due to economic hard times and the influence of Christianity, polygyny legitimizes sex with multiple partners concurrently and is a risk factor for HIV transmission (Orubuloye et al., 1994; Caldwell, 1994). Having a significant number of sexual partners is perceived as evidence of masculine virility. Apart from being sexual risk bearers ('dangerous masculinity'), cultural norms inhibit the use of condoms since it is antithetical to cultural values that extol fertility and the production of male offsprings as a symbol of masculine virility (Leclerc-Madlala, 2009; Orubuloye et al., 1994; Caldwell et al., 1994). Men however, sometimes use condoms with some and not with other partners (Mah & Halperin, 2008). This inconsistency as well as the preference for "skin-to-skin sex" expose them and their partners to HIV infection. On their part, women are compliant and lack the power to negotiate safe sex since requesting that a husband use condom during sexual intercourse raises suspicion and is culturally unacceptable. Compounding the situation is that women are keen on having children as a way of cementing their place within the patrilineage and as a mark of their identity (Leclerc-Madlala, 2009). Similarly, young girls in the Eastern Cape often give birth at tender age as proof of their fertility and as a sign of love to their partner in the hope that having a child could lead to marriage.

5.3.3 Multiple Partnering and Intergenerational Relationships

Alongside multiple partnering, many older men prefer younger women for sexual intercourse. The latter are often believed not to be infected and to be "tight" whereas there is a higher prevalence rate of HIV infection among them. In the Eastern Cape region, the rate of sexual debut before 15 and among 15–24 year old stood at 7.7%, 6.7% and 7.8% in comparison to a national average of 5.0%, 8.4% and 8.5% over the three national surveys undertaken in 2002, 2005 and 2008 respectively (Phaswana-Mafuya et al., 2017). The rate of multiple sexual partners among 15–49 year old was 12.1%, 8.1% and 13.1% in contrast to 9.4%, 9.8% and 10.6% nationally within the same period. Ironically, in 2008, 70% of sexually active individuals of all ages surveyed stated they used condoms at last sexual intercourse (Phaswana-Mafuya et al., 2017). A disproportionately higher rate of HIV infection was reported in the 15- to 24-year age group, quadrupling that of young men and accounted for 90% of new infections in that age group in 2007 (Rehle et al., 2007). Assuming that the older men would have been sexually active for several years, and likely to be infected with STDs including HIV, young (women) are especially at risk of infection because of their lack of leverage to negotiate safe sex (Leclerc-Madlala, 2009; Orubuloye et al., 1994). They are often pushed by poverty and the need for consumer goods to indulge in sexual intercourse with working class older men ("sugar daddies"). These transactional liaisons are one factor militating in favour of teenage pregnancies in the region. As a 19-year-old teenage mother stated:

> I did not love the old man but had to survive and take care of my needs. I also had a young man of my age who is the one responsible for my pregnancy, although I told the old man he was the one and he has continued to support me.

5.3.4 *Gender Inequality and Gender-based Violence*

Women's greater poverty and their inability to negotiate safe sex in their relationships with men in general and especially those in intergenerational relationships expose them to greater risk of HIV infection than men. An analysis of data about intergenerational relationships for instance suggests that having a sexual partner 5 years older poses a high HIV infection risk for youth (Shisana et al., 2012). The economic, food, health, personal or political security of women and young girls are particularly endangered "due to their physical, emotional and material differences and due to the important social, economic, and political inequalities existing between women and men" (Kristofferssen, 2000: online). Female-headed households of which there are many in the Eastern Cape region are particularly exposed to the risk of infection by HIV/AIDS. The lack of assets including land or income to feed her family may put a woman in a vulnerable situation. Because of the likelihood of being "coerced into sex in exchange for money and resources" (Kristofferssen, 2000: online, Ulf, 2000), she is exposed to HIV infection. HIV/AIDS is "also further entrenching poverty, weakening the productive capacities of [regions and] countries, overwhelming already over-extended healthcare systems and threatening both national and continental security" (The Centre for Conflict Resolution, 2005: 8; Pemunta & Obara, 2011; Ulf, 2000). We obtained reports of older men and schoolteachers coercing young girls into having intercourse with them as a natural right leading to teenage pregnancies and female school dropouts.

5.3.5 *Teenage Pregnancies*

The South African Demographic and Health Survey (SADHS) showed an increase in the number of teenage pregnancy between 1998 and 2008. The number of the learner population who became pregnant in some provinces including the Eastern Cape Province almost doubled to 16% (STATS SA, 2016; Mynda, 2013). The Eastern Cape Department of Social Development and Special Programmes, (2016) has summarized the intertwined factors responsible for teenage pregnancies in the region into four categories: (1) the exposure to sex ;(2) cultural factors; (3) psycho-social factors, and; (4) economic factors. First, while young women have a propensity to experiment with sex, early sexual debut is associated with less likelihood to use contraceptives (Geary et al., 2008), and an increase in incidences of unwanted pregnancies (Baumgartner et al., 2009). The significant proportion of teenage mothers engaging in sex for pleasure and transactional sex, usually with older men, exacerbates this situation. Rape (either statutory or explicit) is widespread in the province. Secondly, the cultural practice of femininity performed through childbearing fuels teenage pregnancy and exposes teenage girls to the risk of contracting HIV/AIDS. Additionally, the cultural practice of *Ukuthwala* expose girls to sex. Other factors that predispose teenage girls to unplanned pregnancies include—early marriages usually to older men who are capable of paying the *lobola*. Thirdly, it became evident through discussions that whereas the role of family is very important during adolescence, most parents feel talking to their children about sex and sexuality means encouraging them to have sex. This lack of sex education allows young boys and girls to learn about sex from their peers, from the media and through experimentation. Fourthly, partnering with multiple partners by teenage girls which serves as a means of alleviating deeply entrenched poverty is a widespread practice in the Eastern Cape Province (Eastern Cape Department of Social Development and Special Programmes, 2016). Higher community unemployment alongside higher levels of residential mobility as obtains in the province, are negatively associated with teenage pregnancy (Mkwananzi, 2017: 1).

An inverse correlation has been consistently established between women's schooling and their fertility. Often, educated women generally start bearing children later and bear fewer children, than do their less educated counterparts (Bledsoe et al., 1999; Castro Martin, 1995; UN 1995). Two explanatory models—cognitive and instrumental change models—have been offered to explain the influence of education on female fertility behaviour. The former concedes that education alters people's values and ways of perceiving the world. In other words, it transforms women's perspective, ideas and modes of thought (van de walle, 1992). Education is believed to "transform the mental frameworks that women use to evaluate the world and make decisions about it, more than they do the objective conditions under which these decisions are made" (Johnson-Hanks, 2003: 154). The latter by contrast emphasize that "schooling changes the objective conditions under which decisions are made, for example by increasing the opportunity cost of women's labour" (Johnson-Hanks, 2003: Ibid.). From a macro-economic perspective, educated women, making exactly the same type of rational choices as uneducated women, will put to birth fewer children as their relative cost increases (Johnson-Hanks, 2003: 155). Teenage pregnancy comes with several far-reaching long-term consequences:

> Social concerns about the implications of premature parenthood arise for several reasons. One is the potential health consequences for very young women of pregnancy and birth if their physiological development is incomplete. Other consequences may include premature exit from school, reduced earnings prospects, reduced chances of community participation and the acquisition of social capital, a heightened possibility of divorce or single parenthood, and a greater risk of living in poverty. These other consequences of early parenthood are likely to be greater for young women than young men; in most societies, women have the primary responsibility of child care and childrearing, and parenthood for them often coincides with a shrinking of opportunities and reduced scope for independent action.
>
> (Lloyd, 2005: 507)

5.3.6 *Substance Abuse*

In South Africa, there are significant health inequalities between whites and blacks. For instance, life expectancy between the former and the latter is approximately 20 years (Flint, 2016). The contributing factors are the result of a conjuncture between poverty, inadequate and poor nutrition, alcohol and substance abuse, high levels of violent crimes, and poor access to healthcare. Many of these factors stem from colonial legacies. There is also a higher rate of HIV/AIDS prevalence rate among black South Africans—15% as opposed to 0.3% among white South Africans (Shisana et al., 2014: xxiii, Flint, 2016). Poor diets have led to skyrocketing hypertension rates, and growing rates of diabetes among the black population (Aliber et al., 2018).

The most widely abused substance in South Africa is alcohol, preceded by cannabis. In 2007, 8% of South Africans were reported to be abusing alcohol/drugs. A further 8.4% (an estimated 2.2 million) of the country's population used cannabis in 2004 and 3.2% in in 2008; a marked increase of approximately 20%. Simultaneously, one in four pre-teens have experimented with psychoactive drugs (Department of Social Development: ND). Widespread substance abuse (alcohol, tobacco and marijuana) has also been reported in the Eastern Cape region among high school learners (grades 10–12) (Manu et al., 2017). Alcohol and drug addiction, are often associated with physical, sexual and domestic violence, as well as HIV/AIDS-risk behaviours (Flint, 2015). Drugs inhibit consciousness and individuals take sexual risk, usually without protection under the influence of these substances.

5.3.7 *Cultural Factors: Initiation Rituals*

Among the Xhosa, (including the Mthembus speaking peoples), there has been a resurgence of initiation rituals meant to transform boys into men and to uphold women's dignity by policing their sexuality. This return to tradition is happening within the larger context of the re-affirmation of the African personality that preceded the fall of apartheid in 1994 in South Africa. Despite modernization, the *ulwaluko*, the gateway initiation ritual into manhood remains sacrosanct and is associated with responsibilities. The ritual transforms an initiate from a child/boy (*inkwenkwe*) into an adult and confers an individual the right to take part in male activities including tribal gatherings/meetings. The initiation process involves the surgical removal of the foreskin by a traditional surgeon (*ingcibi*). The seclusion period that lasts for approximately the first seven days is characterized by food taboos. The second phase lasts between two and three weeks and culminates with the burning of the initiates' belonging and a ritual bath marking their transition from childhood to full adulthood and personhood. This ritual initiation process sometimes leads to high morbidity and mortality, owing to complications and penile amputation. These deleterious effects are attributed to the incompetence of traditional practitioners (ritual experts) (Rijken, 2014; Meintjes, 1998).

Conservative estimates have it that since 1995, 969 initiates have reportedly died from complications resulting from the ritual initiation. In addition, the number of penile amputations roughly doubled the number of deaths and complications (Rijken, 2014). Other serious risk of adverse effects include exposure to HIV/AIDS infection and hepatitis B when the ritual is undertaken in non-clinical settings. The use of the same surgical instruments on a number of initiates can spread the transmission of viruses. Despite the palpable health risks and efforts at medicalization, there is still a wide preference for traditional circumcision because of its association with masculinity, ethnic identity and personhood (Peltzer & Kanta, 2008). A 2009 study showed that 70% of medically circumcised Xhosa men felt they could be stigmatized because of their choice of medical over traditional circumcision (Peltzer & Kanta, 2008).

5.3.7.1 Ukuthwala

Since about 2009; South Africa is witnessing a dramatic drop in marriage rates (Rice, 2008; Smit, 2017). This is "due to a changing economy and high bride wealth demands." Simultaneously, there has been a resurgence of *ukutwala* in impoverished rural communities (Smit, 2017: 56). It is a Xhosa word meaning "to carry" (Mubangizi, 2012; Smit, 2017) ('abduction marriage' or bride abduction') that is often characterized by gendered violence (Rice, 2008; Mubangizi, 2012). Historically, *ukuthwala* among the Zulu and Xhosa were staged elopements, in which the display "of male force and feminine resistance served to sustain and reproduce dominant scripts of masculine assertiveness and feminine modesty" (Rice, 2018: 395). The aim was to oblige the family of the young woman to enter into bride wealth (*lobola*) negotiations with the abductor's kin. If the bide price negotiation process turned out to be successful, as was usually the case, both families sealed the marriage but if unsuccessful, the girl's family was paid damages (Mubangizi, 2012).

The transformations and the increasingly violent nature of this institution has been associated with the decline of the migrant labour system that has led to masculine economic marginalization because of unemployment and the inability to pay bride price. Additionally, there is a growing desire among young women for autonomy in spousal choice ('love marriages') (Kheswa & Hoho, 2014). The violence and rape sometimes associated with this ancient practice exposes women to trauma, STDs and including HIV/AIDS infection. The targeting of young girls (12–15 years) by older men is regrettable and can lead to the transmission of STDs and HIV because they would have already had sex with a large number of partners that exposes them to the risk of infection and the transmission of venereal diseases.

5.3.7.2 Virginity Testing

The practice of virginity testing (*Inkciyo*) entails the physical examination of a girl's genitalia to ascertain whether the hymen is intact. If found intact, then, the girl is considered a virgin. If however, the hymen is broken, then the girl is perceived as loose and immoral. "In the southern African context, virginity testing refers to a process in which unmarried young women are examined by older women in order to ascertain whether they remain virgins" (Thonberry, 2015: 131). Unlike in the past when virginity testers were primarily close relatives (mostly mothers and aunts), today the task is performed essentially by elderly women who are recognized in their communities as such (Thonberry, 2015: 131; George, 2008: 1455; Mubangizi, 2012). Virginity testing festivals re-emerged in the 1990s as one of several traditional "native antidotes" to the spiraling HIV/AIDS pandemic and as a way of upholding feminine values of respectability (Pemunta, 2011) by ensuring purity before marriage through the delay of sexual debut (Pemunta, 2016). It also serves as a safeguard against sexual violence (Pemunta, 2016; Thornberry, 2015; Swaartbooi-Xabadiya, 2010). A further motivating factor was the boomerang effect of the passage into law of the 2005 Children's Act in South Africa. The Zulu and Xhosa-language media particularly radio stations such as uKhoziFM and Umhlobo Wenene, and the newspapers *iLanga* and *iSolezwe*, widely portrayed this Act as an attack on parental authority as well as African custom or tradition. This perceived chasm between "the rights of the child" and parental authority led to resistance and an increase in virginity testing below the legal age of 16 years (Thonberry, 2015).

Elizabeth Thonberry concedes that in the Eastern Cape, the nostalgia for custom is a testament of the loss of sexual autonomy that accompanied colonialism. Whereas, the rhetoric justifying virginity testing in the precolonial and colonial eras were deeply patriarchal, the practice ensured the protection of female sexual autonomy and provided protections that the colonial legal regime undermined and that are still to be replaced (Thonberry, 2015). The crux of her argument is that colonialism and apartheid reshaped customary law in the sense that although virginity testing was a means of regulating consensual sexual activity, in practice it served to protect young women against rape and empowered older women to police the sexual morality of young girls. This was independent of the "discursive emphasis on male authority" (Ibid.: 131). Colonialism undermined the system in which norms regulating female sexuality subordinated female consent to familial control and simultaneously disempowered older women through the principle of individual autonomy (Pemunta, 2011; Thornberry, 2015: 130). "During the colonial period, the replacement of "customary" forms of virginity testing by the testimony of medical experts in colonial courts made it significantly more difficult for women to achieve redress in cases of sexual assault. The same process, meanwhile, expanded the power of the colonial state at the expense of the older African women who had previously served as experts on female sexuality" (Thornberry, 2015: 131). In the region, participants cited the preservation of Xhosa culture, pride and the enjoyment of community support as the reasons motivating their participation in *Inkciyo* (see also Nduna, 2014; Swaartbooi-Xabadiya, 2010). A controversial scholarship scheme was introduced in the coastal provinces by Dudu Mazibuko, the mayor of the Uthukela district of KwaZulu-Natal for girls who kept their virginity and remained virgins all through their studies as a mechanism to curb the high rate of female pregnancies and HIV/AIDS. The Commission for Gender Equality however ruled the scheme as unconstitutional and a violation of women's rights because boys were not also expected to be virgins. Despite this, public authorities including the Zulu King has instructed families to constantly "test" their daughters. This public support has driven attendance at public virginity testing ceremonies.

It is an infringement of a woman's right to privacy, bodily and psychological integrity (Mubangizi, 2012). In a bid to keep their boyfriends while continuing to be virgins, young women, we were told, sometimes have anal intercourse that expose them to HIV/AIDS. A further risk of the practice of virginity testing is the widespread belief based on myth that sleeping with a virgin provides therapy against HIV/AIDS whereas it is one mechanism fuelling the spread of the virus.

5.4 Conclusion

This chapter has demonstrated that the historic neglect of the Eastern Cape region through the apartheid and post-apartheid policy of unequal development in terms of healthcare and other infrastructure is responsible for the region's low human development indicators and higher burden of disease including HIV/AIDS when compared to the rest of South Africa. The lack of employment opportunities has for instance led to gendered and deeply entrenched poverty, the increased migration of people in their prime productive years who go out to work in the mines and may return infected with STDs and HIV/AIDS, and the breakdown of family bonds. In the post-apartheid era, this extra-local factor has connived with community norms of sexuality and individual level factors shaping norms of masculinity and femininity. These sexual practices include gender identity and unprotected sex, multiple partnering and intergenerational relationships, gender inequality and gender-based violence, teenage pregnancies, substance abuse and the upsurge of cultural practices (especially *ukuthwala* and virginity testing) partly resulting from the South African government's policy of a "return to tradition" and predispose people—especially women to HIV/AIDS infection. It further accentuated the debate on the relevance and necessity for the integration of both systems of healthcare.

CHAPTER 6

The Debate on the Integration of Traditional Medicine into the Mainstream Healthcare Delivery System in South Africa

6.1 Introduction

This chapter examines the pros and cons for the integration of traditional medicine into the mainstream healthcare delivery system in South Africa. The medical landscape in the country, like in many other African countries is characterized by a pluralistic system of healthcare. South Africa's pluralistic healthcare system is comprised of an institutionalized biomedical system based on scientific procedures and a variety of non-conventional therapies. In Africa, nonconventional therapies are often based on indigenous knowledge systems, beliefs and traditional practices. Traditional medicine is the oldest and perhaps the most diverse of all medical systems. Africa's rich biological and cultural diversity is well pronounced when it comes to healing practices (Gunrib-Fakim, 2006).

One of the problems that usually arise in debates about traditional healing relates to the failure to separate traditional healing practices from other forms of medical therapy including witchcraft. This is because it is difficult to assign one definition to the broad range of characteristics and elements of traditional medicine and healers. Despite the crisis encountered in explaining traditional medicine, a working definition remains essential. The South African Traditional Health Practitioners Act defines Traditional Health Practice (medicine) as "the performance of a function, activity, process, or service based on a traditional philosophy that uses indigenous African techniques and principles that include traditional medicines or practices, including the physical or mental preparation of an individual for puberty, adulthood, pregnancy, childbirth ("sexual and reproductive health, and death") (Act 22, p. 5). Traditional medicine however includes a concatenation of myriad products and practices that may involve herbal treatments, animal products (such as snake, fats, oils, and skeletons), beliefs and meditations as well as inexplicable practices such as spiritual therapy. In South Africa, traditional medicine encapsulates myriad health practices, approaches, knowledge and beliefs. These include plant, animal and/or mineral based medicines, spiritual therapies, manual techniques and exercises applied singularly or in combination to maintain well-being (*impilo*), as well as to treat, diagnose and prevent illness (Marlise, 2003; see also Lamla, 1981).

This implies that it is a concatenation of diverse ethnic practices and the fact that it has not developed into a unified system, but rather practiced according to specific ethnic groups and cultural context further poses an obstacle to integration with biomedicine. Within this diverse ethnic configuration, attempts at integration bespeaks of increasing the hegemony of biomedicine and the erosion of time-tested knowledge systems and medical practices because biomedicine is taken as a standard for the evaluation of traditional healing practices. To judge traditional healing knowledge and practices using biomedicine's values, philosophies, accountability standards and efficiency measures as a barometer is at odds with local realities (Mutabazi, 2008: 221). This remains the case even if so-called objective medicine is significantly influenced by the dominant values of time and place (Foucault, 1975). The failure to consider the diversity of practices that make up traditional medicine, the historical context within which it has developed in South Africa, where the apartheid system of governance ridiculed and castigated it as backward, and then banned it, while successive post-apartheid regimes have either paid only lip service to it or been inconsistent makes the goal of integration a rather herculean task.

Global and regional policy initiatives have led to an increase in support for traditional medicine. The Alma-Ata (in Kazakhstan) conference of 1978 on making health care available to the poor further strengthened the development of traditional medicine. The Declaration of Alma-Ata called for a new emphasis on primary healthcare and on the participation of locals in the design and management of health systems (Nkwi, 2006). It envisaged healthcare coverage for all: "health for all by the year 2000." The shift from hospital-centered to people-centered healthcare gave medical anthropologists and traditional healers a window of opportunity as it acknowledged the importance of traditional medicine and encouraged nations to develop official policies on traditional medicine (Saleh, 1993: 2122; Summerton, 2006). Although the Alma-Ata movement was an attempt to draw attention to the biomedical paradigm's lack of attention to various social influences and indicators on health and healthcare ("health for all by the year 2000"), it has been roundly criticized for it was purportedly subverted by political forces, as well as "by the bacteriological emphasis of the late nineteenth and early twentieth centuries" (Heggenhougen in Mckenna, 2010: 7). The focus on bacteriology further serves to obscure the significant role of socio-economic disparities on health. The Bamako Initiative—Africa's interpretation of the Alma-Ata declaration—called for "health for all by the year 2000" and this further opened an opportunity for medical anthropologists to study local systems of medicine and traditional healing practices. Thereafter, the integration of traditional medicine into mainstream healthcare delivery has instead stagnated in the legislature of African countries including South Africa. As of 2001, of 44 African countries surveyed, 61% had legal statutes regarding traditional medicine and despite this, traditional medicine has remained on the margins, as these statutes have never been implemented (WHO, 2001). In tandem with WHO's Traditional Medicine Strategy 2014–2023, calling on Member States to develop safe and effective policies on traditional medicine (TM), they should be supported in "harnessing the potential contribution of traditional therapies to health, wellness and people-centered health care; promoting the safe and effective use of TM by regulating, researching and integrating TM products, practitioners and practice into health systems, where appropriate" (WHO, 2013: 12). Between 1999 to 2012, the number of Members States with TM policies and those regulating herbal medicine rose from 25–69 and 65–119 respectively (WHO, 2013: 21).

South African healers have since created over a 100 different THPs associations all over the country and steps are underway to bring the country's over 200,000 THPs under a single statutory body. Apart from The Traditional Health Practitioners Act 22 of 2007 that is responsible for setting practice standards through the registration, training and conduct of THPs, in 2013 the Interim Traditional Health Practitioners Council was inaugurated and came into effect on 1 May 2014. The Council draws its mandate from the Bill of Rights embedded in the South African Constitution, the National Health Act of 2003 and the Traditional Health Practitioners Act of 2007 (Street, 2016: 325). On 25 July 2016, there was the publication of proposed amendments to the General Regulations including the intentions of the prior publication and incorporation of the definition of Health Supplement for Comment during a 3 months period. On 16 January 2017 followed the publication of proposed amendments to the General Regulations Provision for the functioning of the South African Health Product Regulatory Authority (SAHPRA) (see amended Act). The Implementation of General Regulations on traditional medicine followed on 25 August 2017 (TradReg, 2017). Despite these regulatory measures, an incessant debate rages on between advocates and opponents of the integration of traditional medicine in South Africa.

The crux of the debate between both camps revolve around the shortcomings of each system of medicine. This ongoing debate that is taking place against the backdrop of democracy and the HIV/AIDS pandemic is part of the multifaceted debate between cultural rights versus international human rights law. It is encapsulated in the "Return to tradition policy" and in relation to the right to available, accessible, affordable and culturally appropriate and good quality healthcare (Office of the United Nations High Commissioner for Human Rights and WHO, 2018) as stipulated in the South African Constitution. Prejudicial views and false premises as well as problematic and questionable dichotomies including the fact that modern medicine is based on science and traditional medicine on the supernatural and superstition are without merit because there is also recourse to faith and prayer in modern medical practice. Both also suffer from issues of safety and efficacy (see Chapter 1). The debate is therefore, rather about the need for complementarity between both systems of healthcare. It is swayed by the perceived differences in the philosophical underpinnings of both systems of healthcare, and the lack of legal protection for THPs. We however, argue that since both systems of healthcare are complementary and embedded in cultural beliefs and practices, the way forward in breaking the deadlock is to do away with the dominant culture as ignorant framework that dominates the mindset of the biomedical establishment. We further highlight the challenges facing biomedicine and militating in favour of traditional health practices and vice versa. These challenges include the acute human resource shortages in providing formal healthcare and the changing pattern of disease necessitate co-operation between both systems of healthcare. We then illuminate collaborative initiatives/attempts to work across both systems in tackling the HIV/AIDS pandemic and the need for bridging by biomedical practitioners to facilitate the integration of both systems. This is because unlike biomedical practitioners, THPs are willing to embrace biomedical approaches to treatment.

6.2   The Debate for and against Traditional Medicine

Some supporters of the integration of biomedicine and African traditional medicine often opt for an intermediate position. They point out that both medical systems are complementary. Despite the endless emotional debates between advocates and those opposed to traditional medicine, traditional healing has remained resilient partly because it is not only readily available; it is also entangled with the cultural heritage, identity and custom of its users. This implies that it deals with the social, cultural and psychological aspects of disease. It is unlike biomedicine, which is concerned only with the physical body—the anatomy, physiology and biochemistry of the human body. In other words, medical staff and other healthcare professionals including nurses, pharmacists, and therapists treat symptoms and disease with the use of drugs, radiation or surgery. Diagnoses usually involves a therapeutic interview and/or laboratory tests. Biomedical therapy entails the application of biological and physiological principles to inform clinical practice. It is based on the scientific procedure—the investigation of biological processes and the causes of disease through careful experimentation, observation, laboratory work, analysis, and testing (CBRA, 2018). Additionally, biomedical knowledge whose basis is the scientific procedure is public knowledge that is available in standard textbooks on physiology and human anatomy as well as on a standardized curriculum. Opponents of integration point out that traditional healing knowledge and practices are shrouded in secrecy and can therefore not be easily disseminated. It is closely guarded and may only be revealed to close family members or initiates. This poses an obstacle to effective regulation and generates resistance on the part of THPs (Street, 2015). They are not only secretive about the source of their knowledge, they keep their prescriptions secret. They depend on knowledge handed down from generation to generation of healers. Memory lapse can result in vague doses. Compounding the situation is the fact that even self-medication with herbal medicine can lead to the overuse of some remedies, resulting in severe health consequences that could include stomach upsets, liver damage and in extreme cases, kidney failure. *Aloe vera* is one widely used natural health product that has been associated with adverse health effects. Nothing indicates to patients that "too much a good thing could be dangerous" (Gouws, 2008: online). In Africa (especially in countries like Zambia, Swaziland, Zimbabwe and South Africa), cancer bush (*Sutherlandia frutescens*) is widely used in the treatment of diseases such as HIV/AIDS and TB, and is believed to generally improve quality of life in patients. It has, however, "been shown to lower the plasma levels of the ART drug, atazanavir, to sub-therapeutic levels when they are taken together, thereby reducing its anti-HIV efficacy" (Gouws, 2008: online, Babb et al., 2007).

Opponents of integration further point out that unlike biomedicine with its bacteriological emphasis, traditional healing practices are based on a different notion of disease and health and on a different worldview. In traditional medical practice, diagnosis consists of a dual interrelated process. First, the healer establishes the organic or physical cause of the sickness through careful examination and questioning of the patient or members of his/her "therapy managing group" (Hsu, 2008). Secondly, follows a divination of the spiritual or mystical cause of the illness. During this therapeutic session, the THP consults the 'spiritual world' to identify the cause of the disease or to find out if the sick individual has violated a taboo and the appropriate sacrifices, spiritual cleansing/protection, appeasement of the gods, or exorcism as the case might require to be made to bring him back to good health. Apart from or in the course of the therapeutic interview, some healers may request for a medical history of the patient. Furthermore, some healers use traditional faith healing practices such as prayers and spiritual techniques to diagnose, cure and improve the health and wellbeing as well as the physical and spiritual health of their patients. Critics of traditional healing practices, however, often question "the legitimacy of healers by maintaining the inefficiency of their ritualized practices. They contend that faith healers use fraudulent healing techniques that reduce access to modern medicine and result in high mortality rates" (Kühn, 2009: 61; Gouwe, 2014). Although both personalistic and naturalistic disease causation theories sometimes co-exists in traditional health practices, personalistic causation sometimes predominate. Good health is about appropriate behavior, conformity with the values and norms of society (Iroegbu, 2005: 82), maintaining harmony between spiritual and physical wellbeing and, having a good relationship with one's ancestors (White, 2015; Omonzejele, 2008; Setswe, 1999: 56–60) because they are believed to have an overbearing influence on social life (Mbiti, 1992; Omonzejele, 2008).

> For the traditional African, health is not just about the proper functioning of bodily organs. Good health for the African consists of mental, physical, spiritual, and emotional stability [of oneself, family members, and community]; this integrated view of health is based on the African unitary view of reality. Good health for the African is not a subjective affair.
> (Omonzejele, 2008: 120)

Similarly, and as Nyamti (1984) rightly points out, it is sacrosanct to maintain the balance between the visible and the invisible worlds because:

> When ancestors are neglected or forgotten by their relatives they are said to be angry with them and to send them misfortunes as punishment. Their anger is usually appeased through prayers and ritual in the form of food and drinks. [The ancestors long for contact with their earthly kin; that is why they are supposed to visit often] (p. 16).

Additionally, proponents of traditional medicine argue that unlike biomedical practitioners who rely on standardized procedures resulting from clinical practices, traditional healers provide personalized care to their patients. They maintain that even patients suffering from the same ailment are provided unique treatment regimens. This is because healers recognize the differences in the social backgrounds of their patients (Oloyede, 2010: 74–75). These differences led Daniel Lantum to point out that:

Two patients reported to a healer with swollen legs, while one was treated for witchcraft poisoning, the other received a spiritual bath, cleansing him from a spell thrown by his late grandmother whom he had offended.

(Lantum, 1978: 109)

As intermediaries and facilitators of communication with the spiritual realm, diviners ensure spiritual intervention for the treatment of illnesses caused by inappropriate behavior on the part of a patient. This explains why they are variously called "the eyes of the community," traditional healers, priests/priestesses and herbalists (Sarpong, 2002: 103–104; White, 2015). They diagnose both the cause, nature and perpetrators of illness, apply therapeutic regimens, and prevent future misfortunes. Unlike biomedical practitioners, they have a broader social role that includes physical, psychological, spiritual and at times, legal issues (White, 2015).

Opponents of the integration of both systems of medicine point to lack of regulation when it comes to traditional medical practices. They raise questions about the safety and efficacy of traditional medical practices. Unlike modern medicine that is heavily regulated, traditional health practices despite commendable strides are not well regulated in South Africa. This lack of regulation and the ambiguities encapsulated in the Traditional Health Practitioners Act of 2007 highlight issues of patient safety and the efficacy of the drugs dispensed by THPs. Additionally and relatedly, the request for copies of didactic materials as part of the accreditation system for trainers and training institutions for THPs, when the actual process for vetting is not disclosed is contentious. It is furthermore, unclear how that will culminate into a national training programme under the National Quality Framework (NQF) (Street, 2016). THPs often acquire their skills in different ways. This ranges from apprenticeship to visions and dreams. Compounding the situation is the wide division concerning the regulation of traditional medicine. Some individuals want prior regulation before integration into the biomedical healthcare system. They claim that it will protect patients, and lead to the minimalisation of health risks. On the contrary, their opponents point out that legal regulation will "undermine healers who play a highly respected cultural role for a large percentage of the African population" (Kühn, 2009: 61).

Although proponents of traditional healing practices invoke the cultural acceptability of this method of treatment, many skeptics and traditionalists however remain nervous of Western healing practices and their modernized techniques". They instead prefer "to maintain a relationship with a local healer, whose familiarity and religious purpose is preferable" (Kühn, 2009: 61). The result has rather been a strong rejection of the South African government's initiatives to introduce a nationalized Western modern medicine, modernization and commercialization through the adoption of a universal system of healthcare that remains out of the reach of many people and does not address their needs. Two main reasons have been forwarded for the lack of traction. First, it overlooks "the strong regional values and deep mistrust of foreign practices" (Kühn, 2009: 61). This skepticism about foreign practices is rooted in the experience of the apartheid system of racial discrimination and 'medical apartheid.' It should therefore be understood against the backdrop of the ANC government's ambivalent policy of a "Return to tradition" as instantiated through the recognition of cultural rights as protected rights in Sections 30 and 31 of the 1996 Constitution (Mubangizi, 2012). The dominant biomedical healthcare system that the government intends to promote remains inaccessible to most of the population. This disjuncture between law and its practical implementation has left both parties "lost in translation" (Kühn, 2009: 61; Street, 2016). The cultural conflicts surrounding "medicinal practices (however) present ways in which individuals can actually work together to integrate both traditional values and progressive practices" (Kühn, 2009: 61; Du Plooy, 2004). As pointed out by Du Plooy (2004) traditional cultural beliefs and behaviours can be categorized into positive (P), exotic (E) or negative (N). In line with this framework, positive cultural beliefs and behaviours are those that are beneficial in HIV/AIDS and other disease prevention strategies and programmes. The emphasis in the anti-HIV/AIDS fight at the community level should be on positive (P) beliefs and values that can be utilized in HIV/AIDS programmes. In synergy with other stakeholders such as community and faith leaders, THPs should be involved in the design and implementation of these programmes. Success stories of collaboration between various health stakeholders in Africa point to the need for cultural sensitivity as well as the importance of involving the whole community in the fight against the HIV/AIDS pandemic (Du Plooy, 2004).

Opinions and attitudes of people towards traditional medicine vary among users and traditional healers on the one hand and non-users on the other hand because of personal preferences or religious beliefs. These different attitudes, the WHO concedes, range from uncritical criticism to uninformed skepticism (WHO, Traditional Medicinal Strategy, 2002–2005). Those who maintain an intermediate position opt for complementarity between the two medical systems. Traditional medicine owes its popularity first to its holistic vision of the concept of health. This implies its ability to simultaneously address issues of the soul, spirit and the body. Secondly is the shortcomings of the dominant biomedical healthcare system-particularly its inability to fully address people's healthcare needs, especially the upsurge in chronic diseases and its lack of a response to the HIV/AIDS pandemic and other diseases that are non-curable. This is happening at a time when there is widespread resistance to both communicable and non-communicable diseases to drugs. Exacerbating the situation is the fact that the pharmaceutical industry seems to be more business inclined and tend to focus on producing drugs that will bring in more economic returns. As it tends to neglect so-called diseases of the poor, it creates inequality and foster recourse to THPs. Although non-fatal, neglected tropical diseases cause enormous suffering and disability (personal and economic pain), and predispose people to other fatal infections. They include diseases such as lymphatic filariasis (river blindness), trachoma, onchocerciasis and leprosy. They survive and thrive on poverty and are widespread in places with unsafe drinking water, poor sanitation and limited access to basic health services in SSA, Asia and Latin America where an estimated 1.4 million people are affected. A conjuncture between improved standard of living in wealthy countries and the emergence of big killers like HIV and TB have pushed these diseases further down the public health agenda. In addition, since drug manufacturers have little profit to make, they have little incentive for investment (Health Poverty Action, 2018, www.healthpovertyaction.org).

It should however be noted that despite the widespread use of traditional medicine, the biomedical healthcare systems in South Africa remains under immense pressure. For instance, the 2016 GHS showed that the first point of access when household members took ill or got injured among some seven in every ten (71,4%) of households were public clinics and hospitals. On the contrary, a quarter of households (27,0%) stated they would consult private doctors, private clinics or hospitals (Stats SA, 2017). These figures may well suggests the underreporting/concealment of visits/failure to report visits to THPs (Molhibe & Sibanda, 2019).

Unlike biomedical practitioners, THPs are generally more accessible and affordable (Kühn, 2009). Respondents constantly pointed out to us that the high cost of allopathic medical care as well as expensive pharmaceuticals have made it to become unavailable and inaccessible to a majority of the population (see also White, 2015; Kühn, 2009) who are obliged to seek care from THPs. In SSA, it is estimated that the ratio of THPs to the population is approximately 1: 500, whereas biomedical practitioners have a 1: 140,000 ratio to the rest of the population. This suggests that there are 80 more THPs to biomedical practitioners. The DoH estimates that 200,000 THPs are active in South Africa alone (Hassim & Berger, 2014). According to Njenga (2005), the doctor-patient ratio in rural Tanzania is 1: 20,000. This is in contrast to 1: 25 to THPs. The human resources for health skills shortfall in South Africa in particular and SSA in general suggests that THPs can help in strengthening health systems if they are appropriately trained to respond to the anti-HIV/AIDS fight. This will be a useful way of "adopting strategies that align traditional healing with the goal of increasing the health standards across the continent" (Kühn, 2009: 61; du Plooy, 2014: 2).

In line with the politics underpinning this study, which is the prospects for the integration of both systems of healthcare so as to achieve health equity and wellbeing for the South African population, we argue that no one system of healthcare can meet all the social and psychological needs of an individual or of all the segments of a population. In other words, both systems of healthcare have their challenges that can only be overcome through complementarity.

Advocates of conventional medicine argue that traditional medicine is not effective and cannot work in isolation. They claim that traditional medicine has problems of imprecise dosage, poor diagnosis resulting from lack of sophisticated technology, charlatanism, exaggerated claims of abilities and inadequate knowledge of anatomy, hygiene, and disease transmission (Saleh, 1993). Although THPs sometimes overlook the importance of dosage, which can cause harm to patients and even lead to death, critics who point to the side effects of traditional remedies are oblivious of the fact that traditional remedies including those involving plants products, like many pharmaceutical industry products, may also have associated side effects. Through interviews, herbalists admitted their awareness of the fact that the toxicity of plants varies with season- a realization that tends to explain the low dosage forms of some traditional remedies. They pointed out that processes such as heating, grinding and pounding may eliminate some toxins, and kill micro-organisms. The chemical change brought about by heating might also increase toxicity. To make traditional medicine more systematic, there is the need to identify the pharmaceutically active compounds to make the methods more systematic and reliable. To critics, the shortcomings of African traditional medicine put South African patient's health and lives at risk. A number of traditional healers share these concerns and do admit their limitations (Fyhrquist, 2007). As one healer pointed out:

> You cannot be a know-all doctor. Those who claim to treat all types of diseases are actually doing a disservice to the vocation of traditional healing. We can learn from modern medical doctors and they can learn from us. Some refer patients to us and vice versa.
> (Mundam, Interview of April 10, 2010; Qokwelni Location)

Those traditional healers who admit limitations are eager to improve their medicinal knowledge and co-operate significantly with practitioners of conventional medicine. It is however a pity that some traditional healers believe that conventional medical practitioners and research scientists simply want to condemn their efforts and steal their secrets (Okpako, 2006).

Apart from the lack of accurate diagnosis, a further challenge of traditional medical treatment regimens that critics constantly highlight is the erroneous assumption by many consumers of traditional remedies who automatically equate "natural equals safe." A further problem is that in their quest for relief, patients often combine traditional or herbal remedies with prescribed drugs. This could lead to "interactions"—"the effect herbal medicines may have on the normal uptake, breakdown or activity of prescribed medicines" (Gouws, 2008: online). This mirrors the case of HIV/AIDS patients who make recourse to traditional healing, delay the uptake of ART or are exposed to toxicity and drug interaction culminating in treatment failure and viral resistance (Babb et al., 2007). Concerning ART, Babb et al. (2007) further point out that its use alongside traditional medicine could lead to drug interactions and that patients should make disclosures during ART counselling sessions. This call for the need by scientists to undertake "proper research to understand such interactions" (Gouws, 2008: online, Babb et al., 2007). Consumers also need be to sensitized about these interactions, whether they are good or bad. They should also be able to disclose everything they are taking to healthcare providers. Few countries including Cameroon, Nigeria, and South Africa have incorporated traditional African medicine into new adverse drug reaction reporting systems (Gouws, 2008). Moreover, they indicate that some traditional healers and traditional medical practices can lead to the spread of diseases including hepatitis B, and HIV/AIDS when instruments used for the procedures are unsterilized. Another challenge is that dependence on divination by some practitioners as a method of diagnosis and treatment deter Christians from accessing their services (White, 2015).

The modern healthcare system is also bedecked by several shortcomings: chronic shortage of personnel; geographical inaccessibility of healthcare facilities and urban monopoly at the expense of rural areas; and high cost of treatment (Labhardt et al., 2010). Apart from these shortcomings, modern healthcare is ill-equipped to treat a wide range of illnesses occurring in African communities. In other words, modern medicine's inability to handle certain health problems has created space for intervention based on traditional medical remedies (Lamla, 2007: 80–88; Zubane, 2001).

Despite the widespread use of TCAM worldwide and therefore its increasing visibility and subsequently, its informal "integration" into biomedical settings (by patients and to a lesser extent by biomedical practitioners), it is still practiced on the margins of the mainstream healthcare system. TCAM's marginal status is attributed to its perceived lack of a modern "western scientific" basis as well an outright dismissal of 'other' competing epistemologies and ontologies (e.g. Hollenberg & Muzzin, 2010; Kumar, 1997), and not the absence of an ancient indigenous scientific basis (Basalla, 1967), as found in China or India for example. The dominant hegemonic mindset fails to understand that "what is metaphysics in one culture is science in another" [sic] (Chattopadhayaya, 1990: xvii). And that in the realm of 'science,' differing worldviews and 'ways of knowing' tend to be confined to or contorted towards western science, rather than comprised of knowledge systems and worldviews from a diversity of cultures, and a variety of historical periods (Shiva, 1997; in Hollenberg & Muzzin, 2010).

Furthermore, biomedicine's reductionism of disease to mere physiology (as well as anatomy and biochemistry), with emphasis on bacteriology (McKenna, 2012), "largely ignores broader social, cultural and institutional contexts" (Baronov, 2008: 242). Concurrently, the significance of indigenous and "other subjugated knowledges" including traditional medicine, which offer a more holistic view of health and healing (Kincheloe, 2006:182) are disparaged. Indigenous knowledges appear within the biomedical ontological frame of reference, and reflect how "[w]ith the birth of modernity, the scientific revolution and the colonial policies they engendered, many pre-modern, ontologies were lost" (Kinchloe, 2006: 182). Medical historian Fielding Garrison's statement of the late 1920s poignantly captures the denigration of alternative medical beliefs and practices and their practitioners:

> Disease [was regarded] as something produced by a human enemy possessing supernatural powers, which he strove to wade off by appropriate spells and sorcery, similar to those employed by the enemy himself. Again, his own reflections in the water, his shadow in the sunlight, what he saw in dreams or in an occasional nightmare from gluttony, suggested the existence of a spirit-world apart from his daily life and of a soul or alter ego apart from his body. In this way, he hit upon a third way of looking at disease as the work of offended spirits of the dead...These three views of disease are common beliefs of the lowest grade of human life (P. 21).

The South African government has since acknowledged the significant contributions made by traditional healers towards healthcare. For example, the National Department of Arts, Culture, Science, and Technology funds consortium research projects into traditional medicines (Meyeng, 1999; Clark, 1998). It is ironic that despite this apparent recognition, there is a discrepancy between policy and reality. In reality, South Africa's official healthcare system is monopolized by modern scientific medicine which is largely recognized as legal. In this system, state licensed professionals with formal training dispense healthcare. The present legislation regards any medical act not backed by a license as illegal. This includes traditional healing practices undertaken by many traditional healers without practicing licenses who have continued to carry out their trade undisturbed by law enforcement officers.

Like in most African countries, traditional healers are not given total recognition and protection by the authorities. In the past, the South African government has followed a policy of non-intervention. Such a policy has created a leeway for 'traditional healers' to carry out their activities unchecked. Recently, the government has embarked on a policy to have traditional healers registered but the criteria for registration remains a contentious issue. The government is more concerned with the task of bringing modern healthcare closer to the people (Goudge et al., 2009). This has angered several critics and they have taken the government to task for its non-supervision of traditional healers and their healing practices. Critics maintain that like in many other African countries, South Africa pays insufficient attention to a healthcare system that has continued to be vital and which serves the majority of its citizens (Zubane, 2001). Healers remain unprotected despite the tremendous leverage of, power and interconnections between multi-national corporations including the pharmaceutical industry (Sunder, 2007) and insurance companies and their increased interest in TCAM practices and products (Singer and Baer, 19995) which they are continuously converting through what Fournier (2013: 22) describes as the "pharmaceuticalization of natural health products/remedies." The institutionalization of traditional medicine by global actors including the World Bank through the "setting up of a regulatory mechanism to authorize the marketing of improved traditional drugs" (World Bank, 2004) is part of this pharmaceutization process. On its part, WHO concedes that "herbal medicines are the most lucrative form of traditional medicines, generating billions of dollars in revenue" (WHO, 2008). The involvement of these actors show that traditional medicine and knowledge systems have become global business and may impact on the way that traditional medicine is integrated into biomedicine.

Nowadays, there is a growing recognition that modern healthcare does not adequately address people's health needs. This recognition is common especially in the non-western world. As a result, non-conventional therapies are increasingly in demand. Despite the recognition of the paradigmatic gulf and therefore the core differences between TCAM and biomedical approaches in the developed world, the move towards integrating TCAM into biomedical settings in North America has been referred to as a 'social movement'; part of the 'New Age' or 'Holistic Health' movement (Baer & Coulter, 2008; Baer, 2004).

This movement is underpinned by the increasing use of TCAM (Fønnebø et al., 2007; Hollenberg, 2006) especially by those in the higher socio-economic classes (Baer & Coulter, 2008). This is partly, an outcome of dissatisfaction with biomedical approaches to care and deficiencies in biomedicine (Di Stefano, 2006; Mizrachi & Shuval, 2005; Baer, 2004; Baer, Singer & Susser, 1997). These shortcomings include- the increasing overreliance on technology and pharmaceuticals and biomedical iatrogenesis (Baer, 2004; Singer, Baer & Susser, 1997). In other words, the biomedical paradigm which is based on materiality and rationality is being challenged by holistic medicine which seeks to identify and integrate elements that are presently, generally neglected into a broader understanding. This partly imposes the need for a rigorous and renewed investigation of the nature and influence of the non-material and non-rational influences that are part of our lives (Di Stefano, 2006; Mcfarlane, 2015). Simultaneously, biomedicine has shifted away from subjective human experience towards objective signs and symptoms, as well as controllable and limited variables at a time when Western culture is insecurely obsessed with rational knowledge, objectivity in confronting human values and human experience (Di Stefano, 2006). Both patients and policymakers have acknowledged the omnipresence of TCAM in Western communities: patients patronize it; numerous students of biomedicine are increasingly enrolling in TCAM courses. The proliferation of many of its modalities in the university setting shows that policymakers are favourably supporting it (Di Stefano, 2006).

For economic reasons as well as personal preferences, South Africans of all ethnic groups, socioeconomic classes and demographics do use traditional medicine. Contrary to Africa and most of the less developed world, in Canada TCAM is largely patronized by those from a higher socio-economic class, whereas TCAM practitioners tend to be from lower socio-economic backgrounds when compared with physicians and their clientele (Baer & Coulter, 2008; Baer, 2004). TCAM is not part of the formal health care system in North America, and patients have to pay for it out of their pockets or through private healthcare insurance schemes. It can however be argued that socio-economic factors alongside social relations, personal experiences and perceptions of trust inform the choice of African traditional medicine as a therapeutic recourse strategy. Research findings suggests that in SSA patients are increasingly seeking care from the informal sector thereby putting to question the effectiveness of modern healthcare delivery programmes in the region (Krause and Sauerborn, 2000; Chuma et al., 2009; Porten et al., 2009). Poor diagnosis of disease is often compounded by a limited knowledge of appropriate management. This has resulted into an increase in the rate of self-medication and consequently, a decrease in the rate of formal healthcare utilization (Tupasi et al.,

1989). In many cases of self-medication, perceived quality of care informs the choice of the provider more than cost or distance (Tembon, 1996; Kruk et al., 2009). Most of the estimated 80% of people in Africa who regularly seek care from traditional providers, rather than go to traditional drug sellers do so without proper consultations, and easy access and low cost, among others are important factors (Larbhardt et al., 2010). A survey of patterns of therapeutic recourse in the Northwest and Southwest regions of Cameroon showed that in case of acute illness, seeking care from traditional healers was more often the first choice than consulting a healthcare facility (Adeso-Atanga, 2003). The use of traditional medicine is however, simultaneous with conventional medicine.

Stated otherwise, in their double quest for therapy and relief, patients and members of their 'therapy managing group' (Hsu, 2008) often engage in "syncretic auto-medication." Despite the possibility of drug interaction and negative health consequences (see above), they often combine modern medicine, as well as plant and animal materials obtained from the immediate environment or bought from the "African chemist" for the management of particular illness episodes. The "African chemist," also called "African pharmacy," is comprised of both ambulant and stable street vendors of medicinal plants, who sale plant and animal parts in both solid and liquid form for the preparation of various concoctions (Pemunta et al., 2020). South Africa needs improved and standardized traditional medicine that is regulated by the DoH. It is however unfortunate that incorporating traditional medicine into the mainstream healthcare system still poses a major challenge. Decades of disregard as well as the non-official recognition of traditional healer's contribution to healthcare by the government has created mistrust and antagonism between the practitioners of conventional medicine and traditional healers.

Similar to biomedicine, traditional medicine is embedded in the culture and belief systems of the local people. Biomedicine as practice is of course not void of a deep cultural anchor "in local contexts and in the multiple realities of daily life" (Griffiths, 2001: 102). The deep cultural embeddedness of biomedical practice explain the failure of interventions designed to "restore" the body to normal because the unexamined assumptions inherent in biomedicine may be antithetical to differing culturally embedded visions of individual and collective wellbeing (Lock and Nguyen, 2010: 50). Disease and healing have a cultural dimension (Jacoksen, 2014; Kleinman, 1980; De Stefano, 2006). As Kathryn Jacobsen (2014: 82) rightly concedes "...people with a shared culture may engage in similar health-related behaviors, have similar health beliefs, and have similar preferences about when and where to seek health care." Similarly, Di Stefano maintains:

> Human experience casts long shadows that are now always so easily dispersed by newer interpretations of the nature of the world, regardless of their power to explain phenomena or account for the mysterious. Looking at human disease and sickness in purely mechanistic terms certainly provides us with clear and irrefutable stories of how diseases may arise and how they affect the body, but this is done at the cost of neglecting the many contexts from which we, as humans, draw meaning. The historical and cultural traditions within which we are raised can powerfully shape our view of the world and the forces within it. (Di Stefano, 2006: 119)

Closely related to the foregoing is what might be called the culture as ignorance framework, or better still, the primitivity argument or the colonial mentality paradigm of traditional healers and traditional medical practices as witchcraft. This might also be termed as the arrogant perception of biomedical stakeholders some of whom hypocritically condemn traditional medicine in bright day light, but consult traditional medicine practitioners at night. Mutabazi eloquently states that (2008: 220) this necessitates "…the struggle to decolonize the mind and shrug off the huge blanket of ignorance and lack of depth of analysis that is a hangover from colonization" because "only then can we start making sense of our reality and adopt relevant, context specific solutions that can re-direct our societies on the road to development." Similarly, Bishop states that:

> There is an inability of the orientalist western imaginary to understand traditional medicine outside of the already prefigured beliefs about Africans and their traditional healing practices, as seen in how the media often conflates witchcraft with traditional medicine. In addition, among conventional medical practitioners themselves in South Africa, there is widespread belief that traditional medicines are unproven, scientifically untested, and ineffective. To the degree that there are emerging calls for the inclusion of traditional healers in contemporary HIV/ AIDS treatment, informal discussions with members of the allopathic medical community suggests widespread skepticism and resistance. Media representations of traditional healing both support and challenge the medical establishment. By calling for inclusion, newspapers confront the expert power of doctors. (Bishop, 2012: 557)

Most biomedical practitioners are trapped in the prejudicial notion of traditional African beliefs and practices as "primitive and savage" because they cannot hold up to the perceived rationality of scientific knowledge (see also Hammond-Tooke, 1989: 185). Gumede (1990: 153) expresses the same sentiments by conceding that biomedical practitioners perceive traditional healers as a threat to the health and well-being of their patients. This skepticism is partly the result of lack of knowledge of traditional notions of disease and health, mysticism surrounding the content of traditional medicines, and the administration of harmful traditional healing practices and medicines (Summerton, 2006: 17) by some self-styled healers. Such skepticism that is due to the unorthodox actions of a few make "integration" to be equivalent with the homogenization and monolithicization of "differing worldviews about health and approaches to health care on a global scale" (Fournier, 2013: 6). This implies that the devaluation, contortion and erasure of myriad health beliefs and long-existing healthcare systems could lead to their eventual biomedicalization in the name of integration and the loss of their intrinsic values. Contortion is partly achieved through "The identification of biomedical equivalence, double-blind clinical trials, and attempts at the codification of traditional healing (and traditional medicine)" (Flint, 2015: 4336). "In essence, the evaluation of traditional healing within an assessment framework that is itself a product of the evolution of the biomedical sector condemns the traditional sector from the outset; its practice will always be viewed by stakeholders within the formal healthcare sector as, at best, misinformed" (Flint, 2015: 4336). However, attempts by both policymakers and the biomedical community to codify what is and what is not traditional healing reveals a fundamental misunderstanding of what it is and how it is practiced. For example, the idea of charlatan healers sits uncomfortably within both cultures—in general, failure to find a cure is often viewed as an indication not of fraudulence or misdiagnosis on the part of the traditional healer, but rather of the strength of the supernatural forces aligned against the patient. In such cases, it thus becomes a matter of seeking out a more powerful healer. In South Africa, it tends to be understood that "genuine" healers will only request payment once the patient is healed. A healer demanding payment upfront may sometimes be deemed suspect (Flint, 2015: 4328).

In order to understand the mystery behind traditional healing, one needs to take into account the social milieu and the worldviews of the healer and the patient. As an overlapping cultural system, the context of healthcare creates its own clinical reality, a specific type of social reality-defined as a transactional world in which institutions and relationships are constituted on the basis of systems of symbolic meanings that constitute the context for illness and healing. Kleinman suggests that therapeutic misunderstandings often occur because different health care sectors fail to sanction competing versions of clinical reality. For example, Arthur Kleinman writes, "health professionals usually are insensitive to the views of clinical reality held by other healers, and to the expectations and beliefs of their patients" (Kleinman, 1980: 58). He draws attention to the need to prioritize the lived experience of patients in healthcare over analytic categories imposed by anthropological theory. In other words, to move away from psychiatric discourses that tend to reduce lived experience to a set of narrow professional categories (Kleinman, 1988).

In a number of Asian countries such as China, India and Bangladesh, traditional medicine is considered as one of the most advanced therapeutic systems. Special policies in Asia are against any form of discrimination against the old medical system. Chinese traditional medicine has become part of a free medical care accommodated in hospitals and has rapidly diffused to all parts of the world. Today in Asia, many doctors are specialists in both modern and traditional medical care. Most of such specialists feel that combined treatment is much better than that of either system applied in isolation (Bannerman et al., 1983: 73–74; see also Moore and McClean, 2010). This further suggests the need for a multidisciplinary lens in medical practice. For example, Harvard University-based Arthur Kleinman is both an anthropologist and a psychiatrist- a situation that has placed him in a unique position to bridge the gap between medicine and culture, and academia and the health arena. In an interview granted the Post in April 25, 2008, Professor Daniel Lantum who is widely reputed in Cameroon for combining traditional and modern medical practice stated that:

> I am a civilised African. I mean that I also learned and acquired what we call the folk wisdom of Cameroon, and part of folk wisdom is traditional medicine. I learned about medicinal plants. I was treating people, before I went to secondary school and after that, I decided to do medicine.
>
> One of the reasons was that I had onchocerchiasis and there was no traditional medicine that could treat it; so I had to go and learn modern medicine to treat myself and other people. When I became a medical doctor and eventually a professor, I said wouldn't abandon folk medicine and that is why I combine the two.
>
> Being a modern doctor and scientist didn't help me to be able to do a lot of research on folk remedy, and to prove that they were effective. It also meant that I had to drop the bias that was imposed by colonialism. Anything about Africa was not good. I didn't believe in that, so I said, I will go and see, and I gave a scientific dimension to what was called empirical knowledge.

(I am) doctor of medicine, and as a professor, teaching the thing to modern physicians, that becomes far more open. I earn my living from that one, but all the same, I am fully aware that traditional medicine is important. I have worked with the Ministry of Health and particularly with the World Health Organisation, WHO, and the Ministry of Health is going to adopt traditional medicine and seek ways of integrating it into other health care services. Whether the ministry does that officially or not, in practice it happens. There is no question about that. (Ndi Chia, 2008)

Many European therapeutic practices are not really traditional, since the traditional elements have been diluted over the centuries by official medicine (Hillenbrand, 2006: 16) leading to what might be rightly called "the invention of tradition" (Hobsbawn and Ranger, 1992). We are thus tempted to argue that the success of modern medicine today in Europe has been made possible through the inclusion of old ways into the new system of approach.[1] This dovetails with Terence Ranger and Eric Hobsbawn's paradoxical concept of the "the invention of tradition" which implies that the sharp distinction between "tradition" and "modernity" is often itself invented. This further suggests that even the concept of authenticity is opened to question (Ranger and Hobsbawm, 1983). In the face of the challenges facing biomedicine -the changing pattern of disease as well as the HIV/AIDS pandemic- traditional medicine provides primary healthcare to a large majority of people in Africa.

6.3 Primary Healthcare and the Changing Pattern of Disease

The WHO recognizes African traditional medicine as a significant primary healthcare resource in developing countries and has continuously encouraged governments to adopt policies that officially acknowledge and regulate its practice. In many countries, including South Africa, policy makers are reluctant to lawfully accept traditional medicine (Fyhrquist, 2007). This reluctance and ambivalence coupled with other challenges have led to a critical lack of co-operation between conventional and traditional medical practitioners (WHO, 1990). As a result of, and despite this lack of co-operation, traditional

---

1 Modern medicine is partly the outcome of improvement on traditional medical practices. The father of medicine Hippocrates was using traditional medical practices to cure people of their illnesses. His healing sword was carved in the form of a snake, which remains the symbol of modern medicine today.

healers who are alleged to possess "vague" knowledge of human anatomy manage hospital diagnosed health problems. This puts the lives and health of many citizens using traditional medicine at risk. Since patients use conventional and traditional healthcare simultaneously, without such a dialogue as well as the eventual inclusion of traditional medicine into the national public health strategy, effective healthcare amongst many South Africans who depend largely on traditional health remedies will not be attained.

6.4 Traditional Medicine and the HIV/AIDS Pandemic

The United Nations Programme on HIV/AIDS (UNAIDS) has appraised the contribution made by traditional healers towards the care of patients infected with, and the prevention of the HIV/AIDS pandemic. UNAIDS has called for a synergy between biomedical and traditional health systems so as to foster initiatives that involve collaboration with traditional healers for HIV prevention and care in SSA with "the ultimate aim of improving access to, and quality of, health services for the clients of both systems." In the early 1990s attempts were made to combine the best of biomedicine and traditional medical systems. A wide variety of projects examined the usefulness of traditional herbal remedies for the treatment of HIV-related illnesses. Studies were also conducted to explore traditional healers' perceptions of STIs and HIV infection. The resulting wealth of information gave rise to the setting up of collaborative projects training traditional healers as educators and counsellors to disseminate information on HIV and STIs in their communities and to their peers. For example, in 2000, community leaders of the Inanda-a community in the Valley of a Thousand Hills, Kwa-Zulu Natal, South Africa called for help in strengthening their response to the AIDS epidemic. They identified local traditional healers as having an important role to play. In response to their request, a multidisciplinary team of social scientists and medical doctors began working in partnership with the local traditional healers on HIV prevention projects. Each month, a group of around 16–20 healers attended one-day workshops where they were drilled on HIV transmission, prevention, treatment and care. They also brain stormed on traditional and cultural sexual practices that could prevent HIV transmission and safer sexual practices involving more than just condoms (UNAIDS, 2006: 5; see also Hillenbrand, 2006). Preliminary clinical trials have also be undertaken on a Nigerian herbal medicine that seems to increase CD4-cell (CD4-cells protects the human body from infections. The HIV virus attacks these cells and uses them to make more copies of HIV- in doing so- the CD4 cell is unable to protect the body) counts and improves the well-being of patients with HIV-related illnesses (Rukangira, 2004; see also Tsibangu et al., 2004). In a clinical study involving 33 HIV-positive volunteers over a one year period, K.C. Tsibangu and colleagues (2004) assessed the value and efficacy of traditional herbal medicines commonly used by traditional healers for the treatment of HIV-positive patients. They report "improvement in the overall health condition and immune system, increase in CD4+T cell count and decrease in viral load count" (Ibid.: 499). They further maintain that after four and/or eight months of therapy, significant health improvement was noticed: better physical appearance (80% of patients), increased appetite (65%), feeling of well-being (60%), disappearance of skin marks (70%) and urogenital lesions (100%), resumption of work duties (60%), weight gain (80%), significant reduction in viral load (85.4%, p=0.0015) and significant increase in CD4+T cell counts (226%, p=0.0000). They conclude that the achievement of health improvement within eight months suggests that herbal medicine can be used as supplementary or alternative treatment for HIV/AIDS patients, and that it serves as an obvious immune system booster and probable "virus cidal factor." This is similar to most immune boasters, including ginseng and omega h3 that are produced from herbs.

Traditional healers can often be helpful in delivering successful medical interventions. For example, in the Central African Republic, AIDS prevention training was given to traditional healers who then disseminated this information to villagers who might not have otherwise been enlightened about issues of HIV/AIDS. Somse et al. (1998) report that ninety six traditional healers received 17–36 hour training, which included education sessions about the prevention of HIV transmission and STDs. The programme was assessed through interviews, and it was noticed that information dissemination on the AIDS epidemic was improved by the training of traditional healers. In a community study in South Africa to determine the potential for traditional healers to assist in the treatment of tuberculosis, 63% of the healers (15 out of 24) differentiated between actual tuberculosis (the infectious disease requiring modern medical attention) and *idliso*, which is the toxic poisoning by spirits, believed to be best healed by traditional healers. Most of the traditional healers revealed that they had sent patients who were potentially infected with tuberculosis to the hospital at some point in their career. The study further revealed that traditional healers were willing to co-operate with other healthcare providers in treating patients. The possibility of a productive collaboration between traditional healers and modern tuberculosis treatment seems to be highly beneficial. Suspicion and doubt have historically existed between traditional healers and physicians. It is believed that a common sense of respect and admiration towards one another will provide a potential for partnership (Wilkonson, 1999).

In Malawi, there is an extremely high STI and HIV prevalence rate. Due to existing health challenges exacerbated by high HIV/AIDS prevalence rate, there is an immediate need to incorporate traditional healers into awareness campaigns and management programmes. In a 2002 study that was conducted in the country, 90% of those who had not used condoms lived in villages and had received treatment exclusively from traditional healers. In Malawi, traditional healers are believed to be more empathetic and approachable than physicians. As a result, community members have greater confidence and trust in traditional healing. It can therefore be very beneficial to incorporate them into the HIV control activities and utilize their sites for activities such as condom distribution (Zarchariah et al., 2002). In Cameroon, a study comparing traditional healers and medical professionals based on their personal approach and communication methods was conducted. At one facility, the interaction styles were compared between seven traditional healers and eight physicians. The traditional healers interacted differently with the patients, striving to find a common ground through communication. This flexible approach by traditional healers probably accounts for the high regard and respect for traditional healers in Cameroon. Socio-economically, patients of traditional healers were similar to patients of the physicians. This means that one's economic or social status does not determine the choice to use traditional or modern medicine. However, traditional healers differ in the following instances: they are found to be more "patient centered," concentrating not only on medical questions but also on daily aspects of life and the patient's personal thoughts and feelings. The "patient centered" approach to healthcare used by healers was identified by the patients as superior. Most patients reported that traditional healers inspired them to travel far distances and to pay high fees and costs associated with the healthcare (Labhardt et al., 2010). The result of such studies may help policy makers, programme managers, and healthcare workers to integrate "patient-centered" communication to modern medical treatment.

A study in Zambia that examined the role of traditional healers in treating individuals with epilepsy found that traditional healers apart from acquiring thorough histories of their patients, may refer patients to a hospital if the seizure seems serious or out of their control. However, it was also recognized that stronger collaborative relationship between medical professionals and traditional healers must be fostered in order to improve treatments (Baskind, 2005). Studies in various countries and cultures have demonstrated the importance of partnerships with traditional healers (Okpako, 2006; Lantum, 1977). Traditional healers interact with their patients on a personal and compassionate level, allowing the patient to feel psychologically at ease. However, the reality remains that traditional healing, by itself is usually not enough to cure a disease

(Baskind, 2005). Biomedical practitioners and traditional healers must communicate with one another and work together in order to treat patients in a way that is both scientifically effective and personally sensitive. This suggestion will not be achieved if the current antagonism between traditional healers and physicians is not open for discussion (Labhardt et al., 2010).

In SSA at least 80% of the people rely on traditional healers (Bannerman et al., 1983; Zubane, 2001; Fyhrquist, 2007). This is partly because there are fewer medical doctors and to worsen the situation, droves of medical personnel are migrating to the developed world for better working conditions and salaries at a time when the HIV/AIDS pandemic is inordinately taxing health systems and budgets. The large-scale emigration of physicians from SSA to high-income countries poses serious development challenges that greatly undermine efforts towards the achievement of the UN Millennium Development Goals (MDGs). In Africa, malaria accounts for more than a million deaths annually, with over 80% occurring in tropical Africa, where malaria remains a bane in under-five children (WHO, 2004). Although Africa has 11% of the global population, the continent has 24% of the global burden of disease, and only 3% of the world's health workers and commands less than 1% of global health expenditure (WHO, 2006: 1). Today the continent is faced with a double burden of communicable and non-communicable diseases (Muweh, 2011). According to the 2011 American Medical Association Physician Masterfile (AMA-PM), 10,819 physicians who were born or trained in 28 SSA countries are currently plying their trade in the United States of America (Tankwanchi et al., 2013). Shortages of medical staff, coupled with the migration of skilled health personnel and brain drain (Parker, 2009) have been rightly identified as some of the major impediments to achieving the health-related MDGs and the SDA. For example, Mozambique- one of the poorest countries in the world, has just 548 doctors for a population of more than 22 million. The WHO baseline estimate for achieving health-related MDGs is at least 23 health workers per 10,000 people—against an average of 13 in Africa. Chad has less than one doctor for every 20,000 people and just four hospital beds for every 10,000 patients. The country suffers most with one of the worst health-worker shortages in the world. Although many countries are scaling up and mitigating their healthcare staff shortages with community health workers, Chad has only 154 of these. The country requires 300 percent more health workers because of increased healthcare needs and a reduction in the medical workforce from HIV-related illness or death. Traditional medicine has thus remained an important component of the healthcare system in many African countries including Chad because of the acute shortage and constant emigration of healthcare personnel. This partly explains why an estimated 80–90% of the populations in African countries are dependent on traditional medicine for their primary healthcare needs (Hostettmann et al., 2000). For example in Sudan, traditional medicine plays a major role in healthcare. This is because access to hospitals and other medical facilities is limited and a high percentage of the population consists of nomads (Elegani et al., 2002). In Tanzania, over 60% of people seeking healthcare, see traditional healers as their first point of contact. In addition, there are far too few medical doctors compared with traditional healers. This increases the chances of people consulting traditional healers instead of medical doctors for therapy (Hedberg et al., 1982). Traditional medicine is important even in the big cities of Tanzania, such as Dar-es-Salaam (Swantz, 1974). The number of registered traditional healers in Tanzania has been estimated at about 30,000–60,000. This is in contrast to about 600 biomedical doctors (Mhame, 2000). It is estimated that about 27 million South Africans depend on traditional herbal medicines for their primary healthcare needs (Mander, 1998). In Nigeria traditional healing is well acknowledged and established as a viable profession (Kafaru, 1994). It has been noted that almost all plants seem to have some kind of application to traditional medicine (Babayi et al., 2004). Approximately 70–80% of Cameroon's population consult traditional healers for their primary healthcare needs (MINSANTE, 2002).

As a drawback, it is often argued that South Africa's traditional healers can be instrumental in the spread of HIV/AIDS. Their practices and procedures are sometimes likely to lead to the spread of the HIV (Helman, 2002). For example, the use of unsterilized instruments particularly razor blades on several patients can lead to the transmission of HIV. However, this "culture as harm argument" presupposes that traditional medicine is unchanging-which is false. Research has however, demonstrated that traditional healers are aware of STDs and HIV/AIDS prevention strategies from the logic of transmission and causation: limiting the number of sexual partners, wearing protective charms or tattoos, having "strong blood," using condoms to reduce the risk of "pollution," or undergoing a "traditional vaccination" consisting of introducing herbs in skin incisions (Green, 1992; Green et al., 1993; Nzima et al., 1996; Schoepf, 1992), as well as female and male circumcision. Some studies have reported that the spread of HIV/AIDS could be prevented by upholding traditional values regarding abstinence such as female circumcision, observation of sex taboos and strengthening the roles of women's societies such as Anankungwi in Malawi, which plays a strong role in counselling girls to observe local traditions pertaining to respect of elders and dressing (Bowa et al. ND, see also Orubuloye et al., 1994). In most cases, condoms have become acceptable to traditional healers, especially when they dovetail with their belief system. For instance, many African healers consider semen an important nutritional element for the nourishment of a growing foetus, for the maintenance of the mother's health and beauty, but their concern for family and cultural survival can supersede this belief and allow them to promote condom use (Green et al., 1993; Schoepf, 1992). Traditional medical practices are neither impermeable to change nor incompatible with modern rational science- both can be harnessed and the outcome will be democratic (see also Pemunta, 2011: xviii, Pemunta, 2010).

It is alleged that traditional healers treat most cases of STDs. Experts believe that STDs are major co-factors in the spread of HIV/AIDS. In developing countries where health infrastructure is poor, traditional healers are located in all villages and towns (Helman, 2002). Traditional healers are therefore seen as God sent messengers to Africa's "cash-strapped" health departments (WHO, 1990). Given the high respect traditional healers command as individuals, John Mbiti (1969: 166) referred to them as 'friends of the community' because of the significant role they play in relieving pain and restoring the life and health of members of their different communities. One of the key questions that this study attempts to answer is: How can we create a working relationship between traditional healthcare givers and conventional medicine with the aim of making primary healthcare accessible for all people?

Despite their knowledge and popularity, traditional healers get little attention from the government and receive too little as compensation for their services compared to conventional medical experts. True collaboration, however, requires a measure of respect for indigenous medicine and African culture. It also requires the shedding of stereotypes of African traditional healers. There is need to search for common ground between modern medicine and traditional medicine. Building upon such a common approach, combining efforts with healers to combat HIV/AIDS and promote public health, makes good sense (UNAIDS, 2006; Mngqundaniso and Peltzer, 2008).

In addition to the healthcare crisis engendered by the HIV/AIDS pandemic, another factor militating in favour of traditional medicine is the changing nature of disease. The 20th century has witnessed a tremendous change in pattern of disease. Previously, many people suffered from acute conditions like pneumonia, malaria, syphilis, gonorrhea among others and died relatively earlier. Today, and despite technological revolution people suffer from long-term incurable and chronic degenerative health conditions including HIV/AIDS and cancer- requiring frequent encounters with healthcare practitioners. These practitioners have simply been transformed into caregivers. Despite biomedicine's groundbreaking accomplishments, certain aspects of human suffering call for more than technical skills. "Those living under the shadow of chronic degenerative diseases, or the so-called 'diseases of civilization' know that they can only be propped up for so long with more drugs and more procedures"

(Di Stefano, 2006: 163). Biomedical physicians do not cure but rather, provide care to their patients. This new trend exposes a wide range of psychological and sociological issues that health professionals need to understand if they are to effectively deliver healthcare that meets the needs of communities (Gilbert et al., 2002). As one critique poignantly maintains, this era of scientific progress epitomized by biomedicine has been characterized by "more litigation, dissatisfaction and complaints. Medicine has lost focus on the person and their experience of illness. It responds inadequately to patient's need to find meaning" (Hemmings, 2005: 92). This is due to overreliance on "technical procedures and tests," focus on "technological fixes rather than psychological interventions" (Hemmings, 2005: 92; Gilbert et al., 2002).

Additionally, the change in patterns of disease is directly related to a change in the concept of disease causation. The aetiology of disease causation nowadays has shifted from the monocausal model (often referred to as the germ theory) to a multi-causal approach. While the significance of biomedicine is acknowledged, it should not imply the negation of other systems of healing. Healing remains a multidimensional phenomenon that needs to be tackled from myriad different directions. The wide breadth of traditional medicine as a form of TCAM testifies to this reality. According to the multicausal approach, many of the diseases people suffer from today are caused by a complex interaction between a multiplicity of factors. Biological factors cannot be excluded from and are entangled with psychological, social, cultural and political factors (Hemmings, 2005: 93). The reality of multicausality imposes the need for the biomedical mindset to part with reductionist philosophies, fixed patterns of treatment based upon pharmaceutical and surgical interventions or what we might call the biological reductionism of biomedicine. In the Western world, biomedical practitioners are increasingly recommending acupuncture, spinal manipulation, herbal medicines, psychosomatic approaches comprised of meditation and deep relaxation (Di Stefano, 2006).

In his study of folk theories of malaria, Pemunta (2013) maintains that a complex web of cultural, poor socio-economic conditions and environmental factors account for the prevalence of malaria in Bali Nyonga. He outlines the multiple notions of malaria causation with dirty environment (80.76%) and the mosquito (76.92%) as the leading causes. Other causes are poor hygiene (46.15%), impure sources of portable water (23.08%), malnutrition (15.38%), witchcraft (11.54%), human-vector contact (34.61%), and palm wine drinking (32.69%). The study revealed that any effective management of malaria must be based on an understanding of traditional cultural views and insights concerning the cause, spread and treatment of the disease, as well as gender roles within a given community since women bear a greater burden of the disease than men. His study further underscores the need to incorporate folk theories of disease causation, gender and malaria issues into malaria control strategies in order to improve their coverage and effectiveness in different contexts. Understanding the complex web of factors involved in the disease process therefore requires comprehensive care, which integrates the patient's physical, psychological and social well-being. Since any single health profession cannot provide this kind of care, this call for a multidisciplinary approach based on teamwork. In simple language, the different healthcare providers contribute differently towards the well-being of the patient. It is only a pity that without such interaction and understanding of the various disciplines involved in healthcare, success may be elusive. This calls for a multidisciplinary perspective to healthcare.

Apart from urbanization and intercultural contact, the HIV/AIDS scourge and the collapse of the economy in most African countries that ushered in the structural adjustment programme (SAP) have greatly contributed to the recourse to traditional medicine and healers in Africa. Although South Africa has never been under an IMF/World Bank imposed SAP, under the apartheid regime, the vast majority of people had limited or non-existent healthcare until the 1990s. Since then, South Africa's healthcare system has made great strides under majority rule, especially in its efforts to reach underserved communities. Despite efforts deployed by the government to bring healthcare closer to formerly isolated communities, much remains to be done especially in the Eastern Cape Province where our research was conducted. In some cases, the effort to bring healthcare closer to the local population is hindered by poor road infrastructure thereby leaving the local population with only one choice- to access traditional medicine. Today, South Africa has emerged as a critical battleground for the HIV/AIDS epidemic. However, acute socio-economic inequalities in access to healthcare still abound. In 2005, the South African government introduced a voluntary, subsidized health insurance scheme for civil servants. Notwithstanding the availability of a non-contributory option within the insurance scheme and access to privately-provided primary care, a considerable portion of socioeconomically vulnerable groups remained uninsured (57.7% of the lowest salary category). Noninsurance was highest among men, black African or coloured ethnic groups, less educated and lower income employees, and those living in informal-housing. The relatively poor uptake of the contributory and non-contributory insurance options was mostly attributed to insufficient information, perceived administrative challenges of taking up membership, and payment costs (Govender et al., 2013). The healthcare crisis in South Africa is compounded by the fact that most people have no healthcare insurance. Although depending on income, most services are free, and where people do pay, it is highly subsidized, having effective access is impeded by lack of financial resources, income inequalities, the persistence of colonial and apartheid era inequalities between urban and rural areas, limited availability of services, lack of transportation, understaffing and poor infrastructure.

There is economic slowdown and a high rate of unemployment. With slow economic growth, the South African economy is not generating sufficient jobs. In the third quarter of 2017, the unemployment rate was 27.7 percent. As employers seek skilled workers, youth and unskilled workers endure the most of unemployment. The youth unemployment rate was 38, 6 percent. Poverty rates peaked between 2011 and 2015 (World Bank, 2018: xi). Access to basic public services including health and education is positively correlated with income, with access lowest among the poorest segments of the population. The poor tend to live in overcrowded housing conditions (World Bank, 2018). Living in overcrowded conditions, as studies (World Bank, 2018; Leventhal and Newman, 2010; Lund et al., 2010) have shown has been associated with worsening health and education outcomes. In South Africa, access to health and assets is skewed across income groups. The rich have better access to hospital-based biomedical healthcare than the poor do. For the poorest decile of the South African population in 2015 "33.8 percent lived at least 20 kilometers away from a hospital, 27 percent points higher than the proportion among the richest decile. Consistent with this, poor individuals lived farther way from a hospital compared to the non-poor" (World Bank, 2015: 23). In South Africa, where there is the persistence of past inequalities between urban and rural areas, there is marked inequities between health outcomes in more urbanised and rural provinces such as the Eastern Cape. South Africa's political and economic history has profoundly affected the country's health outcomes and current health policies. This situation has resulted from a history of racial and gender discrimination, the migrant labour system, and huge income inequalities (Schellack et al., 2011: 559). The reasons for this dismal situation include inadequate efforts to address social determinants of disease such as the levels of deprivation (poverty) in rural areas. Furthermore, rural communities experience significant barriers to accessing health care. This includes financial barriers, inadequate transport, and distance to the nearest facility as well as the limited availability of services. Shortfalls in human resources for health (understaffing) and the poor state of infrastructure in many rural facilities further entrench existing inequities (Gaedeim and Versteeg, 2011; Schellack et al., 2011). An analyses conducted using geographical information system (GIS) shows that in the eastern part of the country as well as in urban areas, there is a low coverage in terms of the number of health facilities by the total population per

10 000 population at the municipal level. This is the case although there are more health facilities in urban areas where the total population is also much higher due to migration (Mokhele et al., 2012; Schellack et al., 2011).

Faced with the scourge of HIV/AIDS, public health officials throughout the developing world were forced to reconsider their attitude of suspicion, mistrust and misgivings towards traditional medicine since they came to the realization that it might be instrumental in preventing the spread of the virus, as well as caring for the sick, especially in rural areas where there is an acute shortage of conventional medical facilities and practitioners. The possibility was that medicinal plants might actually hold the key to fighting the virus. In vitro studies of the akaloid michellamine B, isolated from the indigenous Cameroonian plant *Ancistrocladus* Korupensis showed that the compound is active against two strains of HIV (Hillenbrand, 2006: 3). Further studies aimed at its detoxification have since been suspended (Chibale et al., 2012). The AIDS crisis actually brought traditional medicine to prominence in Africa as some governments for political and economic reasons- the fear of tarnishing their country's image and scaring off tourists initially refused the existence of the pandemic (Ajaga, 1999). Traditional healers took advantage of the government's ambivalence and put up billboards in the urban landscape carrying among others, pictures of pale and wasting, scary-looking, infected individuals. Variously nicknamed euphemistically as "slow poison," "maladie d'amour" and associated to malevolent spirits, these billboards claimed that they had a ready cure for the "slim disease," "seven plus one," "nine minus one." Writing on Cameroon, Pemunta (1999) concedes that one of these billboards carried the epithet "Pharmacie qui "traitent" les maladies depassant la medecine moderne" (Pharmacy which treats diseases that are above modern medicine) referring among others, to HIV/AIDS. Given their record of accomplishment in the treatment of venereal diseases, biomedicine's lack of an immediate response to the scourge and the collapse of the health care system in the wake of the SAP imposed by the Bretton wood institutions on many African countries, traditional healers enjoyed a boom.

By outlawing alternative medical practices, colonialism made biomedicine the only formally accepted medical system in most parts of Africa (Mcfarlane, 2015; WHO, 1990). This socio-political configuration bestowed on biomedicine a lot of power, prestige and leverage. All traditional medical practices were categorically condemned as witchcraft, fake or sorcery and then banned (WHO, 1990). The practice of traditional medicine however survived the onslaught of colonialism in secret in many African countries including South Africa partly because of its holistic health vision. Some scholars maintain that Africans still favour traditional medicine because of economic reasons(Gilbert et al., 2005). They turn to traditional medicine because they cannot afford the high cost associated with biomedicine (Lantum, 1978: 78).

Millions of dollars in development aid have been spent on different public health programmes in the Global South- including through initiative to eradicate malaria and polio. Many lives could have been saved had western donors and policy makers shown a little more faith in Africa's traditional ways. At the joint conference of the Economic Commission for Africa (ECA/UN) and the Organization of African Unity (OAU) held in 1984 in Arusha, Tanzania that brought together experts to address the failure of Africa to produce economic and social prosperity after two decades of massive foreign assistance, the neglect of culture as the bedrock of development was recognized. The ECA and OAU acknowledged the marginalization of the beneficiaries of the development process. The final document however failed to acknowledge that the social sciences had also been left out of the process (Nkwi, 2006). In a series of scholarly writings, Michael Cernea (1985) also indicates the importance of culture and people-centered approaches in his writings. Of course, the failure to achieve prosperity in Africa was not only the result of the marginalization of the social sciences in the development process; corruption and ethnic violence both had significant roles to play (Nkwi, 2006). There is need for a policy reformulation as well as re-orientation. The implementation of medical pluralism and the inclusion of indigenous practices into modern knowledge is important (UNESCO, 1994; UNAIDS, 2006: 5). As UNAIDS rightly maintains, differences in philosophies, worldviews, values, concepts and methods are bridgeable. In other words, we need to "bridge the language and value divide between modern western and African traditional medicine, because people make use of both systems" (UNAIDS, 2006: 7). Both local/traditional/indigenous knowledge and scientific knowledge are not antithetical to each other. Indigenous knowledge Lorraine Brookes maintains, encompasses:

> ...facts, concepts, theories about the characteristics which describe the objects, events, behaviours and interconnections that comprise both the animate and inanimate environments of Indigenous peoples. The various types of information and concepts that define an individual's knowledge have been developed through that person's observations of, experiences with, and explanations about the physical environment and living resources that characterise the territory in which they live. The content and extent of knowledge varies from individual to individual and there can be a specialisation in expertise. The knowledge is commonly shared between individuals, which encourages an exchange and critique of both

facts and ideas at any one point in time; and it is transferred from one generation to the next through the oral tradition thus enabling the knowledge base of Indigenous societies to be transmitted and expanded over time ... Even though Indigenous knowledge is not quantitative in nature, it does not mean that it is not precise. In fact, the need to be precise is one of the primary identifying elements of this knowledge base. (Brooke, 1993, 36–37)

Brookes' (1993) reference to indigenous knowledge here is about the sharing of power. It is a demand that "the power base must be shared" (p. 18). Indigenous knowledge in an institutional context implies local participation in decision-making about the mitigation of the impact of climate change to maintain man-nature relationship that are often disrupted by modern environmental management mechanisms such as fortress conservation. We acknowledge the fact that not all indigenous knowledge is the same nor comes out of comparable histories. Fortress conservation generally displaces and disconnect people from the landcapes in which knowledge finds a stabilizing base or is anchored (see Pemunta, 2018).

Local/traditional/indigenous knowledge does not presuppose that it relates to the past. Every system of knowledge is subject to evolution, is dynamic, interacts with other systems of knowledge and therefore can grapple with contemporary human problems including environmental, social and cultural problems (see Stevenson, 1996: 279; Abele, 1997; Brooke, 1993). Both local/traditional and scientific knowledge share an identical purpose: "[they] are intellectual processes or constructions that have evolved for societies to understand the universe" (Cardova, 1997: 32). Hollenberg and Muzzin (2010: 53) have rightly warned against the marginalization of alternative health care practices, beliefs and worldviews that should rather be perceived as "particular sciences of their own" that do not need alteration or proven to foreign groups using foreign, "standardized" measurements, because each system is the outcome of unique histories, strengths and weaknesses.' In other words, there is a disjuncture between the quantification, objectification and measurement of biological data that is considered "more real and clinically significant," but "not considered to be linked to psychosocial data" (Hemmings, 2005: 92).

Traditional medicines/medicinal plants have been shown to be relevant for biomedical research, particularly research for the development of new drugs. This shows the appropriation of traditional knowledge systems for the production of drugs, which leads to the erasure, devaluation, and contortion of African traditional knowledge systems by biomedical hegemony (see King, 2002; Arnold, 1988). Higher plants produce hundreds to thousands of diverse chemical compounds with different biological activities, and the antimicrobial compounds produced by plants are active against plant and human pathogenic microorganisms (Amenu, 2014: 18). According to the WHO plant extracts or their active constituents are used as folk medicine in traditional therapies of 80% of the world drugs are of natural product origin (Kirbag et al., 2009).

There are between 250,000 and 500,000 plant species on the surface of the earth. Only up to 10% of these species have been studied chemically and pharmacologically for their medicinal properties (Verpoorte, 2000). To date only 1% of the tropical flora species on the earth's surface have been studied for their pharmaceutical potential (Gurib-Fakim, 2006). Drugs derived from plant materials have been and are still important sources of medicines. It has been noted that 50% of medical prescriptions in Europe and the United States of America (USA) are either natural products or natural product derivatives (Newman et al., 2003). An estimated 50 different drugs have come from tropical plants (Gurib-Fakim, 2006). Plants, which have continued to be the main components of traditional medicine, are vital sources of substances used for the production of drugs prescribed in hospitals (Newman et al., 2003). People have used plants for centuries and vast information on the medicinal uses of plants has been accumulated especially in the tropical parts of the world. The use of plants for the production of drugs is usually without the recognition of intellectual property rights and constitutes part of the omnipresent processes employed in the erasure, subjugation and distortion of traditional knowledge systems by the biomedical hegemonic alliance (King, 2002; Arnold, 1988).

In Kwa-Mhlanga, South Africa, an African healer has integrated African and modern medicine. He has embraced the concept of medical pluralism by combining traditional therapeutic methods with homeopathy, iridology, and other western healing methods, as well as traditional Asian medicine in his 48-bed hospital (Helwig, 2010; Shiza and Charema, 2012). Shiza and Charema (2012: 59) note that such a holistic approach to health and wellness as practiced in South Africa encompasses the cohabitation of spiritual healing, mental, physical and social healing. They further concede that biomedicine has been criticized for overlooking the relationship of the social and spiritual being to the body as well as the effect of the former on the latter.

The greatest obstacle to the integration of both systems of health care is that of control and regulation. Both systems are based on contrasting philosophies, values and practices. Attempts to regulate traditional healing practices using the standards and principles of biomedicine "is a fundamental flaw in the existing framework" and will fail to achieve its intended goals. According to a key stakeholder, the Secretary General of the National Council of Traditional Healers and Herbalists Association (NACOTHA), the present model of integration being pursued smacks of an attempt to colonize traditional healers by streamlining "their practices under the fold of western medicine":

> .... mixed cultural issues with religion. Cultural issues should not be mixed with religion or modern science. People should leave traditional medicine practitioners to explain these issues. For example, not everyone can explain things like 'ejjembe' or 'emizimu'. While these things are considered horrible, they are not necessarily bad as they are portrayed

This calls for the need for a culturally appropriate institutional and legal framework, without which it will be difficult to regulate traditional medical practices from a biomedical perspective since most biomedical actors are skeptical and cynical about traditional healing practices and their practitioners (Mutabazi, 2008: 206). Closely related to the foregoing is the perceived power differential after integration. Traditional medicine practitioners will remain subjected to the control of the dominant biomedical health care system. The agenda, Morsy, cited in Kagwanja (1997) is that of integrating traditional healers into the political, economic arena and cultural hegemony of biomedicine. Real integration will call for close consultation with traditional healers that will allow them define the type of partnership they are interested in, but will also entail formalization and training.

In the face of this deadlock regarding the form of integration that is characterized by multiple and competing discourses between: 'formalisation,' 'collaboration' and 'co-habitation and co-existence,' Mutabazi (2008) has recommended the need to 'modernize' traditional medicine through a multipronged process comprising of:

1. Autonomy: The granting of autonomy to traditional practitioners so as to achieve the goal of "modernization" given the weak link between biomedicine and traditional therapy globally and in Africa. Modernization is "...a desire to reinforce the position of traditional medical practitioners by granting them autonomy to develop their own knowledge systems, practices, capacities and capabilities through training, documentation, regulation, peer evaluation and monitoring systems, in the light of the diversity and unique circumstances that most practitioners find themselves in" (Mutabazi, 2008: 211). This vision has resonances with self-reliant development. According to him, traditional healers should be accorded the latitude to organize and develop themselves, to grow as an independent system of healing based on unique and culturally relevant practice. They must show an interest in collaboration. Modernization will entail an improvement in other sectors of the economy given the

entanglement of healthcare with other sectors. Such a model, he concedes, will set aside dangerous perceptions of healers "as backward, conservative, and unscientific" (p. 212). It will recognize healers as autonomous agents with significant and unique contributions to national development goals. It will further give them an agency: "evolve local solutions for local problems without much outside interference and programming-to give the practitioners a voice" (p. 213). Additionally, modernization will imply the indigenization of traditional medicine by taking the norms and tenets of society as a regulatory framework. It will further ensure (1) peer monitoring (2) peer evaluation (3) documentation of formal and indigenous training (4) training and regulation.

The outcome will be to have an integrated national movement of traditional healers, not the multiplicity of fragmentary associations found in several African countries today. Such a united front will increase the bargaining power of traditional healers and improve their healthcare practices through systematization, and most importantly, give practitioners the leverage to "confront issues of regulation and enforcement of the regulations that have proved to be a nightmare for public health officials" (p. 215). This will lead to advantages including accountability and self-regulation. "Granting them autonomy is like giving them a stick to police and discipline themselves, which is opposed to the existing model of partnership where the public officials, through their own lens, are trying to govern traditional medicine and practice." This will be contrary to "the past when public officials have always emasculated the sector and demeaned it, regardless of the fact that it plays a crucial role in health care delivery" (Mubatazi, 2008: 216). In South Africa, the 'Traditional Health Practitioner's Bill 2007' maintains that a person who 'diagnosis, treats, or offers to treat, or prescribes treatment or any cure for cancer, HIV/AIDS or such other terminal diseases as may be described, shall be guilty of an offence' (Richter, 2003). This raises the issue as to whether biomedicine holds the key to these diseases, when traditional therapies have proven far more useful and effective in their management and research is currently underway to biomedicalize various medicinal therapies for these ailments.

2. Training: Traditional healers in different communities should be trained given the diversity of traditional medical practices within any given country and to ensure continuity as most healers are increasingly ageing and passing away without passing over their knowledge to a new crop of young healers. Most importantly, training will create "a critical mass of

traditional medicine practitioners that can meaningfully engage with government and other actors in the health sector." Training traditional practitioners will also lead to the identification of diseases that herbal medicines can cure "so as to avoid making traditional medicine appear to be a panacea for all illnesses" (Mubatazi, 2008: 217). Such an initiative will further lead to the development of knowledge and practices around these illnesses and to maximize the resulting comparative advantages in their management.

3. Documentation will ensure the preservation of knowledge and practices for posterity as well as create a data set on indigenous knowledge (IK) systems. This already obtains in countries such as India and China. To ensure effective documentation, there will be the need to offer basic penmanship skills of writing and numeracy to practitioners so that they can develop and systematize IK systems.

4. Peer evaluation, monitoring and regulation: A salient dimension of 'modernization' is to ensure that standards are maintained, and that oversight is provided to traditional medical practices by the healers themselves. Stewardship will specifically entail the exertion of influence on each other, the shaping of individual behaviour as well as the curbing of private desires that are antithetical to the practice of traditional medicine. So far, stewardship has been biased towards the biomedical system as if it is "the be-all and end-all of health care." Compliance could be ensured through "blacklisting, ostracism, and ridicule through songs." Although these social control mechanisms will not turn an individual into an enemy of the people, they could also pose a threat to his/her citizenship and will in all likelihood, be adhered to. (Ibid.:219).

One other milestone towards the regulation of traditional healing practices in South Africa was the promulgation of the South African Traditional Health Practitioners Act 22 of 2007 and its gradual implementation by the DoH. This far, "An Interim Traditional Health Practitioners Council and a dedicated DoH deputy director have been appointed, the appointment of a registrar is being finalised" (de Roubaix, 2016: 160). A nationwide tour to introduce the Act and explain its implications on the practice of traditional healing to groups of traditional health practitioners is underway. In tandem with the Act, there has been the appointment of an Interim Traditional Health Practitioners Council of South Africa with the aim of advancing traditional medicine as a partner that is capable of responding to the needs of South African society. The Act will also ensure the registration of traditional practitioners as a prerequisite for practice (de Roubaix, 2016).

The Act recognizes four groups of traditional health practitioners—diviners, herbalists, traditional birth attendants, and traditional surgeons (de Roubaix, 2016; Flint and Payne, 2013).

The Act has however; come under serious criticism for being vague on training and certification requirements, for the non-scientific approach of traditional medicine to disease, research and treatment that it effectively legitimizes (de Roubaix, 2016). Traditional healing is characterized by divergence in practices, treatments and training. For instance, initiation into traditional medicine (apprenticeship) differs from one healer to the other as well as the source of the healer's powers (ancestors, medium, close relatives, apprenticeship from a master healer). This divergence in approach, treatment and apprenticeship poses an obstacle to the regulation of traditional healing practices (Mcfarlane, 2015; Street, 2016; de Roubaix, 2016).

This 'modernization' paradigm of traditional medicine however suffers from certain shortcomings. The first is the problem of control over an informal sector that might eventually develop into a 'modernized' traditional sector. Those actors who might not wish to be compelled by a moral code of responsibility to fellow practitioners and their clientele might withdraw to the underworld where they might continue practicing or indulging in harmful traditional practices. The second problem is that of linking the sector with other stakeholders in healthcare without necessarily compromising the autonomy and eroding gains that might have been acquired this far. However, the South African government and the leadership of the traditional medicine association might fruitfully handle the question of regulation.

Despite the above-mentioned obstacles to the integration of both traditional and modern medicine, South African institutions have been involved in transnational collaborative research initiatives on the clinical trials of the efficacy and safety of traditional medicines. One of such collaborative initiative brings together the South African Herbal Science and Medicine Institute (SAHSMI) based at the University of the Western Cape in Cape Town, and the host of the famous International Centre on Indigenous Phototherapy Studies (TICIPS), a global movement on indigenous medicine funded by the National Centre for Complementary and Alternative Medicine (NCCAM) of the Washington based National Institutes of Health (NIH). Other partners include the School of Medicine at the University of Missouri in the US, the Nelson Mandela Medical School of the University of KwaZuluNatal in Durban, South Africa, the Institute for Infectious Diseases and Molecular Medicine (IIDMM) of the University of Cape Town, the Medical Research Council (MRC) of South Africa. They are engaged in conducting clinical trials of herbal plants and were engaged in what could be considered the first randomized double-blind, placebo-controlled trial of *sutherlandia* in healthy adults in South Africa (Oloyede, 2010: 82) using the lenses of biomedicine.

6.5 Conclusion

This study argues that collaboration between traditional healers and modern health practitioners will improve healthcare in South Africa in particular and Africa in general. The incorporation of indigenous knowledge into healthcare policy could create effective intervention and improve service delivery. The debate for and against the integration of traditional and biomedicine is a misplaced one. Patients and members of their therapy seeking group often resort to "syncretic auto-medication" (Pemunta et al, 2020) to maximize the prospects of regaining good health and well-being. Knowledge is always co-produced as knowledge systems interact with, and influence each other. The reductionism implicit in the devaluation of other forms of healing knowledge and practices as TCAM makes biomedicine a standard for reference. However, the integration of traditional and modern medicine in Cuba shows the possibilities for bringing together traditional and modern medicine to ensure the health and well-being of people, and not for the benefit of industry and the market (Fournier, 2013: 55). There is the need to move away from the naturalization of biomedicine as evident in World Bank (2004: 3) statements such as:

> At all levels, modern medicine is an evolving medicine that is open to knowledge and progress through continuous research…. In contrast to this dynamic Cartesian medicine(biomedicine), one must admit that from its nature, traditional medicine does not aim at progress. It is not open to innovation, renewal and the progressive modification of its principles, means, and methods. Tradition keeps it static and inward looking and subjected to the passivity of empiricism set rigidly by the elders and followed faithfully by apprentices.

Traditional healing is not static. It is not "a body of knowledge and practices sealed in time" (Flint, 2016: 4326). Engagement with healers from other parts of the African continent and beyond have partly led to changes in the practice of traditional medicine (Ibid.). Tradition remains contested and opened to innovation, and is not static. Assumptions such as the one in the above-mentioned statement that makes biomedicine the alpha and omega of medicine- or better still, the only "real scientific medicine" are troublesome and suggests that the discourse of integrating traditional knowledge systems into biomedicine is a mechanism for the emasculation of the former healthcare system. To continue perpetuating the dominance of biomedicine, traditional knowledge systems and cosmologies are devalued, reduced to the realm of magic or the supernatural and then, later co-opted and packaged in the name of new drug development (see also, Fournier, 2013: 37).

CHAPTER 7

"African Diseases" and the Epistemology of South African Healers' Knowledge

7.1 Introduction

The medical landscape in South Africa is dominated by three distinct forms of treatment—standard Western European medicine ('allopathy and biomedicine') and two forms of complementary and alternative medicine—Indian traditional medicine and African traditional medicine. The taking of control and the creation of democracy led to the re-institutionalization of many ancient practices in a bid to "sustain…culture and beliefs, while accepting the effects of postcolonialism" (Mcfarlane, 2015: 61). Attempts to revalorize African cultural beliefs and practices as well as problems including the inequalities of the apartheid system and the ravaging HIV/AIDS crises led to an intractable debate on the relevance of traditional medicine as well as the need for its integration into the modern biomedical healthcare system in South African society. This was despite differences in approaches to the diagnosis and treatment of disease between both systems of healthcare (see chapter 6).

> The growing utilization of complementary medicine throughout the Western World points to a need to address more deeply such issues as the foundations of human nature, the adequacy of reductionist epistemologies and treatment methods, and the role and influence of mind in both health and disease. (Di Stefano, 2006: 125)
>
> On the one hand, health care is belief-sensitive. The African belief system and the western belief system, stand divided in their interpretation of illness and health. Therefore the South African Government bears the responsibility of accommodating the health care needs of all South Africans in a non-biased manner. This includes those individuals who opt for the traditional healing system as their choice of health care. (Summerton, 2006: 16–17)

The above quotations underscore the paradigmatic gulf between the epistemological basis of traditional and modern medicine as epitomized by differences in beliefs about illness and disease causation as well as the concept of good health. African traditional medicine is based on the concept of maintaining equilibrium in the physical, social, economic, political and psychological dimensions of human existence. On the other hand, biomedicine with its bacteriological focus is about restoring physical health. The belief-sensitive nature of healthcare calls for the need to go beyond the reductionism of biomedicine as encapsulated in the mind-body dichotomy in order to provide integrative healthcare services that meet the social and cultural needs of clients instead of perpetuating biomedical hegemony that favours biomedicine against traditional healing knowledge systems and practices in South Africa.

This chapter provides a broad overview of the African concept of health ("African diseases") as well as a typology of various categories of healers and their specific expertise. This is despite overlap in the roles of these healers. They are often lumped together and described as "witch doctors" thereby giving traditional healing practices and their practitioners a bad name as well as misrepresenting all of them as doing "evil" or killing, rather than healing patients (Bishop, 2012). The chapter further examines the prospects for integrating traditional medicine into the mainstream biomedical healthcare system in South Africa.

7.2 The African Concept of Health

African traditional medicine involves both the body and the mind. This is a translation as well as an instantiation of the African concept of health, which encapsulates physical, psychological, social and economic well-being. The ultimate background of African traditional medicine points to the causes of illnesses. These causes are usually believed to be from outside influences (personalistic agents). The main aim of diagnosis through African indigenous means is therefore to know who or what could have caused the illness episode (Neuwinger, 2000). Contrary to biomedicine which is associated with diseases of the physical body, and based on the principles of [a monolithic]science and technology[even when both are clearly not monolithic], knowledge and clinical analysis, African traditional therapy does not lay emphasis on the disease per se, but rather on the causative agent-evil spirit: "Being ill is connected not only to environmental factors but societal and spiritual influences. Hence, the healing process does not target the disease, but it is applied holistically [as] a community responsibility. Community and social solidarity are the foundations of sustainable social networks and social support provision and coping strategies" (Charema and Shizha, 2008: 60) required in the healing process. For example, the Yoruba people in Nigeria have three explanations for the cause of illness and misfortune: the natural (physical cause), the preternatural (witchcraft, sorcery as causes) and the supernatural (various spirits as causes) (Prince, 1964). These causes of illnesses are shared by many other people in Africa, such as the Zaramo in Dar-es-Salaam (Swantz, 1974). Thus, the physical cause of the disease is treated with herbs, the preternatural cause with magical means and the supernatural cause with ritual sacrifices, offerings or exorcism (Swantz, 1974).

Both natural and supernatural forces can cause illness in the African context (Ngubane, 1977). Pemunta (2013) for instance found out that although malaria among the Bali Nyonga of Northwest Cameroon is believed to be caused, among other factors by the anopheles mosquito, healers sometimes have to begin by treating the supernatural causes before they can restore the patient to good health after a serious attack of malaria. This shows the entanglement of naturalistic and personalistic concepts of disease causation, as well as what Weiss (1988) refers to as the intertwinement of "magic and nature." Once a traditional healer with special skills has identified the cause of the illness, the natural causes are treated in a non-magical and non-religious manner while the supernatural causes are treated with magical power. Illnesses have been classified as "personalistic" or "naturalistic." The former category includes illnesses which are presumed to be caused by an external super-natural agent, whereas, the latter includes illnesses that are supposed to be caused by nature (Foster, 1976; see also Foster and Anderson, 1978). Naturalistic illnesses are likely to be first treated with the use of local pharmacopoeia, especially if the sickness is not perceived as a severe threat. This classification acknowledges the coexistence of empirical and magical/supernatural aspects of indigenous medical cultures (Waldstein and Adams, 2006).

Nevertheless this system of classification forces a dichotomy that does not faithfully represent the overlap between "magic" and "nature" that is present in many indigenous cultures (Weiss, 1998). Weiss suggests placing illness aetiologies within a continuum with illnesses with aetiologies that are clearly personalistic or naturalistic at either end (Weiss, 1998). Later Arthur Kleinman (1980) distinguished three different sectors within healthcare systems: popular, folk and professional. The popular sector includes the self-medication of laypeople or the use of social networks to choose a treatment while the folk sector refers to shamans or traditional healers. The professional sector involves training in medical schools. Both Kleinman's and Foster's classifications are useful in permitting researchers to define more precisely which of these areas is studied (Waldstein and Adams, 2006). In the last decade, the focus of research on indigenous medical culture has broadened, and some scholars have suggested that in many cases the naturalistic components of medical cultures had been underestimated and that strong evidence exists for empirical knowledge in many indigenous cultures (Brett, 1994; Berlin and Berlin, 1996; Waldstein and Adams, 2006). Although Luo aetiology has been described as personalistic (Abe, 1981; OchallaAyayo, 1976; Odhalo, 1962; cf. Prince et al., 2001: 218), such a system of classification ignores the fact that most illnesses are either self-medicated or treated within the family, if at all. Interestingly, people only begin to look for deeper causes or seek professional advice when the condition has become serious (Prince et al., 2001: 218).

The most significant duty of the traditional healer nowadays is to treat "African diseases"- *ukugula kwabantu / izifo zabantu* (Ngubane, 1977: 15). It is believed that these diseases affect only the African people and cannot be cured by physicians. Lamla (1981: 29–37) has given a long list of these diseases among the Southern Nguni people. He discussed conditions and occasions of "African diseases" (also known in isixhosa as "isifozabantu") and how attempts are often made to cure such diseases. African diseases have been classified into categories based on the presumed cause of the disease (Donda, 1997: 21):

- Diseases caused by omen like *Amafufunyane*. This is a disease that affects girls and is believed to be caused by an omen thrown by a sorcerer "isizwe."
- Diseases caused by animals which kick a family member to death. An example of such a disease is *impundulu* (lightening bird). The causative agent is believed to be an invisible bird which is often responsible for many deaths in certain Nguni communities. While implementing field research, we personally attended the funeral of a young boy who was believed to have been attacked by *impundulu* in Sibangweni Location about 7 km away from Umtata, N2 on the way to Durban. Many rituals characterized the funeral. The presiding medicine men called on the ancestors to punish whosoever was responsible for the mishap. The corpse was buried in the bush where the boy died. Outsiders were not allowed to see the corpse because to the family, the wicked ones had taken their son and what they had in front of them as a corpse was fake. Asked why the body was buried in the bush, a local healer said because they never wanted to carry the ill luck from the bush and bring home. To them bringing the corpse home could pollute (Douglas, 1966) more members of the family and they will suffer the same fate.
- Diseases caused by dangerous spells placed on pathways to harm people. This may include illnesses like *Umeqo* and *ibekelo*. People suffering from such diseases develop swollen legs because they have crossed a spell. If they are not cured in time, they often die. *Ibekelo* and *umeqo* are also common in Cameroon among the Bassa people of the Littoral region who refer to it as *mmsousong*. The Bayangi people of the South West Region of Cameroon call it *nnemnor*. Under no circumstances will people suspected of *nnemnor* be taken to modern health units for therapy.

- Diseases caused by a mystical force which creates suffering (*isimnyama*) of any kind such as poverty, misfortune (*ilishwa*), repulsivesnes (*isimnyama*). In such a situation, an individual will be hated by others for no apparent reason.
- Diseases caused by animistic force (*intwaso*) which makes a person to behave as if he or she is mad. The patient is usually believed to be possessed by a bad spirit. This bad spirit causes the person to behave in an abnormal way that is often termed as madness. Among the Bayangi people this is called "barrem."

The traditional healer diagnoses and treats the psychological basis of the illness before prescribing medicines to treat the symptoms. Most healers believe that the body requires treatment with several different plants. It is this combination which produces a healing effect, either through complementary benefits or synergy and potentiation (Neuwinger, 2000). Many African traditional health recipes consist of several plants, or different parts of the same plant since different plant parts are often believed to cause different effects. The magical strength of a healing plant is often introduced into the therapy. Most often, the traditional healer uses herbs according to their analogy and morphological similarities to the ailment being treated. For instance, plants containing red juice are used for everything connected to blood, menstruation problems and bleeding (Neuwinger, 2000). Similarly, Charema and Shizha (2008: 61) maintain that: "Illness is believed to be caused by lack of balance between the patient and his social environment" and that this disequilibrium "determines the choice of the healing process and the herbs that are valued as much as their symbolic and spiritual significance as for their medicinal effect." For example, the colours: white, black, and red are considered especially symbolic or magical (Peltzer, 1999; Ndulo et al., 2001). Seeds, leaves, and twigs bearing these colours are deemed to possess special properties. In addition to plants, traditional African healers may employ charms, incantations, and the casting of spells. In many indigenous African traditional cultures, illness/sickness is thought to be caused by psychological conflicts or disturbed social relations that create a disequilibrium expressed in the form of physical or mental problems (Kleinman et al., 1978). Treatment begins with the identification of the agent (witch and type of witchcraft) responsible. In cases of insanity or conditions suspected to be caused by bewitchment, patients are less likely to be referred to hospital. The cause may be attributed to the vengeance of spirit, gods and breach of taboos, failure to observe taboos, defying parent's orders, turning of back on customs, failure to attend funeral rituals (Charema and Shizha, 2008: 61; see also Evans-Pritchard, 1937). Traditional medicine is underpinned by symbolism-the belief that white medicine provides an antidote against sorcery while red cleanses the blood stream is widespread among African healers.

Furthermore, the characteristics of an animal/plant are also believed to be transmitted to the user: for example, among the Tswana, crocodile skin is used for fever because it is believed that the crocodile being a water creature, symbolizes cooling-off. In the same light, the Zulu use lion or elephant-any strong or fierce animal part- as a potion against anxiety.

The skills, knowledge and practice of traditional medicine are generally transmitted orally through a community, family or individual. Within a particular culture, elements of traditional pharmacopoeia could be applied by a person who plays a particular medical role such as a healer, diviner, midwife to manage health problems (Cumes, 2004). Traditionally, three factors legitimize the role of traditional healers: their own beliefs, the success of their actions and the beliefs of the community (Laguerre, 1987). Laguerre further notes that when the claims of a traditional healer are rejected by a society, three types of adherents may however still use his services. These include (1) those that were born and socialized in the society and become permanent believers; (2) temporary believers who turn to traditional medicine due to individual crises and (3) those who believe in particular aspects of traditional medicine (Ibid.).

7.3 The Process of Becoming a Healer

Sometimes, African traditional healers learn their talent through personal experiences while being treated as patients. Some individuals decide to become healers upon recovery. Others become traditional healers through a special "spiritual calling" and, therefore, their diagnoses and treatment regimens are decided supernaturally (Jones, 2006). Among the Banyangi people of Cameroon, a sign of calling can come from mental disarrangement caused by *baarem*. This is the spirit of divination, through which the healer gains inspiration. Through training, psychological stability is eventually attained (Onwuanibe, 1979).

The knowledge and skills of traditional medicine could also be passed down informally from a close relative such as a father, uncle or aunt, grandmother to another person. Apprenticeship is usually offered by an established practitioner, who formally teaches the trade over an extended period of time and is paid (Thornton, 2002). According to Okpako (2006), the training of traditional healers is complex and depends on the kind of medical practice the aspirant wants to be associated with. Okpako further notes that once the trainees are officially initiated as healers, they become both spiritual and physical beings. Being physical and spiritual, they can mediate between the human and supernatural world and can invoke spiritual power in their healing processes.

7.4 Typology of African Traditional Healers

> To most Westerners indigenous African techniques are at best puzzling and at worst smacks of witchcraft. The West is replete with technological wonders. Our communication network is a veritable marvel with the likes of satellite phones, fax machines, and the internet. Yet ancient African wisdom has a lot to teach us about communication. There is a realm of spirit, but there is also a veil that must be penetrated if we wish to communicate with this potential source of guidance. Most Westerners do not have the techniques to pierce the veil; sangomas do. Sangoma medicine is very practical. If you have lost a cow, the inyanga can throw the bones and tell you where to go and look for it. The techniques are evidential and have stood the test of time. (Cumes, 2010: 1)

Like modern medicine in which there are a variety of specializations including but not limited to obstetricians, gynecologists, virologists, and pediatricians, traditional African medicine also has specializations. Particular philosophies underpin the workings of various categories of traditional healers. Three types of traditional healers exist in South African society—the *Inyangas, Insangomas* and *Umthandazis* (McFarlane, 2015; Peltzer and Mngqundaniso, 2008: 380). There are differences between all three types in the methods they use in healing their patients as well as in the source of their healing powers. *Inyangas* (traditional doctors) are herbalists with deep knowledge about curative herbs and medicines of animal origin. Ninety per cent of *Inyangas* are male (Kale, 1995). *Insangomas* (in Zulu a diviner) 'They determine the cause of illness by using ancestral spirits, and 90 per cent of them are female' (Kale, 1995). Finally, the *Umthandazis* 'are faith healers who are professed Christians' (Kale, 1995: 1170; Peltzer & Mngqundaniso, 2008) and that are affiliated with one of the African churches (Kale, 1995; Chavunduka, 1986). Their primary form of healing is the use of holy water and by touching their patient to heal them (Mngqundaniso & Peltzer, 2008; Mcfarlane, 2015). But for "the *Umthandazis* who are an outcome of the early European missionary visits to Africa, all the others have been a part of African society even before the European conquest of Africa" (Mcfarlane, 2015: 15). Table 1 outlines the differences between the various categories of healers.

TABLE 1   Traditional healing agencies in South Africa

Agent	Skills	Method of Service	Nature of Service	Accessibility
Insangoma: High grade	1. Lower and middle grade qualifications as pre-requisite. 2. 'Call' by spirits. 3. Apprenticed to an expert. 4. Medical skills acquired by inyanga.	1. Essentially diagnostic. 2. Contact with patient not needed for diagnosis. 3. History, symptoms, and nature of problem not revealed by patients.	1. Conflict resolution. 2. Revelation of misfortune and illness. 3. Recommends solution. 4. Provides expertise and leadership.	Access given to a relatively few.
Insangoma: Middle grade	1. Lower grade qualification a pre-requisite. 2. 2, 3 and 4, as above	1. As above. 2. Throws and reads bones. 3. As above.	1, 2, 3, and 4 as above.	Relatively accessible compared with above.
Insangoma: Middle grade	1. Lower grade qualification a pre-requisite. 2. 2, 3 and 4, as above	1. As above. 2. Divination through trance. 3. As above. 4. Cooperation of clients sought.	Confirms patient's beliefs.	Much more accessible.
Inyanga	1. Individual choice to become one. 2. Apprenticed to an expert.	1. Knowledge of symptoms and patient's history necessary. 2. Contact with patient necessary.	Comprehensive, curative, prophylactic, ritualistic, and symbolic.	Freely accessible.
Specialist	Usual family prerogative	Essentially curative.	Consultant, special skills.	Fewer in number
Spiritual healer	Trances and contacts with spirits.	Essentially diagnostic	Lays on hands, prays, provides holy water and other symbols	Freely accessible.

SOURCE: *TRADITIONAL HEALING AGENCIES IN SOUTH AFRICA* (MCFARLANE, 2015: 66)

Isangomas are required to be specifically summoned by the ancestors and then thoroughly trained. An *isangoma* described his calling and the health problems he finds solutions to thus:

> Question: How did you become a traditional healer?
> Response: It was a call. I wanted to go to school and become a social worker or even an engineer. I fell sick and was taken to a healer, coupled with the kind of dreams I used to have. A healer told my parents that I had been chosen by my ancestors to become a healer. I was taken to my mother's brother who then was also a healer. While with him it came to unfold that, I was truly an elect. He trained me; I worked under his supervision and gained a lot of experience. Today, I work on my own and have helped and I am still helping many people who have problems.
> Question: As a member of the community, how do you assist people who are sick or need help?
> Response: We have many problems in our society. Many people are sick; some of them have natural ailments while others are suffering from the wickedness of others. They have been bewitched in one way or the other. Some other people are suffering from the wrath of the ancestors. They failed to perform certain traditional rites, which are very important to build a good relationship with our ancestors. As a healer, I assist in identifying people's problems, I direct them on how to go about solving their problems. I also administer treatment to the sick. All these I do with the assistance of my ancestors. They direct me, they show me what to do and tell me how to get the right treatments [combination of herbs to make concoctions].

They are reputed for distant diagnosis and healing. Unlike modern doctors who are preoccupied with doing away with the placebo effect, "sangomas are masters in enhancing it, using powerful rituals and their own charisma. Placebo is augmented with ceremonies and plant medicines, or *muti*. The *muti* is always prescribed with a heavy application of attention, intention, action and affirmation, which have now become part of a modern, integrative, or holistic, approach" (Cumes, 2010: 19). The Zulu distinguish between *amakhambi* (herbal medicine, implying medicine with healing powers) and *imithi-* "medicines which produce bad results." These healers identify the cause and how to cure an illness. They are also "consulted for medicines that produce either cures or causes illnesses" (Faure, 2002: 24). Some diseases such as *intwaso* however mark the prelude to divinership while those afflicted with HIV/AIDS could readily feign their illness and claim to have been summoned to become *"thwasa"* (healers) and therefore require initiation.

7.4.1   Disease as Prelude to Divinership

Lamla (1981: 10–15) intimates that *intwaso* among the Southern Nguni people, refers to illnesses associated with entry into priest divination. In other words, it is a call to divinership and the subsequent commencement of divinational practices which brittles with complexities. It is still an unresolved mystery, if one remains in the conceptual context of men and women who claim to have received the particular call of divinership. Unless called, otherwise, nobody consciously, wishes to become a priest diviner. The word *intwaso* is actually an abstract noun from the verb, *Ukuthwasa* (coming into view). In the technical sense that is relevant here, the term means that a person is in a particularly close contact with the ancestral spirits. The ancestors make their presence felt through dreams and this compels the individual to avail him or herself to be a priest- diviner. If one can speak of "curing" at all, it is only the most experienced, renowned and omniscient diviners (*izanuse*) who are capable of curing *intwaso* or *ukuthwasa* (entry into, meaning initiation into divinership). A cure for *intwaso* in the strict sense of the word would imply the warding off of the ancestor spirit and their call. In another sense, the "cure" is the initiation of the individual into divinership. In other words, the diviner as a practitioner of the "healing ministry"- if the phrase is permitted- is a person who himself or herself underwent the ordeal of threatening sickness and the agonizing process of being healed. The diviner has therefore interiorized the meaning of sickness as well as what good health means through personal experience.

The novice or initiate into divination often begins by becoming capricious and unpredictable. He or she may be sensitive to all things that are held to ritually defile a person. He/she becomes eccentric and dreams frequently, often about wild and ferocious animals and snakes. Many novices display a highly neurotic temperament. They may also be constantly in a trance. They often become particular about food. They may be thought of as being mad. They are usually fond of snuff and easily get shaken by convulsions. They often shed tears and weep profusely. They may wake up clapping their hands and beating a drum made of cowhide (*ingqongqo*) rhythmically. It might take several years to discover that the ancestral spirits wants an individual to become a diviner. Novices often also, suffer from acidity (*ukubhodla*) and uncontrollable hiccup or hiccough (*ukukhutywa*). The suffering may be resisted for years but the patient will eventually succumb. Others may resist it until they die because there are few (if any) who voluntarily wish to be diviners.

Many neophytes are nervous and hysterical. They could be assumed to be suffering from functional nervous disease. This is an interesting problem for medical scientists and psychologists. The novice often experiences severe pains. In the healing repertoire, some methods of averting severe pains are known, but these are not final cures. They are only a transition measure until the person begins his/her novitiate. This suggests that initiation into the traditional medical profession is bound up with the ancestral religion. Religion, medicine and magic form a complex whole. A form of mental disorder characterizes initiation into this medical profession. Indeed, the matter is of great complexity that it requires comparative interdisciplinary studies.

An individual that is fully aware of infection with HIV/AIDS could instead of making a disclosure "pretends to have received the 'calling' to ukuthwasa, to become a traditional healer" (Wreford, 2008: 10). What this suggests is that 'charlatans'—also fake their calling into the traditional healing profession. Wreford (2008) provides examples of the disguising technique in which HIV/AIDS infected individuals feign to be *"thwasa"* as a way of disguising their embarrassment at their status as infected individuals to family members, friends and the larger community.

As enumerated by Wreford (2008), there are similarities between HIV/AIDS and the calling to become *'thwasa.'* These similarities include emotional disturbances, myriad physical symptoms—wasting, loss of appetite, upsets to digestive system among others. According to Wreford's ethnographic partners, there is a possibility for someone to be called but also, to be concurrently infected with HIV and to display similar symptoms (Wreford, 2008: 13). These similarities complicate matters for real healers to distinguish between pretended(faked) and genuine calls since those diagnosed of HIV can claim to be called and might eventually loss weight and die. They prefer to surrender to death, rather than to disclose their status (Sethosa and Peltzer, 2005: 36) and seek life prolonging drugs such as antirtrovirals.

Traditional healers like modern doctors operate within specializations. Healers differ, with each healer having a distinct feature. Zubane (2001: 29) has noted that African traditional healers can be categorized into three on the basis of their method of treatment. The first category brings together different types of herbalists:[1]

---

[1] On the one hand, the Zulu distinguish between izinyanga, izangoma and abathandazi, as well as charlatans and abathakathi, on the other hand. Charlatans are 'self-styled healers' who claim to possess cures for incurable diseases, magical solutions for every inscrutable social problem as well as magical solutions to economic problems. Abathakathi (singular

PHOTO 1 A herbalist (*amaXhwele*) at work
PHOTO BY TANYI BESONG

Herbalists (*amaxhwele*) are traditional healers who use herbs, skins of animals, tree barks, for curing illnesses. These healers gather and administer herbal remedies for common ailments.

The practice of traditional medicine varies within communities across the African continent. Amongst the Xhosa people of the Eastern Cape, apart from herbalists, ordinary villagers often have knowledge of medicinal mixtures (*imixube*). In some cases, most members of the community may know how to treat a wide range of common diseases and only seek the advice of a traditional healer for the treatment of certain specific diseases if their own treatments have failed. Such individuals may be mother-in-laws (*omazala*), grandmothers (*omakhulu*), who take care of their daughters' babies from birth. They gather and administer herbal remedies for curative and preventive reasons.

These individuals comprise what Arthur Kleinman (1980) designates as the popular sector of healthcare. They are part of the 'therapy managing group' (Hsu, 2008), or what Janzen (1978: 3–4) refers to as "the lay therapy managing

---

umthakathi) is a reference to wizards and witchdoctors. "Unlike izinyanga, izangoma and abathandazi, they specialize in medicines that produce harmful results" (Faure, 2002: 24).

group." In South Africa, common herbal treatments are known and used by the majority of rural communities as well as by many people in the cities. Daily usages of medicinal plants are often included as part of the people's diet. In many cases, there are no clear indications of the extent to which medicinal plants- grown in home gardens- are used by households as opposed to being prescribed by traditional healers (Okpako, 2006). Traditional healers sell their services on a business basis (Swantz, 1974). Among some ethnicities, traditional healers hold most of the medicinal knowledge. In such cases, their knowledge is often inherited or passed on through certain individuals from generation to generation under a system of apprenticeship (Swantz, 1974; Neuwinger, 2000). In Dar-es-Salaam, among the Zaramo, many of the traditional medicine men have learnt their healing talents (*uganga*) from other ethnic groups whom they believe have a stronger (*uganga*) talent (Swantz, 1974). Traditional healers collect medicinal plants from the wild or cultivate them for treatment purposes (Swantz, 1974; Hedberg & Staugård, 1989). Among the Zaramo in Dar-es-Salaam almost every tree, shrub or grass is believed to be of medicinal value (Swantz, 1974).

Herbal vendors (*Ochitha*) gather and sell herbs, barks of trees for the treatment of various ailments. During a research visit to the Eastern Cape, we observed that the local population simply refer to herbal vendors as "Doctors." Among others, they are gifted in the treatment of urinary tract infections, pre-sexual ejaculation for men, abnormal vaginal discharges for women etc. Herbal vendors do not diagnose illnesses. Zubane (2001) argued that the children of herbal vendors often grow herbal medicine. Through this experience, they become acquainted with medicinal herbs. Some of these children eventually come to learn about medicines and medicinal practices "in an informal, experiential and experimental way" (Prince et al., 2001: 211). Another class of herbalists is comprised of those who heal and provide protective amulets/charms (*amakhubalo*) against evil doers and sorcerers. They also treat diseases with various concoctions of herbal remedies including dried and powdered parts of animals and plants. Such remedies are locally called '*izinyamazane*.' In most African countries, herbal mixtures are also sold to the public in little "medicine shops" (Okpako, 2006). These "small medicine shops" are what Pemunta (1999; Pemunta, 2000) refers to as the "African Pharmacy"-an informal institution that neither falls under biomedicine nor traditional medicine.

Traditional healers also sell some of their medicinal plants on local markets, as could be observed in Dar-es-Salaam (Fyhrquist, 2007). In the wake of a severe economic recession between the decade of the mid-1980s and the mid-1990s, many rural women migrated to urban areas of South Africa and resorted to the harvesting and selling of medicinal herbs in the Durban Muthi Market.

PHOTO 2
Ancistrocladus Korupensis (commonly called Cameroonian vine)
PHOTO BY EMMANUEL O. BUEA, CAMEROON

Apart from transforming the relationship with the environment, many ordinary people subsequently set themselves up as 'indigenous healers.' This was happening at a time when job-seekers were increasingly relying on "the extra advantage from indigenous medicines to make one attractive to employers" (Faure, 2002: 26). In 1997, the Provincial Minister of Traditional and Environmental Affairs estimated trade in medicinal plants in the Province to worth R61 million per annum (Faure, 2002: 31; The Daily News, 14 May, 1997). The herbal trade market in Durban is estimated to attract between 700,000 and 900,000 traders per annum from South Africa, Zimbabwe and Mozambique (Green, 1996). Since CAM is excluded from the public healthcare system, this money was paid for out of pocket (Hollenberg, 2007), by those who can afford TCAM. Concurrently, there are ongoing discussions and projects aimed at standardizing how TCAM is introduced into biomedical education (e.g. Canadian Complementary and Alternative Medicine in Undergraduate Medical Education project). Concurrently, smaller herbal markets are dotted in all South African communities. The resurgence of interest in traditional medicine has been further attributed to consumer's preference for natural products and to the unprecedented spread of diseases such as HIV/AIDS (Shiza and Charema, 2012: 60).

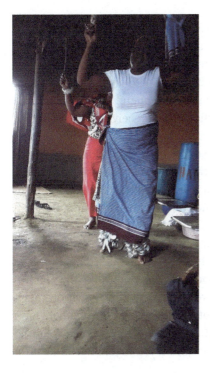

PHOTO 3
A priestess diviner (*amagqirha*).
This woman started her trade at the tender age of about 13. She allegedly had a spiritual and ancestral visitation during which she got her powers.
PHOTO BY ZONA DOTWANA

The last sub class of herbalists is comprised of homeopathic herbalists (*Izinyanga Ezixube Nolwazi ewabelungu*). These are herbalists who have undergone formal western training in the field of medicine. Homeopathic herbalists do consult ancestors during diagnosis. Not anyone can become a homeopath since formal training in a recognized academic institution is required (Okpako, 2006).

The second group of traditional healers is comprised of priest diviners. Diviners (*amagqirha*) get their knowledge as a gift from the ancestors. Following Amakhosi, a participant in the 1915 hearings, "traditionally a healer or diviner found indigenous medicines through the help of his or ancestors" (Chief Native Commissioner's Report, CNC-193–149/1915; cf Faure, 2002: 32).

> Once the medicine had been found, rituals for harvesting- such as prayer and thanks to the ancestors- were performed. In most cases, the person would only harvest the part of the tree or plant (such as bark, leaves, roots etc.) that he or she needed. The rest of the tree would be saved for future use. Medicines were harvested at particular times during the year, mostly during the time when harvesting would do less damage to the tree or plant. The 'just-in-time' nature of the use meant that people only harvested the medicines they needed. (Faure, Ibid.)

The ancestral spirits are believed to reveal the cause and treatment to the diviner for different diseases through visions. In his description of the calling and status of a medicine-man in Africa, John Mbiti (1969: 167) states that "there are medicine-men who believe that spirits or the living-dead have called them in dreams, visions or in waking to become medicine-men." This is doubtlessly an overgeneralization because not all medicine-men receive their calling in a similar way and under similar circumstances. There is, however, recognition that the ancestors are believed to be the source of all medicine. Among the multiple roles of a medicine-man among the Ndebele in South Africa are the supply of medicated pegs for the gates of a new homestead, the combating of witchcraft and magic by preventing their activation and sometimes, by sending them back to their authors, and the striking of the grave of a dead person saying "N.N., wake up! Go and fight" (Mbiti, 1969: 168). Alembi (2003: 81) maintains that the origins, family and kinship ties as well as traditional heritage-folklore and folk belief are important components that determine the practice of traditional healing. Some individuals have acquired healing powers through inheritance from their fathers, mothers or other close relatives who might have inherited same through kinship ties. Masatia's initiation for instance, followed his father's invitation to him in these words: "I want you to join me in the bush to visit our ancestors"

This means that he should come along and be shown the various herbs that the ancestors had shown his father for the management of particular disease episodes. He continued thus:

> Did you see this plant? It is used to treat people, who have been attacked by evil spirits.
> This plant here, it is a bad plant. Evil-doers and witches use it to kill. Never you touch it.
> That plant, that one is good for immunity. When you lick its ashes, nobody can succeed in bewitching you.

As time went on, the novice was taught the names and uses of different medicinal plants. This includes those that could be used for treating people when they are attacked by evil spirits, individuals that have been bewitched, those that can be used in combination to restore love between fighting partners, those that could be used to render people immune and even invisible from witchcraft attacks. This is how the slow and meticulous process of becoming a medicine- man took place (Ibid.). One elderly man stated that:

> The reason for one becoming the target of witches is nothing else but jealousy. Here in Qokoloweni Location, stories about witchcraft attacks

are widespread. Witches kill people, drive others mad or simply make them to become stupid and useless: they will drink excessively, chase multiple women and in the long run, may become infected with HIV/AIDS. Some even divorce their wives. (Interview, Amakwe, December 20, 2010)

The rule of secrecy and the fear of piracy explains why, most healers were reticent even to disclose the names of the various plants or the various components of the concoctions that they use in treating their patients. To gain their confidence, we constantly pointed out to them that we were not interested in their specialized and secret knowledge, which they are usually unwilling to share with cultural outsiders, we informed each participant that we were not interested in their insider knowledge, but rather, only seeking a wider understanding of how they acquired their knowledge (see also Flint, 2008: 32). As one traditional healer clearly stated: "This is a secret only to be revealed to the individual in the family to whom I will bequeath this knowledge when it is time for me to join my ancestors." The skepticism of traditional medicine practitioners is partly attributed to mistrust and suspicion of government's intentions. They suspect the government as conniving with the pharmaceutical industry in dispossessing them and subsequently converting their knowledge into drugs from which they will not benefit. Traditional healers rightly feel that "by divulging their sources of knowledge, documenting it and sharing it, the government will turn it into a gold mine for the pharmaceutical industry and modern physicians" (Mutabazi, 2008: 209). The latter "consider them conservative, subjective, backward and unscientific." They need "protection and the granting of property rights to them for their products" (Ibid.).

Diviners use listening, observation and experience to make a diagnosis aided by the supernatural (communication with ancestors) and the throwing of bones. A person normally does not choose to become a diviner, but rather follows a calling (*thwasa*), which can be disobeyed only at the risk of serious (sometimes fatal) illness. An apprentice (*ngaka*) undergoes an apprenticeship of up to seven years with a fully qualified diviner. Only after a ceremonial ritual and several successful tests of the person's abilities can he start practicing as a qualified diviner. Sometimes the diviner also trains as a herbalist (*inyanga*(Zulu) or *ixhwele* (Xhosa) and can practice both healing vocations simultaneously or separately. The herbalist acts as a druggist, dispensing medicines (*muti*) made from natural substances including bark, roots, leaves, animal skin, blood or parts of animals, herbs, or seawater (Krige, ND:6).

Diviners mediate the worlds of the living and the dead. Donda (1997: 5) classified priest diviners into four sub classes:

PHOTO 4
A bone thrower (*izangoma esichitha amathambo*) at work
PHOTO BY ZONA DOTWANA

1. The "head diviner" (*Iqgirha lentloko*). According Donda (1997), when this type of diviner is consulting a patient, the patient leads him to the correct answer by admitting loudly and often repeatedly when he is close to the truth. Ritter however considers this as pure guess work:

   Chanting his questions, the diviner will require his audience to reply, every one of them, 'we agree' (*siyavuma*). This response guides him to give his divination. (1955: 390)

2. The "bone throwers" (*izangoma esichitha amathambo*) are another group of diviners. Bone throwing is a learned art. The configuration of the bones tells the diviner the unknown secrets of the disease and how to proceed with treatment. The diviner is therefore involved in a process of revelation. They enter the cosmic field and invoke the help of the spirits for healing. This is when the ancestors are invited to assist with the treatment, and the healing process goes beyond placebo and is called distant or remote healing. They use drumming, and mediums of dreams, the divining bones and dancing to help channel the ancestors (Cumes, 2010: 1). "There is mutual understanding between healer and ancestor based on tradition, dreams, and empiricism as to what plant to use for a particular problem. Different tribes and various healers may use the same plant for distinct effect" (Ibid.: 4).

The divining bones are combined with shells, money, seeds, dice, domino-like objects or even domino themselves and other objects chosen by the *sangoma* and the spirit to stand for certain polarities. A miniature car may for instance represent a journey. Most of the bones are from lions, hyenas, anteaters, baboons, crocodiles, wild pigs, goats, antelopes and others constitute objects in the *sangomas's* bag and there are bones representing all psycho-socio-spiritual polarities. These bones stand for all the forces that affect any human being. Particular animals are believed to be endowed with particular attributes when it comes divination: the anteater is associated with "the digging of graves," and its bone "may be used where death is concerned, or it may represent a deceased person or his spirit" (Cumes, 2010: 5–6). The healer invokes the ancestors by giving them snuff, kneeling and clapping, rattling or singing a song, prior to throwing the bones. Sometimes they work in groups and the others will chorus the main healer's reading by chanting the word *siyavuma* (we agree) following each interpretation. The consultation session often begins with a general reading, followed by the asking of specific questions by the patient and/ or members of his or her entourage. Each question is answered by a separate throwing of the bones. Bone throwing as a form of divination is analogous to "interpreting someone's dream, and only the owner of the dream will know if the meaning rings true" (Cumes, 2010: 6).

3. "Whistling diviners" (*igqirha lemilozi*). These diviners who may be regarded as "communicators" are also believed to invoke and use the spirits of the ancestors to communicate directly with a client. Ritter (1955: 391) noted that whistling diviners use a form of whistling (*umlozi*) to communicate with ancestral spirits thereby revealing the cause and treatment of illnesses. Whistling actually serves as a conduit through which the ancestors of the diviner and that of the patient communicate and the diviner only serves as a mediator and communicator.

4. Faith healers/prophets (*umthandazeli* or umprofethi). They use exorcism to eliminate evil spirits from a person or place. Edward et al. (1983: 214) argue that faith healing is an outgrowth of the influence of urbanization, acculturation and Christianity. They further maintain that faith healing is the most potent expeller of evil spirits and that most of the traditional healers' roles of *izangoma* have been taken over by *umthandazeli*.

T.B. Joshua, a self-proclaimed prophet based in Lagos, Nigeria is the founder of the Synagogue Church of All Nations. His Congregation operates a television channel, Emmanuel TV disseminating the miracle of spiritual healing and preaching to a global audience. This Christian minister, televangelist and faith healer is a big giver; his humanitarian works include education, healthcare and rehabilitation programmes. The upsurge of Pentecostal groups is associated

PHOTO 5   Faith healer T.B. Joshua exorcising a patient
PHOTO BY TABI CHAMA

with the 'prosperity doctrine' as an economic message at a time when most African countries are experiencing serious economic crisis. Akoko Robert Mbe (2002: 360) maintains that "… the mainline Pentecostal churches have, with the crisis, shifted their attention to the 'prosperity doctrine.'"

He concedes that the economic crisis has contributed to the flourishing of these churches and that the shift in the economic message of the mainline groups is a survival strategy. Some of them combine spiritual healing with modern medicine. Prophet T.B. Joshua is on record as always recommending medical diagnosis before administering spiritual therapy. Mbe further maintains that the rise of Pentecostalism is a public disapproval by Christians with the way the mainstream Churches are addressing "the spiritual and material needs of their followers. Such increasing disillusionment shows that a swelling number of Christians do not consider it enough for the mainstream churches simply to make critical statements about the worsening economic situation or condemning the few who live in obscene opulence while the majority wallow in misery and poverty" (p. 360). Apart from making use of whatever help put at man's disposal by biomedicine for treatment and relieve, many people readily seek help and assistance through prayer and by going on pilgrimage. This shows that forces that are still beyond our understanding move us (Di Stefano, 2006).

Traditional healers are an integral part of all African cultures. They understand the social environment in which Africans live. They also know how this environment influences people's perceptions. Unlike western-trained medical doctors and health professionals, they have a rather holistic and comprehensive approach to the treatment of health problems. Because of their holistic approach, traditional healers are able to deal with both the physical and spiritual aspects of ailments. In the most remote areas of Africa, people consult the traditional healer of the village in cases of illness. Biomedical care is often beyond reach. It is either too expensive for people to afford or not even available (Verpoorte, 2000). Traditional medicine therefore plays a significant role in the delivery of healthcare to most rural dwellers, who due to poverty cannot afford conventional healthcare.

The healer uses different herbs, barks and roots that often have some medicinal value. In the healer's dispensary could be found his medical arsenal comprised among others of- his goat-skin, a bag (*imihlanti*) in which he carries various medicinal substances that are suitable for the treatment of a variety of diseases. He carries various powders—those made from roots and herbs, parts of animals, reptiles and insects-all of a supposed mysterious nature.

One respondent, a professional nurse with several years of experience told Nolwandle Mngqundaniso and Karl Peltzer:

> We know that some of their muthi (medicine) works. I have seen a patient being saved by traditional healers after the Western medication has failed. ...One example is that of a diabetic patient who came with her glucose levels very low. The doctor was surprised and asked the patient what she took and the patient told the doctor about the traditional healer's medication. She was given a bottle with medication to take for the whole month. The bottle was taken to the laboratory for analysis but they could not find the ingredients of that medication in the bottle even though it was helping. More patients were referred to that traditional healer and were helped. Even with HIV/AIDS and some other STIs we know that traditional healers can be of great help. (Peltzer & Mngqundaniso, 2008: 384)

The above quotation suggests that traditional medicine goes beyond mere herbs and that healers do not sometimes only depend on herbs but also on supernatural powers for the treatment of their patients. Sobiecki (2014: 2) has drawn attention to the association of traditional medicine with religious or spiritual plant use which although "often deemed irrational, non-empirical and unscientific" continues to provide relief to patients. Similarly, the techniques of traditional health practitioners who treat mentally ill patients is assumed to be based on the culturally relevant premises of the patient (Asuni, 1979; Tucker et al., 2011). Stated otherwise, the linkage between the provision of patient-centered, culturally-sensitive healthcare, and the health behaviours and outcomes of patients who experience such care., including for mental illness has been explained in terms of the potential usefulness of the Patient-Centered Culturally Sensitive Health Care Model (Tucker et al.,2011). In the cases cited above, we suggests that behavioural or social gains could be responsible for the positive outcome of the traditional healer's treatment.

It is an acknowledged fact that the development of indigenous herbal products is hampered by lack of scientific evidence to substantiate medicinal claims. While traditional uses may be the point of departure in product development, it is however, unlikely to result in sustainable commercial success in the long term. Examples include *H. hemerocallidea, Aloe vera* and *H. gordonii. Hypoxis* that were subjected to countless studies in the 1970s. They eventually came to constitute the basis of a lucrative trade in so-called "immune stimulants" but there is, however, "no convincing in vivo evidence published in peer-reviewed journals" (Van Wyk, 2011: 826) about their therapeutic utility. Similarly, although *Aloe gel* health drinks are a major international herbal product, they still lack convincing clinical evidence of therapeutic benefits (Van Wyk, 2011: 826). An evaluation of more than 90 of the famous and most promising indigenous South African plants in the context of their potential for commercialization as medicinal products shows they have myriad applications and that 16 of these plants are of particular interest in new product development (Van Wyk, 2011; Van Wyk, 2008). The 16 South African traditional medicines that have been partly or fully developed as commercial crops and products include: *Agathosma betulina, Aloe ferox, Artemisia afra, Aspalathus linearis, Bulbine frutescens, Cyclopia genistoides, Harpagophytum procumbens, Hoodia gordonii, Hypoxis hemerocallidea, Lippia javanica, Mesembryanthemum tortuosum* (=*Sceletium tortuosum*), *Pelargonium sidoides, S. aethiopicus, S. frutescens* (=*Lessertia frutescens*), *Warburgia salutaris and Xysmalobium undulatum* (Van Wyk , 2011: 814).

The degree of his pharmaceutical knowledge remains his own closely guarded secret. He guards his esoteric knowledge from the inquisitive, even at a price. Paradoxically however, it is common to find in a traditional healer's dispensary medicines for diarrhea, scots emulsions, unikasma, disprins, purgatives, liquid paraffin, senna leaves, aspros, vicks, panadol and others undoubtedly obtained from provision stores/modern medicine or pharmacies. This suggests first that traditional healers also practice medical pluralism and are in

PHOTO 6
A diviner's shrine, Upper Ngqwarha
PHOTO BY TABI CHAMA

favour of the integration of both systems of healthcare. Secondly, there is leakage between various systems of medicine both at the level of healers and patients.

We came across a female healer who operates a "modern dispensary" within her traditional medicine clinic. We use the word "modern" in the sense that while there we observed that she also stocks medicines like paracetamol. We further observed *Sutherlandia frutescens* (L.) R. Br., a widely used over the counter complementary medicine and traditional medications by HIV seropositive adults living in South Africa. This is despite the fact that the plant's safety has not been objectively studied. A randomized controlled trial of 56 HIV positive patients showed that *S. frutescens* did not change HIV viral load, and CD4 T-lymphocyte count was similar in the two groups at 24 weeks (Wilson et al., 2015). She comes from Uganda and runs her business in Umtata, Eastern Cape. She is popular in the town. She indicated to us that she could cure STDs, AIDS, bring back lost lovers and enlarge male sex organs with her remedies, and that many people come to see her for these services. We have no way of validating her claim of being able to cure AIDS. Let it however be noted that the existence of medicinal herbs that cure several diseases might have led to

PHOTO 7
The dispensary of a traditional healer
PHOTO BY ZONA DOTWANA

such claims of 'exaggerated' healing abilities by some healers. There is a traditional claim for instance that *Sutherlandia frutescens* (L.) R.Br. [syn. *Lessertia frutescens* (L.) Goldblatt & J.C. Manning] (Fabaceae)-cancer bush, sutherlandia "can be used for almost any disease" (Van Wyk, 2008: 350; Oldham et al., 2013). It is widely used by many cultural groups for the prevention/and or treatment of "fever, poor appetite, unspecified wasting diseases, indigestion, gastritis, oesophagitis, peptic ulcer, dysentery, cancer tonic, diabetes, colds, influenza, cough, asthma, chronic bronchitis, kidney and liver conditions, rheumatism, heart failure, urinary tract infections and stress and anxiety" (Van Wyk, 2008: 350; Oldham et al., 2013). It seems to counteract the muscle-wasting (cachexia) effect of AIDS, reason why it is said to dramatically improve the quality of life of HIV/AIDS patients as suggested by clinical anecdotes (Van Wyk, 2008: Ibid.). It is believed to enhance the immune system's response and to act as an adaptogen. The Medicine Research Council of South Africa has completed a detailed study of the plant and demonstrated that it is void of toxicity in more than 50 parameters tested (Seier et al., 2002; cf. Van Wyk, 2008: 350).

Apparently, scientific medicines provide her with a new and powerful weapon in the same age-old battle between the supernatural forces and the natural means, which are at man's disposal. This traditional healer has learnt modern medicine in order to increase her stock-in-trade of medicinal knowledge and to make more profit. Nevertheless, the new knowledge has not made her to abandon nor even doubt her traditional frame of thought. In fact, it could not because her patients share that frame of thought.

The WHO has recognized traditional medical care as a useful health resource in resource constrained countries, most of which are in the less developed world. However, many countries including South Africa are yet to scientifically evaluate the crude extracts of plants used by traditional healers to determine their pharmaceutical properties, clinical usefulness and toxicological potentials (Kyerematen & Ogulana, 1987). Despite great strides on the testing and commercialization of indigenous South African plants (see above), only an estimated 10.8% of African flora is known to be used in traditional medicine. For southern Africa, the corresponding statistics is an estimated 13.8% of the flora (Van Wyke and Gericke, 2000; cf. Van wyk, 2008) or the exact count of 2 942 species (administered to humans). This represents 13.5% of the flora (Van Wyk, 2011: 813). "Despite the fact that an estimated 10% of the plant species of the world is found in southern Africa, only a few have been fully commercialized and basic scientific information is often not available" (Van Wyk, 2008: 342). Although 'hybridizing' traditional medicine and medical practices to meet the needs of the modern healthcare system represents some form of colonization by every other name, the way forward might be to submit products for biomedical testing of efficacy and dosage, encourage healers to undertake formal training and acquire state licensing to practice.

The lack of basic scientific information on crude extracts of plants used by traditional healers is one factor that could hinder policy formulation and stonewall the eventual inclusion of traditional medicine into the mainstream national healthcare delivery system. According to Wood-Sheldon et al., (1997), 74% of pharmacologically active plant derived components were discovered after traditional healers had used them. Traditional medicine is therefore a foundation for modern medical research. It is relevant towards the ongoing efforts to improve healthcare. Modern medicinal knowledge has evolved from traditional medicine. Certain illnesses are perceived to have magical and supernatural origin (Karim et al., 1994: 3). Such illnesses cannot be treated with modern medical procedures. Traditional medicine, which is also holistic, is culturally designed to respond to such health needs. African traditional medicine is a traditional endeavour to close the gap between illnesses caused by supernatural forces and those of a natural origin.

7.5 Prospects for the Integration of Traditional Medicine into Official Healthcare

Despite the paradigmatic divide between biomedicine and traditional medicine, both medical systems recognize that the activities of the mind can affect the health of the body. Ironically, this recognition of the mind-body intersection has not led to change in medical thinking. In the words of Fritjof Capra, the existing scientific evidence "have failed to have a significant influence on mainstream medical thinking" (Capra, p. 350; cf. De Stefano, 2006). Biomedicine has regrettably and to its own detriment remained trapped in the mind-body dichotomy, which is a consequence of the Cartesian project that separated mind from matter.

Socio-economic realities and a shifting policy emphasis from international organizations-especially the WHO and the World Bank have given impetus to the importance of traditional medicine. However, integrating alternative medicine into a national healthcare programme is challenging. In many countries, there is still resistance in officially accepting traditional medicine. This resistance largely stems from the primary philosophical contradictions between conventional and traditional medicine. Contradictions between the two are based on the premise that biomedicine views illness as a result of pathological agents while traditional medicine accepts that diseases have supernatural causes (Sobieki, 2014; Sobiecki, 2012; Flint, 2008: 20; Sofowora, 1996: 52). While biomedical practitioners may recognize the chemical importance of a herb's active ingredients, they may dismiss or underestimate the comprehensive effect of the mystical aspects of traditional medicine.

Fear and skepticism on the part of scientific researchers emanates from the widespread notion that nowadays, traditional healers are charlatans who claim the ability to cure all heath conditions (Gilbert et al., 2002). In Cameroon for instance, the head of the HIV/AIDS Programme sounded quite skeptical about the possibility of collaboration with traditional practitioners declaring that the majority of traditional healers are unreliable:

> Out of 100, you might only have five who are really good traditional doctors.... The rest might be fake; going around saying they can cure AIDS. We need to work on this before we can embark on any sort of collaboration. (Tzortzis, 2003: 32)

Another problem impeding the integration of traditional and conventional medicine is resistance on the part of the traditional healers themselves. Traditional healers consider their knowledge of plants and medicines to be inherently secretive. To traditional healers, healing is a gift from the ancestors. It is perfected through years of apprenticeship and training. Having suffered to learn their art, they are reluctant to give out information to "uninitiated" researchers. Traditional healers do not easily give out information even if it means that the information sharing might benefit healers themselves or their communities at large. A toxicity study of a traditional remedy in Ethiopia was stopped because the traditional healer whose concoction was being tested for efficacy and safety would not part with the medicine (WHO, 1990: 37). Additionally, interest groups including among others the Complementary and Traditional Medicines Stakeholders Committee have argued that the South African state should follow the footsteps of the Canadian government that has created a special Office of Natural Health Products with the responsibility of registering and regulating complementary and alternative medicines. Interestingly, alternative medicine providers with monetary stakes prefer to maintain a situation where their products will not be "independently validated for safety, efficacy and quality." One reason for this resistance stem from the fact that "the registration process may be costly" (Hassim et al., 2001४: 217). Even more concerning is the tragic reality that some of these stakeholders depend on the desperation of patients, "with their ignorance of medicine, to advertise and sell products" (Ibid.) including "immune boosters and micronutrients" that have been attributed HIV-therapeutic "but are of no value and may often be harmful" (Ibid.). Registration would simply entail forcing most of these medicines off the shelves. Lack of registration however entails the exploitation of a desperate population. Furthermore, the question of how to properly compensate traditional practitioners for their medical and botanical knowledge is a sensitive issue. It has often been reported that the main contributory factor for poor cooperation between traditional and conventional medical practitioners has been the lack of confidence. Traditional healers are usually not protected legally and even denigrated by biomedical practitioners. Worse of all, advocates of co-operation, fail to realize that what they are calling for is not between equals, but rather for the indirect subjugation of indigenous medical practitioners who will be forced into adopting the procedures of biomedicine and its practitioners (Faure, 2002: 37).

There are very few laws that adequately address the issue of traditional medical systems in South Africa. The newly proposed THPs regulations that was opened for public comments from interested stakeholders on November 3, 2015 is replete with ambiguities. Apart from limiting traditional medical practices to South African nationals, it lacks substantive details for the training of THPs, students (*abatwasa*) and/or trainers. It is unclear as to whether "registration will commence simultaneously or in a step-wise manner" (Street, 2016:

PHOTO 8   Leaves and stripped bark of *Prunus Africana* (Pygeum, Wotango, African prune, Red stinkwood)
PHOTOS BY EMMANUEL O. BUEA, CAMEROON

325). Furthermore, "the relationship between schedules relating to registration and training is unclear" (Ibid.). Recognizing the existence of traditional healers is not sufficient. Laws and regulations to empower and protect them have to be adopted and implemented. Ironically, the new regulations requires 'accredited institutions' for the training of THPs to make available 'copies of teaching/learning materials' to the THP's Council whereas even the vetting process remains opaque (Street, 2016: 326). This is quite problematic and raise concerns about intellectual property rights. Legal rights would allow healers to benefit from adequate compensation for their knowledge (OAU/STRC/DEPA/KIPO Report, 1997: 8).

How a researcher approaches traditional healers and what he or she offers can be the key to gaining their confidence and the desired information. Traditional healers operating in an urban society expect to be rewarded for their contribution to healthcare. This is because healers recognize their increased popularity even in western cultures. They tend to suspect that their knowledge will be commercialized. In the process, they may not benefit. The exclusion of natives in the exploitation of Cameroon's *Prunus Africana* (pygeum also called wotango by the Bakweri people of Cameroon) speaks to this pattern of exploitation (Hall et al., 2000). As a result, traditional healers may choose not to cooperate, or they may demand sums of money that researchers may not be willing to pay.

7.6 Enhancing Cooperation between Traditional Healers and Biomedicine

Many difficulties bedeck co-operation between conventional and traditional medicine. This is the case even when some of the approaches to healthcare by modern and traditional healers often show significant similarities (Daly & Limbach, 1996: 48–60). Knowledge is neither totally modern nor traditional; both interact with, and appropriate each other. Many traditional healers have a sophisticated conception of disease, while many biomedical practitioners are able to adapt to other conceptions of health and disease. Consequently, there is hope that as long as the interest in traditional medicine continues to heighten, co-operation between the two sectors is likely to improve. A sensitive approach and full respect for the spiritual and cultural aspects of traditional medicine are necessary if traditional healers are expected to collaborate in a national healthcare strategy. The solicitation of the opinions of healers and their concerns may be a very important step towards co-operation.

In many cultures around Southern Africa, traditional healers are usually regarded as highly respected community leaders. Their beliefs and judgments are valued. Traditional healers are generally compassionate and thoughtful individuals. A good number of traditional healers are reported to be effective in counseling and dealing with psychological issues though some of their behaviours and practices are detrimental to a patient's health (Lambhard, 2010). According to Kale (1995), the fundamental idea of traditional medicine is that "disease" is a supernatural phenomenon governed by a hierarchy of vital powers beginning with the most powerful deity followed by lesser spiritual entities like ancestral spirits, living persons, animals, birds, snakes, plants, and other objects. These forces act together and can either diminish or improve an individual's power. A lack of harmony between the relevant forces may lead to disease. It is often believed that natural substances extracted from plants and animals can help cure the illness or bring harmony.

It is estimated that approximately 200,000 traditional healers are currently practicing in South Africa, compared to only 25,000 medical doctors, and roughly 80% of the black population use the services of traditional healers (NRCATM Report, 2010). Medical schools generally see traditional healing as a somewhat "primitive" approach to medical practice. Some biomedical doctors however observe the approaches that traditional healers employ and then adopt some of their methods if their own are not sufficiently working or if they are in doubt.

At least two nurses in private conversations stated that they had referred patients with advanced hernia to traditional healers because they felt these patients could die if surgery were performed immediately. After the patients had initiated treatment with the THPs for at least two months, the biomedical doctor at the facility was able to successfully perform surgery on them and brought them back to good health. This has resonances in a way to 'modern traditional healers' in Kyle town, southwest Tanzania who are increasingly transcending and destabilizing the boundaries between modern and traditional medicine through 'intentional hybridity' as a way of effectively competing for clients with biomedical professionals whom they accuse of being jealoused of their success in treating clients (Marsland, 2007).

Government health services and directors of healthcare programmes are realizing the need to work together with traditional healers instead of simply ignoring them. While this seems to be a difficult process because traditional healers are not medically qualified or comparable to fully trained doctors, healers remain helpful in tackling critical health problems in most South African communities.

Even though some countries in Southern Africa do recognize traditional healers, their integration in most countries has proved to be a difficult task. An established dialogue between traditional healers and medical doctors is important since the traditional healer's ideas are very useful in the community. It should be noted that sometimes, receiving treatment from a traditional healer can delay medically necessary and important diagnosis and treatment (Somse et al., 1998).

7.7 Conclusion

The African concept of disease like health is broad and all-encompassing. The latter is comprised of physical, psychological, social and economic well-being. Treatment is holistic and is meant to establish equilibrium between the physical and metaphysical realm, between the living and the dead, within the body politic of the community, lineage or family. Contrary to biomedicine which treats the physical body, traditional medicine treats the social body by establishing equilibrium. It is embedded in the African conception of man as communitarian-as defined by "an environing community" (Menkiti, 1984: 173; Menkiti, 2004) (see Chapter 4). Traditional healers are therefore both spiritual and physical beings. They act as intermediaries between the physical and the supernatural realm. However, while some healers have supernatural powers, others do not. There are therefore various specialties within traditional medicine and traditional medicine should not be conflated with magic and witchcraft. This is despite the fact that in Africa, religion, medicine and magic form a single complex. Herbalists for instance, treat patients using herbal medicines comprised of concoctions of plants and animal materials with therapeutic powers. The "Inyangas" for instance are herbalists, usually male, and experts with plants. On the other hand, the "insangomas" are psychic spiritualists, and usually female. They are required to be specifically summoned by the ancestors and then well trained (McFarlane, 2015; Peltzer and Mngqundaniso, 2008: 380). The failure to clearly delineate various categories of healers and their specialties, and the exaggerated claims of some 'self-styled healers' to cure all diseases has discredited the traditional healing profession. The lumping together of all healers independent of their specialty constitutes one of the obstacles to the integration of both traditional and modern medicine. This is the case because some opponents of the integration of both healthcare systems summarily dismiss all healers as quacks and traditional medicine as witchcraft as well as its practitioners as witches and wizards.

CHAPTER 8

The Integration of Modern and Traditional Medicine in Qokolweni Location

> The two systems of traditional and modern medicine need not clash. Within the context of PHC (Primary Health Care), they can blend together in a beneficial harmony, using the best features of each system, and compensating for certain weaknesses in each. This is not something that will happen all by itself. Deliberate policy decisions have to be made. But it can be done successfully. Many countries have brought the two systems together in highly effective ways. In some countries where health systems are organized around PHC, traditional medicine is well integrated and provides a backbone of much preventive care and treatment of common ailments…. (Dr Margaret Chan, WHO Director General, Speech delivered at the WHO Congress on Traditional Medicine in Beijing, November, 2008)

8.1 Introduction

The above-cited statement culled from a speech delivered at the WHO Congress on Traditional Medicine in Beijing, November 2008 by Dr. Margaret Chan, WHO Director General articulates the need for collaboration between the two categories of practitioners because of the complementarity of both systems of health care. In other words, the coercing of medical pluralism through the dominance of biomedicine as in South Africa has some unfettered effects. Despite similarities between medical concepts-for example, Nguni notions of strong and weak blood have similarities with biomedical ideas of the immune system- not all cultural concepts can be translated. This can give rise to inappropriate treatment and frustrations on the part of doctors and patients alike. "The treatment may be ineffective or resisted if it does not fit within the cultural logic of the patient, for instance feeding new born babies only breast milk seemed ludicrous to many African mothers at the turn of the century" (Flint, 2008: 20). Furthermore, this cultural gap has given rise to the present placement of individuals suffering from symptoms of a *twasa*-initiate into psychiatric care institutions by biomedical personnel and patients' therapy seeking group because of their failure to recognize such culture-bound syndromes. The dominance of biomedicine has placed alternative healthcare providers in a marginal position in terms of their rights to practice and to have access to state resources. Moreover, the privileged position enjoyed by biomedicine and the subsequent standards of regulation to which it is subjected, put alternative healthcare providers at a disadvantaged position in terms of both professionalization and regulation. Both healers and HIV/AIDS activists have complained that whereas the efficacy of antiretroviral drugs have been tested, the effectiveness of traditional therapies remains anecdotal (Flint, 2008: 20–21). This calls for the need for culturally appropriate treatments by medical practitioners and the need to translate local idioms into biomedical ideas for effective interventions.

This chapter examines the prospects for the integration of traditional and modern medicine in Qokolweni Location, South Africa. When compared with the rest of South Africa, the region constantly displays poor human development indicators including deeply entrenched and gendered poverty; high rates of infant mortality and overall life expectancy, inaccessibility to existing social infrastructure (see Chapter 5). These are partly the result of apartheid era policies of underdevelopment that led to labour-related migration of the most productive segment of the population into the mines and into richer regions of South Africa as well as the competing disease discourses about the understanding and best management of HIV/AIDS.

The advent of HIV/AIDS led to an intractable debate with traditional medicine being forwarded by the political class under Thabo Mbeki's leadership as a viable strategy for managing the illness while questioning the link between HIV and AIDS and the efficacy of antiretroviral medications (King, 2012; Nattrass, 2005). This highlights the fact that local political dynamics are capable of shaping decision making about treatment since the advent of AIDS and its association with witchcraft as well as the sociopolitical quagmire characterized by instability and unemployment pushed most patients towards traditional healers in their quest for solutions and explanations.

The chapter begins by presenting the demographic and socio-economic characteristics of survey participants. It details how perceptions of health and traditional medicine are shaped by different factors and how local context, cultural factors (beliefs and practices) and historical geographies of decades of underdevelopment and neglect (Farmer, 2006) intersect and shape these perceptions (King, 2012). Differences of opinion among participants as well as among THPs and biomedical personnel, especially nurses on the integration of biomedicine and traditional medicine are analyzed. The analysis shows how despite some regularity in the use of traditional medicine, governmental agencies and other stakeholders have reified its use in ways that fail to reflect local views and practices. The view from below ("subaltern health narratives") (King, 2010: 50) is important in understanding local uses of traditional medicine and highlighting policy failures that might occur as a result of misunderstandings of local practices and knowledge systems (King, 2012; King, 2010: 50).

8.2 Respondents' Opinions on Traditional Medicine

This next section deals with the varied opinions of respondents on the integration of indigenous and modern medicine into the mainstream South African healthcare system. It begins with an analysis of the socio-economic and demographic characteristics of the 50 survey participant's various uses and perceptions of traditional medicine.

Table 2 below shows that a majority of interlocutors were females (60%) while 40% were males-of different age groups. Of the total population of male respondents, 15% have never attained any form of formal education, whereas

TABLE 2   Demographic characteristics of respondents

Sex	Education Obtained	18–20	21–30	31–40	41–50	50+	Sub Total	Total
Male	No formal education	0	0	1	0	2	3	20
	STD 1–3	0	2	0	1	0	3	
	STD 4–7	0	2	3	0	0	5	
	STD 8–10	2	0	1	2	1	6	
	Teriary	0	0	1	0	2	3	
Female	No formal education	2					2	30
	STD 1–3	0	1	0	0	0	1	
	STD 4–7	0	2	0	0	0	2	
	STD 8–10	2	5	0	0	0	7	
	Tertiary	0	6	4	3	5	18	
Total		6	18	10	6	10	50	50

SOURCE: FIELD WORK

15% have attempted Standard 1–3. Additionally, 25% have completed standard 4–7, while 30% have attempted standard 8–10. A further 15% have been to a tertiary formal institution of learning. Of the female respondents, 6.6% have had no formal education, 3.3% (1 person) has attempted Standard 1–3, 6.6% have attempted standard 4–7, 23.3% have completed standard 8–10. Lastly, 60% have attempted tertiary education.

Contrary to other studies (Berhane et al., 2001; Peltzer, 1987), this study revealed that young and educated participants also consulted THPs. Traditional medicine is therefore not medicine for the uneducated. According to Leonard (2000: 43), "Visitors to traditional healers are more educated than the average patient and it therefore seems unlikely they are more ignorant. Visitors to traditional healers are most often people who would have visited a mission hospital or clinic if they had not gone to a traditional healer. They are the sicker and harder to cure patients, not the easier ones." Given the deeply entrenched gendered poverty in the region, we share Kenneth L Leonard's (2000: 43) view that "although poorer people visit traditional healers more often than the non-poor, this is almost entirely due to a geographic effect in which the bulk of the poor have larger additional travel costs to other providers." Research however suggests that although rural dwellers have a range of health care options, the factors shaping health decision making go beyond constraints to access (King, 2012; McIntyre and Gilson, 2002; Scheider et al., 2006) and also include historical processes and historical factors that underpin perceptions of illness and the discourse of health (king, 2012).

In terms of age, the survey revealed that 16% of participants were of the 18–20 age group, 36% were between 21–30 years, 20% were aged between 31–40 years. Furthermore, 12% were aged between 41 and 50 years, whereas, 20% were above 51 years of age. It has been demonstrated that socioeconomic factors including age and sex affect the use and patronage of traditional medicine (Welz et al., 2018; Udezi & Osifu, 2013). Similarly, research suggests that all age groups use traditional medicine for treating illnesses as well as for preventing illnesses and promoting health (Welz et al., 2018; Udezi & Usifoh, 2013).

In terms of marital status and religious affiliation of respondents, table 3 shows that 90% are Christians. This is of course not surprising because most inhabitants of the area profess to be Christians. Only one individual claimed to be a Muslim (2%), while 8% practice their ancestral religion (worship their ancestors). As Brian King rightly maintains, religious beliefs do not determine whether a patient or members of his 'therapy management group' (Hsu, 2002) consults a traditional healer and there are often myriad social pressures to underreport the use of traditional medicine (King, 2012: 1176). In this light, one of his respondents captured this discomfort and ambivalence thus: "We Pray at

TABLE 3 Marital status and religious affiliation of respondents

Sex Marital status		Religious Affiliation				Total
		Christian	Muslim	Ancestral worship	Subtotal	
Male	Single	4	0	4	8	20
	Married	10	1	0	11	
	Divorced	1	0	0	1	
	Widowed	0	0	0	0	
Female	Single	22	0	0	22	30
	Married	4	0	0	4	
	Divorced	1	0	0	1	
	Widowed	3	0	0	3	
Total		45	1	4	50	50

SOURCE: FIELD WORK

the Church in the Day and Visit the Sangomas at Night" (King, 2012: 1173). This shows the varied ways health is understood within local communities and how social, political, and cultural factors shape health decision-making. Similarly, patients do not often report TCAM use to biomedical providers. First, they fear "receiving improper care" (James et al., 2018: 9). Secondly, there is the biomedical provider's "negative attitude with perceived lack of support and understanding that lead to mistrust and stigma from conventional providers" (Ibid.).

In terms of marital status, it was revealed that 60% of respondents were single, 30% were married, 4% were divorced, while 6% were widow(er)s. This finding resonates with Ezeome and Anarado's (2007) study, which revealed that marital status had no effect on the use of CAM by cancer patients. Other factors that do not have an effect on the use of traditional medicine include variables such as age, educational level, religion and socioeconomic status (Ibid.).

8.3   Opinions on Traditional Medicine

Based on spontaneous responses, survey respondents had varying opinions as to what African traditional medicine is all about. This speaks to the different usages for which they make recourse to traditional healers or medicinal recipes as well as their divergent views on the efficacy of traditional healing methods. An estimated 60% of respondents associate traditional medicine with nature. They maintained that traditional medicine is medicine that comes naturally from nature. In other words, unlike western medicine, it is undiluted with chemicals and has been used for many years by their forefathers. Some respondents further added that traditional medicine is any medicine used by Africans to treat and eradicate health problems. To these interlocutors, the various health problems go beyond what can be naturally understood as physical illness. It may be spiritual, mental and lack of peace of mind. Their different viewpoints are represented in Figure 1.

As to what aspect of traditional medicine really makes it "African and traditional," up to 70% of respondents conceded that it is traditional because it is usually not documented. Members of a particular cultural milieu pass it down customarily from one generation to the next. South African healers appropriate "the ideas of tradition to emphasize their authenticity and legitimacy in a multicultural environment where patients may choose from a variety of practitioners and therapeutics" (Flint, 2008: 12). By referring to themselves as "traditional healers," they maintain that their practices have not remained unchanged over time, but are in tune with the practices of their ancestors. This is

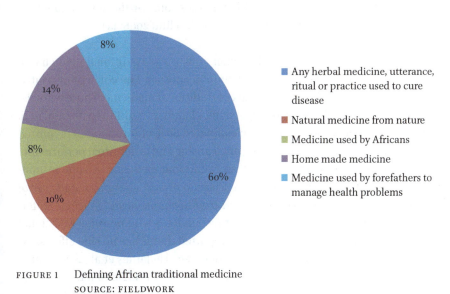

FIGURE 1 Defining African traditional medicine
SOURCE: FIELDWORK
60% = 30 persons
14% = 7 persons
10% = 5 persons
8% = 4 persons

a reference to the intergenerational transmission of knowledge and to the ancestor's intermediatory role in the therapeutic process through dreams, trances and visions. As a double-edged concept, tradition is flexible and can be readily summoned "to support or condemn various actions, practices, and/or beliefs." It is an all-encompassing concept "that connotes the passage of items, images, symbols, events, beliefs, behaviours, customs, or practices from one group to another over the years" (Flint, 2008: 12; see also Leslie, 1992). Tradition is dynamic and as Flint rightly articulates:

> In many ways, traditions are like family recipes, they are not static but subject to change over time. Each generation may improvise to accommodate the availability of ingredients or transformations in technology or to better suit their own tastes, all while attempting to honor the basic recipe. In essence, tradition is like an elastic fabric that is often stretched to meet specific needs. In this way we can see tradition as a cultural construct, subject to change from within and without. While there may be certain values, practices, and symbols that persist over time, there is nothing authentic or essential about them as their importance or meanings shift to reflect society's norms and values. This is not to say that they are meaningless. On the contrary, they have great importance to those who abide by them and possible repercussions for those who do not or for those who are intentionally excluded. (Flint, 2008: 14)

Three respondents (6%) noted that what constitutes traditional medicine in one society could be seen as ordinary flora in another. The concept of relativism is therefore essential when we talk of traditional medicine. Those who disagree with a tradition "may cast aspersions, claiming tradition to be outdated, nonsense, or superstition" (Ibid.). An estimated 60% of interlocutors reported that utterances, ceremonies, bathing or cleansing and other ritual performances are all major components of African traditional medicine. As one respondent rightly maintained:"...*you cannot separate rituals, utterances, and special ceremonies from the practices of African traditional medicine*" (Tsebele, Interview of 20 December, 2010). The 10% of respondents who perceive traditional medicine as "natural medicine" further reported that it has no side effects, except when used with pharmaceutical drugs (see also James et al., 2018). Some herbs are known to interact with pharmaceutical drugs (De Smet, 2002). Despite this recognition, the real frequency of the side effects for most herbs remains unknown "because they have never been tested in large clinical trials and because surveillance systems are much less extensive than those in place for pharmaceutical products" (Bent, 2008; cf. Oloyede, 2010: 77). Furthermore, even the long-standing uses of indigenous medicines neither guarantee their safety nor suggest that their safety and efficacy remain unquestionable (Ibid.). While it is possible to test the efficacy of traditional medicines through clinical trials as obtains for synthetic drugs (Calapai and Caputi, 2007), numerous methodological and logistical problems remain. They include a valid research design, which is a benchmark for human subject research. Yet, there is contention about what exactly constitutes 'a valid study design.' Biomedically trained clinicians would submit that the randomized blind, placebo-controlled trial remains the gold-standard for clinical efficacy (Tilburt and Kaptchuk, 2007; see also Oloyede, 2010: 76–77).

It has been well articulated that attempts to evaluate indigenous therapies using biomedical methodologies is not appropriate and may fail to generate true knowledge since the foundation of that knowledge is a scientific vocabulary that only makes sense within the conceptual framework of allopathic medicine (Fournier, 2013; Oloyede, 2010: 78; Schaffner, 2002; Fabrega, 2002). As Schaffner makes the point: "the standard notion of experimental design criteria represents an imperialistic 'western' mode of thinking." It has been suggested that research on indigenous medicines should ideally employ experimental research designs including RCT, and that despite their imperfections; they are the best methods for enhancing knowledge. While such trials focus on safety and efficacy, they hardly take into consideration the cultural context of such plants (Oloyede, 2010: 78). We maintain that efficacy, like the experience of disease and illness, remains culturally constructed. This suggests the need for a distinction between the emic and etic interpretations when dealing with issues bordering on the efficacy of medicinal plants. While most standard pharmacological evaluations of medicinal plant recipes tend to support the use of traditional medicines, they however, "fall short of suggesting that efficacy must be culturally appropriate. Scientific clininical trials are supposed to provide 'proof' of efficacy and allow these medicines to be admitted into evidence-based medicines" (Oloyede, 2010: 8).

In relation to data in figure 2, most respondents (90%) indicated that they use traditional medicine regularly. There is evidence to the effect that some people use traditional medicines secretly so that their fellow Christians and neighbours do not notice their practices (see King, 2012). Despite European missionary attempts to destroy African traditional religion and medicine because it was allegedly considered as against the Christian faith and moral, most Africans practice religious syncretism. The practice of this "contextual Christianity" (Mokhoathi, 2017: 1) is manifested in people's health-seeking behavior as they shuttle between modern medicine and traditional medicine. Europeans maintained that African religion promoted the belief in witchcraft and that

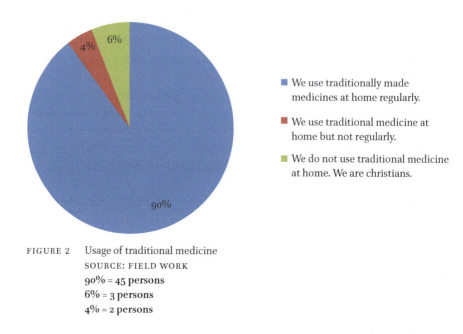

FIGURE 2 Usage of traditional medicine
SOURCE: FIELD WORK
90% = 45 persons
6% = 3 persons
4% = 2 persons

people worshipped their ancestors instead of God. African medicine was further regarded as unscientific and some of its treatment methods were considered anti-Christian. On the other hand, traditional healers were regarded as heathens because of their participation in African Traditional Religion. Thus, Africans who converted to Christianity were discouraged by the church from taking part in African traditional religious rituals and from consulting traditional healers.

This attempt to destroy African religion and medicine has failed. Many African Christians have continued to participate in traditional religious rituals. They have simultaneously continued to consult traditional healers. Stated otherwise, many African Christians have dual membership in the Christian church and membership in African religion. They are syncretic Christians: "many millions of Africans are followers of more than one religion, even if they may register or be counted in census as adherents of only one religion is correct" (Mbiti, 1975: 30). In Southwest Cameroon, a few Christians were temporarily excommunicated at various points in time from the Catholic Church for having allegedly consulted soothsayers. One case involved the President of the revered Catholic Women's Association (CWA) who was wrongly accused of having transformed herself into a venomous snake (mboma in pidjin English) and killed the son of a relative. To plead her innocence and exonerate herself from the accusation, she reportedly consulted a famous oracle based in Nigeria.

Back in the village, the villagers contested her account on grounds that no witnesses from the village accompanied her during the oracular consultation session. When the local priest got the news, she was temporarily suspended from the congregation. Moreover, she was asked to carry sand and to weed the church premises for weeks as retribution. It happened that the church hierarchy allegedly accused her of not having emulated Christ, but rather of having resorted to 'black magic.' Under similar circumstances, other Catholic faithfuls who reportedly consulted soothsayers for one reason or the other decided to boycott the Catholic Church and in protest joined various Pentecostal denominations (see Konings, 2003).

African medicine is inseparable from African religion, for two main reasons. Firstly, Africans have a very broad and general theory of illness; that includes African theology. This theory does not only attempt to explain illness and disease but also the relations between God and the universe. Secondly and, related to the previous one, is that many traditional healers are also religious leaders and vice versa.

Despite attempts by early Christian missionaries and others to suppress the traditional medical sector, it has continued to grow because health care is belief-sensitive and traditional healers are successful in curing a large number of illnesses. Traditional healers use both scientific and nonscientific or subjective knowledge. Scientific medicines are obtained mainly from plants. Many plant medicines recommended by traditional healers, Gordon L. Chavunduka (1986: 240) argues, are correct even when judged by modern scientific methods. This empirical knowledge has been developed through trial and error, experimentation and systematic observation over a long period of time. The major sources of non-scientific or subjective knowledge are the various spirits believed to play a part in health. The social and psychological methods of treatment developed from this unscientific base often bring good results.

Africans are increasingly participating in traditional religions. Although they participate in Christian religious rituals, they also take part in traditional rituals as well as turn to traditional healers in their health-seeking behaviour (King, 2012; Leclerc-Madlala et al., 2009). They therefore seem to be challenging the claims often made by early Christian leaders that many African religious rites and rituals and many of their cultural practices are contrary to Christian faith and morals. In recent years, a number of African scholars (Leclerc-Madlala et al., 2009; Mokhoathi, 2017: 1; Jarvis, 2009) have shown that many traditional practices that Christian churches eliminated or tried to eliminate were not, in fact, against Christian faith and morals. African religion recognizes the existence of witchcraft and the fact that witches that slow human progress exists (Ashforth, 2005; Flint, 2005; Geschiere, 2008). Witches are however, regarded as sinners by religious authorities and it is their duty to talk about witchcraft and to attempt to discourage its practice. African religion does not encourage people to venerate their ancestors instead of worshiping them; members of African religion talk to their ancestors but worship God. African religion says God is for everyone everywhere. God takes very little interest in the day-to-day affairs of individuals. God is not concerned with purely personal affairs but with matters of national and international importance. The ancestral spirits, on the other hand, are concerned with the day-to-day affairs of their descendants. They are the intermediaries between the living and God. People pray to God through their ancestors (Mbiti, 1990).

Many Africans who became Christians found it difficult to abandon their religion and medicine completely. Christian conversion was, therefore, shallow; it did not always change the African people's understanding of life and their relationship to their ancestral spirits and God.

The way forward for Christian churches of all denominations is to examine carefully African religion and medicine and other cultural aspects, with a view to identifying clearly those practices that are not against Christian faith and morals and incorporate them into modern medicine and Christian worship as practiced by the so-called African churches that blend Christian teachings with African tradition. To enable people to act in a more responsible way, "the church can assist in defining and explaining witchcraft" as a form of human behaviour (van Wyk, 2004: 1204).

There is a need for dialogue between the leaders of Christian churches and the leaders of African religion and medicine. Unplanned interaction might continue to create new problems, misunderstandings and conflict. The need is for sound and genuine dialogue; involving negotiations whenever necessary[1] (see also Mbiti, 1966).

Most interlocutors, (94%) conceded that they use traditional and modern medicine simultaneously. They admitted that they encourage others to use the former because it has been "very helpful" to them. This concurs with the findings of previous studies (Welz et al., 2018; Usezi & Osifoh, 2013; King, 2012). However, 6% of users of traditional healing practices reported that although they visit traditional healers, they have misgivings encouraging their relatives and friends to do same. The study further revealed that the 6% of respondents who claimed to be Christians do not use traditional medicine and equally do not encourage their close kins and associates to do same. One of them stated: "I am from a Christian family and we believe in God. I cannot use traditional medicine because it is against the teaching of God." This resonates with Brian

---

[1] see http://www.oikoumene.org/en.

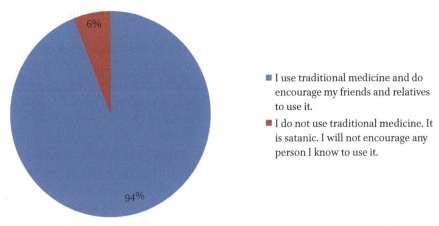

FIGURE 3   Respondents who use and encourage others to use traditional medicine
SOURCE: FIELD WORK
Users = 47 persons
Non users = 3 persons

Kings's (2012) finding that religious belief was one reason for the refusal to use traditional medicine in the Mzinti community that he investigated. On the contrary, some people use traditional medicine because of family tradition (Welz et al., 2018).

Although most respondents appreciated the strengths of African traditional medicine in relieving them of a variety of health problems, a majority of users of African traditional medicine shared a few concerns including—the perceived unhygienic environment in which traditional medicine is administered, and the pain associated with the administration of certain medicines, most notably the making of incision (*ukuqaphula*). Other side effects of traditional medicine include the fact that certain medications are instead presumed to make people sicker. Additionally, some medicines have extremely unpalatable taste and smell, while in some instances; some are governed by the prohibition of sexual intercourse. Furthermore, the prescription by some healers that traditional medicine must not be used simultaneously with western medicine has caused HIV/AIDS patients to drop out of antiretroviral therapy programmes thereby causing them their lives. This suggests that traditional medicine became "a cure and a curse for those sick with AIDS" (Bishop, 2012: 578; Peltzer & Mngqundaniso, 2008). Moreover, the high fee allegedly charged by some traditional healers, exaggerated claims by some healers of their ability to treat all sicknesses, and lack of precise dosage were other concerns. While these concerns form the basis of why some people do not seek help from traditional healers, it also shows how biomedicine is "infused with local discourses of health decision making, which seem to predispose these individuals against seeking out traditional healers" (King, 2012: 1178)..

We also found that people do not only use traditional medicine for therapy, but also for preventive reasons. Some 28% of respondents reported that they visit traditional healers when they have a bad dream or suspect an evil omen (*umhloca*). Three other respondents stated that they visited traditional healers to reinforce their relationships. Others maintained that whenever they encountered something evil, they would see a traditional healer for cleansing and the restoration of peace with the ancestors. This implies that the 'clinical encounter' of traditional healing goes beyond the patient and the healer, and also involves the ancestors of both (Oloyede, 2010: 84–85; Mbiti, 1990). This makes the clinical reasoning of the traditional healer a multilayered process of interaction through which the traditional healer is revealed certain 'signs' including the bodily signs "and interpretations thereof, as well as the consultations with the ancestors for the understanding of the patient's 'disequilibrium' and what to do to bring it back to the 'state' of 'equilibrium.' This 'epistemological complexity' of understanding shows that what is 'prescribed' is specific to the patient as an individual person, not as a body and as such would hardly yield itself to the efficacy sought through clinical trials that are controlled, measured and regarded as valid" (Oloyede, 2010: 84–85; Lantum, 1977).

A young man who buys and sells cannabis or dagga (*umya*) claimed that he has a traditional healer who makes him invisible to law enforcement officers. To him the healer protects him against the police. A soccer player in Qokolweni stated that:

> Soccer is a very challenging career; we make a lot of enemies in the field. To keep myself away from trouble and from bewitchment, before I play any soccer match in advance, I need to consult with my traditional healer. He will tell me the outcome of the match and protect me from sustaining injuries. It really works for me. If you don't protect yourself, sometimes you may see an arrow or a spear coming to you instead of the ball. (Tsewalele, Interview of 15 May, 2011)

Asked about their therapeutic recourse strategies, most interlocutors stated that they often go to hospital first when they are sick. This is however, not the case because most patients start their therapeutic recourse with the taking of common remedies (in the lay sector of healthcare) before engaging with the professional sector (see Kleinman, 1980). According to the GHS data, biomedical treatment regimens (from public clinics and hospitals) was the first choice for an estimated seven in every ten (71,4%) households in the management of

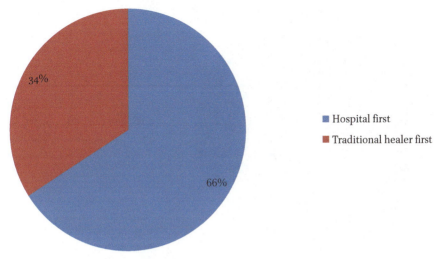

FIGURE 4   Traditional vs Biomedicine
SOURCE: FIELD WORK
Hospital = 33 persons
Traditional healers = 17 persons

ill health or injury. On the contrary, only 27,0% households indicated they consulted private doctors, private clinics or hospitals (Stats SA, 2017).

Regarding the prospects and possibilities for collaboration between modern doctors and traditional healers to improve healthcare coverage and delivery, most participants (62%) maintained that both can work together while 38% of respondents totally disparaged such prospects. Research on factors underpinning collaboration between THPs and CHPs from collaborative initiatives suggests that it is instigated by: the huge number of THPs in most developing countries compared to biomedical practitioners, inadequate or non-existent health facilities, lack of knowledge of THPs and the respect they command in their communities, the cultural acceptability and cost effectiveness of many indigenous medical treatments. Furthermore, collaborative initiatives in research within the context of HIV/AIDS and the political will demonstrated by many Third World governments among others, have also given rise to collaboration between indigenous healers and biomedical practitioners.

Despite the benefits of collaboration, the relationship between the two health care providers remains hierarchical in favour of biomedical practitioners and is characterized by lack of transparency. This imposes the need for mutual respect and dialogue for the exchange of information on the management of illness episodes, materials and technology used in the preparation and dispensing of drugs. It will further entail the recognition of the complementarities of

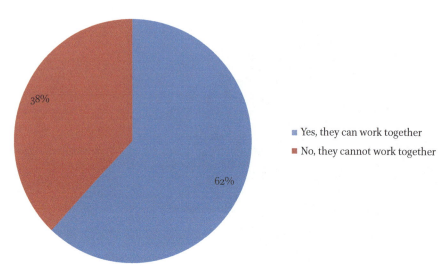

FIGURE 5 Collaboration between traditional healers and biomedical doctors
SOURCE: FIELD WORK
Collaboration is possible = 31
Collaboration is not possible = 19

both systems for referral between them given the multicausality of disease (see Busai and Kasilo, 2010: 5). Similarly, Joy Violet Summerton (2006: 16) captures the complementarity and therefore the need for collaboration in these words:

> The medication given by the traditional health practitioner may not alleviate the symptoms of illness, but the reassurance and the psychological effect of the consultation on the patient might play a vital role in restoring the patient's overall wellness. Similarly, the medication given by the western health practitioner may not provide psychological and spiritual comfort, but may alleviate the physical discomfort of illness. These aspects indicate the interdependent and complementary role that biomedicine and traditional healing play in the healing process.

As to whether or not respondents had experienced any problems while using traditional medicine, a majority, 54% reported that they had never experienced any problems. However, 20% of participants reported that sometimes "traditional medicine does not work." Additionally, 12% of respondents admitted that sometimes there are problems associated with the use of traditional medicine. Another 6% totally dismissed traditional medicine on the grounds that it does not work at all and that traditional healers are quacks.

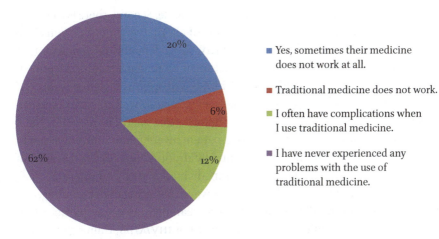

FIGURE 6   Challenges experienced in the use of traditional medicine
SOURCE: FIELD WORK

In a study of western health practitioners' perception of the strengths and weaknesses of traditional medicine for HIV/AIDS patients, Summerton (2006: 15) maintains that on the one hand, the use of traditional healing practices is underpinned by the fact that patients and healers share the same worldview and belief system, the failure of the healthcare system in which case it serves as an alternative, privacy and the absence of time-limitations per consultation, the psychological treatment of patients as well as the relief of scientifically unexplained physiological symptoms of particular illnesses. On the other hand, however, traditional healers are accused of prescribing harmful treatment regimens, especially for HIV/AIDS patients, delaying the seeking of appropriate healthcare: "when their remedies fail to produce the desired effects, destroying the interpersonal relationships of people living with HIV/AIDS through witchcraft accusations, psychological torment by the belief that HIV/AIDS can be cured with traditional remedies." In addition, increasing the workload of biomedical practitioners who are solicited to conduct multiple HIV/AIDS tests after patients have undergone several traditional treatment regimens to cure HIV/AIDS. This implies that traditional healers often fail to recognize their own limitations, thereby delaying treatment, which might be detrimental to the health of the patient (see also Muweh, 2011: 31; Wringe et al., 2017; Summerton, 2006). Three pathways of impact have been identified through which medical pluralism comprising of traditional, faith-based and biomedical health worlds contribute to the care cascade bottlenecks for PLHIV. There is first, delay in access to HIV treatment by the nature of health-related beliefs, knowledge and patient therapeutic recourse. Second, there is the interruption of HIV treatment by the availability of alternative therapies, perceived failed treatment and exploitation of PLHIV by traders and healers who take advantage of them. Thirdly, the combination of biomedical healthcare providers and treatment with traditional and faith-based options fueled tensions and resulted from the fear of drug-to-drug interactions as well mistrust between different providers (Wringe et al., 2017; Summerton, 2006). In KwaZulu Natal for instance, a number of HIV positive patients were using traditional medicine and ART concurrently. They eventually dropped out of ART because of side effects and were using traditional medicine for HIV (Summerton, 2006; Gqaleni et al., 2010; Zuma et al., 2016). As a way of fostering understanding, collaboration and promoting ownership of a meaningful two-way participation between THPs and clinics in the management of HIV/AIDS, training materials have been developed and translated into isiZulua. This is part of various mechanisms of establishing a district health-based collaboration between provincial and local authority clinics and THPs. The overall aim is to capacitate THPs "to document, monitor and evaluate their interaction with patients, and for the referral of patients to these clinics" (Gqaleni, 2010: 295). Concurrently, increasing exposure to HIV/AIDS-related information has led to a shift in the approach of traditional healers in the management of PLHIV. Patient's disclosure of their HIV/AIDS status plays a major role in THP's management of HIV/AIDS patients, permits for referral for testing and care for their patients. They are, therefore, capable of potentially enhancing the success of ART for PLHIV once disclosure is made (Zuma et al., 2016).

Charlatanism remains one of the main negative effects associated with, as well as the risk associated with untested medicinal plant extract and unregulated practices in traditional medicine. Some traditional healers claim expertise in the treatment of every disease. This attitude of know-all healers can delay a treatable medical condition and lead to an irreversible medical condition (Muweh, 2013: 32; Wringe et al., 2017; Summerton, 2006). Fake healing and healers, which obviously poses a significant challenge, is however, not limited to traditional medicine practice. Given that proficient healers render commendable services to a large population, quacks are likely to join the ranks of practitioners (Ebomoyi, 2009; 1982). Similarly, the current economic climate characterized by massive unemployment, has witnessed an increase in the ranks of traditional healers, some of whom are charlatans (Pretorius, 1999: 253; Abdullahi, 2011). The phenomenon of charlatans is intertwined with widespread abject poverty, unemployment and precarious livelihoods (Wreford, 2008; Flint, 2001). These charlatans are keen on getting into the fold of traditional healers through the backdoor by faking their calling.

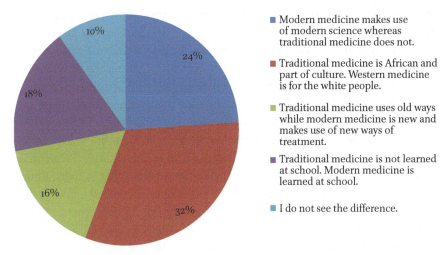

FIGURE 7   Difference between traditional medicine and modern medicine
SOURCE: FIELD WORK

As to the perceived differences between traditional medicine and biomedicine, 32% of respondents maintained that the difference lies in the fact that unlike the latter, the former is embedded in the African culture and worldview. Nevertheless, 10% of interlocutors could not identify any differences between the two systems of healthcare. Furthermore, an estimated 24% of respondents were of the opinion that while traditional medicine does not make use of modern science, modern medicine does. However, our observation in South Africa in particular and in others parts of Africa leads us to the conclusion that traditional medicine is actually being modernized. For instance, healers are increasingly appropriating diagnosis produced by medical laboratories, have adopted modern packaging techniques and are increasingly advertising their products over the mass media (see also Mutabazi, 2008). In South Africa, advertisements for toll-free numbers of traditional healers became legal in 1992. Since then, healers have been selling their services to a modern clientele "by appealing to notions of various traditions" (Flint, 2008: 15). Some 18% of respondents maintained that traditional medicine is not learned at school while modern medicine has a formal system of certification through medical school and medical residency. Additionally, 16% of respondents argued that traditional healers use old ways and procedures while modern medicine makes use of new and modern ways of treatment. Traditional medicine is of course, not cast in stone (Flint, 2016). Its dynamism suggests it is open to modernization.

The choice to use traditional medicine by most women and therefore their individual perceptions, Muweh (2011: 34) maintains, is underpinned by the individual's concept of health and disease. Studies (Potgieter et al., 2015; Mngqundaniso & Peltzer, 2008; Luizza et al., 2013; Voeuks, 2007; Momsen, 2003) however suggests that women are more knowledgeable than men concerning medicinal plants. Consequently, more women than men may be prompted to consult THs. An Ethiopian study for instance points out that unlike men; women have deep knowledge of plants that provide medicinal and veterinary services (Luizza et al., 2013). As caregivers in society, they are responsible for medicating and nursing family members when they are ill. Their broad knowledge and interest in medicinal plants might spur them to consult THs (Potgieter et al., 2015). In some societies including the Lençois community in Baha, Brazil, they are responsible for identifying and naming useful medicinal plant species. They are custodians of the community's ethno-pharmacopoeia (Voeuks, 2007). Furthermore, many useful medicinal plants are often located close to homesteads in home gardens, pastures and croplands (Momsen, 2003). Women are generally those involved in maintaining these areas. They are in constant contact with these areas. We subscribe to Martin J Potgieter and associates' (2015) argument about the Blouberg area of Limpopo Province, South Africa. They argue that since time immemorial, men tend to work further afield, including employment as migrant labourers in mines. Being constantly away from home in the mines suggest they are less intimately involved with local natural resources. They are also less likely to learn as much as women would concerning their uses. The dire underdevelopment of Blouberg with the lowest level of income and highest unemployment rate (90%) in South Africa is comparable to the Eastern Cape where Qwolweni is located. Like in the Eastern Cape, the poor socioeconomic situation has resulted in young men leaving the area in droves to work in the mines in the wealthy parts of the country. Men are generally, more likely than women to work in the mines and therefore to be away from home and leaving the care of the sick in the hands of women.

Those who emphasized on the influence of the supernatural and the spiritual (witchcraft) on their daily lives were more welcoming of traditional medicine in a moment of great anxiety and uncertainty that made the quest for supernatural solutions to look quite normal (Ashford, 2006; Farmer, 2006). This contrasts sharply with those who defined health as "taking care of self," who are more critical of traditional medicine, but are in favour of the development of traditional therapies to meet the healthcare needs of the masses. The major self-reported reasons for seeking help from a THP included a complex of supernatural (do away with bad luck, evil spirit and magic poisoning), or psychosocial problems (depression, anxiety, and sexual dysfunction), chronic conditions comprised mostly of pains in joints, arthritis, hypertension, cancer, diabetes as well as acute conditions and generalized body pains, HIV/AIDS and other STDs—gonorrhea, syphilis, and Chlamydia among others. Most venereal diseases are considered as "diseases of shame." A few respondents maintained that they will prefer consulting a traditional healer because unlike in hospital where their names will be written down, the healer will simply give them a concoction. In other words, most healers do not keep records that might identify them. The nurses with whom we spoke also corroborated this viewpoint. It was further revealed that traditional healers provide HIV positive patients with immune boosters (UNAIDS, 2006; Somse et al., 1998). The consultation of THs for supernatural reasons suggests an emphasis on the supernatural influences (generalized fear of witchcraft) that gripped South Africa in the post-apartheid era and shows how supernatural forces are believed to negatively affect people's daily lives and retard their progress (Ashford, 2006; Farmer, 2006). This situation prompts them to seek explanation and help from THPs rather than from the biomedical sector (Peltzer, 2000; Nelms and Gorski, 2006). People's attitude towards traditional medicine is clearly influenced by their varied health perceptions and needs.

The view of mental healthcare as one area of expertise for traditional healers resonates with the findings of a national survey conducted in South Africa, which showed that unlike modern medicine, traditional medicine plays a significant role in mental healthcare (Williams et al., 2010; Muweh, 2011; see also Lantum, 1977; Muweh, 2011: 34). Mental health illnesses are usually believed to be caused by supernatural agents and only traditional healers are purported to have supernatural expertise to deal with such illnesses. Other diseases reputed to be the domain of, or for which traditional medicine is effective include malaria, sickle cell disease and diabetes mellitus (WHO, 2009). What this suggests is that patients categorise illnesses into "traditional" requiring seeking help from a *sangoma*. On the contrary, other illnesses do not fall into this category and are therefore referred to the clinic or hospital. As one respondent stated: "When I am sick, I look at the disease. I understand the sangoma and others treat some diseases better than the doctor does. If a spirit bewitches one, is there any need to go see a medical doctor?." Another respondent stated: "After one goes to a clinic and does not get better, the next step is to go see a sangoma." This participant's statement suggests that some patients visit traditional healers only after unsuccessfully seeking out treatment from the hospital or clinic. In other words, doctors cannot cure some diseases as well as those that THPs can cure. Once they fail, there is usually recourse to traditional medicine. These different trajectories based on illness causation shows multiple factors inform the choice of healthcare provider even in a poor setting (King, 2012) like Qokolweni.

Figure 8 below summarizes various suggestions put forward by respondents for improving traditional medicine and ensuring collaboration between traditional healers and biomedical practitioners in both urban and rural settings.

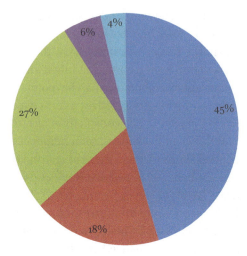

FIGURE 8   Opinions on improving traditional medicine
SOURCE: FIELD WORK

TABLE 4   Effectiveness of traditional medicine

Very effective	Not very effective	Not effective
34	10	6
68%	20%	12%

SOURCE: FIELD WORK

The table above suggests that 68% of respondents perceive traditional medicine as being very effective. However, some 20% conceded that traditional medicine is effective but cannot work in isolation. On the contrary, 6% of respondents dismissed traditional medicine as being ineffective. This diversity of opinion demonstrates the multifacetedness, historical, spatially situatedness, and conflictual nature of perceptions of belief about human health (King, 2012; King, 2010). In other words, there is no unitary perception of disease and health, even within the same community.

Traditional medicine obviously has both its advantages and disadvantages. Patient's perception of traditional treatment regimens often range from fear of adverse side effects of traditional herbs "to traditional medicine fanaticism." Patients who have experienced negative health outcomes with traditional medicine are often more critical of traditional medical treatment. Some however remain faithful to traditional medicine, even after a negative outcome.

Some users of traditional medicine use it only for preventive healthcare- that is; even when they are not sick to maintain their health, but when sick, go to the hospital for proper diagnosis and treatment. This implies that traditional medicine is being used for both preventive and primary healthcare. Yet, other users resort to it only as a last resort when the hospital fails to diagnose their health problems. They start suspecting supernatural causes and that is when they turn to traditional healers for spiritual therapies (Muweh, 2011: 32).

To complement the information that was obtained from the survey, a series of face-to-face interviews were conducted with three traditional healers and in late 2017, we further interviewed 12 nurses in the Qokolweni Location on their perspectives about collaboration between the mainstream biomedical healthcare system and traditional healing practices. These interview excerpts explain how some healers acquired their skills and the wide range of health problems they deal with in their communities as well as their views on collaboration between the traditional and mainstream biomedical system of healthcare. Then follows the opinions of nurses who are at the forefront of service delivery as auxiliary biomedical healthcare personnel.

Excerpts from these three interviews will serve as case studies. In order to keep the names of the respondents anonymous, pseudonyms will be used to represent their different opinions.

8.3.1 *Case Study 1: Vuyo (Fictitious Name)*

Vuyo is a 62-year-old female healer. She is the third child in a family of seven. Her mother originally came from Lusikisiki to marry her father who was a bona fide resident of Libode. Vuyo stated that her mother died when she was still young. Her father later left the home to work in the mines in Johannesburg but never returned. They learned that he had married another woman. Vuyo grew up with her maternal grandmother who was a herbalist and TBA. The latter passed away while she was twenty-two years old. Vuyo who is widowed, has four children and six grandchildren. Most of them live with her.

Vuyo sees herself as an informally trained midwife. She learnt the skill from her maternal grandmother. As a TBA, she provides advice, herbal remedies to pregnant women during gestation (*ukumitha*) and assists them in delivering their babies. She admits that her medicine is effective and has helped many women in need.

8.3.2 *Case Study 2: Bate (Fictious Name)*

Bate is a 35-year-old healer. He is married and has two children, a boy aged five and a daughter who is almost two years old. Bate left formal education at the age of fifteen-at standard eight.

> I received a vision in which I was directed by ancestral spirits on to specific places in the forest to find specific leaves which I used to treat specific illnesses such as umeqo, ibekelo, *idliso* [these are typical "African" diseases]. After the vision, I went to the place. I found the same herbs shown to me in the vision. According to custom, I was a chosen one and had to go through the process of *uku-thwasa*- a form of apprenticeship. (Interview, December 5, 2010)

Literarily, the term *uku-thwasa* means coming into view. In this respect however, the term means that the individual concerned is at an early stage in the process of becoming a diviner. Only the most experienced and renowned diviners are capable of curing *uku-thwasa*. In the case of Bate, it required that he goes through a process of mentorship under an experienced and reputable *igqirha* (priest-diviner). The duration for this training is usually indefinite. It is often determined by the initiate's ability to follow visions and to successfully treat diseases. Bate spent several years with his uncle who was also a traditional healer to get a mastery of what has become his call.

Bate has been a traditional healer since the age of eighteen. As a priest diviner (*igqirha*), he treats bewitched people, people suffering from night poison, and other spiritual sicknesses. During one of several discussion sessions, Bate acknowledged that a greater part of the population use traditional medicine alongside with modern healthcare simultaneously. He also believes that cooperation with biomedicine is possible if traditional medicine is encouraged and accepted as alternative medicine or means of curing many of the ailments, stresses and strains that affect many people.

8.3.3   Case Study 3: Monde (Fictious Name)

Sixty-two-year-old Monde has lived in Qokolweni Location since birth. His parents were traditional healers. As a child, Monde assisted them in collecting and preparing herbal medicines for the treatment of different diseases. Of his parent's seven siblings, Monde is the only one who actually qualified as a priest-diviner. He however claims that the practice of traditional healing is a family thing. The other siblings even without undergoing the lengthy process of *ukuthwasa* know medicinal plants and their myriad usages.

> All my brothers and sisters can make herbal medicine. We were taught by our parents. We used a lot of herbal medicine at home while we were growing up. There were no hospitals close to our home…many of them were far. One had to walk a long distance to find one. They were even just

for the white people. We believed that they could not cure our sicknesses.

Monde is a Christian and worships with the United Methodist Church of South Africa. He believes that God is at the centre of all powers. Although he prepares the herbal medicine concoction, he also believes that medicine without faith in God cannot work. Monde, who was always busy with his patients and church work, did not find any incompatibility in serving God and practicing traditional healing.

Monde admitted the relevance of traditional medicine and the power of God, the creator of all things. To him faith is the key to healing. He encouraged traditional healers to admit their strengths and weaknesses. Monde is critical of healers who exploit sick people and put their lives at risk. He also admitted that he would encourage a fair referral system between practitioners of biomedicine and traditional medicine. The referral system should be based on trust.

Through non-obstructive observation, we kept count of people visiting two popular traditional healers in Qokolweni Location. Tables 4 and 5 represent the number of people who visited the two healer's clinic from Monday the 13th of December 2010 to Friday the 17th of December 2010 and from 10th January 2011 to Friday 15th of January 2011 respectively. Observation took place daily from 8 a.m. to 15:30 p.m.

The category "children" on tables 6 and 7 above refers to all individuals whose ages were estimated to be below ten. While we cannot entirely conclude that all persons observed visiting were patients who needed treatment, it is however worthy of note that people are not known to go to the hospital if they are not ill.

The traditional healers visited during observation were just a few of the many healers found within and around Qokolweni Location. It is unfortunate that the entire community only has one conventional healthcare clinic within the immediate vicinity. There is however, another clinic in the neighbouring Ngangelizwe Township in Mthatha. Most respondents however made mention of clinics in the towns of Mthatha and Tsolo where both biomedicine and traditional healthcare is administered to patients and where patients sometimes receive information on natural plants for the treatment of common diseases when medicine is not available. We visited these healthcare facilities to gain some insights. The number of patients who were waiting for the doctors revealed that there was an influx of patients at the two clinics. The scarcity of medicines in these clinics and nearby hospitals, we suggests could also be a

TABLE 5   Number of patients visiting Obale's shrine

Day	Males	Females	Children	Total
Monday	18	28	4	50
Tuesday	6	15	2	23
Wednesday	7	21	0	28
Thursday	9	11	1	21
Friday	2	16	4	22
Total	42	91	11	144

SOURCE: OBSERVATION DATA COLLECTED FROM MONDAY 29TH NOVEMBER TO FRIDAY 3RD DECEMBER 2010

TABLE 6   Number of patients visiting Enow's shrine

Day	Males	Females	Children	Total
Monday	10	32	0	42
Tuesday	3	21	6	30
Wednesday	10	2	1	13
Thursday	8	17	1	26
Friday	16	13	3	31
Total	47	85	11	142

SOURCE: OBSERVATION DATA COLLECTED FROM MONDAY 10TH JANUARY TO FRIDAY 15TH OF JANUARY 2011

TABLE 7   Number of patients visiting Sangoni community health centre

Day	Males	Females	Children	Total
Monday	21	26	10	57
Tuesday	11	29	18	58
Wednesday	17	36	12	65
Thursday	26	44	22	92
Friday	23	25	7	55
Total	98	160	69	327

SOURCE: OBSERVATION DATA COLLECTED FROM MONDAY 6TH DECEMBER 2010 TO FRIDAY 10TH DECEMBER 2010

factor contributing to the patronage of traditional medicine. In the event of an absence of drugs, nurses at the clinic often prescribe traditional remedies including guava leaves for the treatment of specific symptoms. This has resonances with King's (2012: 1177) findings in the Mzinti community in South Africa. The nurses expressed mixed feelings about traditional medicine and the prospects for collaboration.

8.4 Perception of Nurses and Traditional Healers

Interviews with nurses highlighted mostly mixed but largely negative attitude towards THs. They pointed out that THs lacked training, provided patients with expired drugs, gave improper dosages and were not good at keeping records that can be used to ensure the follow up of patients. As one nurse stated: "These healers cannot tell you what they gave a patient. Some of them even give rotten herbs to patients saying that it is best and works better. Most of them know nothing and sometimes delay patients from seeking proper care from us."

The positive contributions of THs from the perspective of nurses included their contribution to the management of STDs, other minor diseases, and the prospects of them being community counsellors in the fight against HIV/AIDS. On a similar note, THs had mixed feelings towards nurses and medical doctors.

"They give the impression that hospital medicine is the best and never refer patients to us. They also scold patients who visit us, and therefore undermine our work even when they cannot provide therapy" (Traditional healer). They pointed out that biomedical personnel undermine their work by failing to refer patients to them for diseases in which they have expertise such as mental illnesses and that they cast doubt on the efficacy of their treatment. Whereas, THs were willing to learn and improve on their treatment, refer cases to hospitals and clinics, the nurses expressed unwillingness to do same. The negative attitude of nurses towards THs is a key obstacle to fruitful collaboration between the two systems of healthcare and prevents patients who visit traditional healers from telling nurses when they eventually get to the clinic or hospital. It speaks to collaboration between both systems in South Africa as the "education" of healers into biomedical practices (Flint, 2006; Mngqundaniso & Peltzer, 2008).

On collaboration, most nurses felt that it will go a long way to enhance healthcare because healers often maintain close ties with members of society. They stated that THs should refer patients suffering from tuberculosis and cholera to clinics and hospitals. On their part, the nurses stated it is still illegal for them to refer patients to THs. They do however, refer patients to healers for illnesses that they know healers can handle even without stating anything on paper so as to shield themselves from prosecution. They emphasized the necessity for healers to keep records so that in the event of complications, this can help them understand what the patient had taken, or change the medicine they had administered to the patient.

> Most of us healers do refer patients to hospital for infectious, chronic and neurological disorders but medical staff never do the same even when the disease is clearly above biomedicine. Take for instance cases of bewitchment, epilepsy, painful leg and infertility. Despite this, we want to work with them, serve our patients and communities better.

The above respondent is suggesting that each system has expertise in the treatment of particular diseases and that THs have expertise in the psychosocial and spiritual management of patients. He further stated that biomedicine was good for operations, TB and plastering of wounds. THs are expected to refer patients to the biomedical system of health care and not both ways (Green, 2000).

As one nurse stated:

> They do not refer patients because they are afraid to accept failure. They want to make profit all the time by pretending to treat all diseases, which is impossible. Some keep exploiting patients until they die in their care or arrive hospital when the situation is out of hand.

The few nurses who were opposed to collaboration with THs referred to them as "failures," "charlatans" and "people who claimed to cure all diseases." Leonard (2000: 43) seems to counter the view of healers as exploiting patients when he states that "Interactions with a traditional healer are extended over long periods of time because payments are often delayed. If healers sought a temporary placebo effect, they would avoid such lengthy interactions." Some nurses outrightly blamed doctors for the failure of collaboration between the two healthcare systems. "Doctors do not want any collaboration because traditional healers delay care and take patients away from hospitals." One nurse however pointed out that most often when an HIV infected patient shows up, doctors seem to see no hope for their survival. It is usually at this point that some nurses refer them to THs because they will never send them away. A similar attitude of distrust between THs and nurses was recorded in rural Limpopo

Province, South Africa. Nurses expressed low regard for THs and hardly referred patients to the latter (14%). On the contrary, 55% stated they got referrals from THs. The main reason underpinning this referral was the patient's interest, as a last chance against chronic or terminal disease (Pelzer & Khoza, 2002; Peltzer & Mngqundaniso, 2008). Among others, nurses referred cases of HIV/AIDS, cancer, depression, bereavement and psychological problems to THs (Peltzer & Khoza, 2002).

We gathered that most accusations of malpractices levelled against THs is because unlike nurses who have and are obliged to register with the Nursing Council, most traditional healers are still to gain membership into a council in tandem with the recommendations of the 2007 South African Traditional Health Practitioners Bill. Nurses accuse traditional healers of practicing in unhygienic conditions (lack of hygiene), using the same instruments e.g., razor blades for scarification on several patients with the potential to transmit diseases including hepatitis and HIV, failure to keep records, and exaggeration of their healing powers. Other concerns include the lack of precise dosage and expiry dates for their medicine that could be detrimental to the health of patients. These shortcomings of traditional medicine resonate with the concerns of non-users of this therapeutic strategy.

Within the context of HIV/AIDS, THs are seen as community mobilizers and therefore key partners in the fight against the pandemic. They were recommended as a key component of the HIV/AIDS care continuum by the Department of Health (2004). They are perceived as capable of drawing patients into voluntary testing programmes, promoting adherence to drug regimens, sharing their expertise in patient communication with biomedical staff and ensuring patient wellbeing and quality of life. Their holistic approach to patient and disease management has been hailed as appropriate to the problem of immune deficiency caused by concomitant infections, social and psychological isolation, under-nutrition and alcohol abuse. South Africans are reportedly among the highest consumers of alcohol and the country has been worst affected by drunk driving worldwide (Mokolobate, 2017). A 2009 review of alcohol use trends in South Africa over the 12 years preceding the study showed that for both adolescents and adults, the life time, current (past month) use and binge drinking had remained similar over time. Binge drinking was between 7–11% and risky drinking remained stable over the years (6%). There were, however, larger sex, geographic and racial differences. Nationally, risky drinking in pregnant women was 2.5% but particularly high among urban dwellers (4.1%), Coloureds (11.6%) and in the Northern Cape Province (24.9%) (Peltzer, & Ramlagan, 2009). These patterns of behaviour aggravate immune recovery including repeated exposure to HIV and STD infections. A holistic approach to living with HIV and AIDS can prolong life (Department of Health, 2004; Peltzer & Mngqundisa, 2008).

Given their record of accomplishment in caring and treating STDs, including HIV, they could be enlisted for patient referral, treatment and promotion of behaviour change (Green, 2000). Fruitful collaboration between traditional and biomedical practitioners can create complementary systems that will better serve the interests of patients and communities. The paradigmatic gulf between both systems does not preclude collaboration. This is especially the case since THs are willing to train on safety precautions when handling HIV/AIDS, STDs and tuberculosis patients. Many healers with whom we spoke expressed their willingness to collaborate with the Department of Health. It is however, also important that biomedical personnel be trained about the way different traditional healers work, to understand local ethnomedical concepts and to better understand their patients perspective. Trust needs to be established between THs and nurses. Mutual understanding is required for better patient care and the strengthening of the referral system. This is the case because patient shuttle across both systems of health care.

8.5 Conclusion

Despite the paradigmatic gulf between biomedicine and traditional medicine in terms of diagnosis and methods of treatment, patients and members of their "therapy managing group" (Hsu, 2008) often resort to the simultaneous use of both systems of healthcare so as to maximize the chances of restoring the patient to good health. They believe that both systems of healthcare are complementary, with the strength of each system making up for the perceived weaknesses of the other. Patients and their "therapy seeking group" (Hsu, 2002) should be perceived as active agents in their own health (Hsu, 2002; Leonard, 2000). According to Leonard (2000: 43), they analyse significant information before seeking care "react to the incentives they face to provide effort in their own care. It is easy to criticize the apparent ignorance of modern providers to this characteristic of patients, but this attitude is near universal in health care; it is not unique to Africa. This view of patients should be informative in the wider inquiries of health economics."

The particular context of HIV/AIDS and the national policy of a return to African tradition espoused by the ANC-government suggests that local health perceptions, particularly the fear of supernatural forces, are shaped by myriad processes unfolding within contemporary South Africa but also by environmental factors. Whereas the government embraced traditional medicine for

HIV/AIDS treatment, local people have specified views on which category of diseases are to be treated by traditional and modern medicine respectively. This study shows that members of the Qokolweni community often resort to traditional healers only after the failure of biomedical therapy. This contradicts governmental reports about the use of traditional medicine. Moreover, people have varied motives for consulting a THP, including spiritual wellbeing. This suggests that the ANC-government's insistence on an epidemiological approach is at odds with people's lived reality and the diversity of health decision making in rural areas (King, 2012: 1179). This in turn suggests "that health decisions which are deeply rooted and mediated by divergent perceptions of disease and health, are varied and do not align neatly with discourses generated by public health and governmental officials. Health decision making is fluid, pluralistic, and dynamic, and intersects with sociocultural processes in addition to individual biases and spiritual belief systems."

Although medical pluralism is a lived reality at the level of both patients and healers alike, biomedical hegemony remains the norm as most governments, including the South African state provide support and funding only to the mainstream biomedical system, thereby reinforcing its hegemony. Although showing signs of integrating traditional healers, the South African government pursues a fragmentary policy, without a clearly delineated policy framework for collaboration and for translating policy on traditional medicine into practice, a situation that has dogged the government's efforts (Summerton, 2006: 17).

Although respondents have varied opinions on the integration of traditional and modern medicine, 90% of survey participants, most of whom are Christians, regularly use traditional medicine. A significant number of respondents also regularly combine traditional and modern medicines for their healthcare needs. They maintain that traditional medicines are effective against a good number of health problems. Similarly, it emerged from a study of 104 Black Africans sampled from the general public in Limpopo Province South Africa that 68% sought medical treatment for their last illness from THPs, followed by the herbalist (19%) for minor and chronic conditions, the diviner (9%), and faith healer (4%) (Peltzer, 2000).

Most respondents (62%) remained positive regarding the prospects of collaboration between both systems of healthcare. Those who oppose collaboration concede that traditional healers are quacks; they exaggerate both the efficacy of their remedies as well as their skills. Like any system of medicine, traditional medicine has both its advantages and disadvantages. The advantages includes its cost effectiveness when compared to modern medicine, its holistic vision of health when compared to the bacteriological focus of biomedicine, its ability to handle illnesses with perceived supernatural causes, and thus, its cultural and social acceptability among patients and healers. The shortcomings of traditional medicine include lack of precise dosage, its inability to hold up to the biomedicine logic of randomized control trials and "traditional medicine fanaticism"- and therefore the phenomenon of quackery among some healers.

CHAPTER 9

The Daily Use of Traditional Medicine in Qokolweni Location

9.1 Introduction

The main aim of this study was to establish the grounds for dialogue and to articulate the need for collaboration between conventional medicine and African traditional medicine for the general improvement of healthcare. The specific context of democratization and the associated "return to culture and tradition" policy, the sociopolitical uncertainty (marked by dwindling employment prospects and bewitchment), as well as the HIV/AIDS social crises are instrumental and shaped the use of traditional medicine and African belief system in finding solutions or seeking explanations. At the outset of the HIV/AIDS pandemic, the South African government adopted competing policies by refusing the use of life-saving antiretroviral drugs in favour of traditional medicine as a perceived "African solution" to "an African problem" (King, 2012; Nattrass, 2005). This move pushed desperate HIV/AIDS patients keen to seek explanations and solutions to traditional healers. Social crises, uncertainty and disease are all threats to health from an African perspective. This penultimate chapter will interrogate the African concept of health and the daily use of traditional medicine in the Qokolweni Location of the Eastern Cape region of South Africa. It will further summarize the findings of this study and put forward some recommendations for the eventual integration of both biomedical and traditional medicine.

9.2 The African Concept of Health

Many custodians of African culture believe that to maintain health and vitality (*impilo*), people have to address both the natural and spiritual forces in the world. The findings of this study revealed the strengths, weaknesses, opportunities and threats of traditional medicine. We maintain that the traditional healthcare system is full of complexities. Failure to understand and appreciate these complexities often leads to failures in co-operation between traditional medicine and biomedicine. This study has identified various ways of enhancing the strengths of traditional medicine. It recommends the need to research for methods of testing, refining and validating traditional medicine in order to support its integration into the biomedical healthcare system.

9.3 The Concept of Traditional Medicine in Qokolweni

The study revealed that people in Qokolweni have mixed opinions on what constitutes African traditional medicine. A majority of study subjects (60%) perceive traditional medicine to be any herbal medicine, coupled with ritual practice used to cure diseases. Fourteen (14) % of respondents stated that traditional medicine is medicine that is 'home made' and used in the treatment of diseases. Additionally, 10% of surveyed subjects maintained that traditional medicine is simply medicine that comes from nature. To them traditional medicine is medicine that has not undergone any form of industrial processing. Contrary to biomedicine, traditional medicine is relatively independent of high technology. Until recently, complementary medicine was designated as "natural medicine" and it included naturopathy, homeopathy, herbalism, several manual therapies and mind-body medicine (Di Stefano, 2006). Over time, traditional healers are increasingly appropriating the methods of modern medicine to appeal to an urban clientele. Arnold Nyiegwen Muweh describes the appropriation of scientific methods of diagnosis and treatment. His respondents summed up the modernity of traditional medicine as "traditional medical practice which makes use of modern medical techniques" in the diagnosis of diseases as well as in the monitoring of treatment outcome in patients. They maintained that "modern traditional medicine is simply a means to attract more patients and clients" and that traditional healers are capable of improving upon their practice by "acquiring the modern skills and knowledge of biomedicine through education which will then qualify them to become modern traditional doctors" (Muweh, 2011: 29). Faced with numerous cases of post-procedure infection and the need to eliminate complications resulting from circumcision by western doctors over decades of tradition a technology in the form of a precision instrument has been designed for use by traditional healers in South Africa (Bruce, 2002). Still in South Africa, the manufacture of traditional medicine (*muti* trade) is becoming a booming industry, generating an estimated R2.5 billion per annum (Feries, 2000; cf. Bruce, 2002: 165). Traditional medicine offers an alternative way of handling sickness and disease than the methods of biomedicine at far lesser cost. Lastly, 8% of respondents maintained that traditional medicine is medicine used by Africans. This medicinal knowledge is believed to have been inherited from their forefathers in an effort to manage health and to combat diseases.

Like these respondents, commentators (WHO, 1990; Mwangi, 2000; Lamla, 1981) also differ on what traditional medicine really is. The WHO (1990: 1) defined African traditional medicine as "the sum total of all knowledge and practices, whether explicable or not, used in diagnoses, prevention and elimination of physical, mental and societal imbalances." Mwangi (2000) maintained that traditional medicine is a solid amalgamation of dynamic medical traditions and ancestral experiences. For Marlise (2003), traditional African healing involves diverse health approaches, practices and knowledge, mineral based and spiritual therapies used traditionally for healing. While traditional healing may be deplored as being "irrational" and "absurd," it however fulfils an important function in arming harassed people against doubt and misgivings. It imbues the patient with renewed strength. The persistence of belief in traditional healing can be attributed largely to the important role it plays in traditional life which none of the new influences has so far been able to fill satisfactorily (Lamla, 1981: 37). For the average Southern Nguni, modern medical services are too remote from the realities of daily life and therefore do not prove to be an acceptable substitute for traditional medical practices and beliefs. Most knowledgeable observers interviewed were unanimous that traditional healing is likely to remain for some time. They however, also maintained that eventually, it would diminish thereby going the way of many customs, which were once regarded as sacrosanct.

Though opinions on what traditional medicine is, varies, there is general agreement that African traditional medicine is a method of healing that is completely reliant on practical experience and observation handed down from generation to generation through enculturation. Differences in opinion on the issue of the meaning of traditional medicine did not come as a surprise. This is because people use traditional medicine for different purposes. Their notions on what it is will largely depend on what they use it for. This suggests that plants have both sacred and profane usages. As Muweh (2011) reports, some women use it to maintain their health, but when they are sick, they consult a biomedical doctor for treatment, while other women make recourse to traditional therapy only when they suspect the disease to have been caused by personalistic agents.

This study resonates with the finding of previous studies (Gilbert et al., 2006; Di Stefano, 2006) according to which unlike conventional medicines, which is based on the principles of science, and treatment which targets specific pathogens, (virus, bacteria, fungi) traditional medicine relies on history as well as the social and physical milieu of the patient. Additionally, traditional medicine is more comprehensive and it takes into consideration both the physical and the spiritual elements of disease aetiology (Pemunta et al., 2013).

This aspect makes traditional healing a popular healthcare choice in Qokolweni Location and possibly beyond. It is most probably the holistic nature of TCAM that has made pharmaceutical companies to be working tirelessly to thwart its development. Şeref Menteşe, a prominent Turkish herbalist's statement that unlike traditional medicine, modern medical science differs fundamentally in its approach to illness resonates with the situation in South Africa from the perspective of patients: "The [latter] tackles the effects of the basic illnesses and does not deal with the root causes…, most diseases are derivatives of a dozen illnesses. Herbal medicine attacks the roots of these diseases." He has consistently lambasted drug companies, saying the side effects of commonly prescribed drugs have resulted in too many illnesses in the country, costing billions of dollars for the treatment of toxins released from these drugs.

> "As a herbalist who tries to promote the huge benefits of herbal treatment in Turkey, I have been confronted with huge lobbying efforts by big pharmaceutical companies that aim at nothing but thwarting the development of alternative or traditional medicine," he said, stressing that these companies have spent millions of dollars in lobbying efforts to keep doctors, bureaucrats and parliamentarians on their side. "Alternative healing methods based on herbal extracts from nature could potentially save billions of dollars for the state treasury,"[1]

Traditional medicine plays an important role in healthcare. Many respondents maintained that traditional medicine is complex because it involves some aspects of mysticism and the use of plant and animal-based products. Although "the quality of a herbal medicine is believed to be directly related to its active principles," often referred to as "secondary" plant substances, herbal medicines is made up of other substances that are often neglected and poorly understood, which make the ingredients to be "active" as medicinal agents. This explains why, to reproduce the effect of the herbal drugs by isolating its individual constituents and recombining them in the laboratory is often difficult. Apart from generally inactive substances (cellulose, lignin, etc.) there are also "substances of minimal pharmacological interest, such as the bitter or aromatic substances that stimulate the gastric and intestinal secretions thus making the dissolution, and consequently the absorption of the active principle possible or more complete" (Capasso et al., 2003: 11). Similarly, and unlike European herbal medicine, Chinese herbal medicine differs in several significant

---

1 http://www.todayszaman.com/news-237113-big-pharmaceutical-companies-prevent-herbal-medicine-fromdeveloping-in-turkey.html.

ways. Whereas, the Western herbal tradition focuses on "simples," or herbs taken individually, in contrast, traditional Chinese herbal medicine (TCHM) makes almost exclusive use of herbal combinations. More importantly, these formulas are not designed to treat symptoms of a specific illness; rather, they are tailored specifically to the individual according to the complex principles of traditional Chinese medicine. For this reason, TCHM is potentially a deeply holistic healing approach. On the other hand, it is both more difficult to use and to study than its Western counterpart.[2] This research has established that traditional medicine is largely plant-based. For the Qokolweni community as is the case with most African communities, traditional medicine is the most affordable and accessible healthcare system. Thus, it plays an almost inestimable role in healthcare delivery.

The Qokolweni community has only one conventional healthcare centre serving the people of Qokolweni and other neighbouring communities in Mthatha and Mqanduli districts. The transport infrastructure linking nearby communities to Qokolweni is very poor. Respondents reported that sometimes people walk long distances to get care from the healthcare centre. Pregnant women were alleged to have either given birth on the way to these healthcare centres or in some cases, died of pregnancy-related complications. During emergency, even the ambulance services find it difficult to reach out to people who need help. Additionally, the health facility only provides limited healthcare services. A few midwives and nurses with no resident medical doctor staff it. Because the clinic serves people from many communities around Qokolweni, patients often have to wait or stand in long queues before they can get help.

The availability and prevalence of African traditional medicine is a blessing to many local people who need healthcare but sometimes they cannot access it because of a conjuncture between physical inaccessibility and poverty. Lamla (2007: 88) in Nhqeleni observed the same situation. The true test of the role of African traditional medicine lies in testimonies made by its users. This is revealed in table 4 where (68%) of users admit that treatment with traditional medicine is effective. This admission of the effectiveness of traditional medicine as effective highlights the need to take the view from below seriously. That is to take "subaltern health narratives" (King, 2010: 50; King 2012) because misunderstanding of local practices and knowledge systems often lead to policy failures (Ibid.). Also, table 5, 6 and 7 show a picture of what is happening in the community of Qokolweni. Our observations presented in the tables in the

---

[2] http://healthlibrary.epnet.com/print.aspx?token=de6453e6-8aa2-4e28-b56c-5e30699d7b3c&ChunkIID=37410.

preceding chapter shows that many people are likely to visit traditional healers rather than modern healthcare clinics. This suggests the need to take cognizance of local health narratives and decision-making. And how they influence the choice of one healthcare provider over the other—traditional medicine and biomedicine (King, 2012).

Information obtained from respondents revealed that traditional healers have skills to manage and cure a wide range of conditions. These conditions include cancers, AIDS, psychiatric disorders, high blood pressure, cholera, infertility, and many venereal diseases. Traditional healers also claim to cure epilepsy, asthma, eczema, hay fever, anxiety, depression, urinary tract infections, gouts and healing of wounds and burns. This suggests patients and their "therapy seeking group" (Hsu, 2008) categorize illnesses into those that are the province of traditional medicine and those that are better handled by modern medicine.

Most Africans strongly believe that the spiritual aspects of a disease must be addressed before the medical aspects are dealt with (Zubane, 2001). In other words, traditional healers have the ability to diagnose the spiritual aspects of a disease and eliminate them before proceeding with its management (Pemunta et al., 2013). This ability is considered as a gift from both God (*um-Dali*) and the practitioner's ancestors. Traditional healers lay a lot of emphasis in determining the agent underlying any sickness episode which could include bad luck, jealousy or the wrath of the ancestors (Charema et al., Shizha, 2008: 61; Neuwinger, 2000; Prince, 1964). Thus it can be construed that traditional medicine plays an important role in healthcare in Qokolweni Location and South Africa at large.

In addition to treatments used in curing ailments, protection against witchcraft and other ills, new forms of medicinal knowledge have evolved to meet modern demands and new conditions and situations. For instance, there are medicinal herbs for finding employment with effortless ease as well as keeping it. In other words, "some medicines have been modified for use in the new environment" such as medicines traditionally used in courting women. As Veronique Faure eloquently points out:

> Normally, the boy would break a small piece of the root of the medicine and keep it under his tongue while talking to the woman. The medicine was supposed to make his voice sound musical to the woman and thus make her fall in love with him. During the 1980s and 1990s, this medicine was prescribed for people going for interviews, to make the potential employees' voice sound musical to the interviewers and, in this way, make them choose the person for the job. (Faure, 2002: 26)

Other medicines are supposedly used to attract customers to particular beer parlours or illegal taverns or shebeens. Some herbs are believed to "blind" the police so that they may not find a woman's illegal "beer hole" (*Isirhoxo*). Certain medicines can supposedly lead a magistrate to impose a lenient sentence on an offender or even acquit him/her. There are even medicines to obviate the necessity of paying bills. While some medicines are used to protect, others are used to find people's property when lost (Faure, 2002: 29).

It is believed that certain medicinal plants and herbs can cause a famous person to lose prestige while other charms enhance one's dignity. There are medicines to ensure that a newly married wife never abandons her husband and to make her faithful. Other medicines are designed to "fix" a girl to be faithful to her boyfriend (*ubhekamna ndedwa*) against all comers. There are medicines that make a woman to refrain from flirting, while others cure sterility.

Traditional healers have also responded to the exponential increase in the abuse of alcoholic beverages that has gone out of proportion in recent years. They have devised special medicines for making an individual to refrain from taking intoxicating drinks while other medicines are used to make a person stop smoking.

Furthermore, there are medicines for rendering an enemy powerless in a fight while other medicines can render a person invisible. There are medicines for promoting luck especially winning in contests or betting, notably the annual Durban July Handicap or the current national lottery (Lotto) sponsored by the Gidam Company. Certain traditional healers claim to promote wealth by making the rich to become richer. Similarly, Hsu (2002: 299) reports that in Tanzania, patients made recourse to traditional healers for "cases of bad luck in business, protection for imminent travel, search of a partner, and marital problems." While some cases involved witchcraft (*nguvu ya uchavi*), others did not.

This limited survey of occasions when recourse is made to traditional medicine shows with clarity that present-day traditional healers use their skills in a great variety of ways. It shows that they are frequently consulted by their people during all times of need. Obviously therefore, the traditional healers esoteric knowledge covers far wider spheres than those of the physicians whose main aim is to sustain life by curing episodes of ill-health. It is clear that traditional healers no doubt go beyond the curing of physical ailments. Their medicines are used in the social, economic, political and legal domains of everyday life. In this regard then, the word medicine changes its meaning because the application of *amayeza* (medicines) goes beyond the field of medical treatment of physical illness. In fact, the meaning of the word "illness" even changes, because *izifo* (sickness or a kind of social death) cannot be isolated from the rest of a person's life.

Extrapolating from Placide Temples and John Mbiti, philosopher Ifeanyi Menkiti describes the African conception of man as opposed to the Western perspective as communitarian-as defined by "an environing community" (Menkiti, 1984: 173; see also Menkiti, 2004). Similarly, Richard Onwuanibe concedes that the African view of the person is more practical than theoretical: "based on the conviction that the metaphysical sphere is not abstractly divorced from concrete experience, for the physical and [the] metaphysical are aspects of reality, and the transition from one to the other is natural." In this regard, personhood is the outcome of the interplay between the individual and the community. The individual is non-existent, independent of the group: "whatever happens to the individual happens to the whole group" and vice versa (Onwuanibe, 1984: 184). This same vision underpins the quest for diagnosis, illness and therapy. In the Western individualistic worldview, health and illness largely depend on people's living and working conditions. Whilst Africans share this perspective, they also look for the cause of illness and disease from their social relationships: if a taboo has been breached, the necessary course of action-usually involving rites to appease the gods or the ancestors is accordingly identified and embarked upon through diagnosis usually by consulting a soothsayer/witchdoctor. As vividly captured by John Mbiti (1970: 141), the individual does not exist out of society: "I am because we are, and since we are, therefore, I am." Stated otherwise, personhood is articulated in communal terms and is a reference to one's experiences in terms of social relationships. Whatever happens to the individual is believed to happen to the whole group, and whatever happens to the whole group happens to the individual. The individual can only say: "I am because we are, and since we are, therefore I am. This is a cardinal point in the understanding of the African view of man" (Mbiti, 1990: 106).

The relationality of the African personhood, Anthony Appiah concedes is encapsulated in "the general views of a people about the world- social, natural, and supernatural-in which they live" (Appiah, 2004: 26). This demonstrates the centrality of communal experiences. For a critical discussion of the myriad differences in foregrounding the concept of personhood in African philosophy, (see Matolino, 2011; Pemunta, 2011b; Menkiti, 2004; Menketi, 1984). In other words, the individual is rooted in networks of solidarity and community life. "He is seen in his "relatedness" to the physical, environment, others and the unseen world of constructive forces … When any of these relationships is impaired, the human being is "sick". This explains why healing in Africa is not just a biomedical concern, it has to do with preservation or restoration of human vitality in the context of the community and his relationship as a whole. The sense of belonging, solidarity and community life is so strong in traditional society that people do not care so much about what you have as how many people you are able to rally. This for the African is real wealth. People who bring about social disorder and destroy harmony are considered to be witches and wizards. They are said to be "nobodies," no matter how much they own or how wealthy they are" (Mbuy, 2001: 180, see also Pemunta, 2011b: 96).

In practical terms, the relationality of the African worldview is instantiated in the holistic vision of health as manifested in traditional medicine. It has been estimated that 80 percent of Africans independent of socioeconomic and professional backgrounds are dependent on traditional medicine for their health needs (Hostettman et al., 2000; Tabenyang, 2011). It often involves rituals, sacrifices, and the interactions between African metaphysics and cosmology as they shape people's social relationships. Health from an African perspective becomes an all-encompassing condition: a state of complete wellbeing and vitality that permits an individual to express his or her physical, emotional, intellectual, creative and spiritual capabilities in a manner that is harmonious with that individual, others, society and all of life. Good health is associated with success in all human endeavours: soil fertility and high yields, social and biological reproduction-daughters and sons securing marriage partners and giving birth to grandchildren- and professional success among others. In Savage's (1996) description of a holistic vision of health and illness applicable to Bali Nyongans of Northwest Cameroon, she notes that reproductive morbidity, or the inability of a woman to bring forth an offspring, whether through failure to conceive, miscarriage, stillbirth or infant or child mortality is an indication of disharmony with the living and/or between the living and the dead. Health is therefore perceived within the context of traditional society, as a harmonious state where the social/religious or supernatural realm clearly impacts on both physical and psychosocial wellbeing. Pregnancy, par excellence, is one of these states (see also Richards, 2002; Gilbert et al., 2000).

Additionally, sickness cannot be separated from the rest of society and the world in which the person afflicted by *Isifo* (sickness or a kind of social death), lives. "Sickness" in the traditional frame of thought refers to an incapacitated personality. The traditional healer is therefore called upon to restore life (*Impilo*) as "a friend of the community" (Mbiti, 1966: 171). Life in the widest sense refers to the physical, psychological, social, spiritual and moral dimension of human existence and wellbeing. The recourse to traditional medicine and belief system becomes understandable only in the context of such all-embracing view of life and sickness: physical, social and psychological wellbeing that is characterized by success in any worldly undertaking (Gilbert et al., 2000). This is what may be referred to as "African diseases" (*Izifo zesintu*) which physicians cannot treat or cure.

9.4 The Use of Traditional Medicine in Qokolweni

The use of African traditional medicine is a very common practice in Qokolweni Location. Up to 90% of the respondents who participated in this study use traditional medicine on a regular basis. Those who do so, use it simultaneously with biomedicine. We will designate this simultaneous recourse as "syncretic auto-medication." Writing on Tanzania, Hsu (2002: 309) noted that Chinese doctors sometimes provide integrated treatment regimens by simultaneously combining Chinese traditional medicine and biomedicine. According to Kleinman (1980: 59) "the folk (nonprofessional, non-bureaucratic, specialist) sector shades into the other two sectors of the local health care system." Folk medicine is comprised of many different components: while some are intertwined with the professional sector, most are however, related to the professional sector. In the same light, whereas folk medicine is frequently separated into sacred and secular dimensions, in practice, this division is often blurred. Respondents reported that they use a variety of home prepared mixtures for major and minor illnesses. This is the case because beliefs in medical practice are neither personalistic nor naturalistic (Foster and Anderson, 1978). Rather, medical systems are often characterized by both personalistic and naturalistic aspects, and there is the transgression of the fluid boundaries between medical systems as people use and make sense of different medical systems (see also Hsu, 2008: 317–318). While it is believed that diseases are caused by a person's lifestyle/habits of consumption, it is also believed that they are sometimes also caused through the agency and mediation of supernatural factors. In other words, in the cosmology of most African societies, animals, insects and other natural elements do not cause or transmit diseases except when they are used by the gods as punishment against a person, or group (see also Ajala and Nelson, 2013: 82). During both informal discussion sessions and face-to-face interviews, most respondents argued that they often take homemade remedies and when such remedies fail to heal them, they would go to the hospital.

Most of the respondents also admitted that at one point in their lives, they have visited traditional healers. They state that traditional healers often assist in handling major health problems common in the community including HIV/AIDS. This confirms previous findings that a bulk of South African citizens use traditional therapies (Zubane (2001), Karim et al., (1994) and Fyhrquist

(2007)). The continuous use of traditional therapies in the face of advanced biomedicine is a clear indication that biomedicine has not replaced traditional healing.

While a majority of respondents use traditional medicine on a regular basis, a few respondents (4%) argued that though they use traditional medicine, they do not do so on a regular basis. Another 6% entirely refused to admit that they neither make recourse to nor encourage members of their entourage to resort to traditional healing. To this group, traditional healing is not only devilish but it does not produce the desired effect. This group of respondents seemed not to see any element of truth in traditional healing. They disparaged traditional healing on the grounds that it has no accurate dosage. "It is imaginative." "It does not work." "It robs people of their money." "It involves practices that are unhygienic as well as the exaggerated claims by some healers that they can cure every ailment or situation that crops up" (Nwoweh, Interview of 05 December, 2010; see also Muweh, 2011). Some users of traditional medicine share these concerns but they are of the opinion that overall, traditional healing is good, with little or no negative side effects.

The study revealed that most of those who claim they do not use traditional healing are Christians (90%). Further questioning however revealed that at some point in their lives, they had used traditional healing. This brings us to the issue of religious syncretism and division of labour when it comes to therapeutic choice.

People have categorized sicknesses into those that can be cured by traditional medicine and those that can be treated by biomedicine. This categorization however remains fluid and they often resort to both the former and the latter healthcare system simultaneously. This is what Pemunta, (1999) refers to as "syncretic automedication" to maximize the prospects of recovering quickly (see also Hsu, 2000). There are infectious diseases, which are treated with biomedicine, and African diseases which only traditional medicine can cure. This study is therefore in line with the view that modern healthcare has not and may never replace the traditional healthcare system (Labhardt et al., 2010). This explains why traditional healers in Qokolweni continue to provide healthcare to a significant portion of the community.

When asked to evaluate the efficacy of traditional treatment regimens, most respondents (68%) acknowledged using traditional medicine as an effective healthcare system. They admitted the effectiveness of traditional medicine in the treatment of many STDs, and "African diseases" like *isifo sephepha* (Tuberculosis), *isifo sokuwa* (fainting fits), *idliso* (that which has been eaten i.e. poison), *umeqo and ibekelo* (swollen legs), *pleyiti* (severe spasmodic abdominal pain in infancy) *inxeba* (wound), *ukutwala*(to carry or making people rich), *imimoya emdaka* (attack by evil spirits). The above illness episodes are said to have an African origin-that is to be caused by personalistic agents. The aetiology of African diseases cannot be understood from the biomedical point of view. It will not be feasible to seek for a biomedical understanding of the causes of "African diseases." Traditional medicine will therefore remain an important healthcare choice to many South African citizens in Qokolweni and other communities. Medical effectiveness is a 'floating signifier' that is dependent "upon social, ontological- valid categories and their relations- and epistemological-means for constructing valid knowledge-contexts" (Adams et al., 2005; cf. Bode and Payyapplamana, 2013: 14). It is also "bound by individual illness trajectories, objectified disease taxonomies (nosologies) and disease explanations expressed in the words and grammar of a specific medical system (aetiologies)" (Bode and Payyappallimana, Ibid.).

9.5 Attitudes and Perceptions towards African Traditional Medicine in Qokolweni

The attitudes and perceptions of people vary about the use of traditional medicine. Informants were asked how often they use traditional medicine at home. A majority (90%) of respondents admitted that they used it regularly. A few (4%) stated that they do not use traditional medicine regularly. However, some respondents (6%) stated that they do not use it at all. They associated their unwillingness to use traditional medicine on grounds of their religious beliefs.

Asked about which healthcare choice people would first make recourse to when they are sick, most respondents (66%) said they would go to the hospital while 34% said they would first go to a traditional healer. As to the prospects of collaboration between traditional healers and modern doctors to enhance healthcare, while 62% pointed to the feasibility of collaboration, another 38% of informants categorically stated that collaboration between the two healthcare providers was impossible. Even healers do not share a common position regarding collaboration partly because biomedical practitioners are certified through medical education which tends to create a paradigmatic gulf between the representatives of the two systems of healthcare:

> **Question (Vuyo Researcher):** Has it ever occurred to you that if given a chance you can also work in a hospital like a midwife?
> **Answer (Vuyo, Respondent):** Well, we are all doing the work of God. I know that the midwives have been to school, they know their job, I do

admire them but I don't see myself working in a hospital. I am not educated. However, the experience is my stronghold. I would rather see to it that midwives do their job while I do mine.

Question (from researcher) to Bate: Do you think traditional healers like you and modern doctors can work together?

Response (Bate): Modern doctors cannot accept and understand our ways. We healers are not educated like modern doctors. I don't think it is possible to work together.

On his part, when Monde was asked if it is possible for both traditional healers to work in hospital with medical doctors, the respondent confidently asserted that this needs to happen if healthcare needs to be improved. Additionally, he maintained that many clients who come to him have already been to the hospital. He further stated that there are sicknesses, which can better be catered for in the hospital while others must be catered for using simple herbal medicine or traditional stuff. However, to him faith and prayers must accompany all medicine.

He revealed that he actually treats a wide range of sicknesses ranging from flu, cough, spiritual diseases (which is believed to be the province of traditional medicine), STDs like gonorrhea, syphilis, vaginal candidiasis and others. While in his clinic, we observed that he was also managing cases of mental disorder. He also indicated that he treated fevers, patients with erectile dysfunction; he made immune boosters for those who needed them and those who were said to be HIV positive. The healer added that he conducts spiritual baths (*isiwasho*) to people with spiritual problems. This is often accompanied with songs of faith praising God.

Among the main challenges he is facing as a healers is the fact that people are yet to explore the richness of traditional medicine. To him, he felt that there are people who are yet to believe that traditional medicine is an effective healthcare system. He also added that some traditional healers are charlatans. They just go out there deceiving people that they can do everything and treat all diseases. To him this is creating mistrust amongst the many users of traditional medicine as well as hindering the prospects for collaboration. Monde also maintained that unlike modern doctors, the South African government does not support traditional healers. The healer however admitted that some government officials come to him for treatment and divine protection.

He was of the opinion that proper recognition should be given to healers and that their medicine should be processed and used in hospitals. He mentioned a university trained medical doctor with whom he collaborates and who blends traditional practices and modern medical practices. To him, it is working and many patients visit this medical doctor. In his opinion, such practices should be encouraged.

The above-mentioned differences in opinion not withstanding reveal that a majority of respondents use traditional medicine for different reasons. The few who do not do so are all Christians. Christians constituted 90% of our respondents. Only 6% of respondents do not use traditional medicine. This means that most people, irrespective of their religious denominations, still use traditional medicine. Information obtained from fieldwork also revealed that irrespective of the regular use of traditional medicine, 66% of survey participants often make their first therapeutic recourse by seeing trained physicians. This suggests that a working co-operation probably through a system of referral is possible between physicians and traditional healers.

One can rightly submit from the information gathered that despite criticism, many people are not reluctant to use traditional remedies. It would equally be right to say that religious affiliation plays a minor role in determining whether people will use or refrain from using traditional medicine. This is because 90% of the respondents were Christians but only 6% admitted that they do not use traditional medicine. The majority of the respondents were quiet positive. They were of the opinion that traditional medicine can work hand-in-hand with, and therefore, there is the possibility of cooperation between modern and traditional healers. In addition, the understanding is that modern biomedicine can complement but it cannot replace traditional medical practices even in this era of advanced healthcare systems.

9.6 Users of African Traditional Medicine

A closer scrutiny of the demographic characteristics of participants in this study reveals that they were representative of different age groups in the community. They were males and females, with varying levels of education- ranging from lack of formal education to tertiary level. Whereas, some of the participants were married, others were either single or widow(ers).

The ages of participants ranged from 18–50 years and above. They were mostly Christians, a few Muslims and believers in African traditional religion. What this suggests, is that the age, religious affiliation, level of education and income level do not determine who uses or does not use traditional medicine (Berhane et al., 2001; Peltzer, 1987). While this study did not look into the financial or economic status of respondents, education is generally believed to be a predictor of socio-economic status. It is generally accepted that a low level of formal education compromises a person's ability to acquire appropriate paid jobs. Indeed, a significant portion of the informants had attained some basic education to enable them to cope with basic economic requirements.

Traditional medicine is of significant value to a greater portion of the Qokolweni community where independent of age, gender, education and socio-economic background, many people use it. Users of traditional medicine are therefore all individuals in the community who feel that it works for them and are ready to try it. From observation and as collaborated by respondent's accounts, it may be understood that traditional healing combines medicine, magic and religion (see Mbiti, 1999o). Such a triad may appear strange. One thing that is worthy of note is that even our modern scientific knowledge has only recently extricated itself from its original entanglement and alliance with quackery, alchemy and magic. All the same, one thing is common between our modern medical science and traditional healing: both are attempts to control the environment, natural or human. Furthermore, both forms of control are inspired by an interest for society and its various communities. Both exemplify—each in its own way—the old saying: *scientia est potentia* (knowledge is power). However, knowledge is always relative and there are several varieties of truth (Foucault, 1980).

That traditional medicine is, from a western point of view, error, illusion and superstition is beside the point. The point is that traditional healers act on certain beliefs. These beliefs are "true" to them and to their contemporaries. In addition, these beliefs constitute not yet invalidated "knowledge" of the universe from the perspective of modern science. Through action, this knowledge is believed to become powerful, to become a power and force. Therefore, traditional medicine is not mere theory of what things are or do, but it is practical knowledge of how to make things to be or to do what the traditional healers want them to be or to do. The intention, at least, of the traditional healer is to make this knowledge available as well as to use it to control the negative forces in life. His/her knowledge is available to all peoples, in all places and at all times. The creed of the practice of traditional medicine (of the healer) as a communal property in African societies (Mbiti, 1990) is no longer adhered to today. The factors for this change include the monetization of the economy and threats from pirates and fake healers who are keen on laying claim on the knowledge of established healers. The latter have thus become secretive with their knowledge.

The main aim of this study was to establish the grounds for dialogue and to articulate the need for collaboration between conventional medicine and African traditional medicine for the general improvement of healthcare. Specifically, the study sought to articulate the role of African traditional medicine in an era of modern biomedicine; create greater awareness on the notion of traditional medicine; find out people's attitudes towards African traditional medicine; establish users of traditional medicine and explore the different opinions and perceptions of different genders and age groups towards the use of African traditional medicine. This study has investigated the reluctance and critical lack of cooperation between biomedicine and traditional medicine.

The study revealed that:
- The African concept of health is far broader than the biomedical perspective, which concentrates on the physical body.
- African traditional medicine has played and is still playing a significant role in healthcare.
- The majority of people in South African communities use traditional and modern medicine simultaneously in their search for therapy.
- Modern healthcare has not and may not, in the near future, replace traditional medicine. The two healthcare systems can complement one another.
- People are knowledgeable about traditional medicine. They know how it is made, when and how to use it. It is also revealed that though traditional medicine is a vital healthcare resource, it cannot work in isolation due to its own limitations.
- Opinions and attitudes of people towards traditional medicine vary. While a majority of people value and use traditional medicine, a significantly small portion of the population reject traditional medicine for religious and personal reasons.
- The use of traditional medicine cuts across people of all backgrounds. Age, education, gender and economic status do not influence people's propensity to use or not to use traditional medicine.

9.7   Recommendations

Several recommendations that can help healthcare stakeholders to recognize the role of African traditional medicine emerged from the findings of this study.
- The recognition of traditional healers will assist in the formulation of policies that will promote the incorporation of traditional medicine into the mainstream healthcare system. For South Africans of all cultural backgrounds to benefit from maximum healthcare services, traditional medicine must be given due attention and recognized as an alternative healthcare resource. This could only be possible if the government officially recognizes the role of traditional medicine and initiate collaboration with biomedicine.

- There is need for researchers to conduct more interdisciplinary research on African traditional healing practices. Such research may promote collaboration between traditional healing and biomedicine. If this happens, there are chances that there will be appropriate use of the two healthcare resources. Further research in this domain will result in tremendous progress in the control of "African diseases" (*izifo zesiNtu*) and a better distribution of healthcare resources.
- African people have their own common diseases which only traditional medicine can treat. There is therefore a need for the government to support traditional health practitioners to boost their efforts to sustain life. Government incentives to traditional healers may inspire them to be more diligent in their service delivery.
- Traditional healers need to be encouraged to trust researchers and organizations sponsoring research. A healthy relationship between these stakeholders is needed if traditional medicine is to be improved. Research on traditional medicine may improve hygienic conditions, packaging and therefore increase the number of users.
- It is important that the South Africa's National Department of Health formulate policies that will control the use of traditional medicine. Such policies will guide and contribute towards the recognition and acceptance of traditional healers in the mainstream healthcare system in South Africa.
- The establishment of training centres for traditional healers should be given priority. Traditional healers must be trained to handle new contemporary communicable diseases such as HIV/AIDS. The training of traditional healers in the spread of HIV/AIDS and prevention thereof may enhance their efficiency. The government should train traditional healers and use them in the prevention and dissemination of information on HIV/AIDS and other diseases given their numerical strength and proximity when compared to western-trained doctors and other healthcare personnel.
- Training programmes for traditional healers and physicians should be held regularly. Such training is needed to create a forum for understanding and cooperation between the former and the latter.
- The government of South Africa needs to officially recognize traditional healers. This can easily be done by having traditional healers who have satisfied certain ethical conditions to be registered with both the Medical Council and South African Traditional Healers Association.
- Biomedical practitioners need to shift from their overemphasis on the patient as an individual, take note of interconnections by decentering their perspective from a predominantly personal and biological to the role of mental influences, social influences and environmental factors that

influence health. Individuals are entangled in various networks of relationships with other members of society, their family members, communities and the world. Biomedical physicians need to be self-reflexive. They have go beyond disease and its treatment into a deeper understanding of the nature of health, how to support and strengthen it through an awareness of the integrity of the body and mind, explore man's connection with natural forces and spiritual reality as well as the power inherent in healing relationships (Di Stefano, 2006).

– Collaboration between THPs and biomedical personnel on the one hand will keep health personnel abreast with a wide range of patient's therapeutic recourse strategies to enable them provide appropriate advice to their patients. Research evidence suggests that patients rely on health personnel (general practitioners, nurses and pharmacists) as a valuable source of information for all health and health-related problems. On the other hand, collaboration between THPs and biomedical researchers will lead to the validation of the efficacy claims of traditional medical therapies, the assessment of the quality, safety and efficacy of plant materials and the finished medicinal products. Additionally, it is important to tap on the skills of THCPs in the fight against various communicable diseases, including HIV/AIDS and malaria, which are inordinately taxing African health systems given the insider status of THPCs in their communities. Successful collaborations in Mali, Senegal and Uganda show that collaborative initiatives between THPs and modern health personnel "helped to reduce health workers skepticism and strengthened mutual appreciation, understanding and respect between practitioners of the two systems of medicine," the provision of improved and affordable primary healthcare services (Busai and Kasilo, 2010: 4). It is rather unfortunate that calls for integration and the processes themselves are simply a continuation of the struggle between so-called 'rational' western biomedicine and TCAM and approaches to health care that are grounded in the colonial era (King, 2002; Fournier, 2013: 2). This same vision is manifested in the call for surveillance, standardization and regulation of TCAM within the context of an emerging disease paradigm. These calls are "influenced by, and framed within hegemonic biomedical discourses and capitalist ideologies" (Fournier, 2013: 2) but also concealed behind the discursive repertoire of public health and safety (Ibid.). As Cathy Fournier and Robin Oakley (2018: 217) make it clear "the call for regulation, standardisation, and surveillance is obscured by hegemonic biomedical discourses related to public health and safety by international institutions such as the World Bank and WHO." Integration should not imply the contortion of traditional medicine into the dominant health system and the adoption of a reductionist theory of disease in tune with "capitalist ideology and the biomedical model of organization" (Baer, 2001: 6). In fact as pointed out by various commentators (Mckenna, 2012; Baer, Singer and Susser, 1997), the reductionist and behaviourist approaches as well as the overemphasis on technology and pharmaceuticals characteristic of biomedicine shift the emphasis away from the role of socio-economic and political factors that influence health and continues to create inequities. In this regard, integration is a vehicle of governmentality that seeks to control by bringing other knowledge and belief systems under the hegemonic framework of biomedicine and capitalist ideologies (Baer, 2004).

This study has its shortcomings:

> It investigated the role of traditional healers in a modern era. It is highly recommended that a similar study be conducted to understand the perceptions and attitude of modern doctors towards traditional healers in South Africa. Their opinions and attitudes towards cooperation with traditional healers must be understood. Understanding their views will enhance effective intervention. Furthermore, a relatively small sample size was used in this study. It is recommended that other studies in this direction should use larger samples and more standardized research instruments. Additionally, it is also recommended that a similar study should be conducted in a more diversified community with people from different cultural backgrounds. Such a study should involve Black, White, Coloured and Indian peoples. Any similarities in the results would increase the validity of the findings of this study.

9.8 Conclusion

The main aim of this study was to investigate the role of traditional medicine in an era of biomedical dominance. This is despite democractisation that eventuated into the re-valorization of African culture and tradition. This came against the backdrop of the HIV/AIDS social crises that challenged biomedicine's inability to find a solution to the pandemic and the South African government's adoption of traditional medicine as an "African solution" (Flint, 2016: 4332) to the epidemic while simultaneously refusing HIV-positive patients from accessing life-saving antiretroviral therapy. Alongside the sociopolitical quagmire of the time and heightened uncertainty, patients and others turned to traditional medicine to seek solutions to their myriad social and health problems.

The overall aim of this work is to create a platform for cooperation between the traditional and biomedical healthcare systems. As a multi-ethnic country, South Africa has many traditional healers from the different cultural backgrounds. These healers who are increasingly handling hospital diagnosed cases are often alleged to put the lives of fellow citizens at risk. It is also worth noting that despite the sophisticated nature of biomedicine, people of different social backgrounds still use traditional medicine. Some people still believe that certain illnesses cannot be treated in hospitals. Though many people still resort to traditional healing, they share common fears. To them if traditional healing could be improved to meet required acceptable sanitary conditions and measurements, and efficacy standards it could be a proper healthcare choice to millions of people.

There is a lingering belief in the need for traditional healers to continue providing healthcare to people. This is only possible if there is some form of cooperation between biomedicine and traditional medicine. This study will hopefully provide valuable information to all those involved in the healthcare of African people. We believe that if implemented, the recommendations made herein will improve health delivery and cooperation between biomedical doctors and traditional healers in South Africa and beyond. This will hopefully improve the overall standard of living for all and sundry.

Bibliography

Abad, M.J. & Bermejor, M. (2007). *Active antifungal substances from natural sources.* ARKIVOC.

Abdullahi, A.A. (2011). "Trends and Challenges of Traditional Medicine in Africa." *African Journal of Complementary and Alternative Medicine*, 8 (5 Suppl.): 115–123.

Abele, F. (1997). "Traditional Knowledge in Practice." *Arctic*, 50(4): iii–iv.

Adam, J., Hollenberg, D., Lui, C. and Broom, A. (2009). "Contextualizing Integrative medicine." *Journal of Manipulative and Physiological Therapies*, 32(9): 792–798.

Adamo, D.T. (2011). "Christianity and African traditional religion(s):The postcolonial round of engagement." *Verbum et Ecclesia* 32(1): Art.#285,10 pages. DOI:10.4102/ve.v32i1.285.

Adeyini, O.V., Ajayi, A.I., Goon, T., Owolabi, D., Eboh, E., Lambert, A.J.(2018). "Factors affecting adherence to antiretroviral therapy among pregnant women in the Eastern Cape, South Africa." *BMC Infectious Disease*, 13;18(1):175. DOI: 10.1186/s12879-018-3087-8.

African Advisory Committee for Health Research and Development (AACHRD). (2002). Enhancing Research into Traditional Medicine in the African Region, a document prepared for the 21 Session of the African Advisory Committee for Health Research and Development. Port Louis, Mauritius: AACHRD.

Ajala, A.S., Nelson, N.A. (2013). "Local aetiology and pathways to care in malaria among the Ibiobio of south-coastal Nigeria." *Health, Culture and Society*, 4,1,80–90 | ISSN 2161-6590 (online) DOI 10.5195/hcs.2013.102 .available: http://hcs.pitt.edu.

Alembi, E. (2003). "The Calling and work of Wellington Masatia Tambwa: A Traditional Healer from Bunyore, Kenya." *Journal of Folklore*,24:78–90. Available from: http:77www.folklore.ee/folklore/vol24/masatia.pdf.dio:10.7592/FEJF2003.24.masatia.

Aliber, M., Maswana, M., Nikelo N., Mbantsa B. & Bank L. (2018) (forthcoming). *Economic development in South Africa's former homelands and rural-urban linkages*, REDI3x3 Working Paper.

Aliber, M. (2003). Chronic Poverty in South Africa: Incidence, Causes and Policies, *World Development*, 31(3): 473–490.

Amenu, D. (2014). "Antimicrobial Activity of Medicinal Plant Extracts and Their Synergistic Effect on Some Selected Pathogens," *American Journal of Ethnomedicine*, 1, No. 1, 018–029.

Andrew, G.J & Evans, J. (2008). "Geographies of health in nursing Health Practice." *Progress in Human Geography*, 32(6): 759–780.

Andrew, G.J. (2003). "Placing the consumption of private complementary medicine: everyday geographies of older people's use." *Health Practice*, 9: 337–49.

Andrews, G.J & Boon, H. (2005). "CAM in Canada: Places, practices, research." *Complementary Therapies in Clinical Practice*, 11(1): 21–27.

Anlauf, M., Hein, L., Hense, H., Köbberling, J., Lasek, R., Leidl, R., & Schöne-Seifert, B. (2015). "Complementary and alternative drug therapy versus science-oriented medicine," *German Medical Science*, 13(1): 1–47.

Appelbaum, D., Kligler, B., Barrett, B., Frenkel, M., Guerrara, M., Kondwani, K.A., Tattelman, E.(2006). "Natural and traditional medicine in Cuba: lessons for U.S medical education." *Academic Medicine*, 81(12): 1098–1103.

Appiah, K.A. (2004). "Akan and Euro-American Concepts of the Person.," 21–34, Brown, L.M. (ed.), *African Philosophy: New and Traditional Perspectives*. New York: Oxford University Press.

Arnold, D. (2004).*The New Cambridge History of India: Science, Technology and Medicine in Colonial India*. Cambridge, UK: Cambridge University Press.

Arnold, D. (1998). *Imperial medicine and indigenous societies*. Manchester, UK: Manchester University Press.

Ashforth, A. (2005).*Witchcraft, Violence, and Democracy in South Africa*. Chicago: Chicago University Press.

Asuni, T. (1979).The dilemma of traditional healing with special reference to Nigeria, *Social Science and Medicine*, 13(1): 33–39.

Audet C.M., Salato J., Vermund S.H., Amico, K.R. (2017). "Adapting an adherence support workers intervention: engaging traditional healers as adherence partners for persons enrolled in HIV care and treatment in rural Mozambique." *Implementation Science*, 13;12(1):50. DOI: 10.1186/s13012-017-0582-z.

Audet C.M., Blevins M., Rosenberg C., Farnsworth S., Salato J., Fernandez, J., Vermund S.H., (2017). "Symptomatic HIV-positive persons in rural Mozambique who first consult a traditional healer have delays in HIV testing: a cross-sectional study." *Journal of Acquired Immune Deficiency Syndrome*, 1;66(4):e80–6. DOI: 10.1097/QAI.0000000000000194.

Audet C.M., Blevins M., Moon T.D., Sidat M., Shepherd B.E., Pires P., Vergara A., Vermund S.H. (2012). HIV/AIDS-related attitudes and practices among traditional healers in Zambézia Province, Mozambique,*Journal of Complementary and Alternative Medicine*,18(12):1133–41. DOI: 10.1089/acm.2011.0682.

Augusto, G. (2008). "Knowledge free and 'unfree': Epistemic tensions in plant knowledge at the Cape in the 17th and 18th centuries," *International Journal of African Renaissance Studies-Multi-,Inter- and Transdisciplinarity*, 2(2): 136–182.

Babayi, H., Kolo, L., Okogu, J.I., (2004). "The antimicrobial activities of metabolic extracts of Eucalyptus Camaldunensis and Terminalia catappa against some pathogenic microorganism." *Biokemistri*, 16 (2): 106–111.

Babb, D.A., Pemba, L., Seatlanyane, P., Charalambous, S., Churchyard, G.J. & Grant, A.D. (2007). "Use of traditional medicine by HIV-infected individuals in South Africa in the era of antiretroviral therapy," *Psychology, Health & Medicine*, 12(3):314–320.

BIBLIOGRAPHY

Babbie, E.R. (2009). *The Practice of Social Research*. 10th Edition. Belmont, CA: Oxford.

Babbie, E.R. & Mouton, J. (2000). *The Practice of Social Research*. Cape Town: Oxford.

Baer, H. & Coulter, I. (2008). "Taking stock: broadening biomedicine or co-option of complementary and alternative medicine." *Health Sociology Review*, 17: 331–341.

Baer, H. (2004). "U.S Health policy on alternative medicine: a case study in the co-optation of a popular movement." In A. Castro and Singer, M. (Eds)., *Unhealthy health policy: A critical anthropological examination*.(pp. 317–329).Plymouth, UK, Alta Mira Press.

Baer, H. (2001). *Biomedicine and alternative healing systems in America*. Madison WI: University of Wisconsin Press.

Baer, H., Singer, M., & Susser, I. (1997). *Medical anthropology and the world system: A critical perspective*. Westerport CT: Bergin and Garvey.

Bailey, K.D. (1987). *Methods of Social Research*. New York: The Free Press.

Bamford, L.J., Mckerrow, N.H., Barron, P.L., & Aung, Y. (2018). "Child Mortality in South Africa: Fewer deaths, but better data are needed." *South African Medical Journal*,108 (3 Suppl.1): S25–S32.

Bannerman, R.H., Burton, J. and Wen-Chieh, C., (1983). *Traditional medicine and healthcare coverage. A reader for health administrators and practitioners*. Geneva: World Health Organization.

Bannerman, R.H. (1983). The Role of Traditional Medicine in Primary Health Care. In: Traditional.

Bannerman, R.H. Burterand, J. & Wen, R. (Eds.).(1983). *Medicine and Health Care Coverage*. WHO, Geneva.

Baraonov, D. (2008). "Biomedicine: An ontological dissection." *Theoretical Medicine and Bioethics*, 29(4): 235–254.

Baskind, R. (2005). "*Epilepsy Cares in Zambia: A study of Traditional Healers*," Epilepsia, 46. Bioorganic & Medical Chemistry 13 (21): 5892–5908.

Bassala, G. (1967). "The spread of western science," *Science*,156: 611–622.

Bateman, C. (2004). "HIV training of traditional healers limps along." *South African Medical Journal*, 94: 804–806.

Baumgartner, J.L., Geary W.C., Tucker, H., & Wedderburn, M. (2009). "The influence of early sexual debut and sexual violence on adolescent pregnancy: a matched case-control study in Jamaica." *International Perspectives on Sexual and Reproductive Health*, 35 (1): 21–28.

Beck, D. (2004). "Men and ARVs: How does Being a Man Affect access to antiretroviral therapy in South Africa? An Investigation Among Xhosa-Speaking Men in khayelitsha" Centre for social science research working paper 80, University of Cape Town, South Africa.

Benedetto, F. (2008). "Hegemony and Power in Gramsci." In: Howson Richard and Smith Kylie ed. (2008): *Hegemony: studies in consensus and coercion.* New York: Routledge.

Benson, H., Dusek, J.A., Sherwood, J.B., Lam, P., Bethea, C.F., Carpenter, W., Levitsky, S., Hill, P.C., Clem, D.W., Jain, M.K., et al. (2002). "Study of the Therapeutic Effects of Intercessory Prayer (STEP): Study design and research methods." *American. Heart Journal*, 143: 577–584.

Bent, S. (2008). "Herbal medicine in the United States: review of efficacy, safety and regulation- grand rounds at the University of California, San Francisco Medical Centre," *Journal of General Internal Medicine*, 23: 854–9.

Berlin, E.A. & Berlin, B. (1996). *Medical ethnobiology of the highland Maya of Chiapas, Mexico: the gastrointestinal diseases*, Princeton, NJ: Princeton University Press.

Bernard, H.R. (2006). *Research methods in Anthropology: qualitative and quantitative approaches.* Lanham, MD: AltaMira Press.

Bigon, L. (2012). "A History of Urban Planning and Infectious Diseases: Colonial Senegal in the Early Twentieth Century," *Urban Studies Research*, 2012, Article iD 589758, DOI:10.1155/2012/589758.

Bishop, K.M. (2012). "Anglo American media representations, traditional medicine, and HIV/AIDS in South Africa: from muti killings to garlic cures," *Geojournal*, 77, (4):571–581.

Blandy, Fran. (2006). Dr. Beetroot hits back at media over AIDS exhibition. Mail and Guardian Online, 16 August.

Bledsoe, C. (2002).*The contingent Lifecourse.* Chicago: University of Chicago Press.

Bodeker, G., Ong, C.K., Grundy, C.K., Burford, G., & Shein, K. (2005a). Global Atlas of Traditional, Complementary and Alternative Medicine. Kobe, Japan: WHO Centre for Health Development.

Bodeker, G., Kronenberg, F. (2002b). "A public health agenda for traditional, complementary, and alternative medicine." *American Journal of Public Health*, 92(10):1582–1591. DOI: 10.2105/AJPH.92.10.1582.

Booysen, F. (2003). "HIV/AIDS-induced migration: evidence from the Free State Province, South Africa." In Cohen, R. (Ed.), *Migration and Health in Southern Africa.* Cape Town: Van Schaik, pp. 69– 86.

Bor, J., Herbst A.J., Newell, M-I., Bärnighausen, T. (2013). "Increase in adult life expectancy in rural South Africa: valuing the scale-up of HIV treatment," *Science*, 339(6122):961–5. Doi: 101126/science.1230413.

Brooks, K.B., & Katsoulis, L.C., (2006). "Bioactive components of Rhoicissus tridentata: A pregnancy-related traditional medicine." *South African Journal of Science*, 102:267–272.

Bruce, J.C. (2002). "Marrying modern health practices and technology with traditional practices: Issues for the African continent." *International Nursing Review*, 49:161–167. DOI: 10.1046/j.1466-7657.2002.00109.x.

Bryman, A. (2004). *Social research methods*. Oxford: Oxford University Press.

Burawoy, M. (1998). "The Extended Case Method." *Sociological Theory* 16:1 March. American Sociological Association.

Burgess, P. (1999). Traditional Knowledge: A Report Prepared for the Arctic Council Indigenous Peoples Secretariat. Copenhagen. http://www.arcticpeoples.org/.

Burns, R. (2000).*Introduction to Research Methods*, 4th Edition. London: Sage.

Burton, D. (2000).*The Use of Case in Social Science Research*. *In:* Burton, D. (Ed). *Research Training for Social Scientists*. London: Sage.

Burungi, H., Mugisha, F, Nsabagasani, X, Okuonzi, S, Jeppsson, A.(2001). "The Policy on Public-Private Mix in the Ugandan Health Sector::Catching up with Reality," *Journal of Health Policy and Planning*, 16(suppl. 2):80–86.

Bury, M. & Taylor, D. (2008). "Towards a theory of care transition: From medical dominance to managed consumerism." *Social Theory & Health* 6(3):201–219.

Calapai, G. & Caputi, A.P. (.2007). "Herbal medicines: can we do without Pharmacologists?" *Evidence Based Complementary Alternative Medicine*, 4:41–3.

Caldwell, J. & Caldwell, P. (1987). "The cultural context of high fertility in sub-Saharan Africa," *Population and Development Review*, 13(3):409–437.

Campbell-Hall, P.I., Bhana, A., Mjadu, S., Hosegood, V., Flisher, A.J. (2010). "Collaboration between Traditional Practitioners and Primary Healthcare Staff in South Africa: Developing a Workable Partnership for Community Mental Health Services." *Transcultural Psychiatry*, 47(4):610–28. DOI: 10.1177/1363461510383459.

Capasso, F, Gaguinella, T.S., Grandolini, G., Izzo, A.A. (2003). "The Complexity of Herbal Medicines." *Phytotherapy*, pp. 11–12. https://link.springer.com/chapter/10.1007/978-3-642-55528-2_4.

Castro, M.T. (1995). "Women's education and fertility: results from 26 Demographic and Health surveys," *Studies in Family Planning*, 26(4):187–202.

CBRA.(2018). What is biomedical Research? Available: https://ca-biomed.org/wp-content/uploads/2018/02/FS-WhatBiomedical.pdf(Accessed July 30th 2019).

Cernea, M.M. (1982). "Indigenous Anthropologists and Development-Oriented Research" in Hussein Fahim, (ed). *Indigenous anthropology in non-western countries: proceedings of a Burg Wartenstein symposium*. Durham: Carolina Academic Press. (pp. 121–137).

Chakrabarti, P. (2010). *Materials and Medicine: Trade, Conquest and therapeutics in the Eighteenth Century*. Manchester University Press.

Chan, M. Director-General of the World Health Organization. Available from: http:www.who.int/dg/speeches/2008/20081107/en/ (accessed on 20 August 2012).

Chaudhury, R.R. (1997). *Commentary: Challenges in Using Traditional Systems of Medicine*, New Delhi, National Institute of Immunology.

Chavunduka, G.L. (1986). "Development of african Traditional Medicine: The Case of Zimbabwe." (Seminar Proceedings No. 27), 59–72), *African Medicine in the Modern World*. Edinburgh: Centre for African Studies.

Chibale, K., Davies-Coleman, M. & Masimirembwa. (Eds.). *Drug Discovery in Africa: Impacts of Genomics, natural Products, Traditional Medicines, Insights into Medicinal chemistry, and Technology Platforms in Pursuit of New Drugs*, Berlin: Springer-Verlag.

Chopra, M., Kendall, C., Hill, Z., Schaay, N., Nkonki, L.L., Doherty, T.M. (2006). "'Nothing new": Responses to the introduction of antiretroviral drugs in South Africa." *AIDS* 2006, 20:1975–1986.

Clarke, E. (1998). The collaboration between traditional healers and the department of health. Health systems trust update, October, 37:5.

Cockrell, A. (1997). "The South African Bill of Rights and the 'Duck/Rabbit'." *Modern Law Review*, 60 (4):513–537. DOI:10.1111/1468-2230.00096.

Coe, R.M. (1997) "The Magic of Science and the Science of Magic: An Essay on the Process of Healing." *Journal of Health and Social Behavior*, 38(1):1–8.

Cohen, M. & Bodeker, G. (Eds). (2008).*Understanding the Global Spa Industry: Spa Managemnet*, Butterworth-Heinemann.

Cohen, M.S., Chen, Y.Q., McCauley, M., et al.(2016). "Antiretroviral therapy for the prevention of HIV-1 transmission." New England Journal of Medicine, 375:830–839.

Cordova, V.F. (1997). "Ecoindian: A Response to J. Baird Callicott." Ayaangwaamizin: *The International Journal of Indigenous Philosophy* 1(1): 31–44.

Courteny, W. (2000). "Constructions of Masculinity and Their Influence on Men's Well-being: A Theory of Gender and Health," *Social Science and Medicine*, 50 (10): 1385–401.

Cragg, G.M., and Boyd, Michael R. (1996). "Drug Development at the National Cancer Institute." In: Balick, Michael J.E.E, and Laird, S.A. (eds.), *Medicinal Resources of the Tropical Forest: Biodiversity and Its Importance to Human Health*. New York: Columbia University Press. pp. 101–136.

Crawford, T. (1995). "Traditional healers and Psychiatric healthcare." *South Africa Medical Journal*, 85(4): pp. 291–292.

Creswell, J.W. (1998). *Quantitative Inquiry and Research design: Choosing among five traditions*. Thousand oaks (CA): Sage.

Croucamp, A. (2001). Divination: Superstition or Technology? Unpublished colloquium paper, Graduate School for Humanities and Social Sciences at Witwatersrand University, Witwatersrand University, Johannesburg, South Africa.

Crush, J., Williams, B., Gouws, E. & Lurie, M. (2005). "Migration and HIV/AIDS in South Africa," *Development Southern Africa*, 22, No. 3:291–311.

Cumes, D. (2010). "Sangoma Medicine---How it Works." *Conversations in the Field*. 1(6): 1–6.

Cumes, D., (2004). *Africa in my bones: A surgeon's odyssey into the spirit world of African healing*. Claremont (South Africa): New Africa Books.

Dabis, F., Newell M-L, Hirschell, B. (2010). "HIV drug for treatment, and for prevention." *Lancet*, 375(9731):20567.DOI:10.1016/S) 140-6736)10)60838-0.

Daly, D.C. & Limbach, C.F. (1996). *The Contribution of the Physician to Medicinal Plant Research*. In: Balick, M.J., Elisabetsky, E.l, and Laird, S.A. (eds.), *Medicinal Resources of the Tropical Forest: Biodiversity and Its Importance to Human Health*. New York: Columbia University Press. Pp. 48–64.

Dean, M. (1999). *Governmentality, Power and Rule in Modern Society*, London: Sage Publications.

Deb Roy, R. (2018). Decolonise Science—time to end another imperial era. The Conversation, Available from: https://theconversation.com/decolonise-science-time-to-end-another-imperial-era-89189.

Delius, P. (2017). The History of Migrant Labor in South Africa (1800–2014). Oxford Research Encyclopedia of African History. (africanhistory.oxfordre.com). (c) Oxford University Press USA, DOI: 10.1093/acrefore/9780190277734.013.93.

Dell, A.J. & Kahn, D. (2017). "Geographical maldistribution of surgical resources in South Africa: A review of the number of hospitals, hospital beds and surgical beds," *South African Medical Journal (SAMJ)*, 107(2):1099–1105.

Denis, P. (2006). "The Rise of Traditional African Religion in Post-Apartheid South Africa." *Missionalia*, 34(2/3):310–323.

Department of Health/South Africa and Macro International (2002). South Africa Demographic and Health Survey 1998. South Africa: Department of Health/South Africa.

Department of Health KwaZulu-Natal. (KZN) Health 2017/2018 Budget Speech. (2017). Available from:www.kznhealth.gov.za/speeches/2017-2018-budget-speech.pdf.

Department of Social Development. (ND). Snap-shot Survey Report on Substance Abuse in Nine Provinces in South Africa. Republic of South Africa: Department of Social Development. Available: http://www.hst.org.za/publications/NonHST%20Publications/175300445-Snap-shot-survey-report-on-substance-abuse-in-the-nine-provinces-in-South-Africa.pdf(accessed June 28, 2018).

De Robillard, B. (2009). "Girls' and Virginity: Making the Post-Apartheid Nation State." *Agenda: Empowering Women for Gender Equality*, 23(79): 85–93.

De Roubaix, M. (2016). "Healthcare Delivery: The de-colonialization of medicine in South Africa: Threat or opportunity?." *South African Medical Journal*, 106, No. 2:159–161.

Descombe, M. (2003). *The Good Research Guide for Small-Scale Social Research Projects*. Maitland. Philadelphia: Open University Press.

De Silva, T. (1993). "UNIDO development programmes on industrial utilization of medicinal and aromatic plants." *Acta Horticulturae*, 333:47–54.

De Villiers, St. (1985). "(Consideration of) Illness Causation Among Some Xhosa-Speaking People." *South African Journal of Ethnology*,8 (2): 48–52.

Di Stefano, V. (2006): *Holism and Complementary Medicine. Origins and Principles.* Allen & Unwin, Sydney.

Donda, G.H. (1997). *A study of zulu concepts. Terms and expressions associated with Umuthi.* Unpublished masters of Arts dissertation. Memelodi Campus: Vista University.

Du Plooy, F.S. (2004).perceptions of HIV/AIDS prevention workers in Soshanguve of the role of traditional African beliefs in HIV/AIDS prevention. Master of psychology thesis, University of Pretoria, South Africa.

Earl-Babbie, J.M., & Payze, V.B. (2009). *The Practice of Social Research.* Oxford: Oxford University Press.

Eastern Cape Department of Social Development and Special Programmes (2016). Factors associated with Teenage Pregnancy in the Eastern Cape Province. Available: http://www.mmoho.co.za/wp-content/uploads/2016/02/Eastern-Cape-Teenage-Pregnancy-Report-2-ilovepdf-compressed.pdf(accessed June 2018).

Eastern Cape Planning Commission (2014). Eastern Cape Vision 2030 Provincial Development Plan. Province of the Eastern Cape. Available from: http://www.ecdc.co.za/media/1643/ec-vision-2030-plan_271014-2.pdf.

Ebomoyi, E.W. (2009). "Genomics in Traditional African Healing and Strategies to Integrate Traditional Healers into Western-Type Health Care Services- *A Retrospective Study.*" *Researcher*, 1(6):69–79.

Eckstein, H. (2000). "Case Study theory in political Science." In Gomme, R. Hammersley, M. & Foster, P. *Case Study Method.* Sage publication.

Edwards, S.D., Grobbelaar, P.W., Kunene, S.T., Magwaza, A.S., Makhunga, N.V., Nene, L.M., Sibaya, P.T., (1983). "Traditional Zulu theories of illness in psychiatric patients." *Social Psychology Journal*, 121(2):231–221.

Edwards, A., & Talbot, R. (1994). *The hard-pressed researcher: a research handbook for the caring professions.* London; New York: Longman.

Ekpere, J.A. (2000).*The OAU Model law: The protection of the Rights of Local Communities, Farmers, and Breeders, and for the Regulation of Access to Biological Resources- An Explanatory Booklet.* OAU/STRC, Lagos. 100pp.

Eldeen, I., Elgorashi, M.S., Mulholland, E.E., Van Staden, D.A., (2005). "Anolignan B: A bioactive compound from the roots of Terminalia Sercea." *Journal of Ethnopharmacology*, 103 (1):135–8.

Elegani, N.G., El Tohamani, E.I., Muddathir, M.S. (2002). "Antimicrobial Activity of Some Species of the family Combretaceae." *Phytotherapy Research*, 16:pp. 555–561.

Ephraim, C. (2013). Living with HIV/AIDS in King Williams Town, Eastern Cape, DOI: 10.6007/IJARBSS/v3-i11/317, Available from: https://www.researchgate.net/search.Search.html?type=publication&query=HIV/AIDS%20in%20Eastern%20Cape.

Evans-Pritchard, E.E. (1937/1963). *Witchcraft, Oracles and Magic among the Azande.* Oxford University Press. 1976 abridged edition: ISBN 0-19-874029-8.

Fabrega, H. (2002). "Medical validity in eastern and western traditions." *Perspectives in Biological Medicine*, 45:395–415.

Fabrega, H., & Silver D. (1973). *Illness and shamanistic curing in Zinacantan: an ethnomedical analysis.* University Press, Stanford.

Fabrega, H. (1974). *Disease and social behaviour: an interdisciplinary perspective.* Massachusetts Institute of Technology Press, Cambridge, MA.

Fabrega, H. (1997). *Evolution of sickness and healing.* University of California Press, Berkeley.

Farmer, P. (1992). *Aids and Accusation: Haiti and the Geography of Blame.* Los Angeles: University of California Press.

Fanon, F. (1963).*The Wretched of the Earth.* New York: Grove Press.

Faure, V. (2002). "Bodies and Politics: Healing Rituals in the Democratic South Africa." *Les Cahiers de L'IFAS* no.2. French Institute of South Africa.

Flint, A. (2015). "Traditional Healing, Biomedicine and the Treatment of HIV/AIDS: Contrasting South African and Native American Experiences," *International Journal of Environmental Research and Public Health*, 12:4321–4339; DOI:10.3390/ijerph120404321.

Flint, K. (2008).*Healing Traditions: African Medicine, Cultural Exchange, and Competition in South Africa,1820–1948.*Ohio:Ohio University Press.

Flint, A. & Payne, J. (2013). "Reconciling the irreconcilable? HIV/AIDS and the potential for middle ground between the traditional and biomedical healthcare sectors in South Africa." *Forum for Development Studies*, 40(1):47–68. [http://dx.doi. org/10.108 0/08039410,2012.702681].

Foster G. (1976). "Medical Anthropology and international health planning." *Medical Anthropology Newsletter*, 7(3):12–18.

Foster, G.M., Anderson, B.G. (1978). *Medical Anthropology.* New York: McGraw Hill.

Foster, G.M. (1976). "Disease etiologies in non-Western medical system." *American. Anthropologist*, 78, 4:773–82.

Foucault, M. (1975).*The Birth of the Clinic: An Archaeology of Medical Perception*, New York: Vintage Books.

Fournier, C. & Oakley, R. (2018). "Conversions and Erasures: Colonial Ontologies in Canadian and International Traditional, Complementary, and Alternative Medicine Integration Policies." In: Brosnan C., Vuolanto P., Danell J.A. (eds) *Complementary and Alternative Medicine. Health, Technology and Society.* Palgrave Macmillan, Cham. pp. 217–245.

Fournier, C. (2013). *Integration, Conversion or Conflict? A Critical Ontology of the Integration of "CAM" into Biomedical Education by Cathy Fournier Submitted in partial fulfilment of the requirements for the degree of Master of Arts*, Dalhousie University Halifax, Nova Scotia. Available from: https://dalspace.library.dal

.ca/bitstream/handle/10222/42702/Fournier-Cathy-MA-SOSA-December-2013.pdf?sequence=1&isAllowed=y.

Fritzpatrick, R.M. (1986). "Social and changing Patterns of Disease" in Patrick, D. & Scrambler, G. (eds), *Sociology as Applied in Medicine*. London and Baillierre Tindall: Academic Press. Pp.2–17.

Fryklof, L. (1990). "Current trends in self-medication." *Journal of Social and Administrative Pharmacy*, 7(4):149–230.

Fyhrquist, P. (2007). Traditional medicinal uses and biological activities of some plants extract of African combretum loefl., Terminalia L and Pteleopsis Engl. Species (combretaceae). Academic dissertation. Helsinki: University of Helsinki.

Gaedeim, B. & Versteeg, M. (2011). "The State of the Right to Health in Rural South Africa." *South African Health Research* (SAHR). Available from: https://rhap.org.za/wp-content/uploads/2013/11/Chap-9-State-of-right-Rural-Health-pgs-99-106.pdf.

Gavroglu, K., Patiniotis, P, Faidra, S., Ana, C., Ana, D., Maria, P., Sanchez, J., Belmar, A., Nieto-Galan, A. (2008). "Science and Technology in the European Periphery: Some Historiographical Reflections," *History of Science*, xlvi:153–175.

George, E.R. (2008). "Virginity testing and South Africa's HIV/AIDS crisis: Beyond rights universalism and cultural relativism toward health capabilities." *California Law Review*, 96:1447–1517.

George, G., Chitindingu, E. and Gow, J. (2013). "Evaluating traditional healers knowledge and practices related to HIV testing and treatment in South Africa," *BMC International Health and Human Rights*, 13:45 http://www.biomedcentral.com/1472-698X/13/45.

Germond, P. & Cochrane, J.R. (2010). "Healthworlds: Conceptualizing landscapes of health and healing," *Sociology*, 44(2):307–24.DOI:10.1177/0038038509357202.

Geschiere, P. (2008). "Witchcraft and the State: Cameroon and South Africa: Ambiguities of 'Reality' and 'Superstition'," *Past & Present*, 199(3):1:313–335.

Geschiere, P. (1997). *The Modernity of Witchcraft: Politics and the Occult in Postcolonial Africa*, Virginia: University of Virginia Press.

Gesler, W.M. & Kearns, R.A. (2002). *Culture/Place/health*. London and New York: Routledge.

Gilbert, L., Selikow, W.T., (2002). *Society, Health and Disease. An Introductory Reader For Health Professionals*. Braamfontein-South Africa: Ravan Press.

Global Coalition on Women and AIDS. (2005). Progress Report. http://data.unaids.org/pub/Report/2006/20060530_RE_GCWA_ProgReport_2005_en.pdf (Accessed June 2017).

Gqaleni, N., Makhathini, M., Mbatha, N., Buthelezi, T., Mkhize, T., Srnarian, N., Davids, Moodley, I. (2010). "Education and Development of Traditional Health Practitioners in isiZulu to promote their Collaboration with Public Health Care Workers," *Alternation*, 17(1):295–31.

BIBLIOGRAPHY

Good News Bible, (1994). Korea: American Bible Society.

Gordin, J. (2006). "A Country of Living Dangerously." *The Sunday Independent*, December 24.

Goudge, J., Gilson, L., Russel, S., Gumede, T., & Mills, A., (2009). "The household cost of healthcare in South Africa with free public primary care and hospital exemptions for the poor." *Tropical Medicine & International Health*. 14(4):458–467.

Gouws, C.(2008).Traditional African medicine and conventional drugs: friends or enemies? The Conversation, Available: https://theconversation.com/traditional-african-medicine-and-conventional-drugs-friends-or-enemies-92695(Accessed 30th July 2019).

Govender, P.(2009).South Africa to expand AIDS treatment: Zuma. Thomson Reuters News, Available from https://www.reuters.com/article/us-aids-safrica/south-africa-to-expand-aids-treatment-zuma-idUSTRE5B021420091201(Accessed July 13, 2019).

Granich R., Crowley S., Vitoria M., Lo, Ry, Souteyrand, Y., Dye, C., Gilks, C., Guerma, T., De Cocok, K.M., & Williams, B. (2010). "Highly active antiretroviral treatment for the prevention of HIV transmission." *Journal of International AIDS and Society*, 131. DOI: 10.1186/1758-2652-13-1.

Granich R., Crowley, S., Vitoria M., Lo Y-R., Souteyrand, Y., Dye, C. et al. (2010). "Highly active antiretroviral treatment for the prevention of HIV transmission," *Journal of International AIDS Society*, 13(1):1.DOI:10.1186/1758-2652-13-1.

Green, E. (2000). "Traditional healers and AIDS in Uganda." *Journal of Alternative and Complementary Medicine*, 6(1):1–2.

Green, C.E. (1999). "Engaging Indigenous African Healers in the Prevention of AIDS and STDs" in: *Anthropology in Public Health: Bridging Difference in Culture and Society*. pp 63–83.Editor Robert A. Hahn. New York: Oxford University Press.

Green, E.C. (1996), "Purity, Pollution and the Invisible Snake," *Medical Anthropology*, 17(1):83–100.

Green, E., Jurg, A., Dgedge A. (1992). "Sexually transmissible diseases, ethnomedicine and AIDS in Africa." *Social Science and Medicine*, 35(15):261–281.

Green, E. (1995). "The Participation of African traditional healers in AIDS and STD prevention programmes." *AIDSLink*, 36:14–15.

Griffiths, A. (2001). "Gendering Cultures: Towards a Plural Perspective on Kwena Women's Rights in: *Culture, and Rights: Anthropology Perspectives*," Ed. Cowan, Jane K., Dember, Marie-Bénédicte and Wilson, Richard A. Cambridge: Cambridge University Press. pp. 102–126.

Grünkemeier, E. (2013).*Breaking the Silence: South African Representations of HIV/AIDS*. Suffolk: James Currey.

Gumede, M.V., (1990). *Traditional Healers – a medical practitioner's perspective*. Johannesburg: Skotaville Publishers.

Gurib-Fakim, A. (2006). *Medicinal Plants: Traditions of yesterday and drugs of tomorrow. Molecular Aspects of Medicine*, 27:1–93.

Hall, J.B., O'Brien, E.M., & Sinclair, F.L. (2000). *Prunus africana: a monograph. School of Agricultural and Forest Sciences Publication*. Number 18. Bangor: University of Wales.

Hamann, M. & Tuinder, V. (2012). *Introducing the Eastern Cape: A quick guide to its history, diversity and future challenges.* Stockholm: Stockholm Resilience Centre.

Hammond-Tooke, D.W. (1974). *The Bantu-Speaking Peoples of Southern Africa*. London: Routledge & Kegan Paul Publication.

Harrison, A., O'Sullivan L.F., Hoffman, S., Dolezal, C. and Morrell, R. (2006). "Gender Role and Relationship Norms among Young Adults in South Africa: Measuring the Context of Masculinity and HIV Risk," *Journal of Urban Health*, 83 (4):709–22.

Harrison, D. (2009). An Overview of Health and Health care in South Africa, 1994–2010: Priorities, Progress and prospects for New Gains. A Discussion document commissioned by the Henry J. Kaiser family foundation to Help Inform the National Health Leader's Retreat, Muldersdrift, January 24–26, 2010.

Hassim, A., Heywood, M. and Berger, J. (eds). (2014). *Health and Democracy: A guide to human rights, health law and policy in post-apartheid South Africa*. Johannesburg: Siberlnk Press.

Hassim, S. (2002). "'A Conspiracy of Women': The Women's Movement in South Africa's Democratic Transition." *Social Research*, 69(3):693–732.

Health-e News (2008). Health-e News: Eastern Cape poverty – the State is also 'captured' by incompetence.(5th February). Available from: https://www.dailymaverick.co.za/article/2018-02-05-health-e-news-eastern-cape-poverty-the-state-is-also-captured-by-incompetence/#.WzpKDmAzblV.

Health Poverty Action (2018). Neglected Tropical Diseases, Available from: https://www.healthpovertyaction.org/news-events/neglected-tropical-diseases/(Accessed July 31, 2019).

Hedberg, L., Hedberg, O., Madati, P., Mshingeni, K.E., Mshiu, E.N., 1982. "Inventory of plans used in Traditional medicine Tanzania: Plants of the family." Acanthaceae. *Journal of Ethnopharmacology*, 6:29–60.

Hedberg, L., Staugard, F. (1989). *Traditional Medicine in Botswana*. Gaborone: Ipeleng Publishers.

Helman, G.C. (2002). *Culture, Health and Illness*. London: Arnold.

Hemmings, C.P. (2005). "Rethinking Medical Anthropology: How Anthropology is FailingMedicine."*AnthropologyandMedicine*,122:91–103,DOI:10.1080/13648470500139841.

Henning, S. & Akoob, K.(2017). "Motivational factors affecting informal women entrepreneurs in North-West Province," *Southern African Journal of Entrepreneurship and Small Business Management*, 9(1):a91. https://doi.org/10.4102/sajesbm.vi1.91.

Heywood, M., Hassim, A. and Berger, J. (eds.). (2014).*Health and Democracy: A Guide to Human Rights, Health Law and Policy in Post-Apartheid South Africa*, South Africa: Siber Ink.

Hillenbrand, E. (2006). *Improving traditional- conventional medicine collaboration: Perspectives from Cameroon.* American University in Washington D.C, USA.

Hobsbawn, E. & Ranger, T.O. (1992). *The Invention of Tradition.* Cambridge: Cambridge University Press.

Hollenberg, D. & Muzzin, L. (2010). "Epistemological challenges to integrative medicine: an anticolonial perspective on the combination of complementary/alternative medicine with biomedicine." *Health Sociology Review,* 19(1):34–56.

Hollenberg, D. (2007). "How do private CAM therapies affect integrative health care settings in publicly funded health care system?." *Journal of Complementary and Alternative Therapies,* 4(1):1–17.

Hollenberg, D. (2006). "Uncharted ground: patterns of professional interaction among complementary/alternative and biomedical practitioners in integrative health care settings." *Social Science & Medicine,* 62:731–744.

Hostettmann, K., Marston, A., Ndjoko, K., Wolfender, J.L., (2000). "The Potential of African Plants as a source of Drugs." *Current Organic Chemistry,* 4:973–1010.

Hoyler, E., Martinez, R., Mehta, K., Nisonoff, H., Boyd, D. (2016). "Beyond Biomedical Pluralism: characterizing healthcare delivery of biomedical and traditional medicine in rural Guatemala." *Global Public Health,*13(4):503–517.

Hsu, E. (2008). "Medical Pluralism," 316–321, Heggenhougen, K, Quah, S. (eds.), *International Encyclopedia of Public Health,* 4. San Diego: Academic Press.

Hsu, E. (2002). "The medicine from China has 'rapid effects': Chinese medicine Patients in Tanzania." *Anthropology and Medicine,* 9(3):291–313, DOI:10.1080/13648470216335.

Hsu, E. (1999).*The Transmission of Chinese Medicine.* Cambridge: Cambridge University Press.

Hughes, G.D., Aboyade, O.M., Clark, B.L., Puoane, T.R. (2013). "The prevalence of traditional herbal medicine use among hypertensives living in South African communities." *BMC Complement Altern Med,* 2013; 13:38. DOI: 10.1186/1472-6882-13-38.

Hunter, M. (2005). "Cultural Politics and Masculinities: Multiple-partners in Historical Perspective in KwaZulu-Natal." *Culture, Health and Sexuality,* 7(4):389–403.

Hutchinson, P.A. & Mahlalela, X. (2006). "Utilization of voluntary counseling and testing services in the Eastern Cape, South Africa." *AIDS Care,* Jul;18(5):446–55. DOI:10.1080/09540120500213511.

Iroegbu, P., (2005), "Healing insanity: Skills and expert knowledge of Igbo healers," *African Development* 30(3):78–92. http://dx.doi.org/10.4314/ad.v30i3.22231.

Iwu, M.M., (1993). *Handbook of African medicinal plants.*London: CRC Press Book.

Iwuji, C.C., Orne-Gliemann J., Tanser F., et al. (2013). Evaluation of the impact of immediate versus WHO recommendations-guided antiretroviral therapy initiation on HIV incidence: the ANRS 12249 TasP (Treatment as Prevention) trial in Hlabisa sub-district, KwaZulu-Natal, South Africa: study protocol for a cluster randomised controlled trial. Trials 2013;14 (1):230.

Jacobs, W. (2014). "Migration Patterns and Migrant Characteristics in the Western Cape through Differential Urbanisation Lens." Mini-thesis presented in partial fulfilment of the requirements for the degree of MPhil Urban and Regional Science in the Faculty of Arts at Stellenbosch University.

Jacobsen, K. (2014). *Introduction to Global Health*. Second Edition. Burlington: Jones and Barlett Learning.

James, P.B., Wardle, J., Stee, A. (2018). "Traditional, complementary and alternative medicine use in Sub-Saharan Africa: a systematic review," *BMJ Global Health*, 3:e000895.DOI:10.1136/bmjgh-2018-000895.

Jarvis, M. (2009). *Ubuntu Christianity*. Wellington: Fact and Faith Publications.

Johnson-Hanks, J. (2003). "Education, ethnicity, and reproductive practice in Cameroon." *Population-E*, 58(2):153–180.

Johnson, L.F. (2012). "Access to antiretroviral treatment in South Africa, 2004–2011." *South African Journal of HIV Medicine*, 13(1): a156 | DOI: https://doi.org/10.4102/sajhivmed.v13i1.156.

Johnson, T.R. (2002). *Distinguished Native American Spiritual Practitioners and Healers*; Greenwood: Santa Barbara, CA, USA, 2002.

Joint United Nations Programme on HIV/AIDS (UNIAIDS). (2005). *Intensifying HIV Prevention: UNAIDS Policy Position Paper*, Geneva: UNAIDS.

Jones, S. (2006). "From ancestors to herbs: Innovation according to 'the protestant reformation' in African medicine. Ethnographic praxis in industry." *Journal of African Studies*, 15 (1):1–15.

Kafaru, E. (1994). *Immense help from Nature's workshop*: Elika Health services Ltd. Lagos, Nigeria: Academic Press Plc.

Kale, R. (1995). "South Africa's Health: Traditional Healers in South Africa: A parallel Healthcare system." *BMJ*, 1182–1185.

Kale, R. (1995). "South Africa's health: Traditional healers in South Africa: A parallel health care System." *BMJ*, 310:1182.

Kaptchuck, T.J. (2001). "The double-blind, randomized placebo-controlled trial: gold standard or golden calf?." *Journal of Clinical Epidemiology*, 54:541–9.

Karim, S.S., Arendse, R., & Ziqubu-page, T.T. (1994). "Bridging the gap: Potential for a healthcare partnership between African traditional healers and biomedical personnel in South Africa." *South African Medical Journal*, 84:s1–s16.

Kasilo, O.M.J, Trapsida, J-M., Mwikisa, C.N., Lusamba-Dikassa, P.S. (2010). "An Overview of the Traditional Medicine Situation in the African Region." *African Health Monitor*, Issue 4, Brazaville: World Health Organization Regional Office for Africa. Available from: http://www.aho.afro.who.int/sites/default/files/ahm/reports/32/ahm-13-special-issue-pages7to15.pdf.

Kayombo, E.J., Uiso, C., Mbwambo, Z.H., Mahunnah, R.L., Moshi, M.J., Mgonda, Y.H. (2007). "Experience of initiating collaboration of traditional healers managing HIV and AIDS in Tanzania," *Journal of Ethnobiology and Ethnomedicine*, 3–6: DOI: 10.1186/1746-4269-3-6.

Kelner, M. & Wellman, B. (1997a). "Who seeks alternative health care? A profile of users of five modes of treatment." *Journal of Alternative and Complementary Medicine*, 3(2):127–40.

Kelner, M. & Wellman, B. (1997b). "Health care and consumer choice: medical and alternative therapies." *Social Science and Medicine*, 45(2):203–12.

Kew, Y., Chia, Y.L., Lai, S.M., Chong, K.Y., Ho, X.L., Liew, D.W., Moy, F.M., Selvarajah, S. (2015). "Traditional and Complementary Medicine (TCM) among Study Population with Cardiovascular Risk; use and Substitution for Conventional Medicine in Pahang, Malaysia." *Med J Malaysia*, 70(2):86–92.

Kheswa, J.G. & Hoho, V.N. (2014). " 'Ukuthwala' the sexual-cultural practice with negative effects on the personality of adolescent females in Africa." *Mediterranean Journal of Social Sciences*, 5(20): 2808.

Kincheloe, J.L. (2006). "Critical ontology and indigenous ways of being; forging a postcolonial curriculum." In Kanu, Y. (Ed), *Curriculum as cultural practice: postcolonial imaginations* (pp. 181–197). Toronto: University of Toronto Press.

King, B. (2010). "Political ecologies of health." *Progress in Human Geography*, 34(1):38–55.

King, N. (2002). "Security, disease, commerce: ideologies of postcolonial global health." *Social Science and Medicine*, 32:763–789.

King Sabatha Dalindyebo District Municipality (2010). *Integrated Development Plan: 2010/2011*. Mthatha: KSD local Municipality.

Kirbag S., Zengin F., & Kursat, M. (2009). "Antimicrobial Activities of Extracts of some Plants." *Pakistan Journal of Botany*, 41(4):2067–2070.

Kleinman, A. (1986). "Concepts and a Model of the Comparison of Medical Systems as Cultural Systems, *Social Science and Medicine*," (1978),12:85–93;Reprinted in Currer, C, Stacey M, (eds.). *Concepts of health, illness, and handicap*. Geneva: Harwood Academic Publishers.

Kleinman, A. (1980). *Patients and Healers in the Context of Culture. An Exploration of the Borderland between Anthropology, Medicine and Psychiatry*. California: University of California Press.

Kleinman, A. (1984). "Indigenous systems of healing. Questions for professional, popular and folk care." In J. Warren, Salmon, ed. *Alter-native Medicines: Popular and Policy Perspectives*. London: Tavistock. Pp. 138–164.

Kleinman, A., L. Eisenberg and B. Good. (1978). "Culture, illness and care: Clinical lessons in anthropology and cross-cultural research." Annals of Internal Medicine, 88:251–58.

Konings, P.(2003). "Religious Revival in the Roman Catholic Church and the Autochthony-Allochthony Conflict in Cameroon," *Africa: Journal of the International African Institute*, 73(1):31–56.

Krige, D. (ND) Traditional Medicine and Healers in South Africa. The Journal of European Medical Writers,6–9, http://www.emwa.org/JournalArticles/JA_V7_I1_Krige1.pdf.

Kristofferssen, U. (2000). HIV/AIDS as a human security issue: a gender perspective. Expert Group Meeting on the "HIV/AIDS Pandemic and Its Gender Implications", 13–17 November, (Windhoek, Namibia,2000). Available: http://www.un.org/womenwatch/daw/csw/hivaids/kristoffersson.htm(accessed March 16, 2018).

Kühn, B. (2009). *Universal Human Rights vs Traditional Rights. – Topical review Digest: Human rights in Sub-Saharan Africa*. Denver: University of Denver Press.

Kumagi, A. (2008). "A conceptual framework for the use of illness Narratives in Medical Education," *Academic medicine*, 83, No.7.

Kumagi, T., Alswat, K., Hirschfield, G., Heathcote, J. (2008). "Preventative hepatology: minimizing symptoms and optimizing care." *Liver international: Official Journal of the Association for the study of the Liver*, 28(7):pp. 922–34.

Kumar, D. (1997). *Science and the raj: 1857–1905: Delhi*: Oxford University Press.

Kyerematen, G.A. & Ogunlama, E.O. (1987). "An integrated approach to the pharmacological evaluation of traditional material medica." *Journal of Ethno Pharmacology*, 20:191–207.

Labhardt, N.D., Aboa, S.M., Manga, E., Besing, J.M. & Langewitz, W. (2010). *Bridging the gap: how traditional healers interact with their patients. A comparative Study of Cameroon: Tropical Medicine and International Health*, 15(9):1099–1108.

Lamla, C.M. (2007). The search for medical therapy in a local Southern Nguni community in Ugadla: Communicating form Africana4. Mthatha: WSU.

Lamla, C.M. & Simon, M. (1991). "Merging pharmacopoeia: Understanding the Historical Origins of Incorporative pharmacopoeia processes among the Xhosa healers in Southern Africa." *International Journal of Ethnopharmacology*, 33(3):237–42.

Lamla, C.M. (1981). *Traditional Healers and their medicines*, Cacadu: Lumko Musicological Institute.

Lamla, C.M. (1975). "Present Day diviners in the Transkei." Unpublished Masters Thesis. Alice: University of Forthare.

Lantum, D.N. (1978). *The Pros and Cons of Traditional Medicine in Cameroon*. Yaoundé: UCHS/University Yaoundé.

Latiff, S.S. (2010). *Integration of African Traditional Health Practitioners and Medicine into the Healthcare Management System in the Province of Limpopo*. Stellenbosch: University of Stellenbosch.

Leclerc-Madlala, S. (2001). Virginity testing: managing sexuality in a maturing HIV/AIDS epidemic. *Medical Anthropology Quarterly*, 15(4):533–52.

Leclerc-Madlala S., Simbayi, L.C., Cloete, A. (2009). *The Sociocultural Aspects of HIV/AIDS in South Africa 25 years on*. New York: Springer, p. 13–25.

Leedy, P.D. & Ormrod, J.E., (2005). *Practical Research, planning and Design*. Upper Saddle River, New Jersey: Pearson Education.

Leonard, K.L. (2000). African Traditional healers and Outcome-Contingent Contracts in Health Care. Discussion Paper Series No. 9900-02.

Leventhal, T., & Newman, S. (2010). "Housing and child development." *Children and Youth Services Review*, 32:1165–1174.

Light, M.E., Sparg, S.G., Stafford, G.I., & van, S.J. (2005). "Riding the wave: South Africa's contribution to ethnopharmacological research over the last 25 years." *Journal of Ethnopharmacology*, 100(1–2):127–130. DOI: http://dx.doi.org/10.1016/j.jep.2005.05.028.

Lincoln, Y.S. & Guba, E.G., (1985). *Naturalistic Inquiry*. Thousand oaks' (C.A): Sage.

Lloyd, C. (2005).*Growing up global: The changing transition to adulthood in developing countries. Panel on transitions to adulthood in developing countries*. Washington, DC: National Academic Press.

Lock, M. & Nguyen, V-K. (2010). *An Anthropology of Medicine*. Oxford: Willy-Blackwell.

Low, C. (2004). Khoisan Healing: Understandings, Ideas and Practices. D.Phil Thesis, Christ Church College, University of Oxford.

Luizza, M.W., Young, H., Kuroiwa, C., Evangelista, P., Wodere, A., Bussman, R.W. (2013). "Local knowledge of plants and their uses among women in the Bale mountains, Ethiopia." *Ethonobotany Res Appl.*, 11:315–39.

Lund, C., Breen, A., Flisher, A.J., Kakuma, R., Corrigall, J., Joska, J.A., Swartz, L., and Patel, V. (2010). "Poverty and common mental disorders in low- and middle-income countries: a systematic review." *Social Science and Medicine*, 71(3):517– 528.

MacClean, S. & Moore, G. (2012). "Money, commodification and complementary health care: Theorising personalised medicine within depersonalised systems of exchange.' *Social Theory & Health*, Advanced online publication 17 October 2012, DOI:10.1057/sth.2012.16.

Macheke, C. & Campbell, C. (1998). "Perceptions of HIV/AIDS on a Johannesburg Gold Mine." *South African Journal of Psychology*, 28(3):146–53.

Mackenzie-Cook, P.D. (2006). "Challenging the New Orthodoxy in Integrative Medicine." *The Journal of Alternative and Complementary Medicine*, 2(7):679–683.

Magruder, J. & Nattrass, N. (2006). "Exploring Attrition Bias: The case of Khayetlitsha Panel Study (2000–2004)," *South African Journal of Economics*,74 (4):769–81.

Mahady, G.B. (2001). "Global harmonization of herbal health claims." *Journal of Nutrition* 131(3 supplementary):1120–1123S.

Mander, M. (1998). *Marketing of indigenous medical plants in South Africa. A case study of Kwazulu-Natal*. Rome: FAO.

Mander, M. (1998). *Marketing of Indigenous Medicinal Plants in South Africa: A Case study in KwaZulu-Natal.*, Rome: Food and Agriculture Organization of the United Nations.

Mander, M., Ntuli, L., Diederichs, N., & Mavundla, K. (2007). "Economics of the traditional medicine trade in South Africa." In S. Harrison, R. Bhana, & A. Ntuli (Eds.), *South African Health Review* (pp 189–199). Durban, South Africa: Health Systems Trust.

Mann, J. (2002). "Natural products in Cancer chemotherapy: Past, Present and future." *Nature Reviews*, 2:143–148.

Manu, E., Maluleke, X.T., Douglas, M. (2017). "Knowledge of High School Learners Regarding Substance Use within High School Premises in the Buffalo Flats of East London, Eastern Cape Province, South Africa," *Journal of Child & Adolescent Substance Abuse*, v26 n1 p. 1–10.

Marlise, R. (2003).Traditional Medicine and Traditional healers in South Africa. Discussion paper prepared for the Treatment Action Campaign and AIDS Law Project.

Marsland, R. (2007). "The modern traditional healer: locating 'hybridity' in modern traditional medicine, southern Tanzania," *Journal of Southern African Studies*, 33(4):751–765.

Mathew, D. & Carole, D.S. (2004). *Social Research: the basics*. London: Sage Publications Ltd.

Matolino, B. (2011). "The (Mal) Function of 'it' in Ifeanyi Menkiti's Normative Account of Person." *African Studies Quarterly*, 12, 4:28–37.

Maughan-Brown, B. (2007), Experiences and perceptions of HIV/AIDS-related Stigma Amongst People on Antiretroviral Treatment in Khayelitsha, Cape Town, CSSR Working Paper No 185, Centre for Social Science Research: University of Cape Town. Available at http://www.cssr.ac.za/pubs_cssr.html.

Maxim, P. (2006). "Rebuttal of Pro: Should Evidence-Based Medicine Be Used More in clinical practice?" *Western Journal of Emergency Medicine: Integrating Emergency Care with Population Health*, 7(1):1–4.

Mayeng, I. (1999). Integrating traditional medicine into national health care systems, is it an attainable objective? Presented at the WHO consultative meeting on strategy for traditional medicine for the African region 2001–2010, Harare, Zimbabwe, 13–15 December.

Maykut, P. & Morehouse, R., (1994). *Beginning Qualitative Research. A Philosophical and Practical Guide*. London: Falmer Press.

Maylam, P. (1995). "Explaining the apartheid city: 20 years of South African urban historiography," *Journal of Southern African Studies*, 21, no. 1:pp. 19–38.

Mbe, A.R. (2002). "New Pentecostalism in the wake of the economic crisis in Cameroon." *Nordic Journal of African Studies*, 11(3):359–376.

Mbiti, J.S. (1970/1990). *African Religions and Philosophies*. New York: Anchor Books.

Mbiti, J.S. (1975).*Concepts of God in Africa*. SPC: London, UK.

Mbiti, J.S. (1990). *African Religions and Philosophy*. London: Heinemann.

Mbiti, J. (1969). *African Religions and Philosophy*, Oxford: Heinemann publishers.

BIBLIOGRAPHY

Mbiti, J.S. (1992). *African Religions and Philosophy*, 2nd ed. revised; London: Heinemann Educational Books.

Mbiti, J.S. (1970). *African Religions and Philosophies*. New York, USA: Doubleday & Co.

Mbuy, T.H. (2000). African Traditional Religion as the Socio-cultural background of the African of the Third Millennium,"171–182, Nkwi, P.N.(ed.),The Anthropology of Africa: Challenges for the 21st Century. Proceedings of the 9th Annual Conference of the Pan African Anthropological Association. ICCARST Monograph 2.Wenner-Gren Foundation New York.

McFarlane, C. (2015). "South Africa: The Rise of Traditional Medicine," *Insight on Africa*, 7(1):60–70.

McIntyre, D., and Gilson, L. (2002). "Putting equity in health back onto the social policy agenda: experiences from South Africa," *Social Science and Medicine*, 54: 1637–1656.

Mckenna, B. (2012). "Medical education under siege: critical pedagogy, primary care, and the making of 'slave doctors'." *International Journal of Critical Pedagogy*, 4(1), 95–117.

Mckenna, B. (2011). "Medicine's Complicity in the Cruelties of Capitalism," *Counterpunch*, August 30:2011.

Mckenna, B. (2010). "Take back medical education; the primary care shuffle." Invited Editorial for *Medical anthropology: Cross-cultural Perspectives in Illness and Health*, 26(1):6–14.

Meintjes, G. (1998). *Manhood at a price: socio-medical perspectives on Xhosa Traditional Circumcision*. Grahamstown: Rhodes University.

Menkiti, I.A. (2004). "On the Normative Conception of a Person," 324–31, Wiredu, K.(ed.), A *Companion to African Philosophy*. Malden: Blackwell Publishers.

Menkiti, I.A. (1984). "Person and Community in African Traditional Thought," 171–81, Wright, R.A. (ed.), *African Philosophy: An Introduction*. Lanham: University Press of America.

Mercado, L.N. (2004/2005). "The Change in catholic Attitudes towards Traditional Religion," *Dialogue and Alliance*, 18(2).

Metzger, K.L. (2006). "An Existential Perspective of Body Beliefs and Health Assessment." *Journal of Religion and Health*, 45(1):130–146.

Meyer, J.J.M., Afolayan, A.J., Taylor, M.B., Engelbrecht, L. (1996). "Inhibition of herbs simplex virus types 1 by aqueous extracts from shoots of Helichrysum queronites." *Journal of Ethno-pharmacology*, 52:41–43.

Mhame, P.P. (2000). *The role of traditional knowledge (TK) in the National Economy: The importance and Scope of TK, particularly Traditional Medicine in Tanzania*. UNCTAD Expert Meeting on System and National Experiences for Protecting Traditional Knowledge, Innovations and Practices. Geneva: 30 October- 1 November.

Millan, H. (2011). "Cultural curing: Magic in Medicine and the pursuit of Alternatives," *Plaforum*, 12:80–99. Available: https://journals.uvic.ca/index.php/platforum/article/view/10324/2996(accessed June 24, 2018).

Miller, R.L. & Brewer, D.J. (2003). *A-Z of Social Research*. London: Sage Publications.

Mills, W. (1995). "Missionaries, Xhosa clergy and the suppression of African Traditional Custom" In: H. Bredencamp, & R.R. (eds)., *Mission and Christianity in South African History*,pp.153–175, University of Witwatersrand Press, Witwatersrand.

Ministère de la Sante Publique (MINSANTE), (2002). *Stratégie Sectorielle de Santé: Analyse Situationnelle du Secteur Sante au Cameroun*, paper prepared by Ministry of Public Health. Yaoundé: MINSANTE.

Mizrachi, M. & Shuval, J. (2005). "Between formal and enacted policy: Changing the contours of boundaries." *Social Science & Medicine*, 60, 1649–1660.

Mkwananzi, S. (2017). The socio-structural analysis of teenage pregnancy in Southern Africa, A dissertation submitted to the School of Social Sciences in partial fulfilment of the requirements for the degree of doctor of philosophy in demography and population studies, Faculty of Humanities, University of Witwatersrand, and Johannesburg, South Africa.

Mngqundaniso, N.P.K. (2008). "Traditional healers and nurses: a qualitative study on their role on sexually transmitted infections including HIV and AIDS in KwaZulu-Natal, South Africa," *African Journal of Traditional and Complementary Alternative Medicine*, 5(4):380–6.DOI:10.4314/ajtcam.v5i4.31293.

Mngqundaniso, N. & Peltzer, K.(2008). "Patients Consulting Traditional Health Practitioners in the Context of HIV/AIDS in Urban Areas in KwaZulu-Natal, South Africa," *African Journal of Traditional. Complementary and Alternative Medicine*, 18;5(4):380–6.

Mogkobi, M.G. (2013). "Towards integration of traditional healing and western healing: Is this a remote possibility?" *African Journal of Physical Health, Education Recreation and Dance*, (Suppl 1):47–57.

Mokhele, T., Weir-Smith, G. & Labadarios, D. (2012). Development of health density indicators in South Africa using GIS, GISSA Ukubuzana 2012: Academic paper. Available: http://hdl.handle.net/20.500.11910/3226.

Mokhoathi, J. (2017). "From Contextual Theology to African Christianity: The Consideration of Adiaphora from a South African Perspective," *Religions*, 8, 266; DOI: 10.3390/rel8120266.

Mokolobate, K.(2017). Effects of alcohol consumption in South Africa:From the cradle to the grave.Advertorial Special Reports, Available: https://mg.co.za/article/2017-10-27-00-effects-of-alcohol-consumption-in-south-africa-from-the-cradle-to-the-grave(Accessed July 7, 2019).

Momsen J. (2003). *Gender and Development*. London: Routledge Publications.

Moodley T., Sormunen T., Rudenhed L., Maharaj, N. & Sartorious, B. (2016). "Improved pregnancy outcomes with increasing antiretroviral coverage in South Africa." *BMC Pregnancy Childbirth*, 16:35. https://doi.org/10.1186/s12884-016-0821-3.

Moore, R. (2010) "A general practice, a country practice: The cure, the charm and informal healing in Northern Ireland." In: R. Moore and S. McClean (eds.) *Folk Healing* and *Health Care Practices in Britain and Ireland: Stethoscopes, Wands and Crystals.* Oxford: Berghahn, pp. 104–129.

Moore, R. & McClean, S. (eds.) (2010) *Folk Healing and Health Care Practices in Britain and Ireland: Stethoscopes, Wands and Crystals.* Oxford: Berghahn.

Morris, K., (2002). *South Africa tests traditional medicines.* The lancet infectious diseases 2. p. 319. Msimang, C.T., (1882). *Buza ku Mkabayi.* Pretoria: De jager- Haum Publishers.

Moshabela M., Bukenya, D., Darong, G., Wamoyi, J., MCLean, E. Skovdal, M. *et al.,* (2017).Traditional healers, faith healers and medical practitioners: the Contribution of medical pluralism to bottlenecks along the cascade of care for HIV/AIDS in Eastern and Southern Africa, *Sex Transmission Infection,* 93(Supplement 3):e052974.DOI:1011.36/sextrans-2016-052974.

Mpofu, E., Peltzer, K., Bojuwoye, O., Mpofu, E. (2011). Indigenous healing practices in Sub-Saharan Africa. *Counselling People of African Ancestry,* p. 3–21. Available from: http://hdl.handle.net/20.500.11910/3753.

Mubangizi, .J.C. (2012). "A South African Perspective on the Clash between Culture and Human Rights, with Particular Reference to Gender-Related Cultural Practices and Traditions," *Journal of International Women's Studies;* Bridgewater 13, Iss. 3: 33–48.

Mubangizi, J.C. (2012). "A South African Perspective on the Clash between Culture and Human Rights, with Particular Reference to Gender-Related Cultural Practices and Traditions." Journal of International Women's Studies, 13(3):33–48. Available at: http://vc.bridgew.edu/jiws/vol13/iss3/3.

Mutabazi, M.M. (2008). "Should we modernize traditional medicine? Governing Health systems in Africa," 17:(7):201–224. Available from: http://www.codesria.org/IMG/pdf/Chap16.pdf.

Muweh, A.N. (2011). Modernity in traditional medicine: Women´s experiences and perceptions in the Kumba Health District, Southwest Region, Cameroon. Master Thesis Submitted in Partial fulfillment for the award of Master of Science degree in Public Health Sciences, Umeå University, Sweden.

Mwangi, J.W., (2000). *Traditional herbal medicine in Kenya.* Nairobi, Kenya: University of Nairobi.

Mynda, P. (2013). Attitudes, understanding and perceptions of teenagers about the use of contraceptives (Buffalo City Municipality–Eastern Cape). Assignment presented in partial fulfilment of the requirements for the degree of Master in Philosophy (HIV/AIDS Management), Faculty of Economic and Management Sciences Africa Centre for HIV/AIDS Management, Stellenbosch University.

Nasr, S.H. (2007). Avicenna. Encyclopedia Britannica. Online. Archived from the Original on 31 October 2007. .

Nattrass, N. (2008). "Gender and access to antiretroviral treatment in south Africa," *Feminist Economics,* 14(4):19–36.

Nattrass, N. (2005). "Who consults Sangomas in Khayelitsha? An exploratory quantitative analysis." *Social Dynamics*, 31:161–182.

Nattrass, N. (2008). "AIDS and the scientific governance of medicine in post-apartheid South Africa." *Afr. Affairs* 2008, 107, 157–176.

Nattrass, N. (2006). "AIDS, Gender and Access to Antiretroviral Treatment in South Africa." Centre for Social science Research Working Paper 178, University of Cape Town.

Navarro, V. (Ed). (2007). "Neoliberalism as a class ideology, or the political causes of growth inequalities." *Neoliberalism, globalization and inequalities: Consequences for health and quality of Life.* New York: Baywood Publishing.

Navarro, V. (1976).*Medicine under capitalism.* New York: Prodist.

Navarro, V. & Shi, L. (2001). "The political context of social inequalities and health." *Social Science & Medicine*, 52, 481–491.

Ndaki, K. (2009). "Traditional alternatives? In The Virus, Vitamins, and Vegetables: The South African HIV/AIDS Mystery"; Cullinan, K., Thom, A., Eds.; Jacana Media: Sunnyside, CA, USA.

Nduna, N. (2014). "Virginity testing: perceptions of adolescent girls in the Eastern Cape, South Africa," *New Voices in Psychology*, 10(1):16–34. http://hdl.handle.net/10520/EJC160960.

Neuwinger, H.D., (2000). *African traditional medicine. A Dictionary of plant Use and Applications, Part 2.* Stuttgart- Germany: Medpharm Scientific publishers.

Neveen H. (2010). "Herbal medicine in ancient Egypt," Journal of Medicinal Plants Research, 4(2):pp. 082–086, Available online at http://www.academicjournals.org/JMPR.

Newman, D.J., Cragg, G., Snader, K.M., (2003). "Natural Products as sources of New Drugs over the period 1981–2002." *Journal of Natural products* 66: 1022–1037.

Ngubane, H.L. (1977). *Body and Mind in zulu medicine.* London: Academic press.

Nichter, M. (1992). "Anthropology and International Health: South Asian Case Studies." *Medical Anthropology Quarterly*, 6, issue 4, pp. 415–418.

Njoh, A.J. (2009a). "Urban planning as a tool of power and social control in colonial Africa." *Planning Perspectives*, 24:3,301–317, DoI: 10.1080/02665430902933960.

Njoh, A.J. (2009b). "Ideology and public health elements of human settlement policies in Sub-Saharan Africa." *Cities*, 26:9–18.

Njoh, A.J. (2008). "The segregated city in British and French colonial Africa." *Race and Class*, 49:87.DOI:10.1177/0306396808049004060z.

Njoh, A.J. (2008b). "Colonial Philosophies, Urban Space, and Racial Segregation in British and French Colonial Africa." *Journal of Black Studies*, 38(4):579–599, DOI: 10.1177/0021934706288447.

Njoh, A.J. (2007). *Planning Power: Town Planning and Social Control in Colonial Africa.* London: University College London.

Njoroge, G.N., Bussman, R.W. (2006). "Diversity and utilization of antimalarial ethnophytotherapeutic remedies among the kikuyus (Central Kenya)." *Journal of Ethnobiology and Ethnomedicine*, 2(8):pp.1–7.

Nkwi, P.N. (2006). "Anthropology in Postcolonial Africa: The Survival Debate." In *World Anthropologies: Cosmopolitics for a New Global Scenario in Anthropology*.

Nyika, A. (2007). "Ethical and Regulatory Issues Surrounding African Traditional Medicine in the Context of HIV/AIDS," *Developing World bioethics*, 1:25–34.

Nzima, M. et al. (1996). "A targeted intervention research on traditional healers perspectives of sexually transmitted illness in urban Zambia." *Société d'Afrique and SIDA*, 13:7–8.

Office of the United Nations High Commissioner for Human Rights and WHO (2018). The Right to Health. Factsheet 31.

Okpako, D.T. (2006). *African Medicine: tradition and beliefs*. Available online at http://www.pjonline.com (accessed 16/04/2010).

Okpako, D.T. (1999). "Traditional African medicine: theory and pharmacology explored." *Trends in pharmacological Sciences*. 20(12):482–485.

Oldenburg C.E. (2016). HIV treatment and prevention in KwaZulu-Natal, South Africa: individual, couple, and household effects of antiretroviral therapy (Doctoral dissertation), Harvard T.H. Chan School of Public Health. Available from: http://nrs.harvard.edu/ urn-3:HUL.InstRepos:27201745.

Oldham, P., Barnes, C., Hall, S. (2013). Biodiversity in the Patent System: South Africa A country study of genetic resources and traditional knowledge in the patent system of relevance to South Africa, Report Prepared for: Deutsche Gesellschaft für Internationale Zusammenarbeit (GIZ).United Kingdom: One World Analytics. Olive Leaf Foundation. (2017). Mthatha." Retrieved 28 July 2017.

Oloyede, O. (2010). "Epistemological Issues in the Making of an African medicine: Sutherlandia (Lessertia Frutescens)." *African Sociological Review*, 14(2):74–88.

Onwuanibe, R.C. (1984). "The Human Person and Immortality in Ibo Metaphysics," 183–97, OAU/STRC/DEPA/KIPO. *1997 Medicinal Plants and Herbal Medicine in Africa. Policy Issues on Ownership Access and Conservation*. Paper presented at the 1st OAU/STRC/DEPA/KIPO workshop 14–17 April, Nairobi.

Onwuanibe, R.C. (1979). "The philosophy of African medical Practice." *A Journal of Opinion (African Studies Association)*, 9(3):25–28.

Organization of African Unity/Scientific, Technical Research Commission. (1985). *African Pharmacopoeia*,Vol. 1. Ethiopia: Addis Abba.

Orubuloye, I.O., Caldwell, P. and Caldwell, J.C. (1994). "The role of high risk occupations in the spread of AIDS: truck drivers and itinerant market women in Nigeria." pp. 88–100. In *Sexual Networking and AIDS in Sub-Saharan Africa: Behavioural Research and the Social Context*. Eds I.O Orubuloye, John C. Caldwell, Pat Caldwell and Gigi Santow. Health Transition Centre: The Australian National University.

Padayachee, V. (1997)."The Evolution of South Africa's International financial relations and policy:1985–1995," in Michie, J and Padayachee, V. *The Political economy of South Africa's Transition*. London: The Dryden Press.

Palmer, K. (2010). *Spellbound: Inside West Africa's Witch Camps*. New York: Free Press.

Paruk, F., Blackburn, J., Friedman, I., Mayosi, B (2014). "National expenditure on health research in South Africa: what is the benchmark?," *South African Medical Journal(SAMJ)*, 104(7):468–474.

Payyappallimana, U. (2010). "Role of Traditional Medicine in Primary Health Care: An Overview of Perspectives and Challenges," *Yokahoma Journal of Social Sciences*, 14(6):57–77.

Pearce, T.O. (2000). "Death and Maternity in Nigeria." In: Turshen, Meredith (ed.). *African Women's Health*. Trenton. NJ: Africa World Press, Inc.Pp.1–26.

Pegrim, R. (2003). Witchcraft and policing South Africa Police Service attitudes towards witchcraft and witchcraft-related crime in the Northern Province, African Studies Centre Research Report 72 / 2003.

Pelto, J.P. & Pelto, H.G. (1978). Anthropological *Research: The structure of Inquiry*. Cambridge: Cambridge University Press.

Peltzer, K. and Ramlagan, S. (2009). "Alcohol Use Trends in South Africa," *Journal of Social Science*, 18(1): 1–12.

Peltzer, K. & Mngqundaniso, N. (2008). "Traditional healers and nurses: a qualitative study on their role on sexually transmissible infections including HIV and AIDS in KwaZulu Natal, South Africa," *African Journal of Traditional, alternative medicine*, 5(4):380–386.

Peltzer, K. (2000). "Perceived treatment efficacy of the last experienced illness episode in a community sample in the Northern Province, South Africa." *Curationis*, 32(1):57–60.

Peltzer, K. & Kanta, X. (2008). "Medical circumcision and Manhood initiation rituals in the Eastern cape, South Africa: A post-intervention evaluation," *Culture, Health and Sexuality*, 11(1):83–97.

Peltzer, K.; Mngqunaniso, N. (2008). "Patients consulting traditional health practitioners in the context of HIV/AIDS in urban areas in KwaZulu-Natal, South Africa." *Complementary and Alternative Medicine*, 5:370–379.

Peltzer, K.; Mngqundaniso, N.; Petros, G.A. (2006). "Controlled study of an HIV/AIDS/STI/TB intervention with traditional healers in KwaZulu-Natal," *South Africa. AIDS Behavour*, 10:683–690.

Peltzer, Karl. (2009). "Traditional health practitioners in South Africa." *The Lancet* 374, no. 9694:956–957.

Peltzer, K. (2009). "Utilization and practice of traditional/complementary/alternative medicine (TM/CAM) in South Africa, African Journal of Traditional, Complementary and Alternative Medicines," *African Journal of Complementary and Alternative Medicine*, 26(2):175–185.

BIBLIOGRAPHY

Pemunta, N.V., et al. (2020). "Self-medication within the context of medical pluralism in Yaounde, Cameroon," *Pan African Medical Journal*, 37:14. DOI 10.11604/pamj.2020.37.14.17947.

Pemunta, N.V. & Tabi, T.C-J. (2016). "Neoliberalism, Oil Wealth and Migrant Sex Work in the Chadian City of N'Djamena" in Hofmann, Susanne and Moreno, Adi (eds), pp.135–162. *Intimate Economies: Bodies, Emotions and Sexualities on the Global Market. New Palgrave Series Studies in Globalization and Embodiment.*

Pemunta, N.V. & Obara, B.T. (2011). "War, Social dislocation and the double appropriation of women's human security in Sierra Leone." *Journal of Human Security.* 8(2):105–124.

Pemunta, N.V. (2014). "The 'gendered field' of Kaolinite clay production: performance characteristics among the Balengou, Western region, Cameroon." *Social Analysis*, 58, Number 2, summer 2014, pp. 21–41(21).

Pemunta, N.V. (2013). "The Social Epidemiology and Burden of Malaria in Bali Nyonga, Northwest Cameroon." *Health, Culture and Society*, 4, 1:20–36, ISSN 2161-6590 (online). DOI 10.5195/hcs.2013.69 | http://hcs.pitt.edu.

Pemunta, N.V. (2011). Culture, Human rights and Local Socio-legal resistance against Female Genital Cutting practices: An anthropological Perspective. Saarbrücken: VDM Verlag Dr.Müller GmbH & Co.KG.

Pemunta, N.V. (2011a). *Health and Cultural Values: Female Circumcision within the Context of HIV/AIDS in Cameroon.* New Castle upon Tyne: Cambridge Scholars Publishing.

Pemunta, N.V. (2011b). "Challenging Patriarchy: Trade, outward migration and the internationalization of Commercial sex among Bayang and Ejagham women in Southwest Cameroon." *Health, Culture and Society Journal*, 1(1):167–192.|ISSN2161-6590(online)|DOI10.5195/hcs.2011.58| http://hcs.pitt.edu.

Pemunta, N.V. (2010). "Intersubjectivity in Ethnographic Research." *Qualitative Research Journal*, 10(2):38–54.

Pemunta, N.V. (2008). 'Still Fixing Women'?: Female Circumcision and the anti-HIV/AIDS fight among the Ejaghams of Southwest Cameroon.Ph.D Dissertation, Department of Sociology and Social Anthropology. Central European University, Budapest, Hungary.

Pemunta, N.V. (2000).The social and cultural aspects of healthcare delivery: a case study of client's perspectives on indigenous medicines in Yaounde, 62–71, Nkwi, P.N. (ed.). The Anthropology of Africa: Challenges for the 21St Century. Proceedings of the 9th Annual Conference of the Pan African Anthropological Association. ICCASSRT Monograph 2. New York: Wenner-Gren Foundation.

Perez, C.(2008). *Caring for them from birth until death: The practice of community based Cuban medicine.* London: Rowman and Littlefield.

Petrus, T.S., & D.L. Bogopa. (2007). "Natural and supernatural: Intersections between the spiritual and natural worlds in African witchcraft and healing in reference to Southern Africa." *Indo-Pacific Journal of Phenomenology*, 7(1):1–10.

Phaswana-Mafuya, M.N and Peltzer, K. (2007). "HIV/AIDS workplace policies in Eastern Cape tertiary institutions," *Southern African Journal of Higher Education(SAJHE)*, 21(2):308–320.

Phaswana-Mafuya, N., Seager, J., Peltzer, K., Jooste, S., Mkhonto, S. (2017).Social Determinants of HIV in the Eastern Cape. Available from: http://www.hsrc.ac.za/en/research-data/view/4818.

Potgieter, M.J., Du Plessis, H.J., Egan, B.A., Mathibela, M.K. (2015). "Socio-cultural profile of Bapedi traditional healers as indigenous knowledge custodians and conservation partners in the Blouberg area, Limpopo Province, South Africa." *Journal of Ethnobiology and Ethnomedicine*, 11:14.

Pretorius E. (1999). "South African Health Review. 5th Edition. Durban: Health Systems Trust." *'Traditional Healers'* pp. 249–256.

Prince, R.J., Geissler, P.W., Nokes, K., Maende, J.O., Okatcha, F., Gringorenko, E. & Sternberg, R. (2001). "Knowledge of herbal and pharmaceutical medicines among Luo children in western Kenya," *Anthropology and Medicine*, 8(2–3):211–235.

Prince, R. (1964). "Indigenous Yoruba psychiatry," in *Magic, Faith and Healing: Studies in Primitive Psychiatry Today*. Kiev, A. (ed.). London: Free Press, Pp.84–120.

Puoane T., Hughes, G., Uwimana, J., Johnson, Q., (2012). "Folk W. Why HIV positive patients on antiretroviral treatment and/or cotrimazole prophylaxis use traditional medicine: perceptions of health workers, traditional healers and patients: a study in two province of South Africa." *African Journal of Traditional and Complementary Alternative Medicine*, 9(4):495–502. Doi:10.4314/ajtcam.v9i4.6.

Quah, S.R. (2003). "Traditional healing systems and the ethos of science." *Social Science and Medicine*, 57:1997–2012.

Rademeyer, S. (2017). Provincial differentials in under-five mortality in South Africa. Submitted in partial fulfilment of the academic requirements for the degree of Master in Population Studies in the School of Built Environment and Development Studies, University of KwaZulu-Natal Howard College Campus Durban.

Rakodi, C. (1996). "Urban land policy in Zimbabwe," *Environment and Planning*, 28(9):1553–74.

Ralushai, N.V. (1996). *Report of the Commission of inquiry into witchcraft Violence and ritual Murders in Northern Province of the Republic of South Africa*. Pietersburg: Northern Province.

Ran, B.X., Nguyen, N.K., Nguyen, L.P., Nguyen, C.T., Nong, V.M. (2016). "Preference and willingness to pay for traditional medicine services in rural ethnic minority community in Vietnam, BMC Complement Alternative Medicine"; 16:48. DOI: 10.1186/s12906-016-10107.

Ranger, T. & Hobsbawm, E. (ed). (1983). *The Invention of Tradition.* Cambridge University Press.

Rangoon S., Dalasile N.Q., Paruk Z., Patel, C.J. (2011). "An exploratory study of trainee and registered psychologists' perceptions about indigenous healing systems," *South African Psychology*, 41(1):90–100.DOI:10.11.77/008124631104100110.

Rice, K. (2018). "Understanding ukuthwala: Bride abduction in the rural Eastern Cape," *South Africa, African Studies*, 77(3):394–411, DOI: 10.1080/00020184.2018.1464752.

Richter, M.(2003). "Traditional Medicines and Traditional Healers in South Africa," Discussion Paper Prepared for the Treatment Action Campaign and AIDS Law Project.

Rijken, D.J. (2014). Description of the problems accompanying the ritual of Ulwaluko. Ulwaluko.co.za. Retrieved 28 March 2014.

Ritter, E.R. (1955). *Shaka Zulu.* London: Penguin Publishers.

Ross, E. (2010). "Inaugural Lecture: African spirituality, ethics, and traditional healing-implications for indigenous South African social work education and practice." *South African Bioethics Law*, 3(1):44–51.

Roxburgh, S. (2014). Witchcraft, Violence and Mediation in Africa: A comparative study of Ghana and Cameroon, Thesis submitted to the Faculty of Graduate and Postdoctoral Studies in partial fulfilment of the requirements for the Doctorate in Philosophy degree in Political Studies School of Political Studies Faculty of Social Sciences University of Ottawa, Canada.

Rukangira, E., (2004). Medicinal Plants and Traditional Medicine in Africa: Constraints and Challenges. Available at www.sustdev.org/explore/health_soc/articles/edition4.shtml (accessed 13March 2010).

Saleh, A.A. (1993). "WHO/EMRO: Politique Sur la Medicine Traditionelle." In: Grancher, Michel (Ed), *La plante Medicale: de la traditional à la Science.* Paris: Jacques Grancher.

Sarkar, S. &Seshadri, D. (2014). "Conducting recording review studies in Clinical practice," *Journal of Clinical Diagnostic Research*, 8(9):JG01–JG04.

Sarpong, P.K., (1996). *Libation,* Anansesem, Accra.

Savage, O.M.N. (1996). "'Children of the rope' and other aspects of pregnancy loss in Cameroon," in: Cecil, Rosanne (Ed.). *The Anthropology of Pregnancy Loss.* Oxford: Berg, 95–112.

Schaffner, K.F. (2002). "Assessments of efficacy in biomedicine: the turn towards methodological pluralism." In: Callahan, D. (eds).*The role of complementary and alternative medicine: accommodating pluralism.* Washington, D.C: Georgetown University Press.

Schellack, N., Meyer, J.C., Gous, A.G.S. (2011). "Part II. Health and economic context." *South African MedicalJournal,* (SAMJ), 101, No. 8:558–561.

Scheper-Hughes, N. (1993). *Death without Weeping. The Violence of Everyday Life in Brazil.* Berkeley: University of California Press.

Scheper-Hughes, N. (1992). *Death without weeping.* Berkeley: University of California Press.

Schoepf, B. (1992). "Sex, gender and Society in Zaire," *in Sexual Behavior and Networking: Anthropological and Socio-Cultural Studies on the Transmission of HIV*, ed. T. Dyson. Liege: Derouaux-Ordina. Pp.358–368.

Schofield, J. (2000). "Increasing the generalisability of qualitative Studies." In R. Gomm, M. Hammersley, & P.F. (eds.), *Case study method: key issues, key texts.* London: Sage.

Sethosa, E. and K. Peltzer (2005), Evaluation of HIV Counselling and Testing, Self-Disclosure, Social Support and Sexual behaviour Change Among a Rural Sample of HIV Reactive Patients in South Africa, Curationis Feb: 29–41.

Setswe, G., (1999). "The role of traditional healers and primary health care in South Africa," *Health SA Gesondheid* 4(2):56–60. http://dx.doi.org/10.4102/hsag.v4i2.356.

Sharma, U. (1993). "Contextualizing Alternative Medicine: the exotic, the marginal and the perfectly mundane." *Anthropology Today*, 9(4):15–18.

Shin H.K., Jeong S.J., Huang D.S., Kang B.K., Lee M.S. (2013). "Usage patterns and adverse experiences in traditional Korean medicine: results of a survey in South Korea." *BMC Complement Alternative Medicine*, 13:340. DOI: 10.1186/1472-6882-13-340.

Shisana, O.; Rehle, T.; Simbayi, L.C., Zuma, K., Jooste, S., Zungu, N., Labadarios, D., Onoya, D. (2012). *South African National HIV Prevalence, Incidence and Behaviour Survey*; Human Sciences Research Council Press: Cape Town, South Africa, 2014.

Shuster, M.S., Claire, E.F., Paula M., del Rio, C. (2009). "The Cultural and Community-Level Acceptance of Antiretroviral Therapy (ART) Among Traditional Healers in Eastern Cape," *South Africa, J Community Health* DOI 10.1007/s10900-008-9121-9.

Sillitoe, P. (2006). "Ethnobiology and applied anthropology: reapproachment of the academic with the practical." *Journal of the Royal Anthropological Institute* (NS), pp. 119–142.

Silverman, D., (1993). *Interpreting qualitative data: Methods for analyzing talk, text and interaction.* London: Sage.

Singer, M. & Baer, H. (1995).Critical medical anthropology. New York: Baywood Publishing Singer, C., (1928). *A short History of Medicine.* Oxford: Caledon Press.

Smit, J.W.J. (2017). "Rights, Violence and the Marriage of Confusion: re-emerging bride abduction in South Africa," *Anthropology Southern Africa*, 40(1):56–68.

Sobiecki, J-F. (2014). "The Intersection of Culture and Science in South African Traditional Medicine," *The Indo-Pacific Journal of Phenomenology*, 14(1):1–10.

Sobiecki, J.F. (2012). "Psychoactive ubulawu spiritual medicines and healing dynamics in the initiation process of Southern Bantu diviners." *Journal of Psychoactive Drugs*, 44(3):216–223. DOI:10.1080/02791072.2012.703101.

Sofowora, A. (1996). *Plantes medicales et medicine traditionelle d'afrique.* Paris: Editions Karthala.

Somse, P., Chako, M.K., Wata, J.B., Bondha, P., Gonda, B., Johnson, D., Downer, A., Kimball, A.M. (1998). "Evaluation of an AIDS training program for traditional healers in the Central African Republic," *AIDS Education and Prevention*, 10(6):558–64.

South African Department of Health (2004).Operational plan for comprehensive HIV and AIDS care, management and treatment for South Africa. Pretoria: Department of Health.

Srivastava, V., Negi, A.S., Kumar, J.K., Gupta, M.M., Khanuja, S., (2005). "*Plant-base anticancer molecules:* A chemical and biological profile of some important leads." *Bioorganic & Medical Chemistry* 13 (21):pp. 5892–5908.

Stanifer J.W., Patel U.D., Karia F., Thielman N., Maro V., Shimbi D., et al. (2015) "The Determinants of Traditional Medicine Use in Northern Tanzania: A Mixed-Methods Study." *PLoS ONE* 10(4): e0122638. https://doi.org/10.1371/journal.pone.0122638.

Statistics South Africa. (Stats SA). (2018a). Mid-year population estimates 2017. Pretoria: Stats SA.

Statistics South Africa (2017a). South Africa Demographic and Health Survey 2016 Key Indicators Report National Department of Health Pretoria, South Africa South African Medical Research Council Cape Town, South Africa The DHS Program ICF Rockville, Maryland, USA.

Stats SA. (2018b). Mortality and Causes of Death in South Africa 2015: Findings from death notification PO309 3 Pretoria.

Stats SA. (2017b). *General household Survey 2016*. Pretoria: Stats SA.

Stats SA. (2014). *Census 2011 Provincial Profile: Eastern Cape*. Pretoria: Stats SA.

Steinberg, J. (2007). "Finding the meaning of AIDS: ARV treatment in an Eastern Cape Village," *South African Crime Quarterly*, No.21:9–13.

Sterk, C.E. & Del Rio, C. (2008). "The Cultural and Community-Level Acceptance of Antiretroviral Therapy (ART) Among Traditional Healers in Eastern Cape, South Africa," *Journal of Community Health*, 34(1):16–22. DOI: 10.1007/s10900-008-9121-9.

Stevenson, M.G. (1996). "Indigenous Knowledge in Environmental Assessment." *Arctic*, 49(3): 278– 291.

Stock, R. & Stock, F.R. (2013).*Africa South of the Sahara. A Geographical Interpretation*. New York: The Guildford Press.

Stoner, B.P. (1986) "Understanding medical systems: Traditional, modern, and syncretic health care alternatives in medically pluralistic societies." *Medical Anthropology. Quarterly*, 17:44–48. 37.

Stoner, B.P. (2013). "Sociocultural Perspectives Applied to Transdisciplinary Public Health." In *Transdisciplinary Public Health: Research, Education and Practice*; Haire-Joshu, D., McBride, T.D., Eds.; John Wiley and Sons: San Francisco, CA, USA, pp. 141–154.

Street, R.A. (2016). "Editorial: Unpacking the new proposed regulations for South African traditional health practitioners," *South African Medical Journal*, 1006(4):325–326.

Summerton, J.V. (2006). "The Organisation and Infrastructure of the African Traditional Healing System: Reflections from a Sub-District of South Africa," *African Studies*, 65:2, 297–319, DOI: 10.1080/00020180601035708.

Sundar, R.K. (2007). *Biocapital: The constitution of postgenomic life*. United States: Duke University Press.

Swaartbooi-Xabadiya, Zolisa C. (2010).*Attitudes and perceptions of girls in ST John's College about the practice of virginity testing*, MA thesis Submitted to Faculty of Health Science, School of Public Health, University of Limpopo.

Swanson, M.W. (1977). "The sanitation syndrome: bubonic plague and urban native policy in the Cape colony, 1900–1909." *Journal of African History*, 18no.3:pp.387–410.

Swantz, L.W., (1974). *The role of the medicine man among the zaramo in Dar es Salaam*. Doctoral Thesis. P. 387.

Sydara, K., Gneunphonsavath, S. Wahlstrom, R. Freudenthal, S. Houamboun, K. Tomson, G. et al.(2005). "Use of traditional medicine in Lao PDR." *Complementary Therapy and Medicine*, 13(3):199–205. DOI: 10.1016/j.ctim.2005.05.004.

Tabi, C-J.T. (2011). An investigation into the role of traditional medicine in an era of biomedicine: Case of Qokolweni Location (KSDM), Eastern Cape, Republic of South Africa. Master of Social Sciences in Anthropology. Walter Sisulu Unversity.

Tamalaoke, K. (1995). *Herbal medical school advocated*. Ghanaian Times, 20 February, 3.

Tankwanchi, A.B.S., Özden, C. & Vermund, S.H. (2013). "Physician Emigration from Sub-Saharan Africa to the United States: Analyses of the 2011 AMA Physician Masterfile." *Plus Medicine*, DOI:10.1371/Journal.pmed.1001513availablehttp://www.plosmedicine.org/article/info%3Adoi%2F10.1371%2Fjournal.pmed.1001513.

Tataryn, D. & Verhoef, M.J. (2001). "Combining conventional, complementary and alternative health care: A vision of integration," in *Perspectives on complementary and alternative health care*. Ottawa: Health Canada, p.VII.87–109.

Taylor, L. (2013). Herbal medicine versus the FDA. Available: http://www.rain-tree.com/news01132012.htm#.U9LQrfnoR-g.

Tcheknavorian-Asenbauer, A. (1993). "Industrial utilization of medicinal and aromatic plant resources in developing countries." *Acta Horticulturae*, 333:19–46.

The Centre for Conflict Resolution (2005). HIV/AIDS and Human Security: An agenda for Africa, Available from: https://sarpn.org/documents/d0001769/index.php.

Thernberry, E. (2015). "Virginity Testing, History, and the Nostalgia for Custom in Contemporary South Africa," *African Studies Review*, 58(3): pp. 129–148.

Thipe, T. (2013). "Defining Boundaries: Gender and Property Rights in South Africa's Traditional Courts Bill." *Laws*, 2 (4):483– 511.

Thornton, R. (2002). *Traditional Healers and the Bio-medical health system in South Africa*: Summary Report-December 2002 (consultancy report). Medical Care Development International (MDC) for the Margaret Sanger Institute.

Tilhurt, J.C., & Kaptchuck, T.J. (2008). "Herbal medicine research and global health: an ethical analysis of *Bulletin of the World Health Organization*," August, 86, 8 .I8b.

TradReg 2017. Regulation of Herbal and Traditional Medicines. University of Bonn, Germany, Available https://www.bfarm.de/SharedDocs/Downloads/DE/Service/Termine-und-Veranstaltungen/dialogveranstaltungen/dialog_2017/170914/12_Neil%20Gower.pdf?__blob=publicationFile&v=2(accessed July 22, 2019).

Tsey, K. (1997). "Traditional Medicine in Contemporary Ghana: A public policy Analysis." *Social Science and Medicine*, 45(7):pp. 1065–1074.

Tucker, C., Marsiske, R., Kenneth, G.J., Jessica, D., Herman, K.C. (2011). "Patient-Centered Culturally Sensitive Health Care: Model Testing and Refinement," 30(3):342–350. DOI: 10.1037/a0022967.

Tupasi, T.E., Miguel, C.A., Tallo, V.L., et al. (1989). "Child care practices of mothers: implications for intervention in acute respiratory infections," *Annals of Tropical Pediatrics* 9, 82–88.

Tzortzis, A. (2003). *African healers join the AIDS fight: The Christian Science Monitor.* June 30. Available on: http//www.csmonitor.com/2003/0630/p07s02-woaf.html (accessed 11 march 2010).

Udezi, A.W. & Usifoh, S.F. (2013). "Social and economic factors influencing the patronage and use of complementary and alternative medicine in Enugu," Journal of Pharmacy and Bioresources, 10(1):17–24.

UNESCO Report, (1994). "Traditional Knowledge in Tropical Environment," *Nature & Resource*. 30, No2, UNESCO, Paris: Paris University Press.

UNESCO Report. (1994). *"Traditional knowledge into the twenty-first century,"* Nature & Resources. 30, No2, UNESCO, Paris: Paris University Press.

UNICEF. (2017). Health Budget: South Africa 2017/2018. Pretoria: UNICEF South Africa. Available:https://www.unicef.org/esaro/UNICEF_South_Africa_--_2017_--_Health_Budget_Brief.pdf.

United Nation Environment Programme. (UNEP)(2013). Green Economy in a Blue World Full Report. 15 th Global Meeting of the Regional Seas Conventions and Action Plans Montego Bay, Jamaica 30th September – 01st October, Available from: https://wedocs.unep.org/bitstream/handle/20.500.11822/12715/GreenEconomyinaBlueWorld%20FullReport.pdf?sequence=1&isAllowed=y.

Van de Walle. (1992). "Fertility transition, conscious choice, and numeracy," *Demography*, 29(4):487–502.

Van der Geest, S. (1997). "Is there a Role for Traditional Medicine in Basic Health Services in Africa? A Plea for a Community Perspective," *Tropical Medicine and International Health*, 2, Issue 9:pp.903–911.

Van Staden, J. (1999). "Medicinal Plants in Southern Africa: Utilization, Sustainability, Conservation- can we change the mindsets?" *Outlook on Agriculture*, 28:75–76.

Van Wyk, IWC. (2004). "African witchcraft in theological perspective," *HTS Teologiese Studies / Theological Studies* | 60(3):1201–1228.

Van Wyk, B.-E. (2011). "The potential of South African plants in the development of new medicinal products," *South African Journal of Botany*, 77:812–829.

Van Wyk, B.-E. (2008). "A broad review of commercially important southern African medicinal plants," *Journal of Ethnopharmacology*, 119:342–355.

Veloshnee G.V., Chersich, M.F., Harris, B., Alaba, O., Ataguba, J.E., Nxumalo, N.J., Goudge, J. (2013). "Moving towards universal coverage in South Africa? Lessons from a voluntary government insurance scheme." *Global Health Action*, 6:19253-http://dx.doi.org/10.3402/gha.v6i0.19253.

Verpoort, R. (2000). "Pharmacognosy in the New Millennium: Lead finding and Biotechnology." *Journal of Pharmacy and pharmacology*, 52:pp. 253–262.

Von Maydell, H.J. (1990). *Trees and shrubs of the Sahel. Verlag Joseph Margarf:* Weikersheim, pp.63–76 and 393.

Voeks R.A. (2007). "Are women reservoirs of traditional plant knowledge? Gender, ethnobotany and globalization in northeast Brazil." *Singapore J Trop Geo*, 28:7–20. DOI: 10.1111/j.1467-9493.2006.00273.x.

Waldstein, A. (2006). "Mexican migrant ethnopharmacology: Pharmacopeia, classification of medicines and explanations of efficacy." *Journal of Ethnopharmacology*, 108:299–310.

Waldstein, A, Adams C. (2006). "The interface between medical anthropology and medical ethnobiology." *Journal of Royal Anthropological Institute*, N.S.:95–118.

Wallace, D.(2015). "Rethinking Religion, Magic and Witchcraft in South Africa: From Colonial Coherence to Postcolonial Conundrum," *Journal for the Study of Religion*, 28(1):23–51.

Wanyama, J.N., Tsui, S., Kwok, C., Wanyenze, R.K., Denison, J.A., Koole, O., van Praag, Castelnuovo, B. Wabwire-Mangen, Kwesigabo, G.P., Colebunders, R. (2017). "Persons living with HIV infection on antiretroviral therapy also consulting traditional healers: a study in three African countries," *International Journal of Sexually Transmissible Disease & AIDS.*, 28(10):1018–1027. DOI: 10.1177/0956462416685890.

Watson, J. (2005). "Traditional healers fight for recognition in South Africa's AIDS crisis." *Nature Medicine* 11:6.

Watt, J.M. and Breyer-Brandwifk, M.J., (1962). *The medicinal and poisonous plants of Southern and Eastern Africa,* Edinburgh: E & S Livingstone Press.

Weiss, J. (1998). Diagnostic concepts and medicinal plants use of the Chatino (Oaxaca, Mexico) with a comparison with Chinese medicine. University of Texas, Austin. PhD thesis.

Welch, J.S. (2003). "Ritual in Western Medicine and its Role in Placebo Healing." *Journal of Religion and Health*, 42(1):21–33.

Wells, A. (2005). Hegemony: Explorations into Consensus, Coercion and Culture A workshop at the University of Wollongong 14 &15 Feb, Imperial Hegemony and Colonial Labour, Available: https://www.uow.edu.au/~kyliesm/pdf/panel%201%20(wells).pdf.

Welz, A.W., Emberger-Klein, A. & Menrad, K.(2018). why people use herbal medicine, BMC Complement Alternative Medicine, 18:92.

Wessels, W.H. (1992). "Folk healers in South Africa – traditions cannot be ignored." *Salus*, 15 (2):14.

Wessels, W.H. (1992): "Folk healers in South Africa-traditions cannot be ignored." *Salus*, 15(2):14.

Western Cape Department of Health. (2006).*The Western Cape antiretroviral Programme: Monitoring Report*. Cape Town: Provincial Government of the Cape Town.

White, P.(2015). "The concept of diseases and health care in African traditional religion in Ghana," *Herv. teol. stud.*, 71 n.3 Pretoria, http://dx.doi.org/10.4102/HTS.V71I3.2762.

Williams, V.L., Victor, J., Crouch, N. (2013). "Red Listed medicinal plants of South Africa: Status, trends, and assessment challenges," *South African Journal of Botany*, 86:23–35.

Williams, B.G., Taljaard, D., Macphail, C., Gouws, E. (2000). "The Carletonville-Mothusimpilo Project: Limiting transmission of HIV through community-based interventions," *South African Journal of Science*, 86:351–359.

Wilkonson, D., (1999). "Traditional healers as tuberculosis treatment supervisors: Precedent and Potential (Planning and Practice)." *The International Journal of Tuberculosis and Lung Disease*, 3(9): 838–842(5).

Wilson, D., Williams K.K, Gerkovich, M.M. Gqaleni, N., Syce, J., Bartman, P., Johnson, Q. and Folk, W.R. (2015). "Consumption of *Sutherlandia frutescens* by HIV-Seropositive South African Adults: An Adaptive Double-Blind Randomized Placebo Controlled Trial,' *PLoS One*, 10(7): e0128522. DOI: 10.1371/journal.pone.0128522.

Winkelman, M. (2009). *Culture and Health: Applying Medical Anthropology*. San Francisco: Jossey-Bass.

Wood-Sheldon, J., Balick, M.J., Laird, S.A., (1997). *Medicinal Plants: Can Utilization and Conservation Coexist? The New York Botanical Garden*. New York, USA: Bronx.

World Bank. (2018).Overcoming Poverty and Inequality in South Africa. An Assessment of Drivers, Constraints and Opportunities. International Bank for Reconstruction and Development/ The World Bank. Available from: http://documents.worldbank.org/curated/en/530481521735906534/pdf/124521-REV-OUO-South-Africa-Poverty-and-Inequality-Assessment-Report-2018-FINAL-WEB.pdf.

World Health Organization. (1978).*The Promotion and Development of Traditional Medicine: Report of a WHO Meeting* {held in Geneva from 28 November to 2 December 1977},Geneva: WHO.

World Health Organization (2013). WHO Traditional Medicine Strategy 2014–2023, WHO: Hong Kong SAR, China. Available: https://vardgivarwebb.regionostergotland.se/pages/133417/WHO%20strategi.pdf.

World Health Organization (2007).WHO guidelines for assessing quality of herbal medicines with reference to contaminants and residues (Spain: WHO), Available from http://apps.who.int/medicinedocs/documents/s14878e/s14878e.pdf.

World Health Organization. (2002) . Regional Strategy for Traditional Medicine in the Western Pacific. Geneva, Switzerland: World Health Organization.

World Health Organization. (2002).*WHO Traditional Medicine Strategy 2002–2005*. Geneva: Switzerland.

World Health Organization Report. (1990). *Report of the consultation on AIDS and traditional Medicine: Prospects for involving traditional Health Practitioners, paper presented at 1990 Traditional Medicine Program and Global program on AID*. Francistown, Botswana: 23–27 July.

Wreford, J. (2008). Myths, masks and stark realities: Traditional African healers, HIV/AIDS avoidance. Centre for Social science Research, University of Cape Town, Working Paper No. 209.

Wreford, J. (2005). Missing each other: Problems and potential for collaborative efforts between biomedicine and traditional healers in South Africa in the time of AIDS. *Social Dynamics*, 31(2), 55–89.

Wringe, A., Renju, J., Seeley, J., Moshabela, M., Skovdal, M. (2017). *Bottlenecks to AID care and Treatment in sub-Saharan Africa: A Multi-country Qualitative Study*. London, UK: BMJ Publishing Group Ltd.

Wringe, A., Hosegood, Victoria, Seeley, Janet, B. Oliver, O. Kenneth, D. William et al. (2017). Traditional healers, faith healers and medical practitioners: the contribution of medical pluralism to bottlenecks along the cascade of care for HIV/AIDS in Eastern and Southern Africa, Sexually Transmitted Infections, 93(Suppl 3): e052974. DOI: [10.1136/sextrans-2016-052974].

Wright, R.A. (ed.). (1984). *African Philosophy: An Introduction*. Lanham: University Press of America.

World Health Organization (2000). Essential Drugs in the WHO African Region: Situation and Trend Analysis: Final Report of the WHO Regional Committee for Africa, Windhoek, Namibia, 1999. (Resolution, AFR/RC49/R5).

World Health Organization (2014). Fact sheet N°297 Updated February. Available from: http://www.who.int/mediacentre/factsheets/fs297/en/.

World Health Organization (2000). General Guidelines for Methodologies on Research and Evaluation of Traditional Medicine. Geneva: WHO.

World Health Organization (2004). Guidelines for the Registration of Traditional Medicines in the WHO African Region.

World Health Organization (2011). Guidelines on national policy for the protection of traditional medical knowledge and access to biological resources in WHO African Region. WHO Regional Office for Africa, Brazzaville.

World Health Organization (2015). Guideline on when to start antiretroviral therapy and on pre-exposure prophylaxis for HIV; 2017. Available from: http://apps.who.int/iris/bitstream/10665/ 186275/1/9789241509565_eng.pdf (Accessed July 13, 2019).

World Health Organization (2001). Legal Status of Traditional Medicine and Complementary/Alternative Medicine: A Worldwide Review. Geneva: WHO.

World Health Organization (1988). Resolution WHA41.19. Traditional Medicines and Medicinal Plants. Forty-First World Health Assembly Geneva.

World Health Organization (2002).Traditional Medicine Strategy 2002–2005. WHO/EDM/TRM/2002.1.WHO:Geneva.

World Health Organization Regional Office for Africa, Brazzaville. (WHO/AFRO/TRM/2004.1).

Yin, R.K. (1989). *Case study research: design and methods*. Newbury Park, [California]: Sage Publications.

Yin, R.K. (1994). *Case study research: design and methods* (Second edition). Thousand Oaks: Sage.

Zachariah, R., Nkhoma, W., Harries, A.D., Arendt, V., Chantulo, A., Spielmann, M.P., Mbereko, M.P., Buhendwa, L.(2002). "Health seeking and sexual behavior in patients with sexually transmitted infections: The importance of traditional healers in Thyolo. Malawi." *Sexually Transmitted Infection*, 78(2):127–9.

Zubane, S.R. (2001). *Prospect and Scope for traditional medicine in the South African education support services.* Durban: University of Zululand.

Zuma, T., Wight, D., Rochat, T., & Moshabela, M. (2018). "Navigating multiple sources of healing in the context of HIV/AIDS and wide availability of antiretroviral treatment: a qualitative study of community participant's perceptions and experiences in rural South Africa." *Frontiers in Public Health*, 6, Article 73, DOI:10.3389/fpubh.2018.00073.

Zuma, T., Wright, D., Rochat, T. & Moshabela, M. (2016). "Traditional health practitioners' management of HIV/AIDS in rural South Africa in the era of widespread antiretroviral therapy," *Global Health Action*, 10(1):1–12.

Index

abathandazeli 3
abduction marriage 118
accreditation
    procedure 22
    system 127
accusation narratives 88
acupuncture 4, 7, 10, 146
adversarial engagement 17, 98
aetiology 23, 42, 146, 162, 223, 232
African
    concept of health viii, 3, 25, 160, 221, 236
    cultural traditions 1
    custom or tradition 85, 119
    diseases 51, 160, 162, 230–231, 237
    independent Churches 110
    Indigenous Religion (AIR) 59
    personality 1, 117
    pharmacy 67, 135
    problem 1, 27, 82, 221
    quinine 56
    Renaissance project 98
    solution 1, 27, 82, 221, 239
    traditional healers 3, 145, 164–165, 169
    traditional medicine 18, 22, 30, 51, 55, 130, 159, 183, 196, 235
    traditional religion 197
African National Congress (ANC) xvi, 1, 40, 76, 84, 128
AIDS 1, 13, 25, 27, 44–45, 77–80, 82–84, 86–88, 90, 92, 94–96, 98–102, 107, 110, 112, 114, 120, 124, 128, 131, 136, 140–141, 144–145, 147, 149, 169, 181, 184, 191, 201, 205, 217, 219, 221, 226, 237
    Activist Group 81
    dementia 88
    denialists 1, 78
AIR 59
alcohol 88, 94, 112, 116, 217
alkaloid michellamine B 30
allopatic 4, 19, 21, 94
ALMA ATA 5, 12, 69
alternative 2–4, 6, 8, 10, 12, 14, 23–24, 41, 43, 49, 52, 66, 68, 70, 75, 83, 91, 96, 100, 132, 141, 149, 151, 159, 184–185, 191, 205, 212, 222, 224, 236
amagqirha xiv, 3, 89, 173
amagumbi okuxilongela 36
amakhubalo 171
amaXhwele 3
Anankungwi in Malawi 144
ancestors 3, 16, 18, 28–29, 32, 80, 89, 92, 110, 126, 156, 162, 167–168, 173–177, 185, 189, 193, 195, 198, 200, 202, 226, 228
Ancient Chinese 53
Ancistrocladus korupensis 30
Anopheles mosquitoes 64
anthropology 15
anti-colonialism 41–42
antimalarial therapy 70, 86, 91–92
antiretroviral
    agents 83
    drugs 1, 44–45, 77, 191, 221
    therapy (ART) 1, 87
anti-witchcraft ordinances 61, 73
apartheid 6, 14, 23–25, 43–44, 46–49, 52, 55, 60, 63–65, 75, 77–78, 80–82, 85–86, 96, 99, 103–104, 106–107, 117, 119–120, 122, 128, 147, 159, 191, 209
Apicynum erectum 42
apprenticeship 127, 156, 171, 175, 185, 212
Arab doctor 54
archaeological studies 54
ART 1, 78–79, 83, 87, 91–92, 94–95, 98, 102–103, 125, 131, 206
ARV 79, 83–84
Avicenna 54
Ayurveda 4, 50, 53

bacteriological 122, 125, 160, 219
Bamako Initiative 12, 122
belief-sensitive 159, 160, 199
belief system 144, 159, 205, 221, 229
benevolence of colonialism 60
Berlin Medical Papyrus 53
bewitchment 86, 88, 163, 202, 216, 221
Bill of Rights 81, 84, 123
biological knowledge 56

INDEX

biomedical   1, 3–5, 9, 12–21, 23–25, 27–28, 30–31, 34–35, 40–44, 47, 49–50, 52, 58, 67, 71–72, 74–75, 77, 81–83, 87, 89–92, 95–97, 99–100, 102–103, 121–122, 124–129, 131–133, 135–136, 140, 144, 146, 148, 151–153, 155, 159–160, 172, 183–185, 187–188, 190–191, 194, 197, 202–203, 205, 209, 211, 215–219, 221–223, 228, 232, 236, 238–240
   Capitalism   48
   education   28, 172
   healthcare system   1, 5, 6, 27, 31, 76, 127–128, 153, 159–160, 211, 222
   hegemony   96
   model   14, 17, 42–43, 239
biomedicalize   12, 14, 154
biomedically-oriented Randomized Controlled Trials   11
biomedical model, biomedical ontology   51
biomedicine   1–5, 7, 10, 12, 14–18, 21–23, 27–28, 40, 42–43, 45, 47–52, 60, 66–67, 69, 74, 83, 87, 89–91, 93, 96–97, 99, 110, 122, 124–125, 132–135, 139–140, 145–146, 149, 152–154, 157, 159–160, 171, 178, 184–185, 187–188, 190–191, 201, 204, 207, 212–213, 216, 218, 220–222, 226, 230–231, 234–240
biopiracy   6, 37, 56
bio-prospecting   56
black townships   62
bodily wastes   61
Book of Healing   54
breach of taboos   163
bubonic plague   63
Bushmen   29

Caesarian section   57
Cameroon vine   30
Canadian Complementary and Alternative Medicine   172
cannabis   116, 202
Canon of Medicine   54
Cape colony   56
capitalism   12, 40, 48–50, 52
care cascade   205
Cartesianism   50
Cartesian medicine   157
Catholic Women's Association   xvi, 198
causative agent   86, 88, 160, 162
CGE   xvi, 73

charlatanism   130
chemical properties   38
Children's Act in South Africa   119
Child Rights Convention   85
Chinese traditional medicine   230
Christian Bible   53
Christianity   58, 110, 113, 177, 197
Christian missionaries   60, 199
church hierarchy   199
civil and political rights   81
civilizing   52
civilizing health policy   61
clinical
   development   31
   encounter   30, 202
   reasoning   202
clinics   9, 69, 72, 95, 97, 107, 129, 202, 206, 213, 215–216, 226
codification   137
co-existence   13, 16, 28, 67, 153
collaboration   13, 21, 24, 30, 35, 68, 70, 73, 75, 81, 89, 98–99, 128, 140–141, 145, 153, 157, 184, 190, 203, 206, 209, 211, 215–216, 218–219, 221, 232–233, 235–238
colonial civil service   58
   enterprise   49
   era   55, 58, 68, 75, 238
   imperatives   60
   medical apartheid   48
   mentality paradigm   136
colonialism   6, 24, 40, 47, 52, 55–57, 60–61, 75, 77, 85, 96, 99, 104, 119, 138, 149
colonialists   20, 52, 56
colonization   52, 55, 66, 136, 183
coming-of-age rituals   81
commercial farming sector   104
Commission on Gender Equality   xvi, 73
common remedies   202
communication   18, 127, 142, 165, 175, 217
communitarian   188, 228
community   xv, 3, 6, 15, 17, 24, 31, 35, 39, 44, 51, 57, 84, 88, 91–93, 98–99, 112, 115, 119–120, 126–128, 136–137, 140–143, 145–146, 160, 164, 167, 169–170, 187–188, 201, 208, 210, 213–214, 217, 219, 225, 228–231, 234–235, 239
   counsellors   215
   health workers   95, 143
   participation   116

competing policies   221
Concept of Health   221
confidentiality   36
congregation   58, 199
conservation   7, 9, 151
conspiracy theory   88
Constitution   3, 81, 84, 123–124, 128
consultation lodges   36
contextual Christianity   110
conventional medicine   2, 27, 30, 135
Convention on the Elimination of All Forms of Discrimination against Women (CEDAW)   85
convergence   24
corruption   104, 150
cosmopolitan medicine   55, 67
cost effectiveness   203, 219
counter-blame theory   88
critical eclecticism   40
critical medical anthropological approaches   40
Crossopteryx febriguga   56
cryptoccal meningitis   88
cultural acceptability   127, 203
cultural
   complex   56
   practices   22, 44, 55, 58, 61, 78, 86, 111, 120, 199
   rights   84
culture as harm argument   144
culture as ignorance framework   136
culture-bound syndromes   51, 190
culture, place and health   45
Cure and a Curse for HIV   86
curfew laws   63
curriculum   22–23, 28, 67, 125

dangerous masculinity   94
data collection   35–37
democracy   73, 77–78, 84–85
   democratisation   239
   democratic values   84
demon   88
denominations   37, 110, 200, 234
dependency   44, 108
dialogue   24, 40, 75, 77, 140, 188, 200, 203, 221, 235
discourse   12, 51, 63, 99, 157, 193
discrimination   85

diseases of shame   209
Di Stefano   15, 22, 28, 30, 48, 51–52, 54, 67, 134–136, 146, 159, 178, 222–223, 238
diviners   3, 14, 20, 34, 127, 156, 168, 173, 175–177, 212
divinership   ix, xix–xx, 167–168
doctor-patient relationships   8
domination   3, 13, 48
draconian law   63
draughts   57
Dr Rath Health Foundation   1
Dr Ronald Ross   64
drug interactions   90, 131, 206

Eastern Cape   viii, xiv, 3, 9, 13, 23, 25, 27, 30–33, 39–40, 43–44, 46, 48, 77, 83, 87, 91, 102–107, 109, 111–115, 117, 119–120, 147–148, 170–171, 181, 208, 221
Ebers Papyrus   53
economic recession   65, 171
Edwin Smith Papyrus   53
efficacy   1, 5, 7–8, 11, 16–18, 20, 22, 38, 40, 45, 56, 69, 71, 86, 100, 124–125, 127, 141, 156, 183, 185, 191, 195, 197, 202, 215, 219, 231, 238, 240
Egypt   53–54, 70
embeddedness   103, 135
emotional wellbeing   41
Empire   42
empiricism   176, 157
employment   4, 8, 65, 112, 120, 208, 221, 226
enculturation   223
ENE   108
entanglement   25, 45, 49, 80, 154, 161, 235
environmental degradation   57
epidemics   10, 57
epistemology   11, 15, 41
erasure   25, 27, 42, 52, 137, 151–152
Estimate of National Expenditure   108
ethics   39
ethnic identity and personhood   117
ethnobotanists   53
ethnography   9, 21, 32, 34, 77, 89, 169
ethnomedicine   6, 15, 51, 66–67, 92
   definition   15
ethno-pharmacopoeia   208
Euro-American   52
Eurocentric science   51

INDEX

Europe 8, 12, 13, 41–42, 55, 56, 60, 62, 63, 139, 159, 165, 197, 224
European Union (EU) 8
evangelization 61
evidence-based medicine 1
experimentation 51, 115, 125, 199
exploitation 42, 60, 185–186, 206
extended multiple case study method 34
extramarital concurrent partnering 111
Ezekiel 53

face-to-face interviews 23, 35, 211, 230
fainting fits 231
faith xix, 3, 16, 34, 51, 90, 96, 124, 126, 128, 150, 165, 177, 197, 199–200, 205, 213, 219, 233
faith healing 126, 177
fake healers 206, 235
female fertility 115
female-headed 106
folk
  healing 6
  medicine 47, 138, 230
  systems 12
  theories 101, 146
  theories of disease causation 147
Food and Agriculture Organization (FAO) 7
formalisation 13, 153
Foucault 49, 122, 235
friends of the community 3

Galen 55
Galileo 51
Galioungou, Paul 54
Gender-Based Violence viii, 84, 114
gender norms 94
General Household Survey 9, 108, 129
germ theory 42, 146
GHS 9, 108, 129, 202
global ethnography 44
global hegemony 52
Global South 9, 150
gold mines 49, 109
good health 16–17, 26, 50, 125, 157, 159, 161, 168, 188, 218
green economy 4

HAART 89–91, 93, 102
head diviner xix, 176

healers 2, 16, 27, 34, 58, 65, 87, 95, 127, 138, 144, 154, 165, 185, 188, 199–201, 206, 219
Healing Agencies 166
health 1–2, 69, 71–74, 81–83, 91–93, 96–97, 102–103, 106–107, 109, 113–114, 121, 123, 127, 129, 133, 139, 154–156, 180, 185, 190, 217–219, 229, 237
  definition 3
healthcare 1, 3–6, 8–11, 13–15, 17, 21, 23–24, 27–28, 30–31, 35, 43, 45–46, 48–49, 52, 55, 60, 66–69, 78, 80–82, 87, 89, 91, 93–94, 96–97, 99–100, 107, 109–110, 114, 116, 120–122, 124, 127–135, 137, 139, 141–143, 145, 147–148, 154, 156–161, 170, 172, 177, 179, 181, 183–184, 186–189, 202–203, 205, 207–209, 211, 213, 215–216, 218–219, 221, 224–226, 231–238, 240
health supplements 38
health worlds 205
Hearst Medical Papyrus 53
hegemony 3, 13–15, 24, 30, 42, 47–48, 52, 60, 66, 75, 77, 96, 101, 122, 151, 153, 160, 219
  hegemonic biomedical discourses 238
  hegemonic system 14
hepatitis B 117, 131
herbal 1–2, 4, 6, 8, 11, 38, 53–55, 59, 67–68, 70, 89, 92, 121, 123, 125, 131, 133, 140, 144, 146, 155–156, 167, 170–172, 180, 189, 211–213, 222, 224, 233
herbalists 3, 14, 34, 127, 130, 156, 165, 169–171, 173, 189
herbal medicine 11, 53, 55, 67, 123, 125, 141, 212, 222, 224
herbal remedies 1, 38, 54, 67, 131, 140, 170–171, 211
herbarium labels 55
herbs 21, 38, 47–48, 53, 59, 95, 141, 144, 161, 163, 165, 167, 170–171, 174–175, 179, 181, 196, 210, 212, 215, 225–227
Hindu pilgrimage 61
Hippocrates 55, 139
historico-spatial view 43
HIV/AIDS 1, 5, 7, 10, 12–13, 18, 23, 25, 27, 30, 40, 43–44, 64, 69–70, 72, 76–83, 85–103, 105–120, 123, 125, 128–131, 136, 139–145, 147, 149, 154, 159, 167, 169, 172, 175, 179, 181, 184–185, 191, 201, 203, 205, 208, 215–218, 221, 230, 233, 237–239

holistic   14, 43–44, 50–51, 67, 90, 92, 103, 128, 132, 134, 149, 152, 167, 179, 183, 188, 217, 219, 224–225, 229
hospital-based biomedical   148
hospital-centered   122
hospitals   9, 12, 16, 42, 60, 69, 74, 95, 97, 109–110, 129, 138, 144, 152, 202, 212–213, 215–216, 233, 240
human behaviour   200
human development index   25, 109
human development indicators   43, 103–104, 120, 191
humanitarianism   52
human progress   199
Human Resources   82
human security   50
hygiene and sanitation   57, 58
hygienic practices   54
hymen   118

identity   39, 45, 55, 82, 94, 100, 111, 113, 120, 124
ideology of colonial   52
idliso   141, 212, 231
ignoramuses   56
immunity   174
imphepho   9
impilo   2, 121, 221
income inequalities   148
incorporation   28, 89, 91, 111, 123, 157, 236
indigenous   4–8, 13–15, 19–20, 23, 27, 30, 38, 42, 47, 51–52, 54–58, 61–62, 64–67, 69, 71–74, 83, 99, 121, 132, 145, 149–151, 154–157, 160–161, 163, 165, 172–173, 180, 183, 185, 192, 197, 203
    ontologies   37–38
    peoples   42, 52, 99
individual and community level factors   25
industrialism   49
inequalities   25, 44, 47, 50, 64, 78, 86, 94, 104, 114, 116, 147–148, 159
inferior   42, 48, 64
informal settlements   108
informed consent   36, 39
ingcibi   117
initiation rituals   117
inkciyo   118–119
integration   4, 5, 7, 10, 11, 13, 14, 21, 22, 23, 24, 25, 26, 27, 28, 46, 52, 66, 68, 69, 70, 75, 81, 89, 120, 121, 122, 123, 124–125, 127, 130, 131, 137, 152, 153, 156, 157, 159, 181, 184, 188, 189, 191, 192, 219, 221, 222, 238
integrative medicine   10, 28, 41, 67
intellectual property rights   7, 22, 38, 69–70, 152, 186
intergenerational relationships   112, 114, 120
interlocutors   35, 40, 192, 195–196, 200, 202, 207
intermediaries   42, 127, 188, 200
interpreters   36
inter-professional   28
interracial marriages   63
inyanga   58, 59, 165–166, 80, 86, 175
isiwasho   233
izangoma   xiv, 14, 59, 65, 73, 169, 176–177
izinyanga   14, 59, 65, 169

jealousy sickness   88

Kahun Gynaecological Papyrus   53
know-all doctor   130
Kolz, Ludwig   60

laboratory tests   67, 125
labour
    related migration   44, 109, 112, 191
    reserves   106
    taxes   106
    Land Appropriation   48
large-scale forces   43
law enforcement officers   133, 202
lay sector of healthcare   202
lay therapy managing group   67, 171
legalization   40, 96
less developed   2, 24
liberalism   42
Limpopo   9, 80, 104, 108–109, 208, 216, 219
Liverpool School of Tropical Medicine   64
lobola   111, 115, 118
local health narratives   7, 226
local history   51
London Medical Papyrus   53

machine metaphor   50
macroeconomic   24
macro-level   44–45

INDEX

magic 14, 28, 60, 65, 88, 158, 161, 163, 169–170, 174, 189, 199, 208, 235
mainstream 6, 13, 23–24, 68, 81, 99, 121, 123, 131, 135, 160, 178, 183–184, 192, 211, 219, 236–237
malaria 56, 61, 64, 70, 143, 145–146, 150, 161, 209, 238
male circumcision 78, 96, 144
malevolent 29
management methods 41
marginalization 43, 82, 118, 150–151
maritime routes 63
Marlise 2, 51, 122, 223
masculine virility 113
masculinity 93–94, 101, 111, 113, 117, 120
materialism 15
material medica 49
Mbeki, Thabo 1, 45, 78, 82–83, 86, 92, 191
Mbiti, John 3, 16, 145, 174, 228
MDGS 6–7, 12, 143
mechanism 15, 21, 24, 61, 68, 70, 78, 85, 106, 119–120, 133, 158
mechanistic 50, 136
medical aid 74, 109
medical anthropology 66–67
medical arsenal 179
medical education 172
medical pluralism 13–14, 17, 23, 25, 44, 67, 90, 150, 152, 180, 190, 205, 219
medical pluralism 4, 11, 67, 90
medical practice 14, 60, 65, 72, 74, 82, 124–125, 138, 164, 187, 222, 230
medical practices 4, 14, 22, 24, 53, 55, 59, 61, 69, 72, 74, 77, 90, 100–101, 103, 122, 127, 131, 136, 139, 145, 149, 153–155, 183,.185, 223, 233–234
medicinal plants 5, 7–8, 18–20, 30, 40, 55–56, 68–69, 135, 138, 149, 151, 171, 174, 197, 208, 212, 227
medicinal products 8
Menketi 3, 16
mental illness 59, 97, 180
metaphysics 16, 22, 188, 228
methods 3, 11, 16–17, 18, 19, 32, 35, 36, 37, 58, 70, 73, 130, 142, 150, 152, 157, 159, 165, 169, 188, 195, 197, 198, 199, 218, 222, 224
migrant labour 49, 104, 111, 118, 148, 208
Millennium Development Goals (MDGS) 6, 143
mind-body dichotomy 66, 160, 184

miscegenation 14, 63
misdiagnosis 137
misfortune xix, 18, 28–29, 80, 88, 103, 110–111, 160, 163, 166
mismanagement 107
missionaries 60
modern medicine 5, 12, 52, 57, 59, 75, 77, 124, 127, 139, 145, 149, 157, 189, 197, 200, 207, 219, 222
modern Western scientific cosmology 38
mono-causal model 42
Mpumalanga 9
Mqanduli 109, 225
Mthatha xiv, 31–33, 104, 109, 213, 225
multicausality 146, 204
multigenerational families 106
multiple case study 13, 34
multiple partnering 111, 113, 120
multi-scalar 44
muthi 59, 86, 179

National Quality Framework 127
native medicine 58
naturalization of biomedicine 157
Natural Product Alert database (NAPRALERT) 9
networks of solidarity 228
New Partnership for Africa's Development (NEPAD) 71
Nguni 4, 13, 28, 31–32, 162, 168, 190, 223
nobodies 229
nonconventional therapies 121
non-European technologies 41
non-timber forest products (NTFPS) 7
nurses 27–28, 32, 34–35, 40, 124, 188, 191, 209, 211, 215–218, 225, 238

ontology 17, 28, 41, 50, 103, 132, 232
opportunistic infections 70, 98
oracle 198
oracular consultation session 199
oral traditions 54
overcrowding 47, 104

paganism 52, 60
pandemic 1, 5, 10, 12, 23, 25, 27, 30, 40, 44–45, 64, 69, 77–80, 82–83, 85–86, 90, 94, 98–100, 102–103, 107, 118, 123, 128–129, 139–140, 143, 145, 149, 217, 221, 239

papyrus 53
parental authority 85, 119
parenthood 116
Partnership for Africa's Development (NEPAD) 12
Pastorian revolution 60
pathogens 29, 49, 223
pathology-focused 17
patrilineal ethnic groups 31
patriny 111
Pentecostal churches 178, 199
people-centered 122, 150
people living with AIDS 84
perceptions 3, 23, 28, 30, 38, 42, 45, 134, 140, 154, 179, 191–193, 207, 209–210, 218, 232, 236, 239
personalistic 29, 57, 126, 160–161, 223, 230, 232
personalized care 126
pharmaceutical companies 1, 6, 11, 38, 53, 224
pharmaceuticalization
pharmaceutization 5–7, 9, 27, 52, 133
philanthropy 7
philosophical contradictions 184
physiological
    development 116
    principles 125
    symptoms 205
phytochemical 9, 19, 21
phytomedicine 38
phytopharmacological 9, 18–19
pilot study 35
placebo 5, 50, 90, 150, 157, 167, 176, 197, 216
    placebo-controlled trial 157, 197
Placide Temples 228
plantation 41
plants 2, 9, 18–19, 21, 53–56, 70, 74, 130, 144, 151–152, 156, 163, 171–172, 175, 180, 183–184, 187, 189, 197, 199, 208, 213, 223
pluralistic management of AIDS 89
policy 1, 7, 11, 25–28, 45, 48, 62–63, 69, 71, 74–75, 77, 82–83, 100, 120, 122, 128, 132–133, 139, 142, 150, 157, 183–184, 190, 192, 218–219, 221, 225
political
    economy 40, 43, 49, 60, 103
    economy of colonialism 49, 60
pollution 28–29, 32, 58, 80, 144
polycultural amalgam 13

polymath 54
post-apartheid 44, 76, 104, 120, 122
postcolonial 6, 41, 75
poverty 1, 3, 6–7, 43–44, 50, 65, 80, 89, 103–106, 108–109, 111–112, 114–116, 120, 129, 148, 163, 178–179, 191, 193, 206, 225
    poverty-related diseases 47
power 11, 16–17, 22, 24, 29, 39, 44, 47, 49, 61–62, 65–66, 73, 81, 86, 111, 113, 119, 133, 136, 149, 151, 153–154, 161, 165, 187, 213, 235, 238
practitioners 4, 5, 7–8, 10, 12, 13, 16–17, 18, 20, 22, 23, 24, 25, 28, 30, 35, 39, 40, 46, 47, 51, 59, 65, 67, 70, 71, 72, 74, 75, 77, 78, 80, 81, 82, 86, 87, 89, 91, 96, 97, 99, 101, 102, 117, 123, 124, 126, 127, 129, 130, 131, 132, 134, 135, 136, 139, 143, 145, 146, 149, 153, 154, 155, 156, 157, 160, 164, 168, 175, 180, 184, 185, 187, 189, 190, 195, 203, 204, 205, 206, 209, 213, 218, 226, 232, 237, 238
preclinical development 31
priest xiv, 3, 54, 168, 173, 175, 199, 212
priest diviners (*amagqirha*) 3
primitive 6, 136, 187
primitive traditional therapeutics 52
product development 180
professional community 48
professionalization 191
professional sector 161, 202, 230
profit making venture 48
promotion of behaviour change 218
prophylaxis xvii, 56, 79
proscription of the practice of indigenous medicines 65
prostitution 107
protection 22, 29, 38, 69, 70, 79, 85, 86, 110, 117, 119, 124–125, 133, 175, 226, 227, 233
protective amulets/charms 171
proximate cause 89, 98
pseudonyms 39, 211
pseudo-scientific 62
psycho-socio-environmental model 42–43
public health officials 30, 149, 154
purposive sampling 34

Qokolweni ix, xiv, 4, 13, 23–27, 31, 33–34, 36, 38, 40, 44, 46, 109, 190–191, 202, 209, 211–213, 219, 221–222, 224–226, 230–232, 235

INDEX

quackery 59, 220, 235
quacks 189, 204, 206, 219

racial domination 75
racial segregation 48, 62–63
Randomized Controlled Trials (RCTs) 11, 197
rapid effects 10
rational western medicine 52
reductionism 27, 38, 50, 132, 146, 157, 160
  reduction-ad absurdum 12
  reductionist 11, 50, 146, 159, 239
referral 67, 96–97, 109, 204, 206, 213, 217–218, 234
reiki 38
religion 3, 16, 20, 45, 58, 90, 110, 153, 169, 189, 193–194, 197–200, 234–235
reproductive age bracket 107
reproductive health and sexuality 31
research area 32, 38
residential areas 62, 64
retribution 199
return to tradition 1, 64, 77, 86, 117, 120, 123
re-valorization 25, 81, 239
rhino 92
ritual killings 80, 86
Royal Botanic Gardens 42
rural-urban migration 65

sangoma 29, 80, 86, 89–90, 92, 165, 177, 209
sanitation syndrome 62
science-oriented medicine 11
science under capitalism 50
scientific 2–4, 9, 11, 15–16, 18–21, 23, 38–39, 41–42, 47–49, 54, 58, 62, 66, 74, 89, 121, 125, 131–133, 137–138, 146, 150–151, 156–157, 180, 182–184, 197, 199, 222, 235
  medicine 2, 157
  method 15, 19–20, 48, 222
SDA 6–7, 143
self-administered healthcare 67
self-proclaimed healers 47
self-proclaimed prophet 177
semen 144
sexual assault 119
sexual networking 111
shiatsu 38
shingles 88
silicosis 106, 112
single parenthood 116

slow poison 149
Social Sciences Research Council (HSRC) 104
sociocultural context 28, 44–45, 103
  of HIV 110
socioeconomic development 43, 103, 106
  disparities 49, 122
soothsayer 198, 228
Sopona small pox 61
sorcery 28–29, 32, 80, 88, 90, 132, 149, 161, 164
sorcery-induced ailments 57
Sotho 31
South Africa, *passim*
  political class 1, 85
South African Health Product Regulatory Authority xvii, 123
spirits xix, 28–29, 57, 80, 132, 141, 149, 161, 165–166, 168, 174, 176–177, 187, 199–200, 232, 212
spiritual bath 127, 233
spirit-world 132
staged elopements 118
stigmatization 18, 78, 79, 87, 95, 98, 107, 117, 194
stochastic experiments 16
stratified random sampling 35
subaltern health narratives 7, 24, 26, 28, 41, 45, 192, 225
subjugated knowledges 132
Sub-Saharan Africa 5, 134, 143
substance abuse 88, 112, 116–117, 120
substances 2, 47, 51, 71, 117, 152, 175, 179, 187, 224
sugar daddies 114
supernatural 15, 17, 28, 45, 97, 110, 124, 132, 137, 158, 161, 165, 175, 179, 182–184, 187, 189, 208–209, 211, 218, 220, 228–230
supernatural intercession 16–17
superstition 15–18, 20, 51, 52, 58–59, 60, 66, 124, 196, 235
Suppression of Witchcraft Act 47, 81
Supreme Being 57
surgeons 57, 156
surgical interventions 146
suspicious 52
Sustainable Development Agenda (SDA) 6
sutherlandia 157, 182
Swanson, Maynard 62

syncretism 13, 23, 59, 67, 71, 91, 110, 135, 157, 197–198, 230–231
  auto-medication 13, 135, 157, 230, 231
  Christians 110, 198

TCAM 2, 4–5, 7–8, 10–12, 14, 23–24, 27–28, 30, 37–38, 41–42, 50, 52, 97, 131, 133–134, 146, 157, 172, 194, 224, 238
Technological developments in navigation 42
technology 21, 58, 93, 130, 134, 160, 196, 203, 222, 239
teenage 43, 106, 111–112, 114, 120
Teenage Pregnancies 114
theocentrism 51
Theoretical framework 40
therapy seeking group 5, 23, 25, 157, 190, 218, 226
Thomas Aquinas 42
tinkering mechanic 51
TM 8, 55, 70, 81, 97, 123
TMCAM 96
traditional ix, xv, 1–32, 34–40, 43, 44, 46–55, 58, 60, 62, 64, 66–75, 77, 78, 80–84, 86, 87, 89–92, 94–100, 102, 103, 110, 112, 117, 118, 121–147, 149–157, 159–165, 167, 169–175, 177, 179–181, 183–187, 188, 190–213, 215–219, 221–227, 229–240
  birth attendants 34, 156
  Chinese Medicine xvii, 53
  cosmologies 99
  Courts Bill 81, 84
  healers 3, 5, 12–13, 16–17, 20, 21, 23, 25, 30, 32, 34–37, 40, 55, 60, 67, 69, 70–73, 77–78, 82, 86–87, 89, 92, 94–97, 99–100, 110, 122, 126–128, 130, 131–133, 135–137, 140–145, 149, 153–154, 157, 161, 164–165, 170–171, 173, 177, 179, 180, 183, 184, 186, 187, 188, 191, 193, 195, 198–207, 209, 211–215–219, 221–222, 226–227, 230–237, 239–240
  Healers Organization (THO) 81
  health care systems 5
  illness paradigm 98
  knowledge systems 6–7, 9, 11–12, 24, 151–152, 157
  medicine ix, xv, 1–2, 4–15, 17, 18–28, 30–32, 34–44, 46–47, 49–56, 58, 60, 64, 67–73, 75, 77–78, 81–83, 86, 91–92, 96–98, 100–124, 126–139, 144147, 149–150, 152–157, 159–160, 164, 170, 171–172, 175, 179, 181, 183, 184, 187, 188, 190–197, 200–202, 204–210, 212–213, 215, 217–219, 221–227, 229, 230–240
    Definition 2
    fanaticism 210, 220
  traditional pharmacopoeia 21, 164
  traditional vaccination 144
  transactional sex 94, 107, 115
  Transkei 103, 106
  translators 36
Treatment Action Campaign (TAC) 81
treatment regimens 9, 38, 40, 83, 87, 90, 126, 131, 164, 202, 205, 210, 230–231
tropical medicine 61
Tshabalala-Msimang, Manto 81
tuberculosis 60, 79, 106, 112, 141, 215, 218

uBhejane 92
ubhekamna ndedwa 227
Ubuntu 16
Ukuthwala 81, 115, 118, 120
ukuzila 81
UNCTAD 7
underdevelopment 40, 43, 48, 103, 191, 208
unemployment 25, 65, 72, 105, 107–109, 115, 118, 148, 191, 206, 208
UNEP 7–8
UNIDO 7
unsterilized 78, 95, 131, 144
urbanization 147
urban planning 62

vaccination 49, 60, 144
Valley of a Thousand Hills 140
Vaughan 61
VCT 107
Vincent Di Stefano 14
viral resistance 131
virginity testing 78, 81, 85, 101, 118–119, 120
  festivals 118
virgins 86, 118–119, 120
virucidal 141
Voluntary Counseling and Testing (VCT) 107

Walter Sisulu University xiii, xviii, 36, 39
Weber, Max 48
wellness 123, 152, 204

INDEX

Western
    imagination 52
    medical models 38
    medical paradigms 52
    medicine 2, 21, 60, 66
    trained medical doctors 179
whistling diviner 177
whiteman's invention 88
white reservations 65
widowhood rites 81
WIPO 7
witchcraft 19, 25, 28–29, 32, 40, 45, 48, 55, 61, 72–73, 76–78, 80–81, 83, 86–89, 92, 98, 101, 110, 121, 136, 146, 149, 161, 163, 165, 174, 189, 191, 197, 199–200, 205, 208, 226–227
    poisoning 127
    theory of HIV/AIDS 45, 78, 88
witchdoctors 25, 58, 170, 228
witches 28, 32, 40, 52, 73, 80, 174, 189, 199, 229
witch's snake 88

wizards 32, 52, 170, 189, 229
Wolf, Eric 44
Women's League 84
World Bank 6, 11, 24, 28, 109, 133, 147–148, 157, 184, 238
World Health Organization (WHO) 2–4, 6–8, 11–12, 18, 23–24, 28, 42, 47, 51–52, 68–70, 79, 82, 89, 102–103, 123–124, 128, 133, 139, 143, 145, 149, 152, 183–185, 190, 209, 223, 238
World Intellectual Property Organization (WIPO) 7
worldview 3, 29, 42, 48, 50, 125, 205, 207, 228–229

Xhosa 31, 109, 117, 118–119, 170, 175

yoga 4

Zulu 31, 59, 84, 85, 91, 118–119, 140, 164, 165, 167, 169, 175
Zuma, Jacob 1, 78, 91, 98

Printed in the United States
By Bookmasters